Highways anc
from Leeds

A local history of routes to Harrogate, Selby, Wetherby and York

by

John Gilleghan

Sketches by Simon Dacre

Kingsway Press 1994

First published in 1994

by The Kingsway Press, Leeds

Cover transparency of Oakwood Clock by the Author

ISBN Paper 0 9519194 1 5

Printed by BAF Printers Ltd., Leeds LS6 2TG

The Author at Whitkirk Church (Photograph: Leeds Skyrack Express)

Best wishes, John Gillegham.

THE AUTHOR

JOHN GILLEGHAN was born into a family of Halton chemists, his father and mother running the Halton Pharmacy on Cross Green Lane (Whitkirk View) from 1926 until 1958. Both his grandparents were pharmacists: on Roundhay Road and Woodhouse Lane. Walter Thomas Castelow was still working a full day in his shop opposite the BBC at the age of 95. He died aged 98 in 1974.

John attended Cross Gates Primary School for two years and then both the Junior School and Main School of Leeds Grammar School. During his 11 years at this school he was a member of the scout troop, combined cadet force and the chapel choir. In earlier days John sang in the choir at St. Mary's Church at Whitkirk, where his father was buried in 1958.

John gained entry to Bede College at Durham University, where he read Chemistry, Geology, Botany and Zoology. He obtained an honours degree in Botany and Zoology and stayed at Durham University to gain a Teaching Diploma. His interest in the countryside developed at university with many field courses in Wales and the North of England, exploring the flora and geology: Teesdale became a favourite area for exploration. While at Durham University John had an interest in film history and was Secretary of the University Film Society, as well as being film correspondent for the university newspaper "Palatinate". He contributed many articles for the national journal Screen Education and the Yearbook. John's interest in debating and public speaking led to his appointment as Editor of the Durham Union Society.

In September 1960 John was appointed to Temple Moor Boys Grammar School in Halton as a Biology master, a post he held until July 1974. In those years John ran the successful and popular school Film Society, Stamp Club, Biology Club and became an ASM in the large School Scout Troop (3rd. SE Leeds). The award of the Woodbadge led to many other activities in scouting including hiking in Germany and the French Alps, together with the regular Whitsuntide and Summer camps.

Many hundreds of Temple Moor boys were involved in day and weekend outings to the Yorkshire Dales, involving youth hostels and privately hired accommodation. During these visits the three peaks of the Dales: Ingleborough, Whernside and Pen-y-ghent, were climbed many times and the boys were taken caving and explorations included descending Gaping Ghyll pothole.

These activities spread abroad with two week hikes youth hostelling through the Duchy of Luxembourg. These were complemented with many visits to Paris, using accommodation in boarding schools.

School journeys in England for many years at Whitsuntide featured visits to the West

Country staying at a Bristol hotel. There were visits to many sights including Peter Scott's Wildlife Trust at Slimbridge, Bristol Zoo and the Cheddar Gorge and Caves. The popularity of these weeks were so great that John continued with them at Halton Middle School for a few years.

John was appointed as Head of Science at the newly built Halton Middle School which opened in September 1974, with the encouragement of the first headmaster John Rex, a Nature Club was formed with membership of the National Association of School Natural History Societies. John Gilleghan became a northern organiser of national activities including weekends for mainly southern children based at Devonshire Hall in Headingley. Temple Moor and Halton children helped to organise the weekends which attracted full attendances. The Halton Club produced exhibitions of their work displayed at Leeds University and at the Natural History Museum London.

Members of the Nature Club were also members of the Wildlife Youth Service - later the Young People's Trust for Endangered Species - founded by Cyril Littlewood MBE, who visited Halton on many occasions to present certificates to the children. Special plaques were also awarded in recognition of many hundreds of pounds collected by the Halton children for wildlife conservation.

While at Halton Middle School, which closed in July 1992, John ran a successful shop for school funds. A popular regular series of entertainment film shows on Fridays was started in 1975 - a feature at Temple Moor from 1961 - with a great number of school trips both locally and nationally.

John started and trained the school Table Tennis Team, which were Leeds Schools Champions on two consecutive occasions.

John became involved with the Leeds Museum's Saturday Club in 1968 and then became the co-organiser with museum senior curator Jim Nunney. There were hundreds of meetings and trips and a special weekend when Johnny Morris was invited as speaker. Due to falling numbers activities of this once popular children's club were suspended in July 1993. John joined the Leeds Naturalists Club and Scientific Association in 1961, becoming Excursions Secretary and then General Secretary, following in the steps of Dr. John Elliott of Leeds Polytechnic. In 1964 John had the honour of being appointed President and is a life member of this old established club.

John's other academic involvement has included being an examiner for GCE Health Science and as the Science Adviser for a leading educational publisher based in Abingdon. He has written a number of study cards and wall charts with the photography and books for a number of filmstrip and slide series.

In September 1970 John decided to found an adult leisure group with the Yorkshire Dales as the main theme based at a Halton school. This was followed by a similar group at Roundhay School in September 1977. Both these groups are now organised independently and meet with their nearly 200 members at other area locations. The groups invite visiting speakers and have a comprehensive programme of talks, visits, coach outings and weekends coupled with many mainly social occasions. The 21 years of the Halton Evening Group was marked with the presentation to John of a Dales watercolour in 1991.

John's interest in writing - he once wanted to be a journalist - developed with many articles and features for The Dalesman magazine and for Northern Life. He has written the church guides to Aberford, Saxton and Ledsham and the nature trail guides for Temple Newsam and Hazlewood Castle park. He has also written the history of Roundhay Hall and the colour brochure about the building is now a feature of a folder placed in all the rooms at this private BUPA hospital in Leeds.

In 1981 John published the first of three booklets about the Yorkshire Dales called "Introducing the Yorkshire Dales".This success was followed by "Magic of the Dales" and "Time Traveller in the Dales".

A series of radio programmes for BBC Radio Leeds was presented with Mike Levon in the 1980's concerning Leeds parks and the countryside. This success was followed with 60 programmes with minister Frank Pagden - now at The Grove Horsforth - tracing the history of many West Riding churches. These programmes, which were repeated, were accompanied by booklets written by John Gilleghan.

In June 1982 editor David Ward at the Leeds Skyrack Express asked John to write a column of weekly local history to be called "Scenes from the Country". The 600th article was published on December 17th. 1993, featuring the local history of routes around Leeds. The 300th sketch by artist Simon Dacre was published in August 1994. There have been 200 answers to reader's queries and over 100 editions of the weekly Country Quiz. There are annual slide presentations at Whitkirk Parish Hall and a regular series of summertime evenings visiting places of local interest, which are always very well supported by readers. John has established a series of history walks and talks at Temple Newsam Park for the Ranger Service which always attract large appreciative audiences.

John's close links with coach firm David & Catherine Godson started in the 1960's and are now developing a regular series of weekends and day coach tours to many places of scenic and historic interest. Theatre visits and Dales tours are all a part of the visit programme. Sons Richard and Matthew Godson are now taking an active part in the running of this successful local coach firm.

John's interest in world travel started in 1965 with a transAmerica tour and this was followed in 1968 with a first visit to the safari parks on Kenya and Tanzania. In subsequent years over 100 countries have been visited together with a photographic record. His visits to Canada, Sri Lanka, Indonesia, Singapore, Hong Kong, Mauritius and the Seychelles, Iceland, the Baltic countries and St. Petersburg, Alaska, the Caribbean and a cruise to the North Cape of Norway have all been recorded and presented at his talks in afternoons and evenings. The annual November travel evening has always attracted a large audience. His many visits to the Bernese Oberland in Switzerland culminated with slide presentations on behalf of the Tourist Board in many Oberland locations.

John's other leisure interests include photography, wild flowers and the countryside, geology, classical and big band music, especially Glenn Miller and Ted Heath. He has held subscriptions to the winter series of Leeds Town Hall orchestral concerts for many years. Since his retirement John has been able to attend the regular Tuesday lunchtime organ concerts in the Town Hall.

John Gilleghan took early retirement after 31 years teaching Science in East Leeds in July 1991, a year before Halton Middle School became Whitkirk Primary School.

John's mother was 90 years old in July 1994; he has an elder brother Jim who was married in 1958 and is a doctor in a Corstorphine Edinburgh general practice. Their daughter Shona also recently qualified as a doctor.

INTRODUCTION

There was great interest shown in the Skyrack's Local History A to Z series and the subsequent publication of the book "Scenes from East Leeds" in 1992, which sold out in six months. The Skyrack's series "Highways and Byways" commenced in January 1991 with an in depth look at the local history of Hollyshaw Lane and Cross Gates roads. This was so popular with Skyrack readers that historian John Gilleghan decided to spread the area of interest by following the main routes from Leeds to the north and east of the city, initially covering the Skyrack editorial area.
The 100 part series over two years looked in detail at the local history of the roads from Leeds to Harrogate, Selby, Wetherby and York.

This book is a completely revised, updated and more comprehensive version of the articles which first appeared in the Leeds Skyrack Express series "Scenes from the Country".

John hopes that his readers will enjoy the complete version and that it will have wide appeal not only to local historians but to everyone who is interested in the past and the future of a great city's links with its neighbouring towns. This book has intentionally omitted the detailed history of the city of York, which appeared in "Scenes from East Leeds" and concentrates on the outer districts of Leeds.

The sketches are by Simon Dacre who attended both Halton Middle School and Temple Moor High School. He is now 19 years old and in the second year of the BTEC National in Graphic Design at Jacob Kramer College in Leeds. He is hoping to make art his career: he has had many other contracts for his appreciated art work including guide books and church magazines.

John Gilleghan would like to place on record his thanks to all the staff at the Leeds Local History Reference Library who unfailingly provide an excellent service during the many hours of research which is the prelude to the articles every week.

THE ROAD FROM LEEDS TO HARROGATE

PART 1: FROM LEEDS TO THE HARROGATE ROAD

The first toll bar on the 1751/52 Leeds - Harrogate turnpike road was on North Street at Brunswick Place, where the slip road branches off to the Inner Ring Road. The original start of North Street was at Lady Lane, where there was the North Bar of the Medieval village of Leeds. The bar stone was until recently in the wall of the Vicar Lane bus station until an amusement arcade was completed; in the 1920's the bar stone was in the wall of the premises of Heaps, Arnold and Heaps. The East Bar stone is in the wall of the Parish Church, the Burley Bar stone once on Guildford Street is preserved in a glass case in the Building Society on the corner of Albion Street and The Headrow. The West Bar is now represented by a blue Civic Trust plaque on the Bond Street Centre Boar Lane.

The Hope Inn was once to the north of the MGM Cinema and past the Leeds Inner Ring Road on the east of North Street is the large domed building that was Messrs.Heatons (Leeds) Ltd. of Heaton House: they were costume manufacturers. Heatons started in 1899 as a ladies costume and raincoat manufacturer in York Street. In 1903 they moved to premises on King Street with other premises on Cookridge Street. In 1911 the firm moved to North Street and a year later became a private limited company under Harry Heaton. In 1914 the land at the corner of New York Road and North Street was bought and the new factory was opened in July 1916. In 1926 an extension on New York Road was completed with the factory having an output of 3000 garments a week, including the "Alwetha" raincoat. Heatons sold the premises to H.W.Poole (established in 1888) in 1979, which are now known as Crispin House.

The building north of Trafalgar Street was built in 1899 and Thomas Green's Smithfield Iron Works was north of this property with the facade and clock preserved.

North Street was at one time known as Sheepscar Lane bordered by hedgerows, between which stage coaches travelled northwards from Leeds. The North Street Recreation Ground has been maintained as Lovell Park and is adjacent to the Dispensary on Hartley Hill. The old Dispensary at the junction of North Street and New Briggate was opened in 1867 replacing the earlier building of 1824. The Leeds Public Dispensary was established in 1824 for the treatment of the poor in Leeds in rooms rented in the old House of Recovery on Vicar Lane at £4 a year. In 1829 the Dispensary moved to North Street at North Town End and the institution bought a site in Belgrave Square from Francis Lupton for £1000. The foundation stone for the new £4500 Dispensary was laid by the Leeds Mayor John Darnton Luccock on October 19th.1865 and it was opened by Sir Andrew Fairbairn on June 6th.1867 to designs by Leeds architect William Hill. In 1900 the dispensary buildings were needed for street improvements and the new building on Hartley Hill was opened on May 12th.1904 by Dr.T.Clifford Allbutt built to the designs of Francis Bedford (1866-1904) and Sydney Decimus Kitson (1871-1937), the youngest son of Sir James Kitson of Elmete Hall. The old dispensary was not demolished and it was initially suggested as a police station and insurance offices but is now the Grade II listed Chest Clinic. North Street Park was once the grounds of Campfield House, home of the Rhodes family, Richard Bramley and later owned by Arthur Lupton. The five acre site between North Street and Camp Road included the House, which became the Corporation Hotel. The park became the Smithfield Cattle Market when the Leeds Corporation bought the site in 1853: it opened on May 15th.1855. The market held on Wednesdays housed the cattle in iron roofed sheds built in 1865 and 1876: a further plot of land to Claypit Lane was bought in 1867 for the horse fairs. An annual fair for horses was held in July and another for cattle/sheep in November. In 1873 a seven year old boy John William Dunning was killed misbehaving in a swinging gondola at the Leeds Fair Ground at Smithfield.

Smithfield Market closed on May 27th. 1886 and moved to the new market site on Gelderd Road which had been established in 1883. The area was landscaped and opened as a public park in 1888, being nicknamed Sheeny Park: it once had a bandstand and the bowling green is still a feature of Lovell Park.

The Smithfield Market was remembered in Thomas Green's "Smithfield" works on North Street and in the "Smithfield" public house, which ceased to be an inn in the early 1900's becoming part of the ironworks. The facade of the inn, Grade II listed in August 1975, has been restored and is now used as offices: it was built in 1848/50. Thomas Green had worked in a blacksmith's shop and was to establish his iron works on the site in 1835. The firm manufactured steam trams and steam rollers together with the world famous lawn mowers. An agreement was signed in May 1830 by Edwin Budding of Gloucestershire for the manufacture of his invention of the lawnmower - his first customer was Regents Park Zoo London. The expansion of the North Street premises incorporated the site of St. Thomas Church School and the Smithfield Hotel with the clock. The manager of the Smithfield Iron Works for a few years was John Thyne who died in 1882 aged 55. Thomas Green died at the age of 81 in 1892 and the firm was continued by William Penrose-Green who became the Chairman of the company in 1900. The extensive works covered a wide area across Bridge Street but these were demolished when the firm closed in Leeds in 1975 and the land was redeveloped.

Sheepscar Hall on Hartley Hill was demolished in 1968 and had been built by William Etty for Nathaniel Denison a clothier of Great Woodhouse. The hall was later Bischoff House, bought by Bernard Bischoff from Switzerland from the

Denison family. His eldest son was John James Bischoff who lived at the House and when he died in 1806 James lived at the House - he died in 1845.

The Leylands was an area bounded by Skinner Lane, North Street, Regent Street and Lady Lane. The name derived from a farm in the area at the start of the 18th.century. It was in a slumlike area with back to back houses that the dedicated and hard working Jewish community of Leeds lived and prayed. The first purpose built synagogue was opened on Belgrave Street in 1860, being consecrated in August 1861 and rebuilt in 1877 following a fire. An office building now stands on the site where the synagogue closed in 1983. Other synagogues were founded in Back Nile Street, New Briggate(1869), Byron Street (1890), Concord Street (1888) and in Hope Street - between 1908 and the 1930's about 17 synagogues were opened in Leeds.

Jewish immigrants from Russia and Poland settled in The Leylands, most attracted to the clothing industry - started by John Barran in 1856. The Russian pogroms of 1881 brought more Jews to Leeds and the community was about 20,000 by 1914. One of these immigrants was Michael Marks who lived in Trafalgar Street and started his market stall in Leeds in 1884. Education in The Leylands was served by the board schools; Leylands School on Gower Street was opened in 1876 designed by Richard Adams and closed in 1919, then demolished; Lovell Road School was built in 1901 to designs by Walter Samuel Braithwaite, changed its name to Woodside School and closed in the early 1990's - the school is now derelict and is the only old building on Wintoun Street; Darley Street School built in 1895 by architect John Mitchell Bottomley produced the artist Jacob Kramer who worked in Leeds until his death in 1962 - the City Art College is named after this son of Ukrainian immigrants. The fourth board school was at Newtown in Cross Stamford Street opened in 1875 to designs by Richard Adams.

The Jewish population moved north from The Leylands which were gradually demolished from 1907/08 starting south of Trafalgar Street: New York Road was opened on the area on July lst.1910. and the first synagogue in the new area was on Roundhay Road in 1907, followed by the synagogue on Francis Street in 1913. In 1937 the remainder of The Leylands was demolished and Regent Street was widened: in that same year a new synagogue opened in Moortown. By the outbreak of the last World War the Jewish Community was centred at Chapeltown: the New Synagogue on Chapeltown Road was opened in 1932 and closed in 1985 becoming the Northern School of Contemporary Dance.

There were two Anglican churches in The Leylands area: St.Thomas's Church on Melbourne Street was built using polychrome bricks and consecrated on February 2nd.1852. The church on a 36 acre site was designed by William Butterfield (1814-1900) costing £7000 and paid for by the Rhodes family, who owned the area on which the church and school were built. The architect also designed St.John's

Church at Huddersfield in 1851. The foundation stone for the chancel was laid on November 14th.1891 by the Countess of Harewood and it was consecrated on April 25th.1893.
St.Luke's Church on the corner of Skinner Lane and North Street was consecrated on October 4th.1841 and was intended to serve the nearby barracks. It was designed in stone by architects William Perkin & Elisha Backhouse. Their other work included New Manston Hall for the Waud family, St.Matthew's Church, Chapel Allerton and St.James Church, Manston. The new ecclesiastical parish was created in 1861 but the church has been demolished with offices now standing on the corner site:a section of the old stone boundary wall is still to be seen to the west.
The west side of North Street had a hospital for Horses and Dogs; Lovell House the home of Dr.Joseph Stewart and the Golden Cross Hotel near the junction of Meanwood Road. One of the few buildings to remain at Golden Cross is the corner building that once was the Midland Bank: the pub was demolished for road building. Sheepscar Bridge was originally in this area and the Sheepscar,Woodhouse Carr and Meanwoodside Turnpike Trust had a toll bar for this road opened in 1829/30. The tolls were freed on the Leeds/Harrogate, Leeds/Roundhay and the Meanwoodside turnpikes on January lst. 1867.
The Baptist Chapel on Wintoun Street was built in place of the old chapel on Call Lane, demolished to make way for New Market Street. The foundation stone for the chapel off North Street was laid in 1870 and the chapel cost £4500 to designs by architect Alexander Crawford :this Baptist Chapel was supplemented with the North Street Chapel on the corner of Byron Street. The Wintoun Street chapel was closed in 1895 and was converted into the New Central synagogue in 1924 but has been demolished. The New Central merged with the Vilna Synagogue and moved to the old Kingsway Cinema.
The Leeds College of Building now stands between Byron and Concord Streets and originated as the Leeds Mechanics Institute from 1824. The Leeds School of Science was formed and in 1868 moved to the Leeds Institute building on Cookridge Street. In 1908 the Leeds College of Technology was formed having 8 departments in 1930. In 1931 the Department of Building was based in Cross Stamford Street Board School. In 1946 the move was made to the old Darley Street School and the previous school site was used as an annexe. In 1960 the Branch College of Building was created now in two old school buildings. On May 15th.1967 building started on a new college on North Street, which was finished in August 1969: the Darley Street School was then demolished. The next phase of the new college opened in March 1971 and the Cross Stamford Street site was vacated. The College was finally completed on November 18th.1972 having been called the Leeds College of Building from April lst.1970. The architects for the

North Street college was The Building Design Partnership and cost £252,225. The White Stag on Whitelock Street north of Skinner Lane and the listed Eagle Tavern on North Street/Benson Street corner are two old established public houses in Leeds. The present White Stag replaced a previous inn on the site and The Eagle Tavern is one of the oldest unaltered public houses in Leeds. The inn started as stonemason James Bussey's private house in 1826: James's son Robert Bussey took out a licence and it became an alehouse in 1832; it was known as The Builder's Inn,The Ordnance Arms - because of the nearby Barracks and The Golden Eagle.

Where North Street has the junction with Roundhay Road and Chapeltown Road was the site of the second toll house and bar on the extremity of the old Sheepscar green. The bar stood on the corner where the Sheepscar Archives now occupy the old branch library. There was a library on the site from 1877 and the later 1938 library closed on June 4th.1976. The Chapeltown Branch Post Office is now the premises of the Ramgarhia Board. The Post Office closed for business in December 1985. The toll bar was a pentagonal cottage, which was demolished to make way for the Fire Station, Police Station and Post Office.
The Sheepscar Interchange was approved in 1980 and the vast road/lights layout was opened in June 1983, which involved the demolition of much of old Sheepscar. Sheepscar or Shipscar derives from the old Norse "kjarr" meaning a marsh. Sheepscar Beck, having already accepted the waters of Gipton Beck, flows under Timble Bridge east of the Parish Church and then into the River Aire. Sheepscar Beck was once described as one of the dirtiest waterways of Leeds, mainly due to the Sheepscar Dye Works at Sheepscar Bridge.
Sheepscar Mill was west of the bridge and was converted into a corn mill from grinding redwood and was also used for making rape seed oil. In later years the Mill became a Paper Mill for the making of "Emporetica" paper, which was used by chapmen to wrap their goods. Chapmen were the itinerant traders who sold many items, including popular books.

Chapeltown Road, as part of the Leeds/Harrogate Turnpike Trust was constructed by Blind Jack Metcalfe of Knaresborough. Jack was born in 1717 and lived until the age of 93, being buried at Spofforth Church. He was blinded by an attack of smallpox at an early age and became noted as a road builder, violinist, guide, carrier and bridge builder. One of his contracts was for the Harrogate-Boroughbridge Turnpike Road in 1758 and there is a record of a 25 mile stretch costing £3250.

St.Clement's Church was south of the Barrack Street junction and was designed by the architect George Corson (1829-1910) who was also responsible for the Leeds

Grand Theatre and the Leeds Municipal Buildings. The foundation stone for St. Clement's Church was laid on April 24th.1867 by the Mayor Andrew Fairbairn and was a product of the Leeds Church Extension Society, founded in 1864. The congregations were enhanced with attendances from the barracks: there were 804 sittings for a population of 6290. The Church was in the Early Decorated Gothic style with a tower and 140' spire. St.Clement's Church was consecrated on September 10th.1868 and had cost £10,000: the parish was created in 1869.
An inscription on George Corson's parish room was "This stone was laid by HSH Prince Adolphus of Teck May 16th.1895". The Prince was Queen Mary's brother and was stationed in Leeds with the 17th. Lancers at the Barracks. The room and Sunday School were opened on January lst.1896.
St.Clement's Church built from Weetwood and Potternewton stone became a listed building in 1975 following its closure in November 1974 but was demolished in 1976: the site becoming part of the Sheepscar interchange development.
The Roscoe Place Methodist Chapel stood on the corner of Roscoe Mount and was designed by Pritchard of Darlington in 1861/62 in the Gothic style at a cost of £5500. The Sunday School was designed by the architect George Francis Danby in 1882. He was the son of a cabinet maker and built many Wesleyan chapels including one at Cross Gates on Austhorpe Road in 1882. The chapel was demolished in 1974 for re-development. The Roscoe public house on the corner of Gill's Court was built in 1831 as a private house, becoming an alehouse in 1857. It was first known as The Roscoe in 1872 but closed and was demolished in 1982. A small plaque was unveiled in 1983 to mark the site of this once popular public house with Irish connections.

The United Hebrew Congregation's New Synagogue was opened in 1932, designed by J.Stanley Wright of Albion Street in the Byzantine style with dome and minaret: when it closed in 1985 it became the well known Northern School of Contemporary Dance, the distinctive minaret was taken down and some of the fittings were taken to the synagogue on Shadwell Lane.
The house adjacent to the old synagogue was built in 1835 on the south west corner of the New Town development on the Squire's Pastures estate. The land had been sold in 1825 by Earl Cowper to a partnership but he repurchased the land in 1828 when the partnership became bankrupt. This listed house was later used as offices by the United Hebrew Congregation. The Holy Rosary Catholic Church and the relocated Roscoe Methodist Church are a part of this redeveloped area to the east of the Recreation ground. The foundation stone for the Holy Rosary Church was laid in 1936 and the church was opened on September 30th.1937 in the gardens of Ashbourne House: the architects were Marten and Burnett of Leeds, who also designed St.Augustine's Church at Harehills. The first Mass at the Holy Rosary

Church was celebrated by Bishop Poskitt of Leeds and Bishop Shine of Middlesborough. The first Parish Priest was Rev.P.O'Meara in 1951. The Roman Catholic Congregation first met in 1886 on the top floor of the Rosary School on Barrack Street. The first ideas for a new church were suggested in 1927 and the church initially served an expanding Irish population. St.Dominic's Catholic Middle School opened on Leopold Street on September 6th.1971. The school, designed by Weightman & Bullen of York, was planned as the infants department of a projected Junior School for the Rosary Parish and was completed in August 1971. Following the reorganisation of Catholic schools the school became Holy Rosary & St.Anne's RC Primary in 1989. The school replaced St.Anne's School in Woodhouse Square and Holy Rosary on Lofthouse Terrace.
West of the main road is the Buslingthorpe Recreation Park: five acres of land bought by the Leeds Corporation about 1906 in connection with the development of the Mexborough estate.
The new brick built Roscoe Methodist Chapel opened on October 5th. 1974 and as a plaque indicates "continues the Methodist congregation on this site in the preaching room of Willow House of Benjamin Vickers and continued in Roscoe Place Chapel 1862-1974". Roscoe Place Chapel was founded in May 1861 and was built at a cost of £5500.
The Forum Cinema on the corner of Savile Road and Chapeltown Road once stood on the site of the present Forum Service Station. The cinema was designed by Percy Robinson and opened on Monday October 12th. 1936 with the Ruby Keeler film "Colleen" (US 1936 Directed by Alfred Green and also starring Dick Powell, Jack Oakie and Joan Blondell). The opening included a musical stage show with BBC star Len Bermon with two piano accompaniment and was billed as "the most modern and luxuriously fitted cinema in the country". The opening ceremony was performed by the Lord Mayor Ald. Percival Tookey Leigh: he was a dentist by profession with a practice in Park Square Leeds. He was the Chairman of the Libraries Committee - Cross Gates branch library was named after him in 1939 - and he died at the end of October 1938 aged 74.
Percy Robinson, the architect of the brick built Forum Cinema, was born in Leeds in 1868 and built Rawcliffe's Store on Duncan Street in 1905 and The Leeds Exchange in Briggate in 1907. He died in 1950 having had the author William Alban Jones as a partner in his practice.
The Forum Cinema closed on December 24th. 1959 and was demolished soon afterwards. The electronic organ installed for the opening was replaced in 1946 with a Christie organ from the Capitol at Tunbridge Wells - this organ was broken up when the cinema was finally demolished. The last film to be shown at The Forum was "Salome" with Rita Hayworth,Charles Laughton and Stewart Granger: the film was released in the USA in 1953.

The site of the Savile Service Station is now a shopping complex, while the Chapeltown Business Centre occupies the building of the LICS - the North Street branch had opened in February 1860 having new premises in 1897.
On the corner of Francis Street is Browning House with an impressive iron arcade over the gateway. Browning House remembers the Rev.Percy T.Browning who was inducted as the vicar of All Soul's Church Woodhouse in late 1918. He was concerned with the Clarendon Road St.Faith's Hostel and died in 1948.
The large Victorian "Farnville House" was the home initially of William Hornby, tobacco and cigar manufacturer of Meanwood Road. It then became the home of William Fentiman and Amelia Smithson who had 18 children of whom only 13 survived. William Fentiman Smithson was a cloth and stuff merchant:his firm was Henderson & Smithson Co. of Hall Ings Bradford. His wife Amelia ran the milliners and stay makers shop in Bond Street Leeds: she died in January 1932 aged 90. William Fentiman Smithson died at his home at 26 Harehills Avenue on March 2nd.1918 aged 76: he was buried at Woodhouse Cemetery on March 6th. He was a keen Conservative and a Past Grand Warden of the West Yorkshire Masons.
The house was acquired by St. Faith's House of Rescue in 1915, in connection with the Church Penitentiary Society. The house became the Hope Hospital and used for the maternity ward. In 1950 it became Browning House Mother and Baby Home. It is a registered charity and nursing home which can house 18 girls and 15 babies. It aims to offer pregnant girls and women and mothers with babies and very young children a home, when they are under stress and need a loving caring environmnent.
Browning House is run under the auspices of the Church of England (Diocese of Ripon) by voluntary committees. The chapel at Browning House is complemented by visits from the vicar of St.Martin's Church.
The headquarters of the Rugby Football League occupied a house that once belonged to Dr. Alexander Anderson, while Newton Park Congregational & Baptist Union Chapel, designed by Archibald Neill and opened in 1887 is now a Sikh Temple.

The entry to Newton Park is guarded by two large stone pillars and was designated the St. Mary's Conservation Area. The development was built in the 1870's and 1880's on land owned by the Lupton family, who lived at Newton Hall. The plans for this area were commissioned by Francis and Darnton Lupton who appointed architect George Corson whose plans were abandoned and later Charles Chorley. Corson laid out the Newton Hall estate in 1871 and Chorley was building houses at Newton Park in 1885: Newton Park House was built by Chorley for the Luptons about 1886 and demolished about 1920. In 1894 architect Stephen Smith was

engaged at Newton Park - he built the Grand Arcade in Leeds in 1896.
Many years ago there was a square hole in a wall on Chapeltown Road opposite Sholebrooke Avenue with a stone dish to hold vinegar and accepted money for the victims of the plague. The date on the stone was 1666 although the stone is possibly dated to the beginning of the 17th. century. The stone was once in a garden on Reginald Terrace.
A 1926 guide stated that: "Newton Hall on Newton Hill has uncertain age and the once pleasant meadows sloping from the Hall are being absorbed by the builder". Ralph Thoresby referred to Newton Hall as a "venerable fabric". The only reminder of Newton Hall is the lodge house, now isolated on the main road east of St.Martin's Church: the lodge dates from 1886. In 1892 the Hall was the home of Ann Greenhow.

St.Martin's Church was consecrated by the Bishop of Ripon on Easter Tuesday April 19th.1881. The church was built to the designs of Richard Adams and John Kelly of Leeds using local Potternewton stone and cost £8500. Present at the first service were W.L.Jackson the future Lord Allerton and Robert Benson Jowitt of Elmhurst.
In February 1882 the wooden parish hall came into use, where the Yorkshire Penny Bank operated on Saturday evenings. In 1883 a section of St. Clement's Sheepscar and St. Michael's Buslingthorpe was assigned to St.Martin's parish and known as the Mission District - a new mission room had been opened. The vicarage was based at St. Martin's Villa Newton Park. The Mission at Buslingthorpe was complemented with the dedication of St.Columba's Church on October 30th.1886: the carved oak altar had been donated by H.W.Cribb of the Leeds furnishing firm. The Sunday School building was opened in February 1880 by Mrs.W.L.Jackson. St.Columba's Church on Buslingthorpe Lane was closed following the last service on Sunday August 25th. 1940 due to the vulnerability from air attack and shortage of staff. The Victoria Memorial Hall designed by Percy Robinson was dedicated on January 31st.1904 by the Bishop of Richmond and the opening ceremony followed on February 4th. The memorial cross on the south side of the church was transferred from the demolished St.Clement's Church Sheepscar.
The furnishings of St.Martin's Church include the pulpit of Caen stone presented by James Walker JP of Newton Park and the brass lectern dating from 1881. This lectern was presented by Mrs.John Cadman in memory of her husband and shown in the Paris Exhibition of 1881. The murals and stained glass windows have all been recently cleaned and the organ has had a complete overhaul. The East Window is in memory of John Jowitt who died in December 1898 - he was the father of Robert Benson Jowitt who dedicated the window. The West Window is in memory of William Pepper of Newton Green Hall and dates from 1897. The

Baptistry was erected in memory of Richard Bullock who was Vicar of St.Martin's Church from 1892 until 1896 - he died on December 30th.1896 in his 37th.year. East of the main road is Newton Green Hospital opened in 1975 and developed in the grounds of the demolished Newton Green Hall. In February 1994 the £10.7 million Chapel Allerton Hospital was opened having been built in two years on a former field next to the Newton Green Wing. Approval was given in March 1991 for the new 285 bed block and departments and wards were transferred from the old Chapel Allerton Hospital, Ida Hospital Cookridge and the Royal Bath Hospital Harrogate.

At the end of the last century Newton Green Hall was the home of William Pepper, the owner of Monk Bretton Colliery. It became the home of Sir Wilfred and Lady Hepton: Sir Wilfred Lawrence Hepton was the son of William Hepton, Coppersmiths of Hunslet Lane. Sir Wilfred became Lord Mayor of Leeds in 1907/08. He was the director of Hepton Bros Ltd Wholesale Mantle Manufacturers of Oxford Row Leeds. Sir Wilfred Hepton was drowned in the south of France in May 1911 aged 53. He was the President of the Leeds Golf Club at Roundhay, a churchwarden of St.Clement's Church Sheepscar and was knighted in 1908 by King Edward while on a visit to Leeds. Sir Wilfred Hepton was buried with due ceremony in St.Matthew's churchyard following a well attended service at Leeds Parish Church. Lady Hepton died at Newton Green Hall in November 1918. A brass plaque in Leeds Parish Church remembers Sir Wilfred Hepton: born October 16th.1857 and died May 5th.1911.

The lodge to the hall has been demolished and a stone gate pillar is now part of the Polish Church boundary.

The Polish Catholic Church was opened on December 11th.1976 by Gordon Wheeler Bishop of Leeds: the architects were John Brunton & Partners of Leeds and builders were M.Harrison & Co.Ltd. The foundation stone is set into the north wall and the altar came from the demolished church of St.Mary's Quarry Hill. The Polish Centre and Church serves a community of about 1500 in the Leeds area,

Woodfield became the Polish Catholic Centre in 1965 having moved from Claypit Lane. The main entry to Woodfield was by Newton Hill Road with the main front of the house facing south, set in tiered gardens. The stables were demolished in early 1994 allowing access to the other Polish Centre property. This house is "Gledholt", which at the end of the last century was home to Mary Micklethwaite and later to Dr.W.Warnock - it is still known as the "Doctor's House".

Woodfield was the home of the Misses Jowitt in the 1880's and of the clothing manufacturer Andrew Wilson in the 1890's until it was sold to Arthur and Mary Gilliat, who moved from Allerton Lodge. Harold Gilliat followed Arthur, when he died in 1935 aged 80 (Mary died in 1954 aged 88) as the Vice Consul for the Netherlands. Harold Gilliat MC JP was a drysalter with the firm of E.G.Jepson of

Crown Point Road and he sold the House to the Polish Community. In later years Harold Gilliat lived in the top flat within the House and he died in 1961 aged 73. North of Woodfield on the corner of Harehills Lane is the large house known as Newton Hill House, once the home of Joseph Dobson a maltster in Hunslet and in 1916 belonged to Harold Bowers of the firm Kirkby & Bowers stock and share brokers of Albion Street. Partner Charles Kirkby lived at Oxley Hill in Moor Allerton. Newton Hill House is now the home of the East Leeds Womens Workshop.
The start of Harrogate Road is at the junction of Harehills Lane, Potternewton Lane and Chapeltown Road. Newton Hill was once known locally as "Mitchell Hill" due to the small shop run by the Mitchell family on this corner. The property was demolished when the road was made into a dual carriageway.

Kingsway Cinema

THE ROAD FROM LEEDS TO HARROGATE

PART 2:HARROGATE ROAD TO THE RING ROAD MOOR ALLERTON

The start of Harrogate Road is the junction of Harehills Lane and Potternewton Lane. The Chapel Allerton Hospital is Gledhow Grove, built 1835/1840 by architect John Clark for the Leeds merchant John Hives. He was a partner in the firm of Hives & Atkinson of Bank Mills. John Hives and Moses Atkinson were flax spinners at their premises on East Street Cavalier Hill. In 1876 Robert Tennant of Scarcroft Lodge became a partner in the firm. John Hives was born in 1774 and died on September 17th. 1843: his wife Mary Ann died aged 48 in April 1834. Five of their children all died before attaining the age of 21.

In this century Frederick James Kitson, eldest son of F. W. Kitson and the nephew of Lord Airedale and the Hon. Hilda Kitson - Frederick's sister in law - lived at Gledhow Grove: she was the promoter of the "Flowers for Leeds" project and died in 1944, having given the Gledhow Valley woodlands to Leeds. Chapel Allerton Hospital was opened in the grounds of the mansion in Summer 1926 as a Ministry of Pensions Hospital. It superseded a temporary hospital of wooden buildings at Beckett's Park known as the 2nd. Northern General Hospital. This hospital cared for many thousands of wounded men during and after the First World War. The new

Gledhow Grove

Pensions Hospital had five wards for war pensioners and specialised in appliances and false limbs. During
the Second World War there were eight emergency wards and an extension of the nurse's home. By 1960 there was a decline in the need for war pensioner's beds and administration was taken over by Leeds Group A.
The five main wards on the site were moved to the new Newton Green Hospital by Easter 1994.The Gledhow Grove site was first placed on sale in 1992 and again in January 1994 by the United Leeds Hospitals NHS Trust. The listed Gledhow Grove mansion with the stone entrance will remain following the redevelopment of the 18 acre site. The stables of Gledhow Grove remain as listed buildings on Gledhow Park Drive.
The Gledhow Grove site was sold in July 1994 for a multi-million pound figure to Leeds based Rushbond Group and Lincoln based property developers Simons Group. Managing Director of Rushbond of St. Martin's House - adjacent to the hospital Jonathan Maud stated that plans would include housing with the mansion being converted into flats or offices. The Rushbond Group bought the Aberford almshouses and restored them as offices.
The name "Chapel Allerton Hospital" was transferred to the Newton Green Wing, where there are six wards in the old block and five in the new development. The Duchess of Kent officially opened the new Chapel Allerton Hospital on Friday July 22nd.1994.
Harehills Grove stands on the south side of Harehills Lane and became the public Potternewton Park. The house was built for James Brown JP DL(WR) in 1830 and was set in 700 acres of parkland. James was born in 1786 and in 1811 married Charlotte Rhodes of Campfield. Their son was James Brown born in 1814 who eventually left Harehills Grove to live at Rossington near Bawtry and Copsgrove Hall at Boroughbridge. James Brown was the son of James Brown and Anne Williams: they died in 1813 and had two sons James and William Williams Brown, the Leeds banker who lived at Allerton Hall.
"Harehills" became the home of the Quaker industrialist John Jowitt of Beech Grove Terrace by 1860. Jowitt's of Leeds was founded in the 1780's by John Jowitt, the great grandfather of Robert Benson Jowitt. Robert Jowitt was John's son and he married Rachel Crewdson, who died in 1856. He took his two sons into partnership but one died leaving John Jowitt Jnr to run the firm. John Jowitt JP had married Deborah Benson but retired in 1883 and died on December 30th.1898 - the east window in St. Martin's Church is a memorial to John Jowitt bequeathed by his son Robert Benson Jowitt.
Robert Benson Jowitt, who moved from Elmhurst Newton Road to Harehills Grove, was a wool merchant at 39, Albion Street Leeds and the Swan Arcade Bradford with an office in London - the firm dealt mainly with Australian wool. Robert Benson

Jowitt was also a JP, a trustee of Leeds Parish Church, a governor of Leeds Grammar School, Chairman of the Leeds General Infirmary and Chairman of the West Riding Magistrates. He married Caroline McCulloch and they had four sons John Herbert, Robert, Edward and Frederick McCulloch Jowitt.

The Harehills Grove estate was sold by the trustees of the late James Brown in 1893 and it was Robert Benson Jowitt who sold the estate to Leeds Corporation in 1901 for £35,000. He moved to the south of England and he died aged 75 at Tunbridge Wells on November 9th. 1914.

The 27 acre park was opened on October 10th.1906 by the Lord Mayor Edwin Woodhouse, in the last month of his mayoralty. The mansion became a museum housing the Howgate Art Collection and providing refreshments for visitors. William Howgate was a chimney sweep and became a well known art connoisseur and dealer. During a long lifetime he accumulated a valuable collection of rare engravings, old prints and other treasures. He was engaged in arranging and classifying the collection when he was taken ill at Potternewton Mansion and died in 1906: he gave the City his great collection. In 1920 it was proposed that the Mansion be offered to the Leeds Education Committee to be used for the Yorkshire Training College of Housecraft as a hostel for 40 female students with lecture room accommodation. In 1921 the mansion was adapted for use as a preparatory school with 200 boys. The hall was subsequently an annexe to Park Lane College. Potternewton Mansion is now the Management Studies Centre for the College.

Potternewton Hall was built by the Earls of Mexborough of Methley Hall, who demolished the old home of the Mauleverer family when they moved to York. They rebuilt Potternewton Hall in the mid 17th. century and in the 19th. century the hall was the home of Samuel Leathley Nussey (1835-1895) with his wife Agnes and daughter Mary. One of those living at the first Hall was Thomas Hardwick, a lawyer who died in 1577 - there is a monument to Thomas and Anne in Leeds Parish Church.

Potternewton House was the home to John Rhodes in the late 19th. century and to John Schunk. The Schunk family were in the engineering business making railway wagon wheels etc and the daughters married into both the Kitson and Lupton families: Edward Schunk died in 1889 and was buried at St. John's Church Roundhay.

The House became the home this century of the wealthy Leeds accountant and stockbroker John Gordon who became Lord Mayor of Leeds in 1899. When his wife Mary died in 1914 her memory was perpetuated in a steam boat on Waterloo Lake Roundhay called the Mary Gordon. This boat was rediscovered in a boatyard at Knutsford after being used on the River Thames in the 1930's and has been restored by a Leeds businessman. The Hall was bought by Leeds City Council in 1966 and was demolished - the site is now Riviera Gardens.

Ald. John Gordon was born on November 12th. 1854 at Kirriemuir Forfarshire, being educated at Leeds Grammar School, leaving at the age of 15 to join George Young. In 1870 he became a clerk to his uncle John Gordon Snr. and five years later was made a partner. In 1884 he married and from 1886 to 1895 represented Mill Hill Ward. He was a member of the Leeds Rifles retiring in 1887 with the rank of Captain. He lived at first at Church Lane House Adel and in 1892 became a Leeds Magistrate. Following four years illness when he was confined to Potternewton House, John Gordon died aged 71 on Tuesday December 22nd. 1925. He left two sons Cpt. Charles Gordon and Lt. Alec Gordon. His funeral was at Adel Church and a service was held at St. Matthew's Church Chapel Allerton.
Potternewton House has been demolished and the site became Potternewton Heights in 1961. The converted stable and lodges remain on the Lane and the entrance gates are seen on the corner of Henconner Lane and Potternewton Lane.
South of the Lane was the Queen Anne style mansion of Scott Hall, home of the Scott family with William Scott being the last member of this old family. The old hall was demolished and the site used for extensive stone quarrying by the firm of Ingham and Fletcher. The stone was supplied for many city buildings and was eventually filled in and became the playing fields. Scott Hall School has been demolished and the site is probably to be the new police headquarters. Scott Hall Road was built in the 1930's and the name reminds us of this family.
The Chapeltown Tram Depot was closed for service trams on April 23rd. 1955, although it was used to store tramcars for breaking up until August the following year. The depot was substantially rebuilt for the Leeds City Corporation Supplies Depot and later for commercial purposes. The Chapeltown horse-tram service started on November 11th. 1874 terminating at the Queen's Arms Inn - this date was the completion of the line from Boar Lane. There were stabling facilities at the Bowling Green Tavern and a smithy. London's first trams began operating in March 1861 from Bayswater: the cars were designed by a Mr. Train from New York
Steam replaced the horse tram to Leopold Street in March 1894. In January 1900 the no. 2 service electric trams worked the route to the Queens Arms and two years later reached Moortown and Canal Gardens, where they turned back. The circular route started in the mid 1920's until March 1956: the service ceased in 1957.
The large area bounded by Harrogate Road, Potternewton Lane, Stainbeck Lane and the beck to the west was once known as Chapeltown Moor. In the mid-17th. century it was reported that the "air on Chapeltown Moor was healthy and invigorating".It was the site of the racecourse and during both the 17th. and 18th. centuries horse racing would have taken place. The moor was enclosed in the early 19th. century and the area marked by the landowners for development. One of these aristocratic landowners was the Earl of Mexborough holding the land from Leeds to Chapel Allerton. The public house and street names reflect this one time ownership -

Methley Drive, Savile Drive and Mexborough Street.
Three men said to have been concerned with the Farnley Plot of 1663 were hung in chains on Chapeltown Moor in the presence of a large crowd. They were decapitated and their heads placed on the Moot Hall in Leeds for "all to witness and be warned of the fate of treason"
The first recorded cricket match in Leeds was held on Chapeltown Moor on Shrove Tuesday 1757. In 1776 Chapeltown Moor saw a match between the Married Men and the Bachelors and four years later a Leeds theatre was featuring a new dance called The Cricketers or the sports of Chapeltown. Nationally a bat and ball game has existed since the 13th. century but it was in 1711 that a Kent team played All England and in 1735 a match was played between the Prince of Wales team and the Earl of Middlesex. The MCC was established in Thomas Lord's ground in 1787.
On May lst. 1745 a run was held on Chapeltown Moor with a first prize of £3. Registration by intended runners was to be at the "Three Owls" inn: with a minimum of three runners entering. In the late 17th. century Edward Preston made news by running around the Chapeltown Moor four mile course twice in 14 minutes. He died as a result of an accident in January 1770. On June 30th.1794 General Edmeston's regiment of Yorkshire Rangers of 800 men were inspected on the Moor by General Grant - this was followed by a free tankard of ale for each man, on August 29th.1794 the men of the Leeds Gentlemen Volunteer Corps marched from the Leeds White Cloth Hall to the Moor to receive their new colours from the Mayor.
In October 1793 a meeting of the Society of Yorkshire Archers took place on the Moor and afterwards the men dined at the Bowling Green. There was a royal review by Prince William of Gloucester of the Volunteers on December 30th. 1795. The Moor was enclosed in 1809 and these events soon came to an end.
The Mexborough Inn was built on the site of the "Bowling Green Tavern" or the "Three Hulats" or "The Savile's Arms" -owls- feature on the Savile coat of arms - which dated back to the early 18th. century. In heraldry the Hulotte is an owl and derives from the French. The Savile family lived at Methley Hall and today the 8th. Earl of Mexborough John Christopher George Savile lives at Arden Hall near Helmsley. The largest bowling green in Yorkshire finally closed in 1978 and the site became a car park. The area was redeveloped as the Kwik Save supermarket which opened on Tuesday June 14th. 1994: the builders were Boyle Construction.
The first long low white washed inn was further to the north near the corner of Blake Grove, which became a small garden surrounded by railings and maintained by the brewery. The old inn doubled as a polling station and there are a few who remember voting in this building in the 1920's. Plans were announced in 1924 to rebuild the public house, which followed in 1925.
The Chapel Allerton branch of the National Westminster Bank opposite The Mexborough, opened on May 31st. 1926 as the "Westminster Bank" on land leased

from the Barran family: the freehold of the building designed by architects Clark and Lessors was bought in 1928. The Harehills Branch opened on July 5th. 1928 as the National Provincial Bank and was transferred in September 1955 to the present location. The Westminster Bank office in Leeds first opened in 1759 and was rebuilt on Park Row in 1857 - the present headquarters was built in the 1970's. The Dominion Cinema opened on January 4th. 1934 to designs of architect William Illingworth, whose family owned a Bradford store in 1871. The cinema was one of the circuit run by West Leeds Amusements, who opened The Lyric in 1922 and the Kingsway, Clock and Rex cinemas. The first film shown was "Cleaning Up" starring George Gee. The cinema suffered extensive fire damage on June 23rd. 1941: the fire was discovered at 11pm by a wartime fire watcher and took two hours to put out. Masonry crashing into the road caused a few folk to be advised to leave their homes. The Dominion was rebuilt in 1953 but was eventually sold for £65,000. The Dominion cinema closed in March 1967 with the film "The Quiller Memorandum" starring Sir Alec Guiness and George Segal - the film was made in Britain in 1966 and was written by Harold Pinter and directed by Michael Anderson. The Dominion became a Mecca Bingo and Social Club, which it remains today.
The Chapeltown Board School was built in 1879 as a stone plaque informs and was designed by Richard Adams, the Leeds School Board architect from 1873 who died in 1883.
The row of houses north of the board school once was the home of Chapel Allerton Girl's High School. The school entered their new buildings on King Lane in 1939 opened by the Princess Royal with the school now known as Allerton High School. The row was renovated and made available as offices in Summer 1994.
The site of the old St. Matthew's Church is south of the Memorial Cross in Chapel Allerton village. It is thought that the Kirkstall Abbey Cistercian monks founded a chapel at Allerton in the village of Chapel Town. The chapel was established as a chantry during the 14th. century by John Mauleverer and became a chapel of ease to Leeds Parish Church. St. Matthew's Church was built in the mid 18th. century on the old turnpike route via Church Lane and Woodland Lane: in 1751 the route was changed to the present line of Harrogate Road. The old church was enlarged in 1819 and 1840 when the spire was added and there were further alterations by William Perkin in 1866, who had built the church school in 1872. The tower of this old church was rebuilt at the expense of William Williams Brown of Allerton Hall.
In 1880 the old Sexton's Cottage on the north side of the churchyard was demolished and a Roman altar was discovered the altar is now on display at Leeds City Museum with its inscription "To the Mother Goddess deservedly".
The old St. Matthew's Church was demolished in 1935, although the new St. Matthew's Church was consecrated in 1900 having been designed by George Bodley. Chapel Allerton Hall east of the village was built in brick possibly between 1826 and

1830 and became the residence of Thomas Benson Pease. Ald. Pease was born in 1782 and died at Chapel Allerton Hall on May 23rd.1846.He had come to Leeds from Darlington in 1802 and was a principal of the mercantile firm of Aldam Pease & Co.,He was the uncle to William Aldam MP Leeds and was for many years a borough alderman. When he died Thomas Pease left estates in Durham and Yorkshire: he was buried in Woodhouse Cemetery.

Chapel Allerton Hall was the home of clothier Sir John Barran, who was responsible for the purchase of Roundhay Park for the City of Leeds in October 1871 when he was Mayor. This he achieved with the support of the Leeds NE Ward councillor Thomas Mosley - he died in December 1871 aged 62 two months after the purchase of Roundhay Park. His monument in Beckett Street cemetery reads: "Thomas Mosley - this monument has been erected by a few friends and admirers as a mark of their appreciation of his services in originating and earnestly advocating the purchase of Roundhay Park for Leeds and for his persistent advocacy of the people's cause".

Sir John Barran was born in New Wandsworth Surrey on August 3rd. 1821 and married twice: in 1842 to Anne Hirst who died on January 15th. 1874 aged 52 and to Eliza Bilton in 1878. Dame Eliza Barran was born on December 28th.1829 and died on May 4th.1917.Major Barran was the son by the first marriage being born on December lst.1846 and died on September 21st.1866. Sir John Barran was the MP for Leeds 1876-85 and created a baron in 1895. He was a devout Baptist and died on May 3rd. 1905 and was buried in Burmantofts Cemetery, where his gravestone is inscribed "Sir John Barran JP LLD who represented Leeds in Parliament 1876-1885 and the Otley division of Yorkshire 1886-1895".

John Barran came to Leeds to be a pawnbroker but soon brought the multiple clothing trade to the city. He opened a pawnbroker shop at Leeds Bridge but soon added the business of tailor and clothier. He devoted his energies to the development of the ready made clothing trade and saw advantages from the sewing machine: he entered into partnership with Nussey of Carlinghow Mills Batley and then succeeded to the entire business. He moved to Park Row and John Barran & Sons removed to their newly built premises on St. Paul's Street in 1878, designed by Thomas Ambler. In 1898 a new factory opened on Hanover Lane where each of the four floors accommodated 300 workpeople.

It was John Barran who was instrumental in turning Boar Lane into a respectable thoroughfare and this Mayor of Leeds laid the foundation stone for Leeds Bridge - it was opened by Ald. Oxley in 1873. John Barran was knighted in the New Year Honours of 1895 and was JP for Leeds and a West Riding magistrate. The last public function he attended was the degree ceremony of Leeds University on October 6th. 1904 at which he was awarded the degree of Doctor of Law.

Sir John Barran's grandson John Nicholson Barran (born 1872) assumed the title

when Sir John died - his two sons had predeceased him - and it was because his wife was a Canadian that the streets in the old hall grounds were given a Canadian flavour - Montreal, Ontario, Alberta, Toronto, Winnipeg and the Dominion Cinema. The old drive from the main road followed the line of King George Avenue. The Barran family moved from Leeds after the First World War and the estate was sold. Sir John Nicholson Barran lived at Sawley Hall Ripon. Edward Nicholson Barran of Ackworth Grange near Pontefract was the younger son of Sir John Barran 2nd. baronet of Sawley Hall - he died in 1994 aged 84. His elder brother the 3rd. baronet died in 1974 and his younger brother Sir David Barran was the chairman of the Midland Bank. His late sister was the wife of Viscount Mountgarret. The mansion has been converted into 15 flats and the Grade II listed stables now contain 6 flats - an original planning application for their demolition was refused.
A Military Hospital was opened in Chapel Allerton Hall on October 30th.1916 with 35 beds and closed in April 1919 with 59 beds. There were 1320 wounded servicemen who were cared for at the Hall over three years.
Manor Lodge on the corner of Gledhow Lane and Woodland Lane was the entrance to Blue Villa or Allerton Park. The house was demolished in the early years of this century and Allerton Park is now an exclusive road with impressive dwellings. In October 1901 the new road of Allerton Park was being excavated and a large stone coffin complete with lid was discovered. The site of the discovery is marked by an eroded stone set into a house garden wall in Allerton Park and the coffin is now on display in the grounds of St. Matthew's Church on Wood Lane.
Low Gables in Allerton Park was the home of James Henry Braime, the joint managing director of the Hunslet engineering firm Messrs. T. F. & W. H. Braime being pressed steel and metal works. When he died aged 62 in August 1930 his funeral was held at Rothwell Church. Low Gables was also once the home of Francis Martineau Lupton. The son of Francis Lupton, Ald. F. M. Lupton died on February 7th.1821.
The Elms is one of several large houses on Church Lane and was the home of the clothier family of Bucktons. George Buckton was one of the three trustees of the Roundhay Bridge/Collingham turnpike in 1881 - the other two trustees were Francis Lupton and John Rhodes of Potternewton. The Elms was the home of Joseph Lupton in the 1870's to the 1890's although owned by the Nicholsons of Roundhay Park. In later years it became the home of Austyn Barran who was the Leeds food controller in the last War. The executors of the Roundhay estate placed The Elms and Chapel Allerton Hall on sale on June 24th.1871.
The oldest part of the present Allerton Hall remains as the west wing of the mansion between Wensley Drive and Stainbeck Lane. For over 300 years the original house was the home of the Kitchingman family until 1755 when it was sold to merchant Josiah Oates. Captain Laurence Edward Oates was a member of this family and was

immortalised on the Scott Antarctic expedition, when he died alone in a blizzard in 1912 aged 32. A brass plate remembers this brave man in Leeds Parish Church.
The Hall became the home of William Williams Brown. He founded the Leeds Union Bank on January lst. 1813 - the licence was issued on January 15th.- with partners Thomas and Stephen Nicholson of Roundhay Park, the London merchant Joseph Janson and Timothy Rhodes: the object was to supply banking facilities to the woollen cloth trade. A London branch was also opened which was known as Nicholson, Janson & Co becoming Brown, Janson & Co. When Thomas Nicholson died in 1821 and Stephen Nicholson retired from the partnership, William became the senior partner of the bank on Commercial Street Leeds that bore his name. In 1823 Henry Oxley entered the business and was involved in the management until his death in 1890. Henry Oxley was the Mayor of Leeds in 1872 following Sir John Barran: there were three generations of Oxleys in the Bank.
William Williams Brown was the son of merchant James Brown who married Anne Williams. He married Margaret Brockden Duncan of the United States of America in 1812. They had three children Ann Williams Brown, who married Thomas Benyon of Gledhow Hall, Margaret Brown and Samuel James Brown who was born at Allerton Hall on October 25th. 1814 and died at Durness in the north of Sutherland near Cape Wrath in 1891. Samuel James married Jacobina Maria Radcliffe and they had eleven children. William Williams Brown died in 1856 and the bank was taken over by Lloyds Bank on July 17th. 1900. On the same day the London bank and Cunliffes, Brooks & Co Manchester were also taken over by Lloyds. William Williams Brown was a generous benefactor of old St. Matthew's Church.
The 60 room mansion of Allerton Hall was mostly demolished when it was bought by William Jackson MP. He became the First Lord Allerton in 1902: born in February 1840 and died on April 4th. 1917. He was buried in old St. Matthew's churchyard on April 7th.: his wife Grace, who died aged 64 in 1901 and was buried in the family grave. Lord Allerton left £250,000 in his estate and the title was inherited by his son George Herbert Jackson.
The Rt. Hon. William Lawies Jackson LLD FRS was a JP, Chairman of the Great Northern Railway, the Mayor of Leeds in 1895/96, preceding Sir James Kitson and became an Honorary Freeman of Leeds on October 31st. 1908. He was the Financial Secretary to the Treasury: a cabinet minister in Lord Salisbury's government. Jackson was a tanner and currier of Buslingthorpe having patented the Scouring and Butt Striking Machine; the firm had been established in the early 19th. century by his father. William Lawies Jackson was the son of William Jackson and was born at Otley in 1840 becoming the MP for North Leeds and a Privy Councillor in 1890: he had married Grace, daughter of George Tempest in 1860 and they had five daughters and two sons the eldest being George Jackson who lived at The Firs in Wetherby. He married Kathleen Wickham of Boston Spa and later lived at Walton House: he

was married again to Christina Joyce Hatfield, whose family lived at Thorp Arch Hall. When her husband died she lived at the Hall: she died in 1953 and her son Edward Lawies Jackson died in 1982. The third and last Lord Allerton was the son of George and Kathleen: George William Lawies Jackson died in August 1991 aged 87: he had inherited the title in 1927 on the death of George Herbert Jackson and lived at Loddington Hall in Leicestershire.

Rt. Hon. Frank Stanley Jackson GCSI (Knight Grand Commander of the Order of the Star of India) GCIE (Knight Grand Commander of the Indian Empire) was the second son of Lord Allerton born on November 21st.1870 at Allerton Hall. He was educated at Harrow (Winston Churchill was his "fag") - he was the chairman of Harrow School governors from 1942 - and Trinity College Cambridge, captaining the school eleven in 1889 and the university cricket team for two years and played for England. He was Captain of England in 1905 when he retained the Ashes and headed the batting and bowling averages. He played 20 matches for England and scored 1415 runs: he toured India under Lord Hawke in 1893 but never went abroad again. He became the Chairman of the Test Selectors.

He played for Yorkshire from 1890 until 1907 when Lord Hawke was captain. he scored 21 centuries in 328 innings with a total of 10371 runs and an average of 33.89: he made 1468 in the 1899 season. Jackson took 506 wickets with his fast-medium right handed bowling including 25 five wickets in an innings. He maintained strong contacts with his father's firm W.L.Jackson & Sons Ltd. of which he was a director. His playing for Yorkshire was fitted into a busy programme of business and military commitments: he served in South Africa and was Captain in the 3rd. Royal Lancasters.

The Hon. F. S. Jackson was Governor of Bengal from 1927 to 1932 where he survived an attempted assassination in February 1932: he succeeded the Earl of Lytton in the post. Sir Frank Stanley Jackson became Conservative MP for North Leeds and then was MP for Howdenshire from 1915 to 1926 and was elected as the Chairman of the Conservative Party in 1923. In 1922 he was the Financial Secretary to the War Office and was knighted in 1927.

He married Julia Henrietta Harrison-Broadley in 1902: she was the daughter of Col. H. B. Harrison-Broadley of Welton House Brough who was the MP for Howdenshire. Sir Frank Jackson was to follow her father in this post. They had one son who married Diana Beddard in 1927.

The Rt. Hon. Sir F. S. Jackson was appointed President of Yorkshire CCC in 1939, following the forty year presidency of Lord Hawke. He held that position until his death on March 9th. 1947 aged 76. In 1946 he had been knocked down by a taxi and was badly injured: he died at Pont Street London SW1 of heart failure and was buried at Welton cemetery. A memorial service was held at St.Michael's Church Chester Square London.

The grounds of Allerton Hall were infilled with the flats of Wensleydale Court and the old West Lodge on Stainbeck Lane has been demolished and replaced with more modern dwellings.
Some members of the Kitchingman family are also found buried in old St. Matthew's churchyard. The tombs include those of John Kitchingman who died in 1818 - the same year that his wife Martha and son Elijah died. His children were Maria, Diana and Levi, who all died between 1852 and 1847. The Wibsey Bradford branch of the family is represented by the blacksmith John Charles Kitchingman who died in 1881. In Burmantofts Cemetery is the grave of Walter, son of Charles and Martha Kitchingman who died in 1901: Charles was a cab proprietor and died in 1904.
The family were also concerned with Leeds civic life: Thomas Kitchingman was Mayor of Leeds in 1688, in 1702 James was Mayor, Thomas in 1705 and in 1722 James Kitchingman became Mayor of Leeds. Thomas Kitchingman who was twice Mayor of Leeds is buried with his son Thomas in Leeds Parish Church: the grave slabs are to be seen in the chancel floor. Clough House on Stainbeck Lane was opened as "The Mustard Pot" public house in 1979. Hand made bricks were used to build this house in the mid-18th. century, although there had been a previous house dating from 1635: inside there is the date 1650 with the arms of the Benson family. The owner earlier this century was Florence Colman, whose name gave the mustard link, although there was in fact no connection. It is said that there is an underground passage from Clough House to Allerton Hall, with a bricked up cellar doorway being the entrance.
Stratford House was the home of clothier Henry Barran and of the Wilson family of Stanningley cloth makers. The house is now derelict and Springvale adjacent to Stratford House on Stainbeck Lane was a Home for the Blind and is converted into a new NHS Medical Centre.
The Yorkshire Bank has two properties in this area: the branch of the bank opened on March 22nd. 1937 and the Computer-Data Centre opened in 1969. The lodge to Allerton House was here: the House was once the home of engineer William John Naylor JP.
The corner of Town Street and the main road is the Police station, Fire Station and Library built on the site of some cottages which were demolished. Planning permission was granted in November 1901 for a new station. The building was designed by W. H. Thorp FRIBA and was opened by the Lord Mayor Arthur Currer Briggs JP on Thursday January 28th. 1904. The opening ceremony included the presentation of a casket to the Lord Mayor from the Library Committee. Ald. Currer Briggs died at his home Gledhow Grange on August 31st.1906 aged 51.
There would originally have been a fire cart and horse stabled at Chapel Allerton run by the fire police. Progress was made in 1866 when 16 policemen were detailed to attend Leeds fires and in 1868 the men were placed on separate fire duties. The

Insurance Companies Brigades were still playing an active part in fire fighting in Leeds. In 1872 three horses were bought and stabled at the Fire Station in the city with equipment retained in a shed by the Town Hall. A new steam fire engine was bought and used for the first time in July 1876: a second steam engine came to Leeds in 1882. The Central Fire Station in Park Street was established in 1883 and by 1885 the brigade consisted of 30 men who were all members of the Police Force. The first motor fire engine in Leeds was bought in 1910 and it was not until June 1923 that the last two of the Fire Brigade's horses was sold. The Fire Brigade staff in 1932 numbered 37 and there were 54 fire tanks in Leeds and 12358 fire hydrants. In 1948 the Leeds City Fire Brigade operated independently from the Police. The Eastern Sub-Station opened at Gipton in October 1937 and the Stonegate Road Station was opened on May 14th.1957. The original police station at Chapel Allerton contained fire fighting equipment, was opened in 1872 adjacent to the chapel in Town Street and was used as a section station until replaced by the new building. The site is now a house on Town Street Walk. In 1930 it became C Division HQ when the Sheepscar station closed and became known as Chapeltown Police Station. The station today is known as AC Division and with the 200 strong force covers an area from Regent Street to the villages of Scarcroft, Thorner, Boston Spa, Clifford, Bardsey and Collingham. The Chapeltown station has the CID in a new building adjacent to the new Methodist Church and Local Intelligence. The old fire station which closed about the First World War is used by the Police and retains the hay loft and stables accommodation from the early days.

In April 1994 it was announced that the new Chapeltown Police Headquarters will be built on the site of the demolished Stainbeck Middle School. A smaller local station would be built on Chapeltown Road, which will involve demolition of some buildings. It was suggested that £5 million be spent on a state of the art building on the same lines as the new Killingbeck station.

To the east of the Police Station is the Nag's Head public house: this 18th. century coaching inn on the original route of the turnpike retains the horse mounting block outside. The old Bay Horse inn which faced Town Street has been demolished: it was from this inn that a service ran to Leeds in 1750.

The growing number of Methodists in Chapel Allerton necessitated the building of a chapel in 1794 and land was bought at The Croft on Town Street. The date now seen on the present Community Centre was once the position of a clock. In 1805 a Sunday School was built behind the chapel which was demolished in 1835. The Sunday School was held in a basement room which was excavated and opened in 1836. In 1852 the Trustees took it over from T. B. Pease of Chapel Allerton Hall: they bought it for £1200 in 1867 and until 1870 it was a Wesleyan Day School.

In 1872 the Trustees found a site for a new chapel on the main road, being the house and garden of Major Pilsworth - the land was owned by the Gott family of Armley

who sold it for £1700. The new Methodist Chapel was built to the designs of architect C. O. Ellison. The foundation stone was laid on May 26th. 1874. The new chapel was dedicated and opened on March 15th. 1876. The newly refurbished youth and community centre was opened by the Minister Rev. W. Stainer-Smith and a year later Chapel Allerton became a Stewardship Church.
The church hall was built south of the church to designs by architect F. Danby by Joshua Richardson at a cost of £865: the foundation stone was laid in June 1907 and it was opened in September: the building was demolished in 1982 together with the church.
An approach by a developer in 1970 led to the idea of demolition and rebuilding. The approval for demolition was granted in August 1976 but only started in January 1982.The building of the shopping centre started in March and was finished in January 1983. The new Methodist Church opened on February 12th. 1983 on land once occupied by a builders yard and cottages. The foundation stone of the second church laid by Edward Jackson - he ran a Hatter business in Vicar Lane in May 1874 is now incorporated into the new church entrance.
The Chapel Allerton Co-op building was opened in 1901 the foundation stone was laid on March 23rd. by Co-op director Walter Jenkinson. The Regent public house was built in the early 19th. century, while The British Workman in the same street is no longer a public house.

The foundation stone of St. Matthew's Church on Wood Lane was laid in the east wall of St. Luke's Chapel on October 13th.1897 by John William Naylor in the presence of Rt. Rev. William Boyd Carpenter, the Bishop of Ripon and Rev. Edgar Charles Gibson the Vicar of Leeds. The church was consecrated on February 3rd 1900 by Rt. Rev. John Pulleine Bishop of Richmond. The church cost £20,500 and was built to the designs of architect George Frederick Bodley. G. F. Bodley (1827-1907) was born in Hull and designed four churches in West Yorkshire: St. Mary at Horbury, St. Aidan's Skelmanthorpe, St. Edward's Church Holbeck Leeds in 1902/04 and St. Matthew's Church. He also extended the chancel at St. Mary's Church Whitkirk for Mrs. Meynell Ingram. It was Bodley who built the large sandstone church at Hoar Cross as a memorial to Mrs. Meynell Ingram's husband, who died in 1871 - the church was finished in 1876. When Mrs. Meynell Ingram died in 1904 she was buried with her husband at Hoar Cross in Staffordshire.
The oldest inclusion in this church is the font from the old demolished church. It is dated 1637 and is inscribed with the quotation from Chapter 4 verse 5 of Ephesians: "ONE LORD ONE FAITH ONE BAPTISM". The splendid Oak chancel screen was made by the Leeds firm of Marsh, Jones & Cribb in 1900 and the Oak pulpit has steps made from Derbyshire fossil marble. The pulpit is in memory of Queen Victoria who died in January 1901 - as the inscription reads. There is a plaque on the

north wall of the chancel to John Primatt Maud Bishop Suffragan Kensington. He was the perpetual curate of Chapel Allerton from 1900 - 1904 and afterwards was the Vicar of St. Mary Redcliffe at Bristol he died aged 71 on March 21st.1932.

St. Matthew's Church Hall was dedicated by the Bishop of Ripon on April 23rd.1978.

St. Matthew's C of E School was built in 1872 to designs by William Perkin and Elisha Backhouse: the school on Woodland Lane was eventually demolished to be replaced with flats of the Leeds Federated Housing Association. The Primary School became a Middle School in the 1970's and in 1992 reverted to being a Primary School again. The present school building was dedicated on Wood Lane on June 20th. 1975.

The first school in Chapel Allerton was on School Lane rebuilt in 1836 and was demolished in February 1963, having ceased to be a school many years ago - it became a private school in 1891.

The Chapel Allerton Recreation Ground on Woodland Lane is a 6/7 acre site bought by the Leeds Council in 1897 and opened by the Lord Mayor Ald. John Gordon on July 2nd. 1900. The site included a bandstand and has 4 tennis courts, flower beds and a fine bowling green. John Gordon lived at Potternewton Hall and was a Leeds accountant and JP: he was deputy Lord Mayor in 1895/96 when Lord Allerton was the first Conservative Leeds Mayor since 1836.

The "Black Swan" inn was by the gates of the Recreation Ground: the house originated during the 17th. century and probably was a farmstead. The corner of Woodland Lane and Harrogate Road was once The Queen's Arms public House. The inn once had stables and was opened in the 18th. century to serve the turnpike trade. In the 1880's the innkeeper was Elizabeth Kitchen. In 1897 the inn became one of Tetley's public houses - the conveyance mentions Lord Allerton. In 1933 the brewery sold the inn to Herbert Webster of Harehills Road and the present Queens Arms Inn was designed by Sydney Kitson and opened on December 13th.1934.The last landlord at the old Queen's Arms transferred to the new inn and while there Fred Harrison founded the bowling green club. The land on which the new public house was built had been the Chapel Allerton Athletic soccer pitch and in summer was used by New Park Cricket Club. The Queen's Arms has a large bar, restaurant and function facilities and is a landmark of North Leeds.

The old Queen's Arms became a newsagents shop and now the block contains the restored Heritage House. The corner of Woodland Lane and the main road also had a convenience and garage - it is now Eldan House.

On the west side of the main road opposite the junction are the lodge and gate pillars to Westfield. This large building now has access from Wood Lane and was converted into flats. Westfield was the home of Charles Ryder of Tetley's Brewery in the late 19th. century. Charles Ryder became a partner with Francis William Tetley in October 1858, having been working at the Leeds brewery for a few years.

Charles Ryder was Francis William's brother in law - Francis had married Isabella Ryder daughter of Arthur Ryder in 1847. The Ryder family were London traders and Charles came to Leeds from China, where he represented a tea firm in Canton. He was a great success at the Leeds brewery and by 1865 his share of the profits was increased to 40%.
Westfield became the home of Eliza Barran and later of John Croysdale by the end of the 19th. century. Later Westfield became a home of the Delius family who were keen to help local boy's cricket - they provided the kit and transport for the so called Delius XI. Daniel and Rudolf Delius were wool, noil (short separated pieces of wool) and yarn merchants of Union Warehouses Bradford
Moor Allerton Bottoms, once the site of the pinfold, is the area at the junction of Gledhow Valley Road and Harrogate Road. The woodlands of the Gledhow Valley, often called Pollard Woods were presented to Leeds by the Hon. Hilda Kitson of Gledhow Hall. The Hall became a Kitson residence in 1878, having been the estate of Edward Waddington from 1671: it was Waddington who built the Spa which was restored in 1985. In 1764 the Hall became home to Jeremiah Dixon, who became Lord of the Manor and rebuilt the Hall in 1768 - the date and initials JD are seen on the archway across Gledhow Lane.
The Kingsway Cinema was opened on Monday June 28th.1937 by Osbert Peake MP for North Leeds: Osbert Peake was later created Viscount Ingleby. The cinema was designed by James Brodie of Pudsey and was built in the gardens of Allerton Lodge. This house was the home of John and Ann Myers - John died aged 49 in 1816 - Walter Battle in the 1880's and of Arthur Gilliat from 1892 until 1933.Arthur Gilliat died in 1935 while his wife Mary lived until 1954 when she was 88 years old.
The opening film at the Kingsway was Jessie Matthews in "Head over Heels", a newly released film directed by Sonnie Hale and also starring Robert Flemyng. The film was exhibited in Mirrophonic Sound: Sir Edwin Airey sent his best wishes on the opening night.
The last film to be shown before closure on August 23rd.1959 was Marlon Brando in "Sayonara", this 2½ hour picture was directed by Joshua Logan from the popular novel by James A. Mitchener.
The old cinema opened on September 4th. 1959 as the New Central Vilna Synagogue - named after the founders from Vilnius Lithuania, a centre of Jewish and Polish culture which was occupied by Russia in 1939. The congregations of the New Central Synagogue on Wintoun Street and the Vilna Synagogue on Camp Road combined to worship at the old cinema premises. The New Central Vilna Synagogue closed in October 1991 and the site was sold to a developer as possible offices in the building. In March 1994 Leeds Planning Department agreed to allow flats to be built on the site with the demolition of the old cinema. The original settlement of Moor Allerton or Moortown was concentrated in the area which was the Broomhill estate.

Broomhill Farm was run by John William Pollard and was adjacent to the large house of Broomhill. The Pollard family had many farming interests in this area with Charles Pollard at Allerton Grange and William at Gledhow Grange at the end of the last century. Only a small part of a wall and outhouse remains of the Broomhill Farm and a parade of shops is now on the site. Broomhill was built in 1838 for the Skelton family - Thomas Skelton was a partner in the firm of Skelton & Naylor maltsters of Little Holbeck. The property became the rented home of the Ambler family in the late 19th. century and was sold by W. S. Chantrell to Herbert Ambler in 1921: Broomhill was the home to the Leeds architect Thomas Ambler (1838-1920) and his wife Jane who died in April 1935.Ambler set up his practice in Park Row Leeds and in the 1890's took George Bowman as his partner. Thomas Ambler was responsible for the Temperance Hotel Boar Lane, St Pauls House as a factory and warehouse for Sir John Barran in 1878 and in 1883 designed Parcmont for the Barran family - it is now a hotel.

Thomas Ambler died at Broomhill aged 81 on January 13th. 1920 having been in business from 1860. He was married twice and had a son Herbert and four daughters including Gertrude, Mrs. Florence Rowlandson and Mrs. Fawcett. His second wife died in 1918.Thomas was a member of the Leeds City Council from 1884 until 1892 and was a Liberal and a Freemason.

In August 1949 Gertrude Ambler and Florence Rowlandson sold Broomhill to the trustees of the Roman Catholic Diocese of Leeds, who included Bishop Poskitt and the Rev. Joseph McShane. The house became the presbytery of the Immaculate Heart parish, which it remains today.

The Church of the Immaculate Heart opened with Pontifical Mass by the Rt. Rev. John Carmel Heenan Bishop of Leeds on the Feast of St. Gregory March 12th.1956.The church, designed by R. A. Ronchetti, was consecrated by the Rt. Rev. George Patrick Dwyer Bishop of Leeds on June 16th.1959: enclosed in the high altar are the relics of the martyrs St. Valerian and St. Felicity.

A Mass Centre was opened in 1942 at the Queens Arms Hotel from the Holy Rosary Parish: this became inadequate and The Grange at Moortown with 3½ acres of land was bought in 1945 for use as a chapel and presbytery. The first Parish Priest was Father Joseph McShane from the Holy Rosary parish and he bought two wooden huts from Dewsbury Corporation for £500 which were opened by Bishop Poskitt at The Grange as the Church of the Immaculate Heart of Mary on August lst. 1946. Attendances at the Masses were increased by POW's at Shadwell and the Corner House at Moortown was used for social functions.

When the Broomhill estate was bought The Grange was sold to the Sisters of the Cross and Passion and it became a convent and private school. The school expanded and in 1957 the old church was adapted as a girl's grammar school. The Grange is now the St.Gemma's Hospice - the third largest hospice in Britain.

The new church of St. Paul at Alwoodley was opened by Bishop Heenan in 1953 and it became a new parish in 1954. In 1954 a new parish hall at the Broomhill site was built by volunteers and is known as the Queen's Hall.
There is a memorial in the grounds to the Rt. Rev. Msg. Canon Joseph McShane born April 25th.1903 and died August 23rd. 1981: he was interred at Killingbeck. The inscription reminds us that Father McShane was the founder and parish priest of the church 1945 and of St. Paul's Church Alwoodley 1953.
The St. Andrew's RC Primary School in the grounds of the church opened as a Middle School in 1977 but was reorganised as a primary school in 1990.
The Grange was built as a private house, being the home of the barrister Thomas West in 1881 and then Charles Francis Clark, born in 1862 who was to live at Shortacres Moortown from 1900 - he died in 1935. Alexander Murray McQuat from Driverholme Douglas Lanarkshire (Strathclyde) - was the next resident of The Grange - he died aged 86 on February 13th. 1936. Alexander McQuat ran a firm of Leeds wine merchants. The Grange was sold in 1945 to the Catholic Diocese of Leeds and in 1949 the Sisters of the Cross and Passion opened a convent and preparatory school. This was adapted in 1957 as the St. Gemma's Girls RC Grammar School and on March 12th. 1978 the school was rededicated as a hospice. The appeal fund for St.Gemma's was opened in 1977 at Leeds Town Hall. The official opening of St.Gemma's Hospice was on April 12th. 1978 by Bishop Gordon Wheeler and Msg. Joseph McShane and Canon Joseph Lyons.
The new building at St.Gemma's Hospice started on July 4th. 1979 with the foundation stone being laid by HRH Princess Alexandra on June 10th.1980. In June 1981 the purpose built hospice was opened on one floor only. To mark this occasion the Bishop of Leeds Rt. Rev. Gordon Wheeler presented a bronze bust of St.Gemma sculpted by Dr. Arthur Fleischmann. The official opening of the £2 million extension providing 45 beds was by the Prince and Princess of Wales on March 30th. 1982. In his speech Prince Charles said:"What has happened has been the translation into reality of a vision held by a small number of very determined, enthusiastic and compassionate people."
On September 12th. 1991 Princess Diana returned to St.Gemma's Hospice to officially open the £300,000 Elizabeth Prout Study Centre. This is named after the founder of the religious order which runs the Hospice and the internationally known teaching centre providing courses for doctors, nurses, ministers and other caring for the terminally ill.
The Hospice is 80% funded by charity and costs about £2 million a year to operate. It is the third largest Hospice in England and the second teaching hospice providing courses for folk from around the world. St.Gemma's Hospice caters for about 750 in patients every year and also about 800 are cared for in their own homes. The Day Centre which provides vital therapy to the patients, over 2000 attending every year.

On March 12th. 1993 was the official opening of the £500,000 purpose built St. Patrick's Residential Home by the Duke and Duchess of Norfolk and the Bishop of Leeds the Rt. Rev. David Konstant. It provides own room accommodation for nine frail and elderly folk and was built on the site of the former schoolhouse, which became the city's first nine bed hospice in 1978. The motto of St.Gemma's Hospice is "Love knows no measure".
Farming was known in the area from the 12th. century, when the monks of Kirkstall Abbey opened their farm at Allerton Grange. This was still a farm early this century on Lidgett Lane and stood opposite Allerton Grange High School and Moor Allerton Hall - now a Primary School. Allerton Grange County Secondary School opened on February 23rd. 1955. In 1899 the farm was run by Charles Pollard and the Hall was the home of Lt. Col. Lambert and later of R. B. Hopkins.
Street Lane in the mid 19th. century was a quiet country lane and even by the turn of the century had only a few farms and Sportsmans Hall. This was a meeting place for the folk who lived on the nearby estates. The Hall faced south on Street Lane and the verandah offered a good view across the countryside. The row of eight houses west of the Hall site was built in 1870, offering dwellings for workers at the brickworks - the site was on the corner of Lime Tree Avenue and Allerton Grove. The site near Sportsmans Hall became Street Lane Nurseries following the sale of land in 1930 and both were replaced by a parade of shops and the Beth Hamedrash Hagadol Synagogue. This synagogue moved from the corner of Bridge Street and Nile Street, which opened in 1908, to Newton Park Road in 1937. The Street Lane synagogue and community centre was consecrated by the Chief Rabbi Dr. Immanuel Jakobovits on March 9th.1969: stones were laid by Alexander Rose and Bernard Lyons JP on the same day. There is a memorial garden dedicated in May 1970 and a memorial to the fallen of two world wars: the 6 million martyrs.
The Moortown branch of the Yorkshire Bank opened on July lst. 1955. The Corner House was opened on November 28th. 1938 as a cinema but closed after a short life on January 6th. 1940. The building was the design of Pudsey based architect James Brodie: the first film shown was "A Yank at Oxford" with Robert Taylor and Vivien Leigh. There was a squash court, club, dancing and a cafe at the Corner House, which offered teas after a matinée - the shows included two newsreels and shorts with admission in 1939 being 6d and 1/-.The cinema was not licensed for showing feature films and in December 1939 was showing "Overcoat Sam" but the failure to display a category board in the entrance led to a court case. Crawshaw Gardens Estate Ltd. was convicted of an alleged offence in respect of the display and the closure was forced upon the company, who needed to show features to remain open. Later advertising included asking would be patrons to write in for the programme which will be "sent by post on request".
Following the closure of the Corner House as a cinema, it became known as the

Assembly Rooms and was well known for dancing. One of the most popular orchestras of the 1930's was that of Ralph Fidler. Patrons were also invited to join the Corner House Club. The property was sold in 1954 and again in 1972: the property is now the Continental Casino Club.

The only building between Street Lane and Shadwell Lane was the Simpson's tea rooms at the turn of the century. In later years the rows of shops were developed: these included Knapton's Bakery established in 1937 by Herbert Knapton of Holbeck. His daughter Gladys married Cyril Hardy and they ran the Harrogate Road business. Their son Ian Knapton Hardy is the family member who runs the present business.

The branch of the Leeds & Holbeck Building Society opened on Harrogate Parade in 1970. This followed the opening of their branch at Chapel Allerton five years earlier. The Leeds Union Operative Land and Building Society opened in the old school room Marshall Street Holbeck in January 1845. In 1852 the Second Leeds Union Operative Benefit Building Society was founded in the Sweet Street school rooms: this terminated in 1864. In June 1857 a third society was formed which ended in 1870. In 1864 the Holbeck Benefit B.S. was founded and in March 1870 the Leeds Union O.B.B.S. was established until 1883. These five Terminating Societies were a great success and the Building Societies Act was passed in 1874. The sixth society was founded in 1875 on a Permanent basis in the Holbeck Mechanics Institute - the bankers were William Williams Brown & Co. of Park Row. Premises were bought in 1886 on Albion Street and the Head Office was established. - the Leeds & Holbeck Building Society was formed, with the word Permanent removed in 1929.

In the 1920's with the development of The Headrow a nearby corner property was acquired which incorporated the Burley Bar stone - this is displayed in a glass case in the present building. The new building was extended in 1963 and opened by E. J. Loy Wooler, who was to be the Leeds Lord Mayor. Further extensions westward on The Headrow were completed in 1970.

Near the corner of Allerton Grove and Harrogate Road was Moortown Motors followed by a Fine Fare supermarket: the garage transferred to the corner of Regent Street/Skinner Lane. The nearby Marks & Spencer store was opened in October 1992.

South of the Chained Bull public house was Moor Allerton House. In the early 19th. century Moor Allerton House was the home of John Skelton: his wife Ruthetta died aged 24 on June 9th. 1812 and has a memorial in Holy Trinity Church Boar Lane Leeds. The House became the home of Ald. Sir John Ward, who became a Leeds alderman in 1886 and concerned himself with much needed improvements in the local rivers and streams. Ald. Sir John Ward died in 1908 and Moor Allerton House was replaced by the Arncliffe Grange flats.

The Chained Bull inn was originally a low two storey 18th. century turnpike public house being nearer to the main road - it was mentioned in a 1768 survey. It had extensive stabling facilities, a coach house and barn with a smithy: this was run by Thomas Scurrah in the early times of this century. The present larger brick built public house was built behind the site of the old inn: the plans to rebuild were announced in 1924, when the new Ind Coope inn was to be placed about 80 yards to the rear of the old building. Behind the inn was the Moortown (Brunswick) cricket ground, bowling green, tennis courts and between the inn and the smithy was the first Moortown Post Office.

The Midland Bank branch opened in Moortown in 1928 - the branches in Oakwood and Chapel Allerton were opened in 1901.In that year the bank was known as the London City and Midland Bank Ltd and by 1928 had changed to Midland Bank. The Midland Bank has been represented in Leeds from the early 19th. century. The banking firm of Perfect & Co was established in 1809 and the firm was acquired in 1834 by the newly established Yorkshire District Bank - later the Yorkshire Banking Co.

In 1890 the Midland acquired the Exchange & Discount Bank established by John James Cousins in 1860 and also the Leeds & County Bank on Park Row, which had been formed in 1862. In 1901 the Yorkshire Banking Co. was acquired by the Midland.

On Shadwell Lane is Moortown Primary School which was opened in 1889 as Moortown Board School designed by John Peacock Kay. The adjacent building was built in 1882 as the United Methodist Free Chapel, now converted into commercial premises. Donisthorpe Hall was known as Holly Bank and the property of George Edmund Donisthorpe. He ran a firm of wool combers and merchants at the Larchfield Mills on Hunslet Road - his main interest was in the invention of combing machines. He died in 1875 and there is a bust of him in the Bradford Cartwright Museum.

Holly Bank was the home to Edwin Simpson in the mid 19th. century and then to Harry Greenwood. The Holly Bank Estate was sold in 1870 and by the start of this century it was the property of the Watson family of the Leeds soap firm, who changed the name of the hall. By 1916 the Hall was the property of Henry Berry, a hydraulic engineer of the Croydon Works Hunslet. Henry Berry was born in March 1853 and died in February 1919: his wife Sarah died in 1947 aged 87; their daughter was Constance lived from 1887 until 1910. A few years later Donisthorpe Hall was the home of Thomas F. Braime of a firm of Hunslet stampers. In 1955 Donisthorpe Hall became a Jewish Old People's Home and a Convalescent Home opened in 1967. Moorfield House on Stonegate Road was the home of William Cooke in 1890 and later of Edmund G. Arnold (1902-1954). Moorfield Farm was for many years run by the Umpleby family. The Moor Allerton Memorial Institute on Stonegate Road was opened on November 25th. 1920 - the institute was a hut originally given by the North family to the South Camp, near the original racecourse at Ripon. It was removed and re-erected to commemorate the services of all from the parish who served in the First World War. The institute was opened by J. E. Maude of The Mount. The Bowling Club opened in 1926 and a new pavilion was built in 1980; Moortown Lawn Tennis Club opened in 1921. A new Memorial Hall was opened on September 4th. 1971 by the Lord Mayor.

The row of houses from Sand Hill Lane to the Ring Road once included the Post Office (no.498) and the Police Station next door. Providence Square and Providence Place were once a part of this row of houses in High Moor Allerton. There are records of four stone tablets set into the walls of the houses here including religious texts. One inscription was on an archway:"Providence Place S. D. Middleham 1829".The others included religious tracts. In the garden of "Alwoodley Gates" is one of these plaques inscribed:"PROVIDENCE PLACE S MIDDLEHAM AD 1839" the text reads: "Be not wise in thine own eyes. Fear the Lord and depart from evil". This is from Proverbs Chapter 3 verse 7.

There were 20 stone houses around two small greens, one of which was the largest: Providence Place. This part was demolished in 1938 to make way for the Ring Road dual carriageway from Harrogate Road to Shadwell Lane.

The last houses before The Mount were William Hall blacksmith and agricultural engineers Thomas Scurrah, demolished to build the Ring Road in the 1920's.

St John's Church, Moor Allerton

THE ROAD FROM LEEDS TO HARROGATE

PART 3:FROM THE RING ROAD MOOR ALLERTON TO HAREWOOD

The Leeds Ring Road was developed during the 1920's taking some of the land from Moor Allerton church for the dual carriageway. The section from Tongue Lane to Harrogate Road was completed in 1924, as was the section from Shadwell Lane to Roundhay Park Lane. The Moor Allerton District Centre was built on the King Lane/Ring Road corner, with Sainbury's Store opening in October 1981. It was not until 1938 that the section from the main road to Shadwell Lane was completed, having used the old cricket ground in the grounds of The Grange during construction. The continuation of the dual carriageway from Shadwell Lane eastwards and a flyover junction on Harrogate Road were abandoned by the Ministry of Transport in March 1994.

St .John the Evangelist Church was consecrated on December 13th. 1853 by the Bishop of Ripon, being one of the many churches that were built in the programme by Dr. Walter Hook, Vicar of Leeds. The architect was Joseph Thompson of Leeds and the land on which the church was built had been given by Sir Thomas Beckett: subscribers to the building fund included the Earl of Harewood, the Lane Fox family who were Lords of the Manor, John Gott and the merchant John Purchon.
Sir Thomas Beckett also gave the land for the burial ground, the vicarage and the school which was opened in 1855 with a schoolhouse - the school closed in 1881 and the school master's house was demolished in 1939. The old school is now the Parish Hall and has extensive uses. The church was enlarged in 1889 when the present chancel was completed and the vicarage demolished in 1939 - the present rectory was built in 1953.
There are few memorials in the church, although there is a brass plaque on the north nave wall to Joshua Bower Brooke, a trustee and churchwarden who died in March 1914 "in the hunting field". The north transept window was also placed in memory of this local character, who lived at Nunbrooke, south of The Grange (now St.Gemma's Hospice) on Harrogate Road. The wood reredos and sanctuary surround was placed in memory of Ann and architect Thomas Ambler with their son Herbert in 1930. Two windows in the south chancel are in memory of George Watson and his wife Mary Anne - George died aged 65 in 1905 and his wife died a year afterwards. The south transept window remembers John Benson (1819-1889), who is buried in the north graveyard with his father Robert Benson (1784-1859): the family lived at Burley in Wharfedale. The organ was given in memory of Emma Benson of Oswaldkirk Hall: Emma was John Benson's widow who died

in May 1910 and is buried in the family grave.
Increased population ensured the development and growth of the parish: St. Stephen's Church was dedicated in October 1954 and St. Barnabas Church Alwoodley was dedicated in 1962, having developed from Alwoodley Hall. The foundation stone of the Archbishop Cranmer Church Middle School was laid by Sir Kenneth Parkinson on April 28th. 1975 and the school opened in September 1976: the official opening was on December 6th. The school became a Primary School in September 1992.
St.John's Church was reordered in 1988/89 and rededicated on April 15th. 1989: commemorated by the planting of a tree in the churchyard. The War Memorial by the roadside in the church grounds was built in Portland stone by J. T. Wright & Sons for £480. The cross was unveiled on October 8th. 1921. The lychgate was built in 1913 and erected at the expense of Elizabeth Booker in memory of her family. The sundial memorial is to Annie Sagar-Musgrave who died in March 1937 - her family lived at Red Hall Shadwell.
In the churchyard is the grave of James lst. Baron Milner of Leeds who died on July 16th. 1967 aged 78 at his home The Grove North Lane Roundhay. He was born in 1889 the son of J. H. Milner, who was the Leeds City Coroner. He was educated at Easingwold Grammar School and took the degree of Bachelor of Law at Leeds University in 1911. He became a member of Leeds City Council in 1923 and was Deputy Lord Mayor in 1928/29. He was commissioned from the ranks during the First World War and won the MC and Bar. He was wounded and taken prisoner and attempted to escape to Switzerland: his leg was amputated as a result of his injuries. He was awarded the degree of Doctor of Law at Leeds in 1953. Lord Milner was a former Deputy Speaker of the House of Commons and was MP for Leeds South-East from 1929 until 1951. For 50 years James Milner was a partner in the firm of J. H. Milner Solicitors. He retired in 1963 and was awarded the freedom of the City of Leeds in October 1966 - this was conferred in his absence through illness. James Milner was created a Baron in the Dissolution Honours List in 1951.
Lord Milner of Leeds was the President of the Leeds Civic Trust and the Vice-President of the Thoresby Society. In 1917 he married Lois Brown, the daughter of Thomas Brown of Roundhay. Baroness Milner died in April 1982 aged 94: they had one son and two daughters and daughter Zaidee died aged 61 in 1980.
The land east of the church once belonged to The Mount estate: the south facing hall was built in 1790 and included 40 acres of land with the cricket field, polo field, herbaceous walk and a lake. The Mount was the home of the Maude family: James Edmund Maude was born on June 9th. 1847 and was educated at Leeds Grammar School. He joined his father's firm of Leeds timber merchants in The Calls. His brother William Henry Maude also attended Leeds Grammar School

and entered the family firm: he became a JP for the West Riding and lived at Middleton Lodge.
James Edmund Maude died on November 4th. 1933 aged 86 - his wife Annie had died in September 1926 aged 81 and the Hall became Ingledew College. The school was started at 8 Ingledew Crescent Roundhay for boys and girls by Reginald Welch in 1924. When he died in 1934 the school was taken over by Mr & Mrs John Edward Gimlett, who stayed at Ingledew Crescent for three years. In 1937 the school moved to The Mount, the old home of Col. Maude. The boy's preparatory school was run by John Gimlett and the girl's school by Elizabeth Gimlett, who took over as headmistress on the death of her husband in 1961.The school closed on July 17th.1964 and Elizabeth retired from teaching - she died in March 1981.
The house was demolished and the grounds of the estate were sold for redevelopment. The old entrance opposite Fir Tree Lane became Sandringham Way and the lodge demolished. The blocked up gate further to the north was a side entrance to The Mount. There was also an entrance on Shadwell Lane with access into these extensive grounds, which were once opened to the public at weekends.
Fir Tree Lane was the access to both Fir Tree Farm and Beehive Farm.
The Etz Chaim Synagogue was opened in September 1980 and was consecrated by the Chief Rabbi Sir Immanuel Jakobovits on December 6th.1981: there is a stone laid by David Shiffer the Honorary Life Member of the Congregation. The name of this synagogue was obtained as a result of a public competition - it is the Hebrew for Tree of Life.
There was a small building known as Pepper Hall by the west main road side and on the eastern side of the road are Pepper Hills Flats built by the Leeds Housing Association.
The toll bar for this section of the Leeds/Harrogate turnpike was sited at the north end of the Nursery Lane/Harrogate Road junction.
The Moortown service reservoir at 536'OS was completed in 1872, enlarged in 1892 and again in 1926. The first reservoir was 9' deep and held 1,325,000 gallons; the second was 18' deep holding 4,184,000 gallons. There are now three reservoirs distributing to many areas and feeding the Garforth tower by gravity. The 100' Moortown tower - there are 118 steps to the top - was built in August/September 1922 and opened in 1923, standing 616' above sea level: the water has a depth of 16' in the ferroconcrete tower. It is the oldest city water tower with a capacity of 75,000 gallons and was renovated recently.
The Yorkshire Water Authority came into being on April 1st. 1974 as one of ten regional authorities. In 1989 the Water Act transferred responsibilities for water and sewage disposal to ten major privatised companies. Yorkshire Water PLC

employs 4500 people and provides water services to 4.4 million domestic customers as well as 140,000 industrial and commercial customers. The company serves an area of 139,000 sq. km. and supplies over 308 million gallons of water every day.

Yorkshire Water now operates 719 reservoirs and water towers, 149 water treatment works, 1265 sewage pumping stations and 626 sewage treatment works. Of all the water supplied 41% is from the reservoirs, 22% from boreholes, 34% from rivers and 3% is bought from other companies.

Nursery Lane was the access to the Heath Nurseries, north of Pykeley Hill Farm. The nurseries were run by the Rider family: William Rider ran the concern in the 19th. century and he died aged 70 in 1875.The Green family took over at the Nursery prior to closure. The area which included the Pykeley Hill Farm became the Moor Allerton Golf Club, which was founded in 1923 by a group of Jewish community leaders and was the first Jewish Golf Club outside America. The course was designed by Alister MacKenzie and the first clubhouse was the stone built Pykeley Hill farm house, until 1928 when a new wooden building was erected. A £50,000 new club house was officially opened on April 27th.1958 and was used until 1970.In October 1970 Moor Allerton Golf Club moved to the Coal Road, on land which had been bought at auction with the help of Bernard Lyons: the new club house opened in 1971. The new course was designed by the American Robert Trent Jones.

The club house on Nursery Lane was sold to Cameron's Brewery and became The Allerton Hotel: this became a Berni Inn and Warwick Suite PLC (Leeds Masonic Temple) bought the property from GrandMet in 1989. The catering franchise is with John Gilpin Ltd, who have their head office at Harewood. The course was redeveloped and the street names reflect the famous golf courses of Britain: Turnberry, St.Andrews, Birkdale, Wentworth and Gleneagles.

In 1900 the only buildings from Nursery Lane to Alwoodley Gates were the toll bar, Hawk's Nest Farm with Hill Top to the east and Lucy's Cottage to the west.

Moortown Golf Club was formed in 1909 and is set in 75 acres of contrasting woodland and moorland. The course was laid out by Dr. Alister MacKenzie - he designed the famous American course at Augusta Georgia. One of the first Chairmen was T. F. Braime of Donisthorpe Hall. A new clubhouse was opened in 1915 and by the mid 1920's the course assumed the layout which was to exist without major alterations for over 60 years. The old clubhouse was converted into a private house in 1918. In 1929 Moortown Course was host to the first Ryder Cup match, which Britain won. In 1989 the course was re-designed with two new holes created beyond the practice ground. The Club now has a course of 7020 yards and is proud of its history and traditions.

The "Jester" public house was opened in November 1956: John Smith's transferred

the licence for the inn from the "Alexandra" on Green Road. The "Jester" was bought from John Smith's /Courage in 1991 by Mansfield Brewery. Mansfield Brewery was founded in 1855 in Mansfield Nottinghamshire. The brewery now has 440 of its own houses and 1000 free trade customers from Scarborough to Coventry and along the eastern Pennines across to the East Coast.
The company was established in 1854 by farmers William Baily and Samuel Hage with brewer John Watson. By 1901 the company was owned by three families of Baily, Chadburn and Titley - William Baily died in 1874 and his son in 1903. A new brewhouse was completed in 1983 and in 1991 29 John Smith's public houses were bought from Courage. In 1991 a new £3 million head office at Littleworth was opened. In 1992 another 88 John Smith's pubs were bought and 6 Whitbread inns were also bought. In March 1993 11 public houses were acquired from Scottish & Newcastle.

Alwoodley Gates was a separate hamlet in the township of Wigton that once had a Wesleyan Chapel, also used as a day school administered by James Kitchingman. The chapel closed in the 1960's and was converted as a private dwelling: it was sold for £6000 in 1984 and demolished to be replaced by new flats.
The village smithy was on the corner of Harrogate Road and Alwoodley Lane: the blacksmith and farrier was Thomas Burley who died in 1797 aged 46 - and in this century the smith was John Horner. The Horner family also ran the village shop converted from the "King's Arms" Inn, which still stands on the corner: James Kent was the innkeeper, who died in 1845 aged 73.Grove House Farm is a working farm, bought by the Leeds City Council from the Harewood estate. The dairy farm is now run as a mixed beef, sheep and corn concern and was once tenanted by farmer John Umpleby.
Wigton Grove Farm on the north east corner of Alwoodley Lane and the main road ceased to be a farm in the 1950's and Leeds University bought the land when the Harewood estate sold it in June 1951 - the property was then tenanted by Arthur Lupton. The new development of housing is known as Wigton Gates.
The large house "Alwoodley Gates" stands in 4½ acres of land on the south east corner of the junction. It was built in 1935 on land once used for meetings of the Bramham Moor Hunt until 1932. There is a stone built into the south wall inscribed with initials and date. The house was built for James Arthur Sykes, golfer and managing director of the Yorkshire Copper Works. The house was built of Newton Kyme quarry stone - there are many shades of this limestone in the walls - on land sold by the Earl of Harewood's estate. The inscribed stone from Providence Place is part of the garden steps and there is a small sculptured stone over the east door, representing members of the Sykes family. There is also a large S over the west doorway and a metal plaque on the garden wall inscribed:"This

wall was built of stones forming part of the Roman Road which ran towards Shadwell through the site of this garden".This was the road to Adel and Ilkley. In 1976 the house was bought by Leeds United Chairman Manny Cussins, who was also the chairman of John Peters - Manny Cussins died in London aged 82 on 5th. October 1987. Manny Cussins was born in Hull and was to build up the Cussins Group, which was sold in 1954 for £1 million. By 1975 his John Peters chain had 53 furniture stores, 38 tailoring shops in Scotland, 30 men's clothing shops and 11 clothing factories. The group became known as Waring + Gillow and Manny Cussins set up Arncliffe Holdings in 1971.
The derelict cottage in the garden corner was once the home of Leslie Bond the gardener to the Sykes family and the building predates Alwoodley Gates. There is also a sunken factory boiler in the garden, used during the war as an air raid shelter.
Wigton Lane with the Alwoodley Golf Club founded in 1907 and an abundance of new quality housing on the north side, was once known as Alwoodley Lane to Slaid Hill. The lands at Wigton were enclosed in December 1797 and comprised a scattered township, not mentioned in the Domesday Book. In 1327 the hamlet was known as Wigton cum Brandon in Harewood Parish and the then Lord of Wigton was the Prior of Bolton Abbey. It was Peter de Marton who had granted Wigton and Brandon to the Wharfedale priory. The Alwoodley Golf Club was founded by certain members of the Headingley Golf Club at a formation meeting on January 24th. 1907. The first committee included F. W. Tennant the first Chairman of Committee, Arthur Sykes, the Yorkshire cricketer Hon. F. S. Jackson of Allerton Hall, Hon. R. E. Beckett and Dr.Alister MacKenzie who became the first Hon.Secretary. Another member of the first committee was Tom Launcelot Taylor who played cricket for Yorkshire between 1899 and 1906.He was born in Headingley on May 25th. 1878 and died on March 16th.1960. T. L. Taylor played 122 innings for Yorkshire CCC scoring nearly 4000 runs.
Arthur Sykes Snr. was elected Hon. Treasurer but left this post in 1910 and died in June 1929.The Earl of Harewood was invited to become the President: he had leased the land to the Club. The course was laid out by Mr. Toogood of Ilkley Golf Club and in October 1908 the clubhouse was opened by the Earl of Harewood. The Club became the freehold owner of the clubhouse in 1928 and the course with Wigton Moor Whin was bought in August 1967.The practice course was bought from the Harewood estate in 1972.The old clubhouse was demolished in February 1994 and the new clubhouse, designed by Norfolk architect Charles Morris, is scheduled to be opened in early 1995.
West of the Gates on Alwoodley Lane is one of the oldest houses in the area: Moss Hall is the first house west of the Sandmoor Golf Club and is a listed Grade II building. It was built in 1583: the mullioned windows and attractive garden setting

are complemented by recent building in sympathy with the main dwelling.
Sandmoor Golf Course was created on land farmed by Henry Barran, who found no success with his farm and had a private course designed. This became Sandmoor Golf Club in 1926 and the No.1 fairway is the site of the Roman road - for many years this was known as Caesar's Fairway. The footpath signposted from Alwoodley Lane east of the clubhouse entrance is an old route to Alwoodley Old Hall. This now demolished building on the south side of Eccup Reservoir was the seat of the Franks family.
In the 14th. century Alice, daughter of Roger de Alwoodley who held a mill and land in this area, married William Franks. The estate assumed greater importance and this was enhanced with a marriage into the Gascoigne family: William Gascoigne of Gawthorpe Hall married Agnes the daughter of Nicholas and Alice Franks in the 14th. century. It was William Gascoigne who bought Harewood lands from Robert de Insula in 1363 and was granted the custody of Harewood park. William and Agnes Gascoigne's family included Sir William the Lord Chief Justice and Nicholas Gascoigne who released the park to Sir William de Aldeburgh. The coats of arms of both the Alwoodley and Franks families are seen in Barwick in Elmet church: over Sir John Gascoigne's grave stone in the north aisle is a coat of arms of Sir Nicholas Gascoigne. Sir John was the grandson of William and Agnes and Sir Nicholas was the son of George, one of John's 15 children. The coat of arms of the Franks features three silver hawks on a red background and a black horizontal line dividing the birds. The Alwoodley crest includes eight golden stars. The coat of arms of the Franks once featured in Kiddal Hall: Helen Ellis, sister of Sir John Ellis the first of his family to live at Kiddal, married Nicholas Franks of Alwoodley. In the 18th. century the only son of John More, builder of Austhorpe Hall was Nicholas who married Susan Franks of Alwoodley.
In 1638 the manor was bought by Sir Gervase Clifton of Clifton south of Nottingham near Ruddington, who married seven times and died in June 1666.Sir Gervase was a Knight of the Bath at the coronation of King James lst in 1603: the King created Sir Gervase a Baronet in May 1611.Sir Gervase Franks supported the Earl of Strafford of Wentworth and Ledston Hall during his trial, which ended with Strafford's execution in 1641.
In 1661 the estate was bought by Cornelius Clarke and a year later was sold to Roger Jackson. Alwoodley Old Hall was the main feature of the hamlet, called Aluuoldelei in Domesday possibly referring to a personal name or a hilly district. By 1285 the area became known as Alwaldley, where the Earl of Albemarle held some land. In later years the land and mill were granted to the monks of Embsay, who moved to Bolton Priory in Wharfedale.
The later Hall was built in 1825 on the site of the older building being a farmhouse

Alwoodley Hall

and home to the Midgeley family for four generations. It was said that the timber from the Old Hall was once used to make repairs at Scarcroft Mill near Thorner. Robert Benson the first Lord Bingley bought the Old Hall in 1729 and left the estate to his daughter who married George Lane Fox in 1762. The Alwoodley estate was left to Sir John and Lady Goodricke and in 1792 the estate reverted to the Lane Fox family, with whom it remained. The old hall, which had been abandoned was finally demolished in 1969.

A 128 acre site east of Harrogate Road is planned to become the relocation for Leeds Grammar School. The site is bounded by Manor House Lane and the main Harrogate Road, with a main entry controlled by traffic lights. The land at Alwoodley Gates is owned by Leeds University who plan to exchange it for the Leeds Grammar School lands at Moorland Road - the listed buildings would be preserved - the Junior School on Clarendon Road and the playing fields at Lawnswood. The multi-million pound project involves a common site for the 1270 boys with the Junior School and playing fields on the same campus.

A proposal by H. R. Abraham for the creation of a reservoir at Eccup in 1834 used a tunnel under Adel Moor to Seven Arches aqueduct and then by a conduit to Weetwood Reservoir on the site of the filter beds. After the 1837 Leeds Waterworks Company Act was passed, the building of the reservoir started in 1840 and in 1841 water was not taken anymore from the River Aire: the works were completed in 1843.In 1847 water was taken from Stub House Beck by agreement with the Earl of Harewood. In 1850 the Eccup reservoir embankment was raised by four feet allowing storage of 263 million gallons.

In November 1852 Leeds Corporation bought the Leeds Waterworks Co. for

£222,730, when the population of Leeds was 171,000.In 1867 a Cornish engine pumped water from the Wharfe to Eccup at a rate of 4 million gallons daily. The pumping was stopped in 1902 and the engine was scrapped in 1935.
The construction of Eccup reservoir as it is today started on September 29th.1879.The spade which Alderman Croft used to turn the first soil was inscribed marking the creation of Eccup New Reservoir. The new reservoir was completed on March 15th.1885 although there was a delay until April 1898 due to a leak being discovered. A new embankment was built by engineer Edward Filliter between 1890 and 1897. In 1897 a second tunnel was made under Adel Moor with the use of a cast iron main to Woodhouse Moor, which was rented from the Manor of Leeds in September 1840 - the land was bought by the Corporation in 1938.
Recent figures from Yorkshire Water state that Eccup covers 79 hectares with an average depth of 19 metres and holds 6,410,000 cubic metres of water (about 1½ million gallons).
The Eccup Filtration Works and pumping station were built in 1964 supplying high levels of the City. Eccup Reservoir was declared to be an SSSI (Site of Special Scientific Interest) in July 1987: bird watching is a popular activity although there are no water sports.
The other reservoirs owned by Leeds are Lindley Wood (1875), Swinsty (1876), Fewston (1879), Leighton (1929) and Thruscross (1966).

Between 1870 and 1880 parts of the Eccup estate were bought and in 1927 the first farms were purchased: in 1950 the estate covered 208 acres and there were three tenancies. In that year 504 acres of the Harewood estate were bought by Leeds Corporation and today the Eccup estate has 712 acres and 14 tenancies.
Eccup village was mentioned in the Domesday Book as Echope meaning Ecca's Hop - a hop was a piece of enclosed land in the middle of fens. The village today is small with its farms and isolated New Inn. The chapel, smithy, shop have all closed - the school closed in 1942.The village had no electricity, gas or water until the mid-1950's and there was some consideration given to the possible abandonment of Eccup village.

North of Alwoodley Gates is Millfield House by the impressive Alwoodley Lodges entry to Harewood Park built in the mid/late 18th. century. The main entrance to Gawthorpe and Harewood House was at Lofthouse Lodge, by the Coal Road/Harrogate Road junction. The lodge, gates and walls are all listed buildings designed by John Carr in 1755: the main entrance in Harewood Village was not built until 1803.This was designed by John Muschamp and Peter Atkinson based on original ideas by Humphry Repton.
The Lofthouse entrance vista was enhanced about 1755 by John Carr with the

building of Lofthouse Farm which he described as an "eye-catcher" for the main entrance to Gawthorpe Hall.
The two roads leading east to Wike are Fortshot Lane and the Coal Road. Fortshot House was the home of Thomas and Ann Wade - he died in 1874 aged 81.
Wike was known as Wic in 1086 derived from old English for a Dairy Farm - the name is seen in Giggleswick and Appletreewick in the Yorkshire Dales and Wyke south of Bradford. The manor of Wike became Harewood property in 1804 and in 1857 there were 131 folk living in Wike, of which many were part of the ten farming families. In the mid-19th, century Wike had two shops, a smithy and "The Globe" public house. The inn was known as "The Chequer" by 1822 with J. Hudson as licensee. Some of the timbers from this inn were used to repair Moor Hill at Harewood, when it became the residence of Moorsom Maude in the early part of this century.
Wike today has about 70 people living in around 25 scattered dwellings. The population has declined since 1900 when there were 108 people.
Wike was divided in early times into two ecclesiastical parts: the Harewood part in 1275 was held for 40 years by the Prioress of Syningthwaite and in later periods both Arthington Nunnery and Pontefract Priory held land at Wike.
The Bardsey section was held by the Cistercian monks of Kirkstall Abbey, whose abbot became the Lord of Wike. The area, together with Collingham and Bardsey, was granted by King John in 1209 to Kirkstall.
Wike School was one of Lady Betty Hasting's Charity Schools on School Lane. The school and schoolhouse were endowed in 1726 and were a part of this charitable lady's Trust set up on December 14th.1738.Lady Betty Hastings left £5 a year to the schoolmaster of Wike. The initial trustees included Lady Betty, the Hon. John Dawney, Sir John Bland and Sir William Lowther. The trustees of the Charity in 1900 were Granville Charles Hastings Wheler, Robert Gunter of Wetherby Grange, Rev. Benjamin Hemsworth of Monk Fryston Hall, the Earl of Crewe and John Davison Bland.
One of the conditions that was placed on the schoolroom by Lady Betty was that it was to be used as a chapel - Wike Church services are still held regularly in the schoolroom and conducted from Bardsey. When the school was operating the children would clear their desks every Friday afternoon to prepare for the Sunday service. This process was reversed every Monday morning.
This church charity school was restored in 1878 and in 1901 there were 70 children attending under the care of headmistress Annie Ware, who was appointed on July 22nd. 1897.There were further improvements made to the school in 1914.The resident headmistress in 1927 was Miss Wormald, who received a letter in that year from the Lady Betty Hastings Trust indicating possible closure: the school finally closed in 1931.

School Lane is now the access to the Leeds Golf Centre, opened in 1993.The Lane has been extended to the Wike Ridge and Oaks Courses and the David Leadbetter Golf Academy.
The listed mid-18th. century Manor House Farm on Town Street was sold in recent years and has been much restored and extended with a new stone entrance - it is now called "Sandown". Once farmed by the Goodall family Manor House was sold by the Harewood estate in 1951. The village smithy closed in the late 1970's and was sold by auction - this property was again sold by the estate in 1951. Forge Lane is a reminder of this once important village facility for many years run by David Hartley. Many past Wike villagers were buried at Harewood Church and included John Brewerton (died 1846 age 86), Joshua Wiggin (died 1847 age 88), Joshua Geaves (died 1858 age 27) and George Smith (died 1854 age 20).
Piped water only came to Wike during the 1940's when some POW's helped to dig the trenches through the village. The village wells were until then the main source of water: Burble Well on Brandon Lane and Gin Well on Town Street were well used by all the residents. The Gin Well was restored and a plaque placed over the waters, which no longer flow. The North Sea Gas pipeline passes south of Wike, although no houses in Wike have this energy source.
In 1836 James Dent discovered an old pot containing 2000 old coins in an old Wike house. This hoard was mainly from the 14th. and 15th. centuries and were some of the possessions which survived the Scots raids of 1316.
The entry into Wike from the Coal Road joins with Backstone Gill Lane and past the Manor House cottages: Forge Lane crosses Grace Beck past Hillcrest Farm and the road becomes a part of the Leeds Country Way past Lofthouse Farm.

Old Smithy, Wike

The Harrogate Road from Lofthouse Lodge passes Wallside Plantation and Lofthouse Grange Farm to the east: Hollin Hall further to the east possesses a large pond, which can be admired with its wildlife from a public footpath via Harewood Avenue to join with the Leeds Country Way. Thomas Shiers tenanted Hollin Hall in the mid 18th. century - he died in 1795 aged 70 and in the 19th. century the tenant was Thomas Bickerdike. Hollin Hall was the location used for the TV series "Follyfoot".
It was in the parkland through Lofthouse Lodge - a popular footpath with access to Stank and Harewood Village on a round walk - where in 1962 was discovered the site of Lofthouse hamlet, finally demolished in 1810.There are records of the Scott family living at Lofthouse - Anthony Scott who died in 1789 and Robert Scott who died in 1854.
South of the footpath is the Greystone: an ancient meeting stone in prehistoric times. On the north face of this gritstone block is a cup and ring mark and flints and an axe from 1500/2000 BC have been found in this area near the Greystone. It has been suggested that the word Harewood has been derived from Grey Stones Wood as Harawuda - Hara Stanes Wudu - means a wood by the stones. The area was known as Hareuuode in the Domesday Book - in Old English "haer" meant stony ground and "har" meant grey.
The small derelict house opposite Gateways School and part of the estate boundary wall is Ivy House. It is dated 1675 and was possibly used as a lock-up and in later times used as a keeper's house.
Gateways School occupies a dower house of the Harewood Estate known as Moor Hill, with the present entrance on Harewood Avenue. Moor Hill was the home of the Hon. Arthur Lascelles in 1841: he was one of the sons of the 2nd. Earl of Harewood. A few years later the son of the 3rd. Earl, the Hon. George Lascelles was living at Moor Hill while by the start of this century it was the home of the estate agent Moorsom Maude. Later it was the home of Henry, who was to become the 6th. Earl of Harewood. Moor Hill then became the home of the surgeon Carlton Oldfield and Michael Oldfield. In 1923 the Earl of Harewood leased Moor Hill to Carlton Oldfield and for another five years in 1932.On April 29th.1937 Peter Oldfield, the son of Mr & Mrs Carlton Oldfield was married at St. Margaret's Westminster to Elisabeth the daughter of the Earl and Countess Dunmore.
The school was opened in 1941 on Sandmoor Avenue Alwoodley by Nancy Simpson and Lilian Cox - they first opened a private nursery/kindergarten for 15 girls and boys but soon needed larger buildings: they moved to Moor Hill in 1945.Nancy Simpson left the school in 1955 to marry Sir Alfred Wort and Lilian Cox continued as headmistress. The school began admitting secondary school girls and Lilian Cox retired in 1963 with Jean Gardner becoming the new

headmistress. The school started a Sixth Form and Gateways became girls only. In 1972 expansion included permanent buildings for the Infants and the conversion of a stable block to provide science laboratories, kitchens and dining rooms. The school is still expanding and caters for day girls between the ages of 3 and 18.In March 1989 the new Watson Centre was opened by Lord Marshall. A new Junior School called "Youngers" was opened by the Earl of Harewood on September 27th. 1993. The Gateways Educational Trust, a registered charity, was formed in 1961 and the school motto is "Gate to Opportunity".

THE ROAD FROM LEEDS TO HARROGATE

PART 4: HAREWOOD

The Tadcaster/Otley turnpike of 1752/53 joins with the Leeds/Harrogate turnpike in Harewood Village. The original route of the Harrogate road was through Harewood Park past the vicarage and church through North Park to Harrogate Lodge and the toll bar south of Harewood Bridge. The road route was altered to include Harewood Castle within the estate wall creating Harewood Bank, further realigned in 1954/55.

Prior to the Medieval borough of Harewood, the original village would have been nearer to the Church. Archaeological investigations have revealed earthworks of the settlement 460 yards north east of Harewood Church. This shift in focus was similar to Leeds, where the development of the burgess plots along Briggate caused a change of centre from the Parish Church. At Harewood a clue to the original site came from the name "Bondmanholes" recorded on a 1698 map, meaning the strips of land in the open field of the peasant landowners. Bondgate is still an important part of the present Harewood village.

In the 18th. century Harewood village was described as "a town of one street with a regular approach to the gateway and has been rebuilt to exclude the appearance of dirt and poverty".In that period the tollbooth or market house with six butcher's shops, was in the middle of Harewood Avenue near the junction. It was demolished about 1768 and the market cross which stood nearby was taken down

Harewood House

in 1804: the cross was on a stone pedestal with seven steps and had been re-erected in 1703 by John Boulter of Gawthorpe Hall; there was a depiction at the top of the cross of the game of knur and spell. Harewood was awarded a market charter by King John and the market was held on Mondays near the baiting stone and ring. In October was held the annual sheep fair until the 19th. century. There were many weavers, spinners and dyers who once lived in the Harewood cottages and in 1755 Edwin Lascelles built a large house on The Avenue which became a ribbon factory for a few years - it was converted into four cottages in 1770, after closure of this business in 1766.
The main entrance to Harewood Park was built in 1803 by the village mason John Muschamp - there are many members of this family buried in Harewood Church. To accommodate this new entrance some houses were demolished on the west side of the main road.
Harewood Avenue has a Post Office and the United Anglican Methodist Chapel: the Methodists met in a house from 1772 until the chapel was made in 1815 from two houses. The Literary and Scientific Institute at Harewood was founded in 1853 and closed in 1959.The chapel moved in 1964 to the premises of the old village institute. These houses, in common with many other John Carr houses at Harewood, are listed buildings.
The "Harewood Arms" hotel was built in 1810 - there were six inns at Harewood at one period. The Crown and The Star were on Bondgate, Red Lion and Black Bull near the square and the White Hart on Lodge Green.

Harewood Arms Hotel

The Harewood Arms Hotel was taken over by Sam Smith's Brewery in 1977 and was refurbished in 1985. The Barrett family ran the inn in the 19th. century: Stephen Barrett moved from the Ship Inn on Harewood Bridge in 1867. In 1861

Stephen Barrett was aged 57 and was a farmer employing four labourers as well as being the landlord of The Ship Inn. John Barrett ran the Harewood Arms in the 1890's. Gallows Hill rising behind the Harewood Arms would have been the place of execution for those found guilty of serious crimes at the court of justice held in the Great Hall of Harewood Castle.

The Harewood C of E Junior/Infants School was founded in 1768 by Edwin Lascelles and built by John Carr. The school was rebuilt in 1845 by the 3rd. Earl of Harewood, who also supplied all the books.

There are only two 17th. century houses at Harewood that survived the Carr rebuilding: the house opposite Gateways School on the main road and Cutler's Cottage dated 1678 JC = John Cutler, a former owner of the Harewood estate.

The village smithy was on the site of the petrol station: the blacksmith was James Linfoot and later Peter Deakin, who started to sell petrol.

The corner shop on Church Lane and the main road was the place where Anthony Scott started his trade. There are members of this family buried at Harewood Church: George Scott died in 1842 and Mary in 1868.In 1853 Mary Hannah Scott aged 3½ was buried - the daughter of Anthony and Hannah Scott. The shop closed at Harewood in 1981 and the present fashion shop was opened a year later. The family also opened Scott's Corner on the approach to Harrogate.

The Village Hall on Church Lane was opened by HRH The Princess Royal and the Countess of Harewood on September 6th.1959. Nearby is Church Lane Lodge, once the home of cobbler Charles Baldwin. In The Square is the estate office opened here in 1972.Moor House was once the Vicarage dating from 1795 and it became the home of the Oldfield family, prior to their occupancy of Moor Hill. In 1918 Carlton Oldfield was appointed the obstetric surgeon at the Leeds General Infirmary.

The manor of Harewood was one of many that William the Conqueror gave to Robert de Romelli: the manor included Alwoodley, East Keswick, Wigton, Wike and Dunkeswick. Robert's daughter Cecily married the Earl of Chester and the Harewood estates passed to their daughters Alice and Avicia. The daughters married the Earl of Murray and William de Curci. It was William who improved the manor house at Harewood and he probably also built Harewood Church in 1116.

Harewood remained with the de Curci family for four generations: the estates passed to the FitzGerald, Redvers, Earl of Albemarle, Edmund Plantagenet, Lord L'Isle of Rougemont and William de Aldburgh. In 1367 it was William who fortified the manor house: Sir William became Baron Aldburgh in 1371 and he placed his coat of arms with those of Edward Balliol, King of Scotland over the entrance to his castle - the motto "Val Sal Be Sal" is inscribed on his coat of arms. The motto means "What shall be shall".

The twin towers of this ancient castle are visible from Harewood Bank, the ruins are not able to be visited due to the condition of the fabric. In the Great Hall, once decorated with stained glass, rich furnishings and heraldry there is a canopied recess: often thought to have been a tomb it was likely to have been a sideboard. Baron Aldburgh died in 1377 and Harewood was divided between his two daughters Sybil and Elizabeth. Elizabeth married Sir Richard Redman who became the Speaker of the House of Commons in 1415.Sybil married Sir William Ryther and both families lived together or alternately at Harewood Castle for many years. William's son was Robert who married Isobel Gascoigne: she was the daughter of Sir William Gascoigne, son by the first marriage of Lord Chief Justice Gascoigne to Elizabeth Mowbray. Matthew Redman also married another daughter of Sir William Gascoigne, who was living at their nearby family seat of Gawthorpe Hall. The last member of the Ryther family to have lived at Harewood Castle was Robert who died in 1637: following his death the Castle gradually fell into disrepair: before the Civil War it was described as being "decayed".

The approach to All Saints Church Harewood is either through the park or by Church Lane, where there is access to the graveyard. The church is north of the 18th. century Harewood House in an area known as The Grove. There may well have been a church on this site from Saxon times but the first stone church was built by William de Curci. The church was rebuilt in the 14th. century and again a century later. There was further restoration in 1793, when the founder's inscribed wooden beam was lost and Sir George Gilbert Scott rebuilt Harewood Church in 1862/63.

The church is famous for the collection of six alabaster tombs restored in 1981.One of these white tomb chests is that of Sir William Gascoigne, Lord Chief Justice born at Gawthorpe Hall in 1350.He married Elizabeth Mowbray and Johanna Pickering: the two lines thus created lived at Gawthorpe and at Cardington in Bedfordshire. Sir William wears the robes of Lord Chief Justice: the tomb was made in Derbyshire.

The tomb of Sir William Ryther shows his head resting on his helmet - he died in 1426.His wife Sybil Aldburgh is by his side. His family came from Ryther Castle near Selby and his family fought at Agincourt. He married Sybil Aldburgh, whose father had inherited Harewood with her sister in 1392.

The third alabaster tomb is that of Sir Richard Redman and his wife Elizabeth Aldburgh: he was born at Levens and was the sheriff of Cumberland and later of Yorkshire. He married in 1393 and his wife died in 1434 - the sisters were responsible for building Harewood Church in about 1410.

Sir William Gascoigne and his wife Margaret Clarell is the fourth tomb in Harewood Church: he is shown wearing mid 15th. century armour with the Gascoigne pike's head on the helmet. He was the grandson of the Judge and the

son of Sir William and Joan Wyman. He supported the House of Lancaster and died after pardon in about 1465.Margaret Clarell was from Aldwark and married for the third time in 1425. Their eldest son married a Neville and was knighted at the Battle of Wakefield in 1460.
Sir William Gascoigne and his wife Margaret Percy are featured on the fifth tomb: at one time wrongly ascribed to John Neville. Sir William married about 1467 - his wife's father was killed at the battle of Towton. In 1468 he obtained a licence to crenellate Gawthorpe and enclose the lands creating a park: Sir William died in 1487.
Edward Redman and his wife Elizabeth Huddlestone represent the last of the six tombs in Harewood Church. The effigies are perhaps the finest of the set: he was the great-grandson of Sir Richard Redman and succeeded to the Harewood estate in 1482.He supported the House of York and probably fought for the King at Bosworth. He died in 1510 after holding the position of Sheriff of Cumberland and Westmoreland.
There is a memorial within the church to Sir Robert Denison, Judge of the Court of the King's Bench in 1741, who died in 1765.
There are also memorials to the later Lascelles family and one of the most recent burials was that of Mary Princess Royal in 1965.She was the daughter of King George V and Queen Mary: in 1922 she married Henry Lascelles 6th. Earl of Harewood. The Princess Royal died while walking around the lake with her son and grandsons on March 28th.1965: her funeral at Harewood Church was attended by the Royal family, the Lascelles family, estate workers, pensioners and many more.
Harewood Church was placed in the care of the Redundant Churches Fund in October 1978.

The first mansion in Harewood Park was the Medieval Gawthorpe Hall, home of the Gascoignes. The name was probably derived from "Gauk's Torp" - a personal farmstead. In 1135 Maud de Gawthorpe married William Gascoigne and this family lived at Gawthorpe Hall until 1567.The Hall was about 350 yards to the south of the present Harewood House, under Capability Brown's lake. Some of the foundations of the Hall were revealed on draining the north east corner of the lake about 1830.A print of the old hall in 1722 showed it to have extensive gardens, chapel, stables and an orchard. The print also shows that there had been remodelling of the original Gawthorpe Hall to allow it to be more habitable.
The first mention of a Gascoigne living at "Harewood" was in the 13th. century, when William Gascoigne married Elizabeth daughter of William Boulton. In the following century another William married Matilda daughter of John of Gawthorpe and his son - another William - married the daughter of Nicholas Franks of

Alwoodley. It was this William Gascoigne who bought land at Harewood in 1363 and he and his son were granted the custody of Harewood park, wood and hunting rights. In 1373 he entailed his Harewood lands to his eldest son William, who became the Judge. His second son was Nicholas Gascoigne who acquired Lasingcroft in Manston in 1391.The old Lasingcroft Hall was sited to the south of the present farm.

The 16th. Sir William Gascoigne had an only daughter Margaret Gascoigne who married Thomas Wentworth in 1580, who became Lord of Harewood. Their son William inherited Harewood and HIS son Thomas was born in April 1593 and was knighted in the year of his marriage to Lady Margaret Clifford. Sir Thomas was MP for York and his second wife was Lady Arabella Hollis, who was a prominent political figure. He was imprisoned but was pardoned and rose in royal favour. He was created Baron Wentworth in 1628 and later Viscount Wentworth, Lord President of the North. In 1631 he was made Lord Deputy of Ireland and in 1639 became the Earl of Strafford and Lieutenant General of Ireland. After a further troubled life he retired to Gawthorpe but was brought to trial and executed on May 12th.1641.

In 1653 William, son of Strafford sold the Ledston estate to Sir John Lewis and in 1656 sold Harewood to Sir John Lewis and Sir John Cutler: they were London merchants who had married the daughters of Sir Thomas Foote Lord Mayor of London. Sir John Lewis sold his interest in Harewood to his brother in law who became sole owner and he lived at Gawthorpe Hall from 1657 until his death in 1693.The hall became the home of his daughter Elizabeth and her husband the Earl of Radnor, who passed the estates on to John Boulter in 1696 as she had no heirs. It was Edmund Boulter who sold the estates of Harewood and Gawthorpe for £63,827 in 1739 to Henry Lascelles a former Tax Collector in the Barbados, London merchant banker and MP for Northallerton. In 1740 he set up a merchant bank with George Maxwell who had been a Barbados sugar planter. The year after he had bought Harewood Henry Lascelles placed his eldest son Edwin in charge of the estates, while he ran his London business.

Henry's son Edwin succeeded to Harewood in 1753 on his father's death and in 1790 was created Baron Harewood. He was the builder of Harewood House: the first turf was turned to lay the foundations in January 1759 and the foundation stone laid on March 23rd.

The architects for Harewood were John Carr and Robert Adam with Capability Brown landscaping the park. John Carr was born at Horbury in 1721 and was twice Lord Mayor of York. He died at Askham Hall on February 22nd 1807.Robert Adam was born at Kirkaldy in 1728 and was appointed architect to the King. He became MP for Co. Kinross in 1768 and died in 1792 being buried in Westminster Abbey.

The stone to build the house came from a local quarry and a start was made in April 1755 on the stable block west of Gawthorpe Hall in which Lascelles lived until his "new house at Gawthorpe" was completed in 1771.In 1772 Gawthorpe Old Hall was finally demolished and Capability Brown came to Harewood on his first visit. The final bill for Harewood house and grounds was £50,000 being £20,000 more than he had estimated.
Adam designed the interiors from 1765 using mahogany from the family estates on Barbados and the window lead came from the Grassington Mines. The plasterwork ceilings were designed by Adam and executed by Joseph Rose; decorations were by Angelica Kaufmann, Biagio Rebecca and Antonio Zucchi.
Thomas Chippendale worked at Harewood from 1767 until 1778, creating his masterpieces of furniture and inlaid marquetry. The library desk was sold for £43,000 in 1965 to Temple Newsam House, while nine Chippendale mirrors were sold in 1987 for £300,000.This had not been the first sale of Harewood treasures: in 1966 following the death of the Princess Royal £568,000 was raised for death duties.
Capability Brown's landscaping designs included the creation of a large lake, made by damming Stank Beck and covering the site of Gawthorpe Hall.
When Edwin Lascelles died in 1795 aged 82 the estate was inherited by his cousin Lt. Col. Edward Lascelles, who had married Anne Chaloner in 1761.Edward was raised to the baronetcy in 1797 and entered the House of Lords a year later. He was created the First Earl of Harewood in 1812 and died aged 80 in 1820.His second son Henry Lascelles inherited Harewood - eldest son Edward had died in 1814 - and married Henrietta Sebright in 1794. Their eldest son was Henry Lascelles who became the 3rd. Earl of Harewood and married Lady Louisa Thynne daughter of the Marquess of Bath. Their son was another Henry who married

Harewood Church

Lady Elizabeth de Burgh daughter of the Marquess of Clanricarde: their son Henry became the 5th. Earl of Harewood (1846-1929).
Henry 5th. Earl married Lady Florence Bridgeman daughter of the Earl of Bradford and their son Henry became the 6th. Earl of Harewood - he married HRH Princess Royal, daughter of King George V and Queen Mary. The present 7th. Earl of Harewood married the Viennese concert pianist Marion Stein in 1949, who became the Countess of Harewood. The wedding was held at St. Marks Church South Audley Street on September 29th.,to which 200 tenants and estate workers were invited down to London.
The Earl divorced in 1967 and married the Australian Patricia Tuckwell, sister of Barry Tuckwell the well known horn player. Marion married the politician Jeremy Thorpe. George was born in 1923 and succeeded in 1947, when his father died aged 65.In June 1950 at the Queen's Hotel Leeds Lord Harewood placed a third of his estates on sale by auction in 99 lots. Much land was bought by the tenants including John Dalby whose family had been on the estates for generations: 90% of land was bought by tenant farmers. In 1951 the villages of Weeton, Wigton, Wike, East Keswick and Kirkby Overblow were sold and a few years later the estate was down to about 7000 acres. In 1959 another 4000 acres were sold and in 1973, amongst other sales, was the disposal of building lots on Bondgate.
It was recorded in 1822 that the House was open to the public on Saturdays and in 1901 on Thursdays only. Harewood House opened to the public in 1950 on a limited scale and was followed by more rooms available to view after the death of the Princess Royal.
Harewood House was substantially restored starting in 1844 by Charles Barry, who won the competition to rebuild the Houses of Parliament after the fire of 1834.He removed the Adam portico on the south front and replaced it with Corinthian columns. He redesigned the grounds below the south front and laid out an Italian terrace garden which took four years to complete. Barry also transformed the inside of the House: his final bill was £37,000 with decoration and furnishing of the interior completed for £7000 by the London based firm George Trollope & Sons - the work was completed by June 1853.
The House, grounds, bird garden and the collections, which include works by Turner, Reynolds, Titian, Tintoretto and El Greco are administered by the Harewood House Trust. The Terrace Gallery shows works by British and international artists and photographers.
Harewood Bird Garden was opened in 1970 and soon became a very popular attraction, with Butterfly World as a later attraction. An extension was opened in 1981 with a Paradise Garden featuring lizards and other reptiles. The most important aspect of the Bird Garden is the conservation work with a captive breeding programme. The Bird Garden succeeded in rearing the Mauritius Pink

Pigeon in April/May 1994: the curator of the Bird Garden is Jim Irwin-Davies. The mansion was shrouded in scaffolding in 1993 for the removal and reconstruction of a large part of the roof. The terrace and parterre had been in disrepair for 40 years and the nine month project was completed to Barry's original design for the 150th. anniversary on July 7th.1994.The work cost £400,000 with grants from English Heritage, EC and the balance from the Harewood House Trust. The project was assisted by students from Askham Bryan College and the fountains were switched on after a 60 year gap on September 8th. 1994.

THE ROAD FROM LEEDS TO HARROGATE.

PART 5 FROM HAREWOOD TO SPACEY HOUSES

Harewood Bank is the second route for the Leeds/Harrogate turnpike road with the first road through the park down to the bridge. A track avoiding the toll bar once went through the plantation and across the Castle Ford: this was later closed.
Stockton is one of the deserted villages east of Harewood, now the site of the Harewood Hill Climb. The farms today are the only reminders of a once extensive settlement. There was probably a chapel at Stockton about 1400 -1600 and earthworks indicate that it was a larger hamlet in the late 17th. century. The other deserted centres in Harewood include Lofthouse in the park by Lofthouse Lodge which may have been abandoned in the 15th. century; Newall whose exact location in unknown but is near to the present village; Towhouses which developed in the 12th. century and sited north of Eccup Reservoir's easterly end on Sturdy Beck. The site excavated in 1977 revealed desertion about the mid-16th. century.
The two turnpike roads were served by a tollbar south of Harewood Bridge. The toll house was demolished in 1960 as it had been declared as unsafe. In later years the toll bar house sold confectionery, being home for the Barrett, Watson and Walker families this century.
It is likely that there had been an earlier toll house north of Harewood Bridge. The original turnpike road came through the park via Harrogate or Bar Lodge. The fine

Harewood Toll Bar

wooden gates came from Chesterfield House in London. The house in Mayfair on the corner of South Audley Street and Curzon Street had been built in the 1740's by Isaac Ware for the 4th. Earl of Chesterfield and sold to Henry 6th. Earl of Harewood in 1919.
The 6th. Earl of Harewood and the Princess Royal sold Chesterfield House in 1932 and it was demolished in 1936. The two pairs of gates were brought to Harewood and placed at Harrogate Lodge and to the south of Harewood Lodge in the village centre.
There were many initial objections and riots against the imposition of tolls for the turnpike roads. One such riot took place on June 25th.1753, when a group of men led by the Langdale brothers followed their destruction of the barriers at Halton Dial, Beeston and on the road from Leeds to Bradford. They advised Edwin Lascelles of their intention to demolish the Harewood toll bar but Edwin confronted the mob with a band of his own estate workers. He led a group of about 80 and met the Leeds mob on Hill Green. There was much fighting and Lascelles took 30 prisoners, ten being sent to York Jail. The mob leaders threatened to destroy Gawthorpe Hall and support was requested from the dragoons of York, who were barracked at Harewood. The soldiers were soon afterwards sent to Briggate to quell a major riot where 500 protesters were gathered: the soldiers fired after the Riot Act was read and ignored - they killed 8 people and wounded 50 and this was proved to be end of the Turnpike Riots.

Harewood Corn Mill was given by Cecilia, daughter of Robert de Romelli in the 12th. century to the monks of Embsay: they later moved to Bolton Priory on the River Wharfe. In 1656 there was a reference to the mill:"Upon the river of Wharfe there is a Corne Mill with two payer of milstones, the dam of which was almost made new last year and cost near to £100."
Mill Farmhouse dates from the early 19th. century and is a listed building. The old mill at Mill Farm was burnt down on February 20th.1820 and was rebuilt the same year. The mill retains the wooden water wheel although in poor condition: the flour was being ground at the mill until 1976, where corn was also ground for pig food. Charles and Ann Norfolk lived at "Harewood Mills" and Charles died in 1828 aged 68 and was buried in Harewood Church - his wife died in 1884 aged 75. In Arthington churchyard is the grave of Robert Mawson Pullein of Harewood Mills 1859-1932.
Harewood Sawmill was once a part of the Harewood Estate, providing fencing and other materials. The products were for estate use only until 1947: the sawmill expanded in 1957 and was sold in 1972 into private hands. The mills today supply the estate and farmers with fencing and rustic poles, open to both trade and the public.

Harewood Bridge was built in 1729 on an old crossing site. The bridge was widened to the west in 1771 by John Carr, as can be seen under the arches. Two metal plates on the bridge indicate the division between Dunkeswick and Harewood. The narrow bridge has been the scene of many accidents and many suggestions have been made as to the possible resiting of this important bridge. One of the worst recent accidents was on April 5th.1991 when a transporter plunged through the parapet into the river having hit a car.

The house on the north west of the bridge was once the "Ship Inn", although old maps suggest the site was on the east side of the road. The innkeeper in 1822 was Anthony Scott, whose family ran the Harewood village shop and opened Scott's Corner near Harrogate. By 1851 Stephen Barrett had taken over at The Ship and in 1867 transferred to the Harewood Arms. In 1861 Stephen Barrett was described as a innkeeper and farmer with 170 acres, employing five labourers. There are records of 70 folk living at Harewood Bridge in the 19th. century

There are many members of the Scott family buried at Harewood including Mary Hannah, daughter of Anthony and Hannah who died aged 3½ years in 1853: their son Alfred died in 1864 aged 1 year 4 months and Elizabeth had died aged 2 years in 1824.

It is probable that The Ship closed when the turnpike road ceased to operate: the building was divided into three cottages, where one retains well worn steps to the cellar where the beer would have been stored.

Harewood Bridge House is the large complex of buildings on the north east of the bridge and is in the Harrogate District of North Yorkshire. The house was built in the 19th. century and was used as a boarding school by H. Robinson in 1866. It became the home of Col. John Francis Cust and his wife Florence Harriet Cust. Florence was the daughter of Henry Lascelles 3rd. Earl of Harewood (1797-1857) and his wife Lady Louisa, daughter of the Marquess of Bath. Lady Florence Cust was born on October 8th.1838 and was buried with her husband at Weeton Church. The church was founded by Henry 3rd. Earl of Harewood and contains some stained glass windows dedicated to the Cust family. These include windows to Col. John and his wife and also his brother Cpt. Horace Cust.

Colonel Cust was born at Hanover House Middlesex St. Georges on June 6th.1825 and was the eldest son of the Hon. P. F. Cust and Lady Isabella. Lady Cust was given a painting by Turner of Harewood House and following her death on November 18th.1901 the picture was returned to the House collections.

Harewood Bridge House became the home of Robert Percy St. Martin Delius JP, a Bradford mill owner who always sent his own Christmas cards with the inscription:"Happy Christmas from Dunkeswick".In the late 1920's Major Arthur Nicholls made Harewood Bridge House his home, while in the 1930's it became the home of Edward Hudson. Francis Edward "Tony" Hudson lived at the House before his marriage - he became the Chairman of Yorkshire Post Newspapers in 1981/1983 - when he moved to Kirkby Overblow and now lives in Bedale. In 1949 the House became Bridge House School - a boarding school for boys with impaired hearing and handicaps preventing normal educational progress. There were 32 boys resident at Bridge House but the Leeds LEA closed the school in 1987. The site transferred under boundary reorganisation to Harrogate Council and plans were announced in 1994 to convert the building into 16 two bedroom houses.

Old Ship Inn - Harewood Bridge

The site of Rougemont is a few hundred yards west of Harewood Bridge on the north bank of the River Wharfe. This ancient fortified home on the rise of Ridgeman Scar and now enveloped by woodland was the home of the de l'Isle family. The name Rougemont derives from Red Hill and is accessible by public footpaths from Harewood Bridge, from the Dunkeswick/Weeton road and from Gallogate Lane to Weeton Church from the village centre.

The overgrown site retains the defensive ditches with a central house on the rise. The area is 80 yards by 60 yards with a 10 feet high outer mound. The assumption that the buildings of Rougemont were wooden were put in doubt in 1980. In that year the foundations revealed a stone perimeter and there are still some dressed stones to be found on the site today.

Robert Lord L'Isle of Rougemont inherited Harewood Manor in 1260 and built his family home on the river bank. Their family name indicates descent from the de Breant family who held lands in the Isle of Wight and they took their family name

Insula or de L'Isle. The Rougemont family lived eventually at Harewood Castle and were to be followed by William de Aldburgh - he fortified the manor house in 1365. In 1352 mention was made of John de Insula Lord of Rougemont and the family remained at this river site until 1365 - in that year William de Aldburgh married the heiress of the de L'Isle family.

A site near Rougemont Woods was suggested for possible oil extraction, a rig appeared in 1984 but was abandoned in September after two months.

The detached brick houses on the east side of the main road and opposite the Dunkeswick and Weeton road were built of bricks made in a small brickyard in the 19th. century and there are still remains of the claypits and a large pond. An early 19th. century shows two clay pits and are described as being "old".

Dunkeswick was known as Chesuic in earlier days and by 1145 had acquired the prefix Dun- meaning "down" to separate the hamlet from East Keswick: the name refers to a cheese farm. The township was a boundary for the Forest of Knaresborough and the townships of Weeton with Dunkeswick were formed into a parish in 1852 from Harewood. Dunkeswick Common together with Huby and Weeton were enclosed in 1790.

Dunkeswick was a part of the vast Harewood estates until its sale in 1975. The total lots included five farms, 57 acres of woodland in a total of 1274 acres.

The village of farms and cottages was once the home of the Mallorie family - Matthew Mallorie "a man greatly beloved by all men, who dwelt at Dunkeswick" was buried at Harewood Church on April 27th. 1619. The Mallorie family were here in the 16th. century - Sir John Mallorie was the Governor of Skipton Castle. The Harewood churchyard also has the grave of Thomas Bateson the Dunkeswick smith, who died in 1851: he was followed by Samuel Bateson, who died aged 52 in 1864 and by Alfred Bateson. In the 1830's the wheelwright was Charles Bateson and Geoffrey Bateson now lives in retirement at Huby. The old smithy is on the south corner a few yards from the main road to Dunkeswick and has a wall post box.

A chapel at Dunkeswick was founded in 1886 by the Earl of Harewood as a chapel of ease to Weeton and there was a small Methodist Chapel, now standing isolated in the large field near the main road. This preserved building recently lost its roof and during the 1940's had been the home of the tramp called "Darkie Jimmy". Services at this old building were later transferred to the Anglican Chapel in Dunkeswick. This Wesleyan Chapel was demolished after the last service in February 1974, having been sold by the Harewood Estate. All the stones were used to build the present Old Chapel house. There was a private boarding school at Dunkeswick run by Sarah Vickers in the mid-19th. century.

Poplar House Farm is near the main Harrogate Road and was the home of the Michael Dickinson stables until he departed for America in 1989. There was a fire at the stables in 1984 and the property was sold for restoration. There was an

application to develop the site in mid-1994.
The houses set back south from the main lane through Dunkeswick near the old chapel started as a tannery: the old tanning shed is the eastern of the two low buildings and had an outside pool. John Norfolk was a Dunkeswick tanner in 1838 but soon afterwards the tannery ceased to operate and the present house was built by the Williamson family about 1870. The area in the vicinity of the present three cottages could have been the site of other dwellings: pieces of pottery have been discovered in the gardens.
The gardens of the old tannery feature an old mill grinding stone, a large circular stone water trough and parts of an old stone balustrade from Harewood House. On the north side of the lane opposite the old chapel is Sturdy Cottage - a reminder of farmer Cecil Edward Sturdy.
There are two farms on the main street through Dunkeswick: Hawthorn House and Prospect Farms - this farm specialises in organically grown potatoes. The old Highways Depot is now the agricultural engineering concern of the Pickard family. On the roadside is the wooden seat placed to mark the coronation of The Queen in 1953.
West of Dunkeswick off Weeton Lane to the north is Healthwaite Hill which was the seat of the Maude family. The first member to hold property in this area was Edmund Maude, who bought the lands from Matthew Redman in 1550. In 1602 Anthony Maude of Healthwaite was the only executor of the will of Thomas Maude of Holling Hall at Ilkley. Anthony's five children included Robert who married Ann Oglethorpe of Roundhay and was living at Healthwaite in 1631. The Maude left the area for Ireland in 1650. Later members of the family included Sir Thomas Maude created Baron de Montalt in 1766 and his brother Sir Cornwallis Maude created Viscount Hawarden in 1791. The present house has been restored and retains a water pump and old plough on the property.
Haggas Hall is to the north of Healthwaite and was the home of James Fox, who died aged 74 in 1909. In 1917 Herbert Fox farmed at Haggas Hall and in 1936 Harry Fox was the farmer. Haggas Hall was built in 1588 and there is a dated stone on the south front. The present owners have been at Haggas Hall from 1962 creating the gardens, planting hundreds of trees and extended the main Hall to the east. The builder was Les Hanson and he placed his initials and date 1969 on a stone of the side wall. The driveway to Haggas Hall is one of the prettiest in the area and the whole property has been restored including the old barn. Prior to Haggas Hall receiving mains water supply, it was the job of a worker to carry buckets of water from the well two fields distant.

Weeton was known as Widetone in 1086 and was the village where willows were grown. Land at Weeton was granted to Bolton Priory in 1307 and in 1504 Sir Robert

Plumpton held lands at Weeton and Huby. The lands became part of the Harewood Estate in 1721. The village originally would have had a centre around the green: the Sunday School was built on the green in 1712 but was demolished in 1933. Where there is now a memorial seat to Eleanor Walsh, was once the pinfold where stray animals were impounded.

There were two schools in Weeton: the old school on the corner of Weeton Lane and Wescoe Hill Lane was opened in 1856 at the expense of the Earl of Harewood and Lamb's School was an independent concern.

Weeton Methodist Chapel was built in 1796 and the front was rebuilt in 1881 - there was an inscription reading: "The poor have the Gospel preached to them 1796 Benj Winterburn". Services ceased in Weeton Chapel in 1938 - it has been converted into a private residence. The Old Hall is set back to the north of the main street and may have once been a butcher's shop. The Hall was once the home of John Dyson Jnr. - the family lived at The Limes where John Dyson died aged 71 in 1916 - in the early part of this century and he was followed by Major Arthur Lupton and by the Leeds architect John Ellis Stocks FRIBA who died in 1951 aged 67. His wife Evelyn died on Easter Day on April 6th.1958 aged 70: Weeton Old Hall was sold in September 1953.

On December 20th.1909 land was conveyed to build the village institute, which was opened on November 5th.1910 by the Countess of Harewood: application to convert the hall into two cottages by Wharfedale Holdings Ltd. was approved in March 1976. Weeton was sold by the Harewood Estate in June 1951 including the Post Office, Mount Pleasant, Yew Tree and Bridge farms.

It was the coming of the railways to Weeton that led to a rapid population increase. It was the inspiration of Henry 3rd. Earl of Harewood that led to the building of St. Barnabas Church Weeton. St. Barnabas was his patron Saint and it is said that the church was built out of the village in order that the spire could be seen by the Earl from Harewood House.

The Earl appointed George Gilbert Scott and this "Cathedral of Lower Wharfedale" had its foundation stone laid on April 3rd.1851 by the Bishop of Ripon. The consecration of the Church took place on October 12th.1853 in the presence of the Earl and Countess of Harewood and the sermon was preached by the Vicar of Leeds Rev. Walter Hook. The occasion was also celebrated with a feast held on land at The Ship Inn Harewood Bridge: this was attended by 300 folk - distinguished guests were entertained to lunch at Harewood House where there was a sugar model of the church on view - and those workmen involved in the construction were invited to a feast the next day. The contractors were Hall & Brown of Leeds and J. H. Smith of Camden Town was the stone carver.

The interior of Weeton Church is impressive with the East Window (1855) and West Window (1875) being supplemented with attractive stained glass in memory of the

Weeton Church

local Cust family. There is a Benefactions Board which states that William Wade in 1722 left the annual rent of Wescoe Hill Close to the poor of Weeton township. The church displays two volumes of a mid-19th. century family Bible with binding by William Morris. There are plaques in the chancel to the vicars Claude Lambert (1884-1916) and John Biggs (1917-1952), who was the last vicar to live in the adjacent vicarage house - the vicarage in its four acres had been built in 1853.
In 1981 St. Barnabas Church became one of the four parish churches in the enlarged United Benefice of Kirkby Overblow. The other churches are St. John's North Rigton, St. Peter's Sicklinghall and the redundant church of Stainburn.
Weeton became connected with the railway from Thirsk and Ripon in September 1848: the connection to Leeds was hampered with the difficulties of the 2 miles 241 yards long Bramhope Tunnel - the whole line was opened in July 1849. It is said that horses were used to lower a Hunslet built engine onto the railway line at Wescoe Hill. The Leeds & Thirsk Railway was later known as the Leeds Northern and was absorbed into the North Eastern Railway in 1854.
Weeton Station was on the line from Arthington whose first station opened in 1849 and was resited in 1875 - it closed in March 1965. The line crossed the River Wharfe

by the Arthington Viaduct which is 475 yards long, on which work started in November 1846 building the 21 arches. The trains arrived at Weeton's wooden platform after emerging from the 100 yard Wescoe Hill tunnel, stopping at Pannal and by the loop across Crimple Viaduct to Harrogate. The line once had a junction with the line from Wetherby until the line was closed in 1964. The main line from Leeds via Weeton once crossed the river by Crimple Low Viaduct to Starbeck and the line from York to Harrogate.

The station master at Weeton in the mid-19th. century was George Grainger, who died in 1875 aged 59. The station is really in Huby and has a regular passenger service to Leeds and Harrogate. The station yard off the Bradford road has two Station Cottages: the station itself is now unmanned.

The Danish foundation of Huby - the word probably means a village by a hill or could relate to the Viking invader Hubba developed around Strait Lane and there was once a small village green surrounded by thatched cottages. The village was known as Hobi and in the 18th. century as Hewby. Roger de Huby gave Fountains Abbey the income from some land in the village: Marmaduke Huby was one of the last abbots of Fountains Abbey in the 16th. century.

There was a corn mill called Wood Gate Mill - the old mill and Mill Green on Woodgate Lane have been converted into private residences. Woodgate House was the home of William Charles Lupton who was born on February 13th.1849 and became the head of Lupton & Sons wine merchants of Bradford. He was the Bradford Mayor between 1899 and 1902.

The smithy is also converted into a private cottage. The Old Post Office Cottage was Huby Farm and was used as a meeting place for Huby Methodists with Charles and Susannah Atkinson. In 1796 the Huby cottage of John Taylor was licensed for meetings and the first Methodist Chapel was opened in 1840 on Crag Lane/Strait Lane junction for £130. The new Wesleyan Chapel was built in 1889/90 by Thomas Turnbull. There are foundation stones laid by Miss Carr of Kippax, John Sinclair of Otley, Miss Willcox of Burley and Isaac Atkinson of Arthington House - all on April 22nd.1889. The old building was used as a Sunday School and later as a school.

The complex of Sleights Mill, Farm and Cottage are on the corner of the old road from Castley to Weeton.

In later years Rosebourne House on Strait Lane was built adjacent to the old Post Office and in doing so demolished one of the many thatched cottages: the original inhabitants were Misses Skirrow.

Huby was bisected by the development of the Wigton branch of the Dudley Hill-Harrogate-Killinghall turnpike (A658). The original turnpike act creating the Trust was in 1752/53 with the road to Killinghall (B6161) and a turnpike bar at Beckwithshaw but the section between Pool Bridge and Buttersyke Bar was not completed until 1837 and thus called the New Road. The road was served by two

local turnpike bars at Pool and at the junction with the Leeds/Harrogate turnpike road. Travellers visiting Huby prior to the turnpike would approach the village via Castley, Newby and Sleights. The railway line used part of the old track to Weeton village.
Huby Village Institute was built in 1920 and the present Almscliffe Hall was opened in 1978 - the building is well used today.

North Rigton was mentioned as Ristone in 1086 and means a village on a ridge. The area was once a part of a great hunting forest but this changed in the early 13th. century, when land was cleared. In the latter part of the 13th. century North Rigton was part of the lands of Fountains Abbey and the Abbot was Lord of the Manor. In 1311 William de Rigton became the Abbot of Fountains - he was abbot until 1316 - and in 1315 the Abbot of Fountains and Richard Furneaux were returned as Lords of the Manor.
The Scots ravaged Rigton in common with many other villages following their success at Bannockburn in 1318. In 1642 Royalist troops from Knaresborough attacked Rigton. In 1556 the Manor of Rigton was sold to Sir William Fairfax. In 1716 the manor was sold to Robert Wilkes and in 1796 the manor was bought by the Earl of Harewood. The old manor house was north east of the school and the moat can still to be seen measuring about 33 yards by 50 yards: Hall Green Farm remembers this ancient site. The old tithe barn nearly 50' in length has been demolished.
The "Square and Compass" inn dates from the 18th. century and once had a brewery on the site together with a wheelwright. The old inn was a low thatched building until 1896 and was rebuilt this century. The inn became a freehouse in 1950, when the Harewood estate sold the land. The conveyance was signed by The Princess Royal to the Smith family. In common with other former Harewood Estate public houses, the inn once was closed on Sundays - as was the Harewood Arms in Harewood village.
The small village green at North Rigton has the wooden 17th. century stocks. A metal plate states that the site is that of an old 13th. century iron smelting furnace and that the stocks were originally sited by the old pinfold on the top of Rigton Hill. There would have been no seat and "delinquents" sat on a stone flag with their backs to the pinfold wall. The stocks were moved to the present site in 1930 - in 1960 they were restored and a seat was added. The green now has a large stone which is the memorial to the two World Wars, using stone from Almscliffe Crag.
There are several wells in North Rigton including one on Brackenwell Lane and the site of the village pump. Drinking water was taken from this well until 1950. There is another well at Well Cottage complete with cover.
The Methodist Chapel at North Rigton was opened in 1816 and a larger building

North Rigton Church

followed east of the first chapel, using the old stones. The Earl of Harewood laid the foundation stone for the new building in 1932 and the chapel was opened on April 15th.1933. In the mid-19th. century the folk who were listed as residents of North Rigton included corn miller Thomas Dunwell, shoemaker William Gill, rope maker Charles Wilkinson and smith Major England.

Rigton National School was built in 1851 at the expense of the Earl of Harewood and the rector Henry Blunt. A plaque on the extended school records the foundation.

St.John's Church was consecrated by the Bishop of Knaresborough on June 2nd.1911, built by J. T. Wright to designs by architect W. Hill & Sons. Prior to this church being opened for worship, services were held in the schoolroom. A building fund was started in 1904 and in June 1910 the Countess of Harewood cut the first turf. The vicarage was given by the Earl of Harewood, who also gave the site for the new church. The vicarage west of the church was considerably extended in 1914 and is now a private house.

The interior of this church contains many examples of Mouseman Robert Thompson's woodwork. The altar and rails are all by Thompson and the table by the door is a memorial to Joseph Lister. Joe Lister was born in Thirsk into a family of millers on May 14th.1930 and became the fifth secretary of Yorkshire County Cricket Club in 1972 following the 37 years service of John Henry "Jack" Nash. He played four innings for the County in 1954 and scored 35 runs. Joe Lister was the uncle to Yorkshire cricketer George Gibson Macauley (December 7th. 1897 -

December 13th. 1940), who played 318 innings for the county scoring 5717 runs and taking 1774 wickets; he played hockey for Yorkshire and played 24 first class matches between 1951 and 1959.
Joseph Lister became Worcestershire CCC Secretary before being appointed to Yorkshire. He lived at Huby and died in Harrogate on January 28th. 1991 aged 60.
The font is made from stone and marble as is the fine pulpit a memorial to Marianne Rosa Kent of Tatefield Hall at Brackenthwaite. There are the graves of the Kent family in the churchyard at Pannal.
In the graveyard are the tombs of Wilfrid Edmondson Edmondson-Jones (1902-1976) who was the vicar of North Rigton from 1965 until 1972. The architect John Ellis Stocks FRIBA is also buried in this churchyard - he was a partner in the firm of Jones & Stocks of 20 Park Row Leeds and lived at Weeton Old Hall. He was born on October 3rd.1884 and died on December 18th.1951.
Although there is evidence of a small chapel existing at North Rigton prior to the new church, no trace is found although on Chapel Hill some bones were once found in the old cemetery

The hill top village of Kirkby Overblow has a long history for a village name which ends with -by indicates a Danish origin. The "orbauers" or "overblow" was added in the 13th. century and indicates the presence of ore-blowers or smelters in an area once rich in iron deposits. In 1302 the village was known as Kyrkby Orblauers.
In the Domesday Book the village was known as Cherchebi and following the

Kirkby Overblow Church

Conquest the lands belonged to the Percy family. In 1362 Henry Percy willed the foundation of a chantry at Kirkby, in memory of himself and his wife Mary - they are both buried at Alnwick.
All Saints Church today mainly dates from 1780/81 when rebuilding took place. There was a church here in Saxon times and the Normans rebuilt the church. The only reminder of the early Medieval church is the doorway in the north wall, which possibly dates from the Saxon period. The north wall is thicker that the other church walls and the door was often called the Excommunication Door - the exit to unconsecrated ground in early churches. The north transept dates from the 14th. century with its piscina: St. Helen's Chapel was founded by Henry Percy was once the private chapel of the Lords of the Manor. Fragments of old stained glass have been arranged in the chapel window. The chapel was restored and rededicated to St. Helen on November 6th.1966 with the Mouseman furnishings being gifts of the parishioners. The inscription on the 15th. century tower reads "Charles Cooper rector of this parish took care that this falling tower should be restored 1781". The sundial on the tower bears the date 1798 and Victorian restoration costing £1185 was completed by George Street in 1872. More restoration was to follow a fire in the chancel during December 1891. The altar rails are also the work of the Mouseman of Kilburn and were placed in memory of the Rector Dr. Robert Bellamy. The lectern, also in memory of a past Rector, has the mouse displayed on its base.
At one period the Rector of Kirkby Overblow distributed nine bushels of wheat every Christmas to the poor parishioners.
There are memorial plaques to Joe Ridsdale (1866-1910) "in recognition of his labours for the village including six years as Hon. Sec. of the Flower Show Church Warden 1902-1910"; Walter Hudson JP of Low Hall (1875-1953); Thomas Lister Ingham who died in 1910 - a copse east of the hall is still known as Ingham Whinn - and Myles Dodson who died aged 68 on September 19th.1657. Myles Dodson was an early owner of Low Hall and had his coat of arms over the hall fireplace. Low Hall was once the meeting place of the Puritans or non-conformists. They were later to build their own Methodist Chapel in the village.
The oak panelling in the restored baptistry created in 1968 came from the manor house of Low Hall: the Hall today is the home of a racing stable. The Ridsdale family once lived at Low Hall: James died in 1810 aged 59 and his son died in 1812 aged 23. A later occupant was Charles Wardman in the 1860's.
The tomb slab of William Plompton now against the south nave wall, dates from the 15th. century. The slab features the hammers of the Hammerton family and the crest of the Plomptons. In Spofforth Church is a worn effigy of Sir Robert Plompton from about 1324.
There is a memorial to Christopher Bethell (1728-1797) on the south chancel wall. He was the 4th. son of Sir William Codrington and married Ann (1754-1797) the

daughter of Samuel Lord Sandys. This Puritan family lived at Swindon Hall in the 16th and 17th centuries and their home was destroyed by the Royalist forces in the Civil War. Sir Walter Bethell married Mary, daughter of Sir Henry Slingsby of Scriven and their children included Sir Slingsby Bethell, sheriff of London in 1680 and William Bethell Rector of Kirkby Overblow for 38 years: he died in 1685.
The house was rebuilt after the Civil War and again in 1830 being on the road from the village to the main Harrogate Road. There is a grave in the churchyard to George Pickard of Swinden Hall who died in 1921 aged 84.
Swindon Lodge is to the east of Swindon Lane and was the home in the 19th. century of William and Mary Renton and their son John, who died in 1853. The property was sold by the Harewood Estate in 1951.
There is also a memorial in Kirkby Overblow Church to William Symondson who died aged 53 in 1735, one time secretary of the United Society for the Propagation of the Gospel. The memorial to William Lister Fenton-Scott on the north chancel wall records his 16 years as Registrar-General of the West Riding, he lived at Wood Hall near Linton, Wetherby. William died aged 67 on March 27th.1813 and his wife Mary died in October 1815 aged 59. Their large box tomb on the east side of the church bears their initials and in pre-War days was surrounded by iron railings. The other member of this family was William Lister Fenton Scott who died aged 61 on October 8th.1842. It was William Lister Fenton Scott who erected a memorial in the churchyard to Samuel Steel of Sicklinghall, who died in 1834 aged 64.
On May 13th.1981 the Queen confirmed the creation of the United Benefice of Kirkby Overblow to include the churches at Stainburn, Weeton, Sicklinghall and North Rigton. The dedication of a village well to St. Helen also indicates the early establishment of the village. The waters with their healing properties were a trusted treatment: the original well with descending steps is in the cellar of a house, while a spring flows in the grounds of St. Helens near the south church wall. The dedication to St. Helen would have originated in the 4th. century - Helen was Constantine's mother, who had made her pilgrimage to Jerusalem. Emperor Constantine was the first Christian Emperor being declared at York in 306AD. He was born about 264AD and died in 337AD - he moved his capital to Byzantium in 330AD and named it Constantinople.
The village school was opened in 1780 and enlarged and improved by the Earl of Harewood in 1871: the school house was added in 1790 by subscription and extensions to the school occurred in 1900. The old school room is now the assembly hall of the present school which comprises modern buildings. In the 19th. century one of the schoolmasters of Kirkby Overblow was John Christian Brooke.
Kirkby Overblow won the best kept village award in 1965 and has two old public houses, horse mounting steps outside Sycamore Farm and appropriately named Tithe and Glebe Cottages. The old Post Office is also converted into a private residence.

The public houses are the 18th. century "Star and Garter" and the "Shoulder of Mutton". The innkeeper of the Star & Garter was Robert Leatham, who was at the inn for 40 years and died in 1855 aged 85. His son Richard Leatham took over the licence at the inn. The innkeeper at the Shoulder of Mutton was William Lawn in 1838 and in more recent years Alice Appelbee who died in 1980 aged 79. She was followed by David and Molly Parsons, who left to run a hotel in Pickering.
In more recent years Kirkby Overblow was the setting for the TV series "Langley Bottom" and "Parkin's Patch".

Barrowby House is the Ripon Diocesan Retreat and Conference Centre. It was built on the site of Barrowby Grange, administered by the monks of Fountains Abbey who used it as a temporary storage for their tithes to be taken to the abbey by packhorse. During the times of Elizabeth Ist. Barrowby Grange became the home of a Roman Catholic family and would have been under surveillance.
A bungalow was built on the site of the old monastic grange in 1908 for Consuelo Albinia Crompton-Stansfield, who had inherited the estate from her brewer father Col. William Crompton Stansfield of Esholt Hall in 1907. Consuelo obtained her furnishings from other places including panelling from Low Hall and a staircase from Esholt when it was demolished about 1922 - originally at Wallington Hall in Northumberland. The bookcases also came from Esholt Hall and a room was substantially altered to accommodate them. The chapel at Barrowby House was designed by Mr. Hill, who removed the panelling to the church. The chapel was dedicated by the Bishop of Ripon in July 1967.
Consuelo attended services at Kirkby Overblow and struck a friendship with the vicar Canon Malcolm MacColl. He was himself a friend of Gladstone who visited the rectory at Kirkby, although the Rector was more often out of the village. Although an averred bachelor Malcolm MacColl married Consuelo when he was 73 years old and enjoyed three years of married life. Their graves are side by side at the east end of Kirkby Overblow Church - he died in April 1907 and his wife Consuelo died on July 11th.1932. She left Barrowby to her nephew Sir Gilbert Inglefield and in 1950 he gave the house to the diocese as a thanksgiving for his safe return from the War.

Rudding House was built in 1807 replacing an older building standing to the south west. During the reign of King George II (1727-1760) Rudding Park was owned by the Williamson family from Wetherby and they sold to the Craddock family who in turn sold it to James Collins by 1767. He enlarged the old House and planted avenues of trees. Rudding was then purchased by Thomas Wilson, brother of the Bishop of Bristol and in 1788 Lord Loughborough bought the property - he was the Lord Chancellor to William Pitt. Lord Loughborough was created the Earl of Rosslyn

in 1801 and employed Humphry Repton to redesign the park. In 1805 the Earl died and Rudding House was sold to William Gordon.
William Gordon was the nephew of the Earl of Aberdeen and had lived at Stockeld Park Wetherby. It was Gordon who demolished the old mansion and built the present structure. It was bought unfinished in 1824 by Sir Joseph Radcliffe, second baronet; William Gordon died in 1845.
The Radcliffe family took their name from the town east of Bury where they had their home at Radcliffe Tower before 1194. The family was first mentioned in the 12th. century, when Henry witnessed a charter for the foundation of Burscough Abbey. His son William Radcliffe became the chaplain to King Edward Ist.(1272-1307). In the early 17th. century William Radcliffe settled at Milnsbridge and his son devised the estate to his nephew Joseph Pickford, who took the name and coat of arms of Radcliffe.
Joseph Pickford was born in 1744, and he inherited the Milnsbridge estate in 1795 and was raised to the baronetcy in November 1813. He married three times: Catherine Percival by whom he had a son William born in 1763 at Royton Hall. His second wife was Elizabeth Sunderland by whom he had eleven children including the priest Joseph Pickford (1766 - 1804) - he was buried at Acomb York. There were no children by his third wife Elizabeth Creswick. He became the JP for the West Riding, Lancashire and Chester. He died at Clifton in Bristol in 1819. It was his grandson Sir Joseph Radcliffe who bought the Rudding estate.
The son of the Rev. Joseph Radcliffe was Sir Joseph born at Royton in 1799 and the purchaser of Rudding: in 1819 he succeeded to the baronetcy and he married Jacobina Maria Macdonnell, daughter of General John Macdonnell in Edinburgh on October 29th. 1819: they had 12 children. Sir Joseph died at Rudding on November 29th. 1872 and his wife had died on May 10th.1868, both being buried at Spofforth. The eldest son was Sir Joseph Perceval Pickford-Radcliffe who was born on October 4th.1824 and married Katherine Mary Doughty, daughter of Sir Edward Doughty - he became the 3rd. baronet and the builder of Rudding Chapel in 1874, after he succeeded to the estate in 1872.Sir Joseph's brothers were Charles (born 1829), Arthur Reginald who married Georgiana Pickford, Godfrey Edward and his sisters were Jacobina Maria, Elizabeth, Amelia, Flora, Alpina, Henrietta, Georgiana and Laura.
The eldest daughter Jacobina Maria Radcliffe was married on June Ist.1841 to Samuel James Brown: he was the son of the Leeds banker William Williams Brown of Allerton Hall and his wife Margaret Duncan of Philadelphia, who died in May 1820.
The 4th. baronet Sir Joseph was one of 10 children and he succeeded his father in 1908 and after the last War he made Rudding over to his grandson Captain Everard Radcliffe.

Rudding Chapel

The Gothic Revival Catholic church was designed by architect A. E. Purdie FRIBA and built in memory of Sir Joseph's parents: Sir Joseph who died November 29th. 1872 and his mother Dame Jacobina who died May 10th. 1868. The chapel was officially opened on the day that Joseph Edward Radcliffe reached his 21st. birthday on August lst. 1879. There were many celebrations on that day with lunch in the House and a service in the Holy Family Church. There is a plaque on the south wall to this Sir Joseph Edward Radcliffe who was born on August lst.1858 and died on September 29th.1949. His crest is shown together with the family motto:"Virtus Propter Se". He became a Major in the West Yorkshire Regiment and owned about 30,000 acres of land in Yorkshire and Lancashire. On his death the estates were passed to Sir Everard Joseph Reginald Henry Radcliffe of St. Trinians Hall Richmond, who was appointed Captain of Yorkshire CCC in the summer of 1911. Sir Everard was born on January 27th.1884 at Hensleigh Devon and first played for Yorkshire cricket in 1909: he played until 1911 with 76 innings completed scoring 826 runs as well as taking 2 wickets for 134 runs. He had captained Yorkshire during the absence of Lord Hawke (Captain of Yorkshire CCC 1883-1910) especially in the summers of 1909/1910. Sir Everard died on November 23rd. 1969 aged 85 at St. Trinians Hall Richmond, where he had lived for about 20 years. He was educated at Downside and Christ Church Oxford and was a stockbroker in Newcastle upon Tyne for a few years.

On the same wall is the memorial plaque to Bernard Joseph Percival Joseph Radcliffe who was born on November 12th.1869 the 4th.son of Sir Joseph and Katherine and

died on September 29th.1948: his wife Georgina died on December 26th.1941. The chapel also contains memorials to Lt. Percival Radcliffe killed in action on November 25th.1911 aged 20 and to Cpt. Arthur and Francis Joseph Radcliffe.
Today, the chapel is rarely used but retains the Aberdeen marble pillars and a 15th. century statue of St. Hilda. There is a needlework picture of The Last Supper over the west door and the church contains many memorials to the Radcliffe family.
In August 1972 the 2000 acre Rudding estate was sold by Captain Sir Everard Radcliffe to a Northamptonshire landowner John Mackaness of Boughton Hall - the contracts were signed on Saturday August 19th. The sale realised over £1 million and had been forced on the Radcliffe family due to increased taxation and general costs. Captain and Lady Radcliffe left for Lausanne Switzerland with their two month old heir for a period: the house contents were sold later in 1972. The books were sold by Christies in October 1972 and there were other contents sales on November 2nd and 15th.
Hugh Radcliffe, the second son of Sir Everard Radcliffe 5th. baronet of Rudding Park, Milnsbridge House and Royton Hall died in December 1993. He married Maria Pereira, grand daughter of George Lane Fox of Bramham Park in 1937. He served in the last War and was awarded in MBE in 1944. His third son - he had six children - is the Very Rev Timothy Radcliffe a Dominican Friar since 1965 and elected in 1993 as Master of the Order of Dominican Friars.
The Mackaness family formed a Trust with father and three sons - Rudding House Conference and Banqueting Centre was opened on December 8th.1987. Rudding House is a listed Grade I building set in 230 acres of private parkland. The Rudding Holiday Park for caravans and holiday cottages will be complemented with the Golf Course. The £1.5 million Rudding Park golf course is an 18 hole championship course designed by Marton Hawtree and built by John Greasley Ltd. set to open in June 1995, on a daily fee basis. There will also be a 30 room accommodation development at Rudding Park which will add to the conference and dining facilities.

Follifoot is a small village south of Rudding Park: it was known as Fulifet in 1167 derived from the Scandinavian "fola gefecht" meaning a place where horse fighting or racing took place. The first reference to a race meeting at Follifoot was in 1753 when there was a two day meeting in September. Alexander's Hill in this area was settled by prehistoric man: the mound of earth and stones was excavated in 1850 for the sale of stones to repair the road. There were several weapons found together with articles of pottery, bone and bronze.
A chapel was in existence in 1548 at Follifoot as records show that a mass was held in that year. St. Joseph & St. James Church was dedicated on October 22nd. 1848 as a chapel of ease to Spofforth Church. The church is in the parish of Spofforth and Kirk Deighton and the churchyard contains the graves of the Whittertons of

Bramham Hall Plompton, the Leake family of The Poplars later The Priory Follifoot and the two chest tombs on the south side to John and Richard Teale - they died in 1852 and 1860 - amongst the first burials at Follifoot.
The East window is dedicated to the memory of Sir Joseph Radcliffe, founder of the church who was born on June 5th.1799 and died on November 29th.1872. The north and south chancel windows are also dedicated to the memory of Sir Joseph: the north window was erected by the daughters of Sir Joseph's friend James Tripp, Rector of Spofforth. The windows were dedicated between 1879 and 1881. The south nave window is to the memory of William and Mary Leake; the north window to Thomas Leake of The Cedars Hemsworth who died in October 1894. The window was presented by his sister Frances Leake in 1895. The Oak pulpit was made by Robert "Mouseman" Thompson and dedicated to the memory of John James Wood of Crimple in 1956. The small Oak replica of the Saxon village cross stands by the west window and was made by local craftsman Claude Townsend. He also reseated the church in English Oak and made the altar rail and Bishop's chair together with the village bus shelters. The church was re-roofed and a service of thanksgiving took place in December 1993. The sculptured marble reredos features the "Scene at Ammaeus" and was presented to the church by the Leake family.
Follifoot Wesleyan Chapel opened in 1879 and is now a private house. The village has two inns: the Lascelles Arms built in the 17th. century and once called the Harewood Arms. The Radcliffe Arms dates from the 19th. century and was the King's Arms but had changed by the turn of this century. Hilltop House is dated 1796 and was the original King's Arms Inn and retains the cellars and has two wells in its grounds.
The impressive Rudding Gates were once the main entrance to the House along a short drive. The village green at the top of Main Street has a 7th/8th century Saxon cross which had been found in the Park. It was given to the village in March 1967 by Cpt. Sir Everard Radcliffe in memory of his grandparents. The cross was on the top of a mound in Rudding Park for a century: in the private cemetery of the lower wood. The stone pound on Knaresborough Road dating from 1688 was restored in 1975.
The village smithy, kept by the Wood brothers produced the iron gates for Rudding Gates but this trade has ceased along with the wheelwright, flaxspinner, shoemaker, tanner and miller. The village stocks were restored in 1957. in memory of Amy Winifred Robinson of Priory Lodge and Col. Gerard Maxwell Glynton of The Priory. The Priory, formerly The Poplars and home of the Leake family, is an old building and is believed to be the site of a monastery/rest house for monks journeying between Kirkstall and Fountains Abbeys - the present house was built in 1737 as a residence and school for the Catholic priest. Until 1952 there was a holy water stoup outside a door but the school was moved to Knaresborough in 1787 and the house

became a private dwelling. The Priory is adjacent to the recent housing development of Manor Fold. The cellars of The Priory are reputed to have a connection with Duck Nest Farm: said to have been built with stones from Spofforth Castle.
The oldest houses in Follifoot are thought to be Manor Farm cottages dating from the 17th. century: one retains the date 1681.
Follifoot Village Hall on Tofts Lane had the foundation stone laid by Captain Sir Joseph Everard Radcliffe MC on October 17th.1971 and was completed a year later: it was designed by a villager and built by a Harrogate firm. The present Primary School is a 19th. century building: enlarged in 1890 and included a teacher's house. Oakfield House was once a school built in the early 19th. century and a Catholic school in Rudding Lane was closed in 1959.
The Follifoot estate of Aketon in the Crimple Valley was once the home of Sir Kenneth Parkinson, Chairman of Yorkshire Post Newspapers until his death in June 1981. The six bedroom house and 100 acre estate was placed on the market in September 1981: the gardens were created by Lady Parkinson who died in November 1980. The family bought the house, which was built at the turn of the century, in 1938: the setting is east of Follifoot and near to Spofforth.

The main road to Harrogate from the junction of the Leeds and Bradford turnpikes was known as Buttersyke Bar - Moses French was the toll collector in 1841. The bar house was demolished in 1926 as it obscured the road ahead for motorists. The new roundabout was built for the Harrogate-Knaresborough by-pass road. The first phase of this road opened in November 1991 followed by completion in September 1992. The ascent of Swarth Hill past the turning for Burn Bridge (originally Burnt Bridge) - the pre-turnpike route to Harrogate - leads to the Princess Royal Way and the hamlet of Spacey Houses.

Spacey Houses developed with the opening of the turnpike road to Harrogate - George and Isobel Spacie lived in the old inn with their children Roger and Susan. Isobel was buried at Pannal on December 26th.1671 and George Spacie on December 22nd.1695. The Old Spacey House Inn is now a private house opposite the Spacey Houses Hotel, itself an inn in the 1830's. The house is part of Spacey Houses Farm and was built in two sections, as shown by the differing stonework. This turnpike inn became important in the days of coaching and the old stables, coach housing and barns are still intact together with the original cobbled paths. The small garden where folk used to drink their "home brew" is well kept and the old toilets were at the bottom of this garden. The old beer drop with its wooden covers leads into a barrel cellar where other access is by steps from the house or down the hatch. The old inn backyard has also a smith's shop and a well preserved grinding stone - there is also a metal plate placed by the Ordnance Survey as a bench mark.

The front of the house facing the main road retains the hooks for the gates, although the gates and iron fencing were removed for the war effort.
The old inn developed from the farm, which probably originated about 1674 - the house dates from 1714. Records show that Ann Wilkinson was the innkeeper the 1830's and by 1841 her two sons farmed the area. The innkeepers included John Trees who died in 1840 aged 56, William Trees who died in 1867 aged 51 and Ann Trees (died 1887 aged 71). The Trees family are buried at Pannal Church and include William Trees born on July 7th. 1854 and who died on July 24th. 1885.
The Spacey Houses Hotel was also a turnpike public house dating from the 18th. century. The inn was owned by a charity set up by Thomas Richardson in 1765: a Trust was created ten years later through his will. In May 1894 the trustees of the charity "Dr. Richardson's School" sold the property to Alfred Holmes. Alfred died aged 58 on April 11th. 1904 and appointed his wife Sarah as the trustee: she died on December 26th. 1913. Alfred's will also stated that his son should become a trustee when he attained his majority: John Shutt Holmes died in 1900 aged 25. His daughter Priscilla Ethel Holmes became the trustee of the charity: she attained her majority on December 19th.1902 and she died in May 1920. The property was part of her estate which was sold by auction at the N.E.Station Hotel Harrogate on May 31st. 1920 by Renton & Renton: the sale indicated the closure of the Trust.
The new owner was William Ernest Penn of Bradford who paid £8500: the sale also included the New Inn on the corner of Cold Bath Road/Otley Road Harrogate and the site of the slaughterhouse on the Wetherby Road/Hookstone Road corner. The sale of the Spacey House Inn included the cartshed, warehouse, washhouse, coachhouse, stables and garage.
On May 15th.1925 William Penn conveyed the Spacey Houses Inn to William Whitaker Ltd of the Old Brewery Bradford: the sale included the brewery barn, stables, maltkiln and garden. William Whitaker Ltd sold to Joshua Tetley on September 20th.1960.
Pannal Auction Market started trading on the corner site opposite the Spacey Houses Hotel and by the end of the last century was run by Robert Burton: he was a farmer and auctioneer with stock sales on alternate Mondays. The market moved to its present site about 1926 and has regular livestock, horse and car auctions. The present owners bought the business in 1955 and introduced the car auctions in 1966 and horses were sold from 1970.
Pannal Golf Club was formed following a meeting on November 6th.1906 to discuss the rent of land at Pannal owned by Lord Harewood - Harrogate Golf Club had been founded in 1892. By the end of November the 100 acre site was leased for 21 years and a further acre was acquired to build the club house. The Pannal Golf Club was formed in December 1906 with an entry fee of 10/6d and an annual subscription of a guinea. Until the clubhouse was built, members of the Club used temporary

facilities at the Spacey Houses Inn. The Pannal Golf Club Ltd was established on June 28th.1906 and on September 8th.1906 saw the opening of a nine hole course designed by Alex "Sandy" Herd of Huddersfield.
An 18 hole course was proposed on September 25th.1906 and sketches for the clubhouse were prepared by the Hon. Secretary Richard Crosland. The new course was opened on October 12th.1907 and the new clubhouse was opened on November 16th.1907: the official opening of the new course took place on April 11th.1908 with an exhibition match between James Braid and Percy Hills.
In 1908 a letter was sent to the Secretary of the Bramhope Hunt about the "serious damage done to the course" and demanded compensation. The Golf Course was altered and completed by March 1935, opening on May 6th. following advice from Major C. A. Mackenzie.
During the years of the last War, some land of Pannal Golf Club was used to graze 250 sheep and the course also provided land to grow potatoes, oats, wheat and sugar beet. This ceased in 1943 with the sheep taken away in 1946: the course which had been partly ploughed up was reconstructed.
On January 30th. 1950 Lord Harewood announced the disposal of the estate including 124 acres held on lease by Pannal Golf Club. The conveyance was signed on September 7th.1950 through a Debenture Trust Deed to cover the £10,000.
In 1956 Pannal Golf Club held their Golden Jubilee and on July 16th.1972 British Open Champion Lee Trevino played an exhibition match at Pannal.
On Pannal Road stands Follifoot Hall built in 1861 on Follifoot Ridge and was the agent's house for the Radcliffe's Rudding Park estate. Following the departure of Tommy Ives the Hall became a dental practice and then it became Graham's Bathrooms headquarters, Arncliffe Holdings and now is the offices of Moore Estates Ltd. from 1992.
The grounds contain a Saxon burial mound and earthworks by the 18th./19th. century windmill now converted into a private house: it is stone built and has an irregular castellated top.

THE ROAD FROM LEEDS TO HARROGATE

PART 6: FROM PANNAL TO HARROGATE

Pannal was not mentioned in the Domesday Book although Beckwith and Rosset were mentioned. The survey states that "In Roserte Ulf had one carucate and a half to be taxed: land to one plough: waste". The lands became part of the Forest of Knaresborough and the canons of Newburgh held land at Pannal in the mid-15th. century. It has been suggested that the name Pannal derives from Pen Hall - a mansion on a hill or Pan Hall, meaning it was timber built. In 1304 Pannal held an annual fair and a weekly market granted by Royal Charter. The old market cross was once outside the village blacksmith's shop but is now in the grounds of Pannal Hall. About 1257 the Order of St. Robert of Knaresborough and the Holy Trinity came under royal patronage. About 1309 the Earl of Cornwall as Lord of the Forest of Knaresborough, gave the community of St. Robert (1160-1218) the church at Pannal in exchange for a part of the Forest. Until 1539, when the community was dissolved, the brethren appointed the vicar of Pannal. The church also had a Chantry Chapel of St. James, which was not dissolved until 1549.

Pannal Church

St. Robert was born in York, the son of Robert Flower twice Mayor of the city. He became a white monk at Newminster near Morpeth and afterwards a hermit at Knaresborough in the chapel of the Holy Cross. St. Robert's Cave is the location of the hermitage: little remains of the Chapel. The sites of the Priory Mill and the Trinitarian Priory are both occupied by private housing.

The Parish Church of St. Robert of Knaresborough, whose records are complete from 1568, has a tower and the chancel dating from 1297 and a nave from 1772 - the bases of the old nave pillars are used as footscrapers outside the south door. The church was founded in earlier days - there is a record in 1271 of an Archdeacon of Rochester resigning the Pannal rectory. The Scots made the church their headquarters after Bannockburn and afterwards burnt the building. The tower contains three bells which are reputed to have come from Fountains Abbey - they were recast between 1669 and 1702. The marble font, restored in 1975, is also supposed to have come from the Abbey. The original chancel was four/five feet lower that the original chancel and both the piscina and sedilia are well below their former height. The altar was made by local craftsmen with wood from an earlier chancel screen. The main entrance to the church was made in 1883 replacing the north door of 1772: the church was reopened after restoration on February 21st. 1884.

The Jubilee Chapter House was opened in 1977 replacing the old church hall built for Queen Victoria's Jubilee. The choir vestry, whose foundation stone was laid by James Ramsden MP on September 18th.1955 opened in the following year.

The church furnishings are mainly recent and there are five pieces of Robert "Mouseman" Thompson's work. The east window was erected by Elizabeth Penelope Bentley in 1883 in memory of her relations buried in the chancel: the marble grave slabs are to David Smith Wilson of Pannal Hall (died 1915 aged 73), his son W. Wilson-Bentley (died 1908 aged 29), Anne Elizabeth nee Bentley, wife of David Smith Wilson (died 1902) and Marian the daughter of David Smith Wilson (1864-1891).

There is some Medieval glass showing the arms of the Community of St. Robert which may have come from Knaresborough or have been a part of the original east window.

Outside in the churchyard is a large stone coffin, used in the 19th. century to defeat the efforts of grave robbers supplying surgeons with their training corpses. In the south churchyard is also the box tomb of Joseph Thackwrey with the inscription:"Joseph Thackwrey by name, who by the help of God, brought Sulphur Wells to fame. In the year of our Lord 1740 I came to the Crown in 1791 they laid me down. When I shall rise again no man can surely tell; but in the hopes of Heaven I'm not afraid of Hell. To friends I bid farewell and part without a frown, in hopes to rise again and have a better Crown". The Crown Hotel is in Low Harrogate.

James Bray, buried at Pannal Church, was awarded the Leeds, Bramhope and Pannal contracts for the Leeds & Thirsk Railway: they included Arthington viaduct and Bramhope tunnel. James Bray accumulated enough wealth to buy Moor Park at Beckwithshaw. He died on October 17th. 1873 aged 72. The family tomb inscription include Thomas Bray (died 1876 aged 47), Elizabeth (1802-1876) and Hirom (1833-1856).

The graves of the Cluderay family of Spacey House are in Pannal Churchyard and include Esther, wife of Charles Cluderay who died aged 40 on July 14th. 1789 - she was the mother of 15 children. The family were called Clithero and Clideroe: Charles was born in 1744 and died in 1808 and he was a cordwainer. He married Esther Winterburn in 1769 and on her death married Ann Oates. The eldest son from the first marriage was William who became the local miller at Pannal: he married Ann Oddy of Spofforth and their son Charles Cluderay was clerk to the Holbeck Board of Guardians and superintendent registrar. A family descended from this line now live in Barwick in Elmet. There are many memorials in Pannal Church chancel to the Bentley family of Pannal Hall. Those on the north chancel wall include Thomas (died November 27th. 1930 aged 42); William (1780-1843); Melville Guy (1960-1968) and on the south chancel wall to William (1730-1813) and Eliza Penelope described as a Lay Rectoress who died on Easter Even 1884. There are more Bentley gravestones set into the chancel floor and in the graveyard.

Pannal Hall was built by the Tankred or Tankerd family but was replaced by the present building in 1860 built by Thomas Bentley. The family were followed by two generations of Dougill and on August 2nd. 1638 William Dougill conveyed the Hall to Thomas, Charles, James and Philip Herbert. A Philip Herbert was Lord Mayor of York in 1675 and in June 1694 he mortgaged Pannal Hall estate to Robert Bell.

Robert Bell died in 1707 and the estate passed to his son and was then sold to William Pullan and on November 10th. 1724 the Pannal Hall estate was sold to George Bentley. George was born in 1680 and came from Great Rosset near Pannal: he died in March 1765 and was succeeded by his son William Bentley. The estate passed through generations of the Bentley family and in 1866 the estate was devised to William George Bentley's aunt Eliza Penelope Bentley. The now reduced Pannal Hall estate remains today in the possession of this local family.

Pannal school was built in 1816/7 and with the schoolhouse was funded by public subscriptions and donations from the Bishops of Durham and York together with the Earl of Harewood.

Pannal County Primary School on Pannal Green was opened in 1967 with an extension added in 1979.There are eight mixed ability classes with about 250 children. The catchment area includes Burn Bridge, Pannal Ash, Rossett Green and the Fulwith area.

Quarry House was the old vicarage and was built in 1910 but has been a private house since 1978. Adjacent to this house was the old parochial hall opened on May

28th. 1888 to mark the Jubilee. Sandy Bank Quarry was last worked in 1930 providing material for many local Pannal houses. On the hill top is Pannal House - All Saints Court - which once belonged to the Wescoe yeoman family. The house was once a boys school - Pannal College in the 1890's - a nursery school and a college for nannies. It was sold in 1947 and became private housing.
Pannal station master's house was opened as Platform One on October 16th. 1980 - the house dates from 1848. The additional dining accommodation of a pullman car adds colour and interest to a meal.
Pannal Memorial Hall was once known as Oddfellows Hall and dates from the First World War.
The firm of Bintex was opened at Pannal in 1938 until they were taken over by Dunlopillo in 1949. In 1960 the headquarters of Dunlopillo were relocated to Pannal from Fort Dunlop and a year later the new office block was completed. The car park near Pannal Bank involved the demolition of a row of railway cottages.
The 17 acre site of Dunlopillo manufactures Latex foam bedding, car seats, pillows - Latex was invented in 1929 - and in 1994 £¾ million was sanctioned for latex plant improvements at Pannal's factory. The firm had 2 million of export orders in early 1994.
Mill Cottage at the end of Mill Lane is dated to 1765 and nearby is a boundary stone for the Forest of Knaresborough dated 1767.
At Daw Cross on Spring Lane is the Pannal Methodist Church. Meetings were initially held at John Kent's farmhouse in 1773 and in Pannal Hall: by 1784 a new chapel was opened on Hillfoot Lane. The foundation stone for the new chapel at Daw Cross was laid on June 15th. 1904 and the church was opened on January 19th.1905. In 1932 a tablet was placed on the old site dated 1788: the old chapel was demolished in 1905. The present gates of the chapel were hung to mark the bicentenary of the chapel in 1984.
Burn(t) Bridge now merges with Pannal having the cricket ground and the "Black Swan" inn opposite Lockwoods Restaurant. In 1838 Jane Jackson was the licensee of the Black Swan. Burnt Bridge Corn Mill was on the Crimple Beck east of Bunker Hill. The graves of Hannah and Abraham Thackray at Pannal Church describe them as living in Burnt Bridge - they died in 1869 and 1879 respectively.
The large isolated house on the main road to Harrogate near the railway bridge is "Fieldhurst" and was once a boy's school.
Leeds Road Garden Centre was opened by Brian Smallwood in 1962 as an indoor nursery and by 1972 he had built himself a new house. The Centre was bought and developed as a Garden Centre in 1982.
Brookside Nursery was a much earlier site being a nursery from about 1896. The flowers and salad crops grown at the centre had wide appeal but in 1962/63 the hurricanes destroyed the nursery site: it was rebuilt in 1973/74.

Ampher Bridge is now Almsford Bridge crossing the River Crimple - the old stone bridge can be seen to the east of the new road bridge. The new bridge was built in 1930 having been financially possible with a generous donation from W. H. Baxter JP of Leeds and Harrogate. William Henry Baxter lived at Knapping Mount Harrogate and was the director of W. H. Baxter Ltd, makers of stone breaking machinery of Gelderd Road Leeds. He was born in Hunslet in December 1849 and in November 1873 he married Eleanor Colbeck.

During the last War there were concrete bollards half way up Almsford Bank used as a tank trap.

Crimple Viaduct is the Impressive railway feature to the east and was built for the Church Fenton-Tadcaster-Wetherby-Harrogate branch line which opened on August 10th. 1847. The Crimple Viaduct was built in 1846 and is 1873' long having 31 arches. Each arch has a 31' span and the viaduct has a height of 110'.

The railway from Leeds via Bramhope Tunnel, Arthington Viaduct, Weeton and Pannal stations now crosses the Crimple Viaduct - the Wetherby line closed on January 4th. 1964. Trains from Wetherby and Spofforth passed through the 825 yard long Prospect or Crimple tunnel before they crossed the viaduct.

Fullwith Mill was one of a few corn mills on the Crimple: Henry Cullingworth ran this mill and died aged 59 in 1848 and Robert Read was at the mill - he died aged 65 in 1861. Stone Rings Quarry is remembered in the lane to the west at the top of Almsford Bank: the quarry exploited the local sandstone for building.

The junction of the main road and Hookstone Road is now the site for Appleyards and the National Westminster Bank. The bank was once known as Scott's Corner: the grocery firm of Anthony Scott was founded in 1852. They ran the old Ship Inn at Harewood Bridge and later moved into Harewood Village. The Harrogate premises were originally at 13a Hookstone Road and also at High Street Boston Spa, Collingham and at Harewood. In the early 1930's Scott's shop moved to the newly built corner site complete with the familiar clock. The Hookstone Road premises were taken by the Claro Cash & Carry. The shop closed in February 1961 and moved to Harewood for a few years: the shop is now a fashion business. When the Scott family had the Harewood shop they also ran a small farm of about 10 acres with pigs and cows: they had a farm delivery service and were an integral part of the area.

Rev. John Trevor Scott was born at Scott's Corner in 1935 and was a director of the firm until 1961, when he left to enter to train for the ministry. He was a former Harrogate councillor and became the Vicar of Collingham for 8 years and then a popular Vicar of Pannal Church from January 25th. 1978. Rev. John Scott died on November 2nd.1989.

The National Westminster Bank opened on Leeds Road Harrogate in the 1920's as the National Provincial Bank: this had been established in the early 19th. century for

the purpose of extending to England the system of joint stock banking which had taken root in Scotland. The Leeds branch was opened in 1878 through the purchase of the Bank of Leeds Ltd. A few years after Scotts ceased trading at the corner premises the National Westminster Bank, who had acquired the National Provincial Bank transferred their business.
Appleyard's showrooms were opened on April lst. 1968 following those of Glover's of Ripon.
Appleyard Group PLC had its origins in June 1919 when John Earnest Appleyard opened his first showroom on Park Row in Leeds. The first service depot opened in Armley in 1920 but the Park Row showroom burnt down in June 1921. A new depot opened in Albion Street in September that year and a new showroom was built on St. Anne's Street and by 1923 the company employed 75. The North Street depot was opened by William Morris - later Lord Nuffield - in October 1927. In the last War the depot was used to produce aircraft wings and heavy shells for artillery guns: 2000 were employed at one stage. Appleyard PLC now employs 2800 staff with the Harrogate showroom selling Rover cars. It was in 1952 that Austin and Morris merged to form the British Motor Corporation: Rover PLC was formed in 1986.

St. Mark's Church Hall stands adjacent to the "Mile Post" public house, which was known as The Travellers Inn in the 19th. century.
The chancel of St. Mark's Church was completed in 1893 with the nave built in 1903: the architect was John Olrid Scott (1842-1913). He was the son of Gilbert Scott, who was supposed to have based his designs on Fountains Abbey with the high chancel and nave. The church, built of Almscliffe stone, was consecrated on July 29th. 1905. The west end of this church was not completed until after the War in 1948. The planned tower was never built due to lack of available funds.
The font is from 1899 given by the inhabitants of the Oatlands part of the parish. The marble reredos dates from 1911 depicting the Resurrection in St.Luke. There is a Mouseman Thompson Litany desk in memory of George Scott (1878-1947). There are memorial tablets to Edmund Moody, the first churchwarden, who died in 1938 and to the Rev. William Yeadon Potter, the priest of St. Mark's Church from 1893 until 1922. It was through the efforts of this priest that the church was built and consecrated: he was the first vicar from 1905 to 1922 and he died on December 7th. 1933.

The main road now approaches Harrogate Stray being a 215 acre expanse of grass resulting from an Act of Parliament in 1770 providing for the enclosure of the Forest of Knaresborough in which Harrogate stood. The value of the springs to the town was realised and provision made for the Stray to remain unenclosed for ever with public access available at all times. Thus the Stray is the only common land

remaining today of the Forest which until 1893 was stinted pasture. In that year the Harrogate Corporation assumed control over The Stray from the Straygate owners for £11,780. There were at one period 50 cattle gates, which were held by 26 owners - the Ingleby family of Ripley Castle held 12 of these gates. The old stray racecourse was a feature of the Oatlands drive area, laid out by Clement Wolsley in 1793 and was about 1½ miles in circumference.
East of the main road approach to the Prince of Wales roundabout is the Tewit Well, restored in 1973. This chalybeate spring is assumed to have been discovered by William Slingsby of Bilton Hall in 1571. The cover was built to designs by Thomas Chippindale in 1807/08 and until 1842 stood over the sulphur springs of Low Harrogate's Pump Room. The medicinal properties were soon made public and it was Timothy Bright in 1596 who named it a "Spaw" after the town in Belgium.
Harrogate stands on a geological anticline of Lower Carboniferous rock and the faulting of the rock structure has caused the distribution of the springs: 88 springs rise to the surface within a 2 mile radius of the town. 35 of the springs, of which 16 could be used medicinally, rise within the one acre of Valley Gardens - laid out in 1887 as a floral walk between the Old Sulphur Well and the wells in Bogs Field. The Valley Gardens now cover five acres and are the home for the annual springtime Harrogate Flower Show.
St.John's Well in High Harrogate was recognised as being medicinal in 1631 by Dr. Michael Stanhope and a few years later the well attained great popularity. The stone cover was placed in 1656 and the first pump room was opened in 1786 by Lord Loughborough: the present building was erected in 1842.
The Marquess of Granby Hotel was once known as The Sinking Ship and the Royal Oak from 1736. In 1795 it became the Granby with Christ Church nearby. The old church of St.John was built in 1749 and the present church was consecrated in October 1831.

Prior to the turnpike road junction to the west is a triangle of grass, once the site of Harrogate's first railway station. The original line from Wetherby crossed Crimple Viaduct and through a short tunnel - used as an air raid shelter during the last War - terminating at Brunswick Station. This station was opened on July 20th. 1848 but was closed on August lst. 1862: a new line extension was created to the present Harrogate station, which opened in 1862. The land occupied by Brunswick Station became Trinity Stray in compensation for that lost with making the new line. The Railway Company sold further land in 1867 for building plots at The Oval.
Trinity Wesleyan Chapel was opened in 1879 and the Prince of Wales Mansions were opened as Michael Hattersley's Hotel in 1815 - it was called The Crossroads for a period. It was renamed the Brunswick in 1831 - the station took its name from this and became The Prince of Wales Hotel in 1866 following a major rebuilding. This

once busy hotel closed in 1957 and was converted into apartments.
The 9' high sandstone pillar on the road into the town from the Prince of Wales roundabout marks the boundary of the Leeds and Ripon Turnpike Road. The stone was set on this site in 1778 and placed with iron railings surround in 1870. The stone was at the junction of the turnpike to Knaresborough and Boroughbridge and to Otley. Parts of these roads were constructed by "Blind Jack" Metcalfe of Knaresborough.
John Metcalfe died aged 92 on April 26th. 1810 and was buried at Spofforth Church. The tombstone in the north churchyard was erected by Lord Dundas - Jack had spent the last years of his life with his daughter at Spofforth. His wife died in 1772 and was buried at Stockport, where Jack Metcalf had many road making contracts.
His tomb at Spofforth is inscribed:"Here lies John Metcalf one whose fight, felt the dark pressure of an endless night. Yet such the fervour of his dauntless mind, his limbs full strong his spirit unconfined. That long ere yet lifes bolder years began, his sightless efforts marks the aspiring man. Nor marked in vain high deeds his manhood dared; commerce, travel both his ardour shared. Twas his a guides unerring aid to lend, oer trackless wastes to bid new roads extend."
Facing West Park Stray is the United Reform Church (Congregational Church) built in 1861/62, on the corner of Victoria Avenue opened two years before, to the designs of architects Lockwood and Mawson. The tower reaches a height of 130'. On the opposite corner of Victoria Avenue was the "Belvedere" built by Burley banker John Smith in 1861. It became the home of Lord Faber and was the College of Art from 1955: the house is now available as offices.
The separate villages of Low and High Harrogate were infilled by the Victoria Park Company who proposed their plans from 1860. Victoria Avenue was the main feature of the layout: George Dawson lived in the avenue until his death in 1889. George Dawson was the genius who gave Harrogate many of its most prominent stone buildings with his architect J. H. Hirst. In 1841 the Harrogate Improvement Commissioners started their work with the Royal Pump Room.
The house on the corner of Raglan Street and West Park was where Richard Oastler died on August 22nd. 1861. He was born in St. Peter's Square Leeds on December 20th. 1789 becoming a cloth dealer and when his father died in 1820 he managed an estate near Huddersfield. About ten years later Oastler started a campaign against children working in the mills. His main object was a ten hour day, which he achieved in 1847 before retiring from public life. There is a brass plate in the north entrance of Leeds Parish Church to Richard Oastler, which was placed by public subscription in 1925.
Princess Alix of Hesse, Czarina of Nicholas II stayed at Cathcart House when she came to Harrogate to take the waters. She was shot with the family in July 1918 at Ekaterinburg.

The hotel on the corner of Albert Street and Prospect Place was built in 1901: it is now known as Gladstones. The shelter on West Park Stray opposite the hotel was erected in 1895.
The 71 bedroom Hospitality Inn on Prospect Place was originally five Georgian style town houses built after 1820 and became the Grange Hotel by the turn of the century. The Mount Charlotte Hotel Group opened their first Hospitality Inn at Harrogate in 1980 and this now is one of 12 such hotels in the UK. Mount Charlotte Thistle Hotels operates over 100 hotels in the country with 24 in London.
In 1932 the group, now known as Mount Charlotte Investments PLC began trading as Lomah (Rhodesia) Gold Mines Ltd.; interests shifted from Africa to Australia and in 1936 it became Mount Charlotte (Kalgoorlie) Ltd. The Mount Charlotte mine in Kalgoorlie produced more than half the gold ever mined in Australia. By 1954 all the gold mine leases had been sold and the group was renamed in 1958. Between 1957 and 1960 the Mount Charlotte Investments acquired a group of London based restaurants and milk bars from Bettabuys, Walkers and the Black & White Group. In 1961 Nuthalls Ltd was purchased bringing into the group pubs and a cake company. This was also the start of the hotels involvement: the original hotels included locations at Bristol, Llangollen, Guernsey and Jersey. More hotels were acquired during the 1960's and 1970's but it was the acquisition of Gale Lister & Co Ltd a wine and spirit company based in Leeds that brought the Grange Hotel Harrogate into the Mount Charlotte Group. It was during the 1970's that the group sold off its interests in fast food outlets, inns and restaurants and concentrated on developing the hotel chain. In 1979 the Golden Lion and Wellesley hotels in Leeds were bought and in 1980 the conversion of The Grange Hotel was completed by a building company later incorporated into the group as Mount Charlotte Building Services. In 1987 the Leeds Merrion Hotel was included in the takeover of Kingsmead Hotels Ltd. In 1989 32 Thistle hotels from the Scottish & Newcastle Breweries PLC were acquired
The Prospect Hotel started as Prospect House built in 1814 by Nicholas Carter Snr being the first house to be built on Prospect Hill. The house was rebuilt in 1859 by Leeds architects Perkin & Son and enlarged in 1870. The Carter family built the 82' tower with an observatory and remained at the hotel until 1936. The hotel was sold to a Scarborough hotelier and in 1936/37 part of the hotel was demolished to allow for the widening of James Street. The hotel became the 85 bedroom Imperial Hotel, one of the Principal Hotels Group in 1987: the company had been founded in 1985 having originally the St. Nicholas Hotel Scarborough. The Group now own 15 hotels in England including The Metropole in Leeds and the Royal York Hotel.
The 75' high white obelisk marks the centre of Low Harrogate and is a memorial to those who gave their lives in the First World War. The foundation stone was laid by the Hon. Edward Wood later to be Lord Halifax on June 2nd.1922. The unveiling

took place on September lst. 1923 in front of Princess Mary and Viscount Lascelles. The architects were Prestwich & Sons with panels by Gilbert Ledward. The site of Prospect Square was the gardens of the Prospect Hotel until 1920 when it was bought by the Corporation.
St. Peter's Church was consecrated in 1876 to designs by J. H. Hirst and contains a well known organ made by Heinrich Schulze: St. Bartholmew's Church at Armley has another Schulze organ. The tower of St. Peter's Church was added in 1926 to designs by A. Gibson. The Regal Cinema was opened on September 18th. 1937 on the site of the old St. Peter's Church schoolrooms. The crescent building east of Prospect Place was designed by J. H. Hirst and built by George Dawson in 1873/80

The origin of the name Harrogate is probably derived from Herehlawgatte meaning Soldier's Hill Way: Harlow means a grey hill. A community has existed at Harrogate from about 1332 but expansion only came with the discovery of the medicinal springs. The Sulphur springs in Low Harrogate became popular with their cures for rheumatism, gout and skin diseases. Increased numbers of visitors saw the erection of four well heads on the Pump Room site. In 1804 the area was drained, paved, three well heads were removed and the present one left in place being covered with a canopy - now covering the Tewit well. The sulphur water at the Royal Pump Room is the only spring available to the public - the well is in the basement. It was Dr. Edmund Deane who first drew the attention to the strongest Sulphur spring in Great Britain in 1626. The Pump Room was built in 1841/42 to a design by Isaac Thomas Shutt of the Swan Hotel costing £2249.0s.7d. Betty Lupton, the Queen of the Wells, dispensed waters for decades until her death in 1843 at 83 years old: she is buried at Pannal Church.

Pump Room, Harrogate

The public right of access to the springs was recognized by the Stray Award of 1778 and the Harrogate Act of 1841. In 1884 Harrogate was incorporated as a borough by Queen Victoria. The annexe to the Pump Room was designed by Leonard Clarke and opened on June 7th. 1913 by the Lord Mayor of London. The Harrogate Pump Room Museum was established in 1953 and won a design award in 1988.
Valley Gardens were opened in 1887 as public pleasure grounds: they were laid out between the old sulphur wells and the Bogs Fields. There are 36 sulphur and iron springs arising within an acre: the waters were pumped to the Royal Baths and Royal Baths Hospital opened in 1889 by the Duke of Clarence. The Sun Colonnade was opened in 1935 by Lord Horder and the Magnesia Pump Room was originally opened in 1895.
In later years specialised baths and pump rooms were built in Harrogate providing recreational facilities. The Montpellier Baths were built in 1834/35 for Joseph Thackwray of the Crown Hotel. The baths were demolished in the 1890's providing the site for the Royal Baths. In Crown Place once stood a small shop where Joseph Thackwray attempted to divert the waters of the public Sulphur spring into private control by excavating a new well. Jonathan Shutt of the Swan Hotel discovered this on December 1st. 1835 which led to a public outcry and the need to protect the mineral Springs.
Montpellier Gardens were laid out by Joseph Thackwray in 1835 prior to the building of the Spa. The Royal Baths used some of the gardens whose entry was guarded by the small octagonal building still standing. The small pump room by the gatehouse was demolished in 1954 to make a car park, although the gardens were destroyed by the extension of the Royal Baths started in 1936 and opening in July 1939 by Sir Frank Bowater Lord Mayor of London. The wing was designed by Leonard H. Clarke.
The foundation stone for the Royal Baths and Winter Garden was laid on July 10th. 1894 and the building was opened on June 23rd. 1897 by the Duke of Cambridge, having been designed by London architects F. T. Baggalay and F. Bristowe. No more patients were admitted from 1968 and the baths closed in March 1969. Only the Turkish Baths remain in use today and the Harrogate Tourist and Information Office is located in this building. The Kissengen well is sited under the main entrance to the Royal Baths: a strong saline iron concentrated solution.
The Old Town Hall in Swan Road was built in 1805 for the increased number of visitors to the spa waters. The building was remodelled by Arthur Hiscoe in 1875: it has been the Promenade Room, Victoria Room and the Town Hall Theatre, where both Oscar Wilde and Lily Langtry appeared. The building is now the Mercer Art Gallery.
The Royal Spa Concert Rooms and Gardens were built in 1835 as the Royal Promenade and Cheltenham Pump Room for John Williams who owned the

Cheltenham estate: they were built in the classical style by John Clarke of Leeds. The Cheltenham Spring had been discovered in 1818 with a new Pump Room opening in 1970/71 designed by H. E. Bown which became the site of the Kursaal. The six acres of the grounds had a skating rink and lake: they were acquired in 1896 by the Corporation and the Cheltenham Spa Rooms were demolished in 1939 and the site is now used for exhibitions.

Crescent Gardens were laid out after 1890 on the site of the demolished "Crescent"inn, once called The Globe and then The Half Moon. The Festival Pavilion was made in 1990 for the award winning Harrogate garden at the Gateshead Garden Festival and was re-erected at Crescent Gardens in 1992. The statue displayed is that of Cupid and Psyche by Giovanni Bonzoni and first bought by a syndicate of Harrogate businessmen in 1862.

The Victoria Baths were opened in 1832 on Crescent Gardens by John Williams and were replaced by the New Victoria Baths built for the Harrogate Improvement Commissioners in 1871 and designed by James Richardson costing about £35,000. The baths faced Crescent Gardens and rooms were used by the Commissioners during their work. The present council offices were designed by architect Leonard Clarke in 1931 from the baths buildings. It had been originally proposed that a new Municipal Palace be built on Victoria Avenue and the site was prepared. The Carnegie Trust funded the first section and the library opened on January 24th. 1906: the remaining part of the site became public gardens in the 1920's.

The foundation stone for the Kursaal, renamed the Royal Hall during the First World War was laid on January lst. 1902 by the Mayor Ald. David Simpson and the opening was performed by Sir Hubert Parry on May 27th. 1903. The architects were R. J. Beale and F. Matcham. The site of the adjacent Exhibition Halls was the Royal Chalybeate Spa Concert Rooms and Pleasure Gardens opened by John Williams in 1835 - they were demolished in 1939.

The £34 million Harrogate Conference Centre opened in 1982 and £8 million Harrogate International Hotel opened in 1985.

The Harrogate Hotels included "The White Hart" in Low Harrogate dating from 1846 and now an NHS Training Centre. The "Old Swan" was established about 1700 becoming the Harrogate Hydropathic in 1878. The "Crown" Hotel was established by Joseph Thackwray in 1740 and rebuilt in 1847.The hotel was extended by George Dawson in 1870. The "Majestic" Hotel opened in 1900 although suffering fire damage on June 20th. 1924. The "Cairn Hydro" opened in 1890. The "Grand"Hotel opened in 1903 and the "George Hotel" opposite the Royal Hall opened in 1850 following the rebuilding of the original inn.

The Victoria Gardens is the most recent addition to the Harrogate scene which incorporates the Harrogate indoor market. The first stage was opened in October 1992 and the final phase was opened by the Mayor of Harrogate on November

2nd.1992. The neo-Classical complex, owned by the National Provident Institution, was designed by architects Cullearn and Phillips based on Andrea Palladio's Basilica in Vicenza. About 100,000 a week pass through the complex which cost £50 million.

Harrogate Conference Centre

THE ROAD FROM LEEDS, TO SELBY

PART 1 HALTON DIAL TO WHITKIRK

The Leeds - Selby Turnpike Trust was formed in 1740/41, in the hope of increased business between the two towns and thence by boat to Hull and the continent. It was recorded in October 1750 that at a meeting of merchants of Leeds it was resolved to repair the road from Leeds to Selby. The tolls were collected at a small cottage, which operated a weigh house for both wool and coal. This cottage was converted into a shop when the tolls were lifted in 1874 and demolished in 1929. In July 1929 there was a report that the "little squat stone weigh house will soon be seen no more... road improvements demand its demolition and its passing closes a chapter of the turnpike roads." John Barber ran the toll bar in 1849, James Adams in 1853 and Emma Waite ran the shop in 1903 and her son John Edwin Waite was the last shop keeper and he started his Weigh House garage on York Road in 1929.
Killingbeck pond was filled in about 1919 and converted into allotments. After a long period being allowed for the land to settle, the new by-pass road was opened to eliminate the bends in September 1931.On September 25th. a car accidentally used the old route and caused an accident. The line of the old York Road is by the side of the City Lights inn and is now a cul-de-sac. The old road was used by the trams until May 8th. 1933 when the track across the old pond was opened. The new road also necessitated the removal of the premises of the Killingbeck Motor Co.,which in 1924 was selling petrol at 1/4d. a gallon. Killingbeck Bridge over Wyke Beck is also seen on the old road, having now lost some of the coping stones.
The Leeds-Selby Turnpike road started by the old Woodpecker at Quarry Hill: the 1750/51 turnpike to Tadcaster starting at Halton Dial, with the toll bar by Wyke Beck. From earliest days the road from Leeds to Halton Dial has been the "road to York" and thus tolls paid at the Dial were the second from Leeds.
A Dial means a new turnpike, which ascended Halton Hill on an unmade road which was made worse by the heavy cart loads and their narrow wheels: the tolls were increased for these vehicles. Tolls were not paid by folk attending Sunday church services or even for cattle being herded onto a pasture. There was always trouble with the coal transport: Garside's Killingbeck Colliery in Halton Deans paid an annual fee in lieu of more frequent payments; whereas Gascoigne's coal had free passage from Garforth - Sir Edward Gascoigne was a trustee of the turnpike. The act was amended in 1750 to impose tolls on all the traffic due to the increased wear on the road surface. There was trouble at Halton Dial tollbar when a group of men attacked the barhouse objecting to the high scale of charges. This action had been sparked off by the attack on the Harewood Bridge tollbar, defended by Edwin Lascelles and his stalwarts in 1753.

The traffic lights and one way system under the railway bridge date from 1991/92: the bridge was built about 1833.Work on the Leeds - Selby railway started in 1832 and the contractors for the Osmondthorpe/Selby section were Hamer and Pratt of Goole. Despite holdups with both Richmond Hill tunnel and the Halton embankment, the first train left Marsh Lane for Selby on September 22nd. 1834. There were short lived stations at Halton Dial on Saturdays, closed in 1864 and Osmondthorpe Halt, which opened in October 1930 and closed in March 1960.A petition was raised in an attempt to re-open Osmondthorpe Halt in May 1978.Initially trains into Leeds terminated at Marsh Lane, until Leeds New Station was opened in 1869.Marsh Lane was resited in that year and closed in 1958.

The City Lights Inn opened in 1987, when the property was bought from Leeds Corporation by the Loveday family. In 1991 the Weigh House restaurant was built in sympathy with the older building. The inn contains many old photographs of the area including one of the demolished "Greyhound" inn on York Road. The building was first opened on March 31 1932, construction being started in December 1931, to the east of the old weigh house cottage. It was built to house the tramway booster generator station and was one of three: the others were at Chapel Allerton and at Headingley. This was necessary as the Crown Point Road Power Station closed in March 1932 and power was obtained from the Corporation Electricity Department and after 1948 from the YEB. Crown Point station was demolished during the 1950's. A tramway inspection cover was discovered by workmen at Halton Dial in June 1992, in marking out for BT cable lines. The heavy steel cover was offered to the Crich Tramway Museum in Derbyshire.

When the tramway system closed in 1959 the building became the storage depot for the Highways Lighting department The original tram routes were No.23 to Halton, No.24 Temple Newsam; these were changed in 1929 to No.17 Halton and No.22 Temple Newsam; in 1936 Halton became No.20 - these numbers remaining until closure in November 1959.

The tram route to Halton up Halton Hill was single track at first, with the branch to Halton dividing opposite Willow Well Farm. The route terminated at the High Street/Chapel Street junction, until November 8th.1936 when the terminus was changed to the Irwin Arms Inn. This was to coincide with the completion of the Selby Road dual carriageway and tram reserved double track set apart from the two lanes of traffic.

Killingbeck Pond supplied water via a goit to turn the wheel at White Bridge Mill, while in the area north of Selby Road east of the bridge was once a large reservoir, storing water brought by a sluice from Wyke Beck - originally used to power the mill. The water was pumped up Halton Hill by a water wheel from the early 1860's to a circular reservoir on Selby Road at The Crescent. The Whitkirk water tower then continued the water to the Temple Newsam estate and later to parts of Halton

and Whitkirk. Due to the variable quality of the water for drinking purposes, water was later to come from Leeds and the Wyke Beck supply used for non-drinking purposes.
White Bridge Mill was run by James Berkenhout - a descendent of a Dutch Leeds merchant - and Thomas Clark in 1779, who had perfected a way of dyeing linen and cotton cloth in different colours. Parliament had granted them £5000 on condition that they divulged their secret to the public. The concern, using the first power loom in England, made bunting for ship's colours. It is said that when Queen Victoria was inspecting her fleet, she saw a flag made by the Halton firm and asked that they make some more. The firm could not recreate the exact colours demanded and they lost the contract. In 1838 the concern was run by Peter and Thomas Clark, who were both "Ship's Bunting Makers and Corn Millers." Peter and Thomas were the sons of Peter Clark Snr, who died aged 76 in 1831 - son Thomas died aged 45 in 1845 and Peter died in 1865 aged 67. By 1866 the mill house had been converted into two dwellings and was eventually demolished.
The area is occupied by houses and the Wykebeck Hotel: plans were approved in May 1938 for the building of this public house by the Kirkstall Brewery. The licence was transferred to The Wykebeck Hotel from The Greyhound Inn on York Road on April 21st. 1939.

Wykebeck Arms

In 1933 Dunhill Brothers bought 16 acres of land for £1500 on which to build the estate, which carries their name. The Dunhills were completed about 1935.Application was approved in 1937 for an assembly hall - now Crossways Hall. The Dunhill family grave is at Whitkirk and includes Jean 7½ year old daughter of William and Emma - she died in 1967. Joseph Dunhill, builder of houses in Whitkirk and Halton, died in January 1960. In later years he lived at East Keswick, where he ran a grocery shop.
Land for the building of a branch of the Leeds Industrial Cooperative Society was conveyed in August 1931 and was opened at a later date: this store has now been rebuilt.
Whitebeck (sometimes known as Whitebridge) Farm was built in the 1820's near Whitebridge Mill. One of the first tenants was William Scott who died aged 44 on November 24th. 1874 and was one of the first burials in the new cemetery at Whitkirk. His wife Hannah died on March 13th.1919 aged 86 at Park Road Farm Colton - their son John Scott died at the Colton farm in the same year as his mother. For many years there was a "Kit Scott's Field" at Colton. When William Scott died the next tenant at Whitebeck Farm was Joshua Kershaw - he died on March 18th. 1883 and was buried at Whitkirk Church. George Taylor was the Whitebeck Farm tenant - he died aged 73 in April 1914.
William Verity Snr.(died 1893 aged 69) ran the concern - near the site of a garage today - and his son William Jnr. ran the farm. Some members of Verity family came to the area from Upper Nidderdale at the start of this century. Their farms were at Middlesmoor, Summerbridge and Birstwith: in later years Miles Verity took Gilsyke Farm on Selby Road and William Verity Jnr. had a smallholding adjacent to the Halton Congregational Chapel. One of the mistals with a large Templar cross on the exterior, is still used by the scouts, having been offered by Lord Irwin for £100.
The Verity family owned much land on Halton Hill with "William Rise" and "Verity Spur" remembering this farming family. William Verity Snr's sons were unmarried Miles (died 1956),William who died June 8th.1960 aged 64 at Hollinthorpe Farm Swillington: a service was held at Halton Methodist Church on Saturday June 13th.;Richard became a newsagent in Dewsbury. William Jnr. married Mary Whitfield of Colton, who died aged 35 in 1933 - the Whitfield family have run Grange Farm Colton since the 1890's - and their son Edward and his wife lived at Hollinthorpe Farm, which was in the Verity family from 1939.
The Stubbs family lived in Whitebridge Cottages near the farm and many folk remember them as living in "Stubbs Farm".The cottages were near the site of the Wykebeck Hotel.
Spoilheaps from Garside's Killingbeck Colliery have now been removed and the area landscaped as Halton Deans park. The colliery, which had closed by 1887, had access from the main York Road by a railway bridge and there was a ale house in

Primrose Valley run by Thomas Shaw in 1838 to supply the needs of the miners. In 1834 the ale house was also a shoemakers run by John Rollison. Ralph Thoresby writing in the early 18th. century said that "there is a deep valley, a woody tract remembered by old folk ... slag of iron works I saw when I traversed the ground." Osmondthorpe Lodge was south of the Halton Dial railway but was demolished to make room for estate development. Occupiers of the Lodge this century included Abraham Pratt contractor, John Laine and William Hall. The Hall family moved to Halton Moor Avenue from the Lodge and now live in North Leeds.

During the late 1920's and 1930's the Halton Moor estate was developing and in June 1939 the 20,000th. municipal dwelling was opened on Coronation Parade. Catholic families were moving away from St. Patrick's and St. Mary's Churches and the St. Mary's priests looked after the growing Halton estate. Father O'Ryan wrote to Leeds City Council in September 1932 asking for permission to build a new school and church. The council agreed to sell four acres of land by Wyke Beck, the church of Corpus Christi was built and first Mass was said on Christmas Eve 1932.The church presbytery was opened in 1934 and the foundation for a new school was laid in May 1934.The primary school opened in September but on 28th. September 1950 the church caught fire. Mass was said for a time in the Halton Parochial Hall and the church was restored to open on December 17th. 1950. Construction started on a completely new church in January 1960 on the old bowling green. The church was opened on July 8th.1962 by Bishop Dwyer. A new senior school was opened in September 1968 by Denis Healey MP.

Wyke Beck takes its origin as Great Heads Beck and flows through Roundhay Park. The beck forms the early 19th. century Waterloo Lake, flows under Easterly Road and Foundry Lane to Killingbeck Bridge. It flows under the railway and Selby Road on its way to join the River Aire near Skelton and the site of old Thorp Stapleton Hall.

The other White Beck (Wykebeck Farm) Farm was south-east of the beck alongside Halton Hill. In the mid-19th. century prior to Whitebeck Farm was the firm of Joseph Atkinson & Co. manufacturing Oil of Vitriol, Aqua Fortis and Epsom Salts. The farm was known as Elam's farm from 1919, when the family moved from Broomhill Farm near the site of the Shaftesbury Cinema. They moved to Broomhill in 1907 from Rowley Grange Farm at Scarcroft and before this farmed from Osmondthorpe Farm. This farm occupied the site of the Co-op on Osmondthorpe Lane/York Road before demolition to build the estate in the 1920's. Alfred Herbert Elam had three sons and one daughter who now lives near Selby. For one week from March 30th. 1936 Elam's Farm became the stabling facility for four elephants appearing at the Shaftesbury Cinema. The elephants were presented by the Power Brothers and gave a nightly ½ hour show on a specially strengthened stage. On the way to Elam's farm in the dark after the shows, the elephants were provided with lights on their trunks and tails at each end of the line. The elephant shows played to packed houses and were known as Lena, Julia, Roxie and Jennie the dancing elephant - they played cricket, baseball and fencing on stage! After many British performances their last show was in Southampton prior to departure for America before the outbreak of war.

Alfred Elam, who got his first car in 1932 - Ford UB 6512 - died in 1946, following the forced disposal of his Whitebeck Farm to the Council for redevelopment at the start of the War. He moved to Well Green Farm at Garforth Bridge - now the Hilton Hotel and sold the business in March 1941 to the local Bowes family of Swillington. The sale by Thomlinsons included all the farm stock; the Elam family had held sales at Whitebeck Farm in November 1934 and December 1935; the latter included the sale of 30 pigs and 17 horses which were held on a farm possessing their own blacksmith and wheelwright. At one period the farm, with extensive stables, had 40 horses and delivered milk on their horse drawn float. The farm often advertised their dairy products on the screen at the Shaftesbury Cinema.

The Elam family, as tenants of the Temple Newsam estate received invitations to a lunch at the house in June 1906, the 21st. birthday of Hon. Charles Wood in October 1933 and the marriage of the Hon. Charles Wood and that of the Earl and Countess of Feversham at Hickleton Hall in September 1936. They also received Christmas cards, including one in 1930 from Lord and Lady Irwin at the "Viceroy's Camp, India".

On leaving Well Green Farm, the Elam family moved to a smallholding at Birkin, where Alfred died.

The Sutton estate on Halton Hill was started in 1932/33 by the Sutton Housing Trust - formerly known as the Sutton Dwellings Trust. The Trust was founded under the will of William Richard Sutton, the founder of Sutton & Co. Ltd. Carriers of Fountain Inn, Wood Street, Aldersgate Street and later Golden Lane London. By his will dated August 1894 he left the bulk of his fortune for the foundation of a charitable trust providing low rent dwellings for the "poor" in London and other centres of population in England. William Sutton founded his business before 1860 when the railways carried most of the parcels. Sutton's idea was to persuade traders in cities such as Leeds, Manchester and Bristol to order traffic in bulk by his company and then to "bulk" all parcels by rail to their destinations, where agents collected, sorted and delivered. The railway companies took him to court but eventually lost their case. Sutton's main transport developed by road and the business was eventually absorbed as part of BRS Parcels.

The Trust came into being on his death on May 20th 1900 with assets of £1½ million. The first Sutton flats were built at Bethnal Green in 1909. In 1992 the Trust owned 14,388 houses, flats and bungalows in 33 English towns. There are 366 properties at Halton and 246 at Killingbeck, which was completed in 1929.

Negotiations were progressing in 1922 to acquire 20 acres of land that was part of the Temple Newsam estate. There was a delay and the site was bought in 1931: in 1932 plans were prepared for the building of 270 cottages and flats. In December 1932 the contract was given by the Sutton Trust to builders William Thompson of Sheepscar Street North for 265 dwellings on Selby Road. The builders stated that there was enough work for 300 men for a year. The architects for the new estate were Chorley, Gribbon and Foggett of Leeds. In 1934 the estate was formally handed over to the Trust: there is a stone plaque above the estate office door on Carden Avenue - "THE SUTTON ESTATE SELBY ROAD LEEDS These dwellings were erected under the charitable trusts of the will of William Richard Sutton of Golden Lane London EC Carrier who died on May 20th 1900". At the bottom of this inscription is the date 1934.

Four years after the tram service ended to Halton in 1959, the central reservation was grassed over, leaving the lines intact. Willow Well Farm is a tall white building north of Halton Hill, dating from the mid-19th. century. The farm was once run by the Paxtons and then by Frederick Jowitt and his wife: they moved in to Willow Well Farm on January 16th. 1916. They had cows, horses and hens as part of their holding. The farm was sold at auction in 1937 for £1100 and was bought by Gertrude Bray as a 4 bedroom detached house and the outbuildings. The farmhouse was converted into two dwellings by Gertrude Bray in 1938 - planning was approved in December 1937: the housing around the farm was built by Bray (Builders).Gertrude Bray was a co-director of G. Bray Ltd. and joined the Leeds City Council in 1945, being Deputy Lord Mayor in 1964-65. She retired in 1968 and became an Honorary Alderman. Gertrude Bray died aged 85 in January 1992, having retired from the firm in 1976.Gertrude Bray, who lived at the Manor House Whitkirk and later at West Burton, played an important part in the development of East Leeds including Cross Gates and the Penda's Way estate together with its own railway station.

St. Wilfrid's Church was consecrated on 13th. May 1939 on land given by Lord Halifax. In 1853 Sunday evening services were held at Halton School and the brick built mission room on Chapel Street opened on 30th. August 1888, provided through the generosity of Mrs. Meynell Ingram: since recent conversion the chapel has been faced obscuring the foundation stone. In 1892 there were regular Sunday evening services and in 1896 an altar was provided with the start of Holy Communion services.

In February 1917 the Mission Room was dedicated as the temporary church of St. Wilfrid and Hawthorn House - the home of the Graveley family of builders - was used as Church House. It was the home for the priest and used for scouts and a boy's

St. Wilfrid's Church

club. The St. Wilfrid's wooden church hall was dedicated in February 1938.
In July 1936 Halton was carved out of Whitkirk as a Conventional District and in 1937 it was announced that Sir John Priestman, the Sunderland shipbuilder, had offered £10,000 to build a new Halton church. Sir John Priestman donated £20,000 to the Centenary Forward Movement, which divided the amount to build three churches. The architect of St. Wilfrid's Church was A. Randall Wells FRIBA, a clerk of works at Brockhampton, with a London office. He had already built St. Andrew's Church at Roker in 1907.
The ceremony of Breaking the Ground took place on July 5th. 1937 with a procession from the church in Chapel Street to the new site.
The foundation stone was laid on November 6th. 1937 on a rainy day and the new St. Wilfrid's Church was consecrated in the presence of the Bishops of Ripon and Knaresborough with the Dean of Westminster. The font, from Barton Church Doncaster which had two fonts, has a silver gilt bowl - this was an 18th. century punch bowl and was donated to the church by the architect Randall Wells. The statue of St.Wilfrid is by Eric Gill, who also designed the Leeds University War memorial frieze - Eric Gill died in 1939. The chancel curtain is by Evelyn Ross and there was a complete re-ordering of the east end in the 1980's. The church bell was

presented by St. Wilfrid's Church in Harrogate. Between 1944 and 1961 Canon Ernest Southcott was the Vicar of Halton, who made the church a prime mover in the "Parish and People" project. There were many concepts of modern church life pioneered at St. Wilfrid's Church, whose wooden spire is illuminated nightly. The new parish of St. Wilfrid's Halton was formed in July 1939 and extended to Halton Moor Road.
St. Wilfrid was born in 634AD and became a devout and scholarly monk studying the Roman church rites on a pilgrimage to Rome. It was through his persuasions that the decision was made at the Synod of Whitby in 664AD to change over to Roman customs. In 678AD he spoke against a proposal to divide up the Northumbrian diocese and he again travelled to Rome to appeal to the Pope. Wilfrid was granted the Bishopric of Hexham and the monastery at Ripon. There are now about 50 churches dedicated to St. Wilfrid: he rebuilt the monastery at Ripon and the present crypt at Ripon is Wilfrid's building and is one of the earliest Christian survivals in Britain dating from about 670AD.

Many of the houses north on Halton Hill beyond the church were completed by the early years of this century. The sandstone quarry and Copperas works in this area were active in the mid 19th. century. The Copperas works - sulphates of Copper and Iron - were run by Joshua Bernard in the 1830's.
The corner shop of Primrose Lane/Selby Road was run by Albert Scarfe as the Primrose Cash Store in the first years of this century. It was later run by Alice Maria Bonsall - the corner was often known as Bonsall's Corner. This corner and the row of houses by Rock Terrace were demolished for the opening of the Halton Clinic in May 1984.The partly unmade Primrose Lane was known as Back Lane and connected Halton Hill with Cross Gates. In the 1930's and 1940's there was a small factory run by The Acme Jam Co. The firm always accepted empty washed jam jars for Id. from the public.
Temple Newsam Road was once known as Engine Lane leading to the Halton Brick Works, on an area now a landscaped field and play area. A map of 1771 shows a pumping engine on this area and the site of Halton Colliery. In January 1749 there was mention in the Leeds Mercury of "..the coalmine at Halton commonly called by the name of Hell Dyke, late in the possession of John Wilks is now open again and will supply the country with that beautiful bright coal ... John Webb Halton Colliery Steward." In this century Arnold Bedford ran Halton Colliery with three shafts and a drift until the war years. After nationalisation in 1948 the old pit area - between New Templegate and North Plantation Wood - was opencast by Lindsay Parkinson until 1952. The area was landscaped for housing development: Temple Avenue, Rise and Close.
Halton Feast was held in the early 1800's at the end of August and was both a

religious festival and a village fair, which could have had origins in early times. The Feast spread from Marsh Lane, along York Road which was lined with stalls. The Feast was a holiday for the tenants of the Manor of Whitkirk, who held many properties in East Leeds and in the town.

The Irwin Arms public house was known as the "Cock and Cushion" in 1838, when the licensee was William Pawson: it was also called The Irvine Arms. William Bardon followed as the innkeeper and he died in 1861 aged 61. George Fryer of the Irwin Arms died aged 58 in 1903. The nickname is still often used, being the arms of the Lords Irwin of Temple Newsam. In this period there were also the Travellers and the Woodman, shown on a 1765 map. The Irwin Arms was a low building on the site of the present adjacent row of shops and once had a bowling green. Planning approval for a new inn was granted to John Smiths Brewery in May 1936 and an amended plan for the basement in August. The building was completed a few months later and the inn is now one of the chain operated by the Mansfield Brewery. The Mansfield Brewery was founded in 1855 to brew beer for Nottinghamshire miners and they now have 450 public houses.

Halton Police Station opened west of the Irwin Arms in 1953 and was used as a section station until 1965, when it closed and later demolished. The site is now part of the inn car park. There had been a police house on Primrose Road near to Button's hairdressers: Sergeant Cannon in charge.

The land near to the Irwin Arms was the site of Thrift Stores. The store opened in July 1964 and became one of the 160 stores the company administered.Thrift Stores started from two family concerns: Ideal Stores in Wellington Road 1873 and Thrift Store Holbeck 1881. When the new Halton Thrift opened they offered a bucket free to all customers spending 15/- or more. The Thrift had their older branch on Cross Green Lane Halton near the Post Office,which had opened about 1900. The founder member of Thrift Stores was Wright Popplewell who lived in Halton: he died aged 78 in June 1933 having handed over the business to his son by 1914. The present Post Office dates from 1931 replacing a nearby earlier building.

One of the oldest businesses on Halton Parade is Ernest Rudge's bakery. He acquired the business in September 1944 from Minnie Cronk. The bakery is still in the Rudge family. Halton's only bank on the parade closed in 1983.

In this area was Halton mortuary, used mainly for mining accidents and in 1928 when a child Brian Taylor was killed by a collapsing boundary wall at Halton Primary School.

Henry and Ann Stevenson's Park View Farm - William Stevenson in 1912 - was demolished about 1950, stood on Irwin Approach. Nearby was Todd's Garage - Edwin (died in 1952) and son Dennis - and between them the surgery of Dr.William Harold Bean who died in 1976 (Drs. Bean, Shires and Moody) and had been a local GP for 35 years. In the 1930's one of Dr. Bean's partners was Dr. E. L. Brittain. The

surgery was demolished in 1991 and a new dental surgery opened by Peter Rider on December 14th. 1992, transferring from the Grade III listed Dial House on Chapel Street. The old surgery area was the coal depot for Arnold Bedford when he developed his coal merchant business: his office was on Chapel Street on the same row as Schofield's newsagents on the corner and he lived in Colton.
On the corner of Grove Road (Peggy Lane) was the village smithy cottage: the blacksmith was Samuel Joseph Townend.Amy Townend was a costumier who later moved up Selby Road to a bungalow near Wilfred Avenue.
There was a row of shops before the Traveller's Rest inn on the High Street and these included the Halton Co-op Butchers and Grocers and Killerby's Grocers. Richard Killerby had opened his Halton shop in 1877: he died in October 1931 and his son Alfred died in December of that same year.
The house and shop adjoining Killerby's store was the scene of a tragic accident. Joseph Connell and his wife ran a grocery and confectionery shop on the High Street and closed as usual at 9.30pm on Sunday April 24th. 1932. They put their three children to bed and left for a short visit to Barnsley but were delayed on their return. At 2.30am on Monday April 25th fire was spotted by Dr. & Mrs.J. A. Young of Gilsyke House and the doctor ran across the road to try and save the children. His efforts were in vain as Elizabeth Ellen aged 11 and Margaret Annie aged 8 died in the fire and Alfred aged 5 died the following day. Evidence was offered at the subsequent inquest by Dr.Young and Samuel J. Townend: the funeral was held at Harehills Cemetery conducted by the Vicar of St. Agnes Church and attended by a great number of mourners and spectators.
This area became the Halton District Shopping Centre in the late 1980's. The Leeds Co-op Super C store opened on October 27th. 1987.

The "Traveller's Rest" public house was probably built in the early 19th. century: Mary Hawkshaw was the licensee in the 1830's. Alfred Briggs was the innkeeper in the following years and he died in 1878 aged 39: his wife Caroline died in 1900 aged 61. The licensee in 1900 was James Teale. In November 1898 the property was sold by the Hon. Mrs.Meynell Ingram to Mary Jane Dawson and in December 1919 the property was held by Walter and Ernest Dawson. The inn together with the extensive bowling green - now the Halton Centre car park - was bought for £7250 by Joshua Tetley at auction on March 16th. 1925 from Harold Dawson. Plans were presented by Kitson, Parish & Ledgard in 1938, 1941 and 1950 to rebuild the Inn, which never matured although there has been a complete refurbishment and extension . It was in October 1822 that Armley maltster Joshua Tetley bought the business belonging to one of his customers William Sykes: the brewery on Hunslet Lane, which had been established in 1792. Joshua married Hannah Carbutt in 1784 at Sheffield Parish Church and their first home was in Albion Street Leeds. They had five girls and

when they moved to a new home in Park Square their only son Francis William was born. The main branch of the Tetley family lived at Armley Lodge until 1882 there is a memorial in St. Bartholomew's Church to William Tetley who died in 1834. In 1839 the firm of Joshua Tetley & Son was created with Francis. Francis married Isabella Ryder and they had 15 children. In 1862 he commissioned George Corson to build Fox Hill. Foxhill became the home of Moorlands School in 1967 when they moved from their premises on Otley Road. Joshua Tetley died aged 81 in 1859 at The Hollings Hampsthwaite, now a Dr.Barnados school.
Thomas John Barnardo was a Dublin born philanthropist born in July 1845. In 1867 he started homes for some of London's destitute children. They became known as Dr.Barnardo's Homes although he never qualified as a medical doctor.
Charles Ryder joined Francis as a partner, with his son Charles to enter the firm. Charles went to Leeds Grammar School, Harrow and Cambridge and joined the Leeds brewery in 1873 - he died at Gledhow Hill Leeds in 1902. His son Charles Foster Ryder became a partner and had two homes: at Thurlow Hall Suffolk, where he died and at Scarcroft Grange, Wetherby Road.
The first Tetley pub was the "Duke William", which forms a part of the present brewery: it closed in 1953. Melbourne Brewery was taken over in 1960 together with its 245 pubs and the company merged with Walker Cain to become Tetley Walker Ltd. In 1961 Tetley Walker merged with Ind Coope and Ansells and when Tetleys acquired J. Lyons in 1978 the firm became Allied Lyons PLC. In 1993 the company merged with Carlsberg and now the Tetley Pub Company, part of Allied-Lyons retailing is responsible for more than 1400 pubs throughout the North of England.Tetley's £6 million Brewery Wharfe opened in March 1994 within the 22 acre brewery site with the story of the English Pub from the 14th. century monastic brewhouse at Kirkstall Abbey to the Star and Crater pub from the year 2053.
On the south side of the High Street was Gilsyke House with extensive gardens and stables,later three garages. The driveway for Gilsyke House was almost opposite the present Halton Library: Charlie Frame's Butchers in earlier times.
A number of doctors have lived at Gilsyke House including Dr. Edward Windle Tinsdale who was probably the first doctor at Gilsyke when it was built about 1820. Dr. Samuel Joseph Noake in the 1870's and 1880's, Dr. Arthur T. Wills, Dr. Bertram George Mortimer Basket by the turn of the century and Dr. Patricius Wallace Ashmore during and after the Great War: his partner was Dr. Haygarth who lived in Cross Gates.
Gilsyke House became the home of Dr. John Alexander Young, a Canadian born GP who trained at St. Mary's Hospital London. Dr.Young came to Halton in 1923 and was joined by a partner: Dr. Herbert Arnott Eadie, who was killed while riding as a passenger on a 6 ton caterpillar tractor on Post Hill. The driver of the tractor was Arthur Waterman, president of the Leeds Motor Club of which Dr. Eadie was the

MO. In front of 3000 people the tractor nearly reached the top and hit a stone, which caused Dr. Eadie to be killed as it overturned. He was a native of Edinburgh, a Captain in the Royal Army Medical Corps and was a keen rider and golfer. In 1928 he married the lady golf professional at Temple Newsam: he was killed on Sunday September 27th. 1931 at the age of 30. Other partners included Dr. Trevor Owen, Dr. David A. Kidd (1955-1959) and Dr. Robert P. Mattock (1946-1971),who lived on Pinfold Lane. Dr. Kidd came to Halton from Tynwald Mount near the Moor Allerton Centre to live at the old blacksmith's house on the corner of Grove Road for a few years. Dr. Jack Young retired in March 1962 and was presented with a silver owl mustard pot by Major Brooksbank in June. Dr.and Mrs. Young lived in Filey and Rosedale Abbey, where their son John ran the Milburn Arms Hotel. Dr. Young died aged 85 on June 2nd. 1975 and was buried at Scarborough. A post-funeral reception was held at the now demolished Holbeck Hall Hotel.

Dr. J. L. Ramsey joined Dr. Young's practice in 1959 and he lived at Gilsyke House from 1962 until 1966: Gilsyke House was demolished for development in 1967. Dr.Ramsey retired as the senior partner in September 1993. Dr. R. Johnson joined the Halton practice in October 1967 and he retired in early November 1994. The present doctors are Dr. M. Addlestone who joined in 1973, Dr. S. J. Renwick came in 1992, Dr. A.C. Smith from 1993 and Dr. M. Ilyas who joined in November 1994.

Demolition of Gilsyke House was followed by the building of the parade of shops on Selby Road.These were opened in 1967 and include Bloom's Chemists transferring from Irwin Approach and the Leeds & Holbeck Building Society, whose branch was opened in 1976. Gilsyke House is still remembered in the name of the present doctor's surgery.

The name Gilsyke was one of the four ancient fields of Halton. Gill Syke Field covered the south of Selby Road; Cross Field was land north of Selby Road to Hollyshaw Lane; Garth End Field was north of Primrose Lane and New Field created in 1667 from a splitting of Gill Syke.

Netto opened the Halton store in 1990 - their first year of UK operation - following the closure of Grandways, and is a part of the family owned Danish Dansk Group of supermarkets. Netto have 400 stores in Denmark, Germany and Britain with over 60 stores in the North of England and Midlands and a new warehouse at South Elmsall.

East of Gilsyke House was Springfield Place,the site of Clara Rollinson's cafe and confectioners: teas could be taken on the tennis court adjacent to the shop. The shop became George Greenfield's shoe repairers in 1935 and when the house was pulled down, a deep brick lined well was discovered near the front door.

North of the High Street is part of the Halton Centre, with the library opened in August 1987, replacing the older Halton library opened on September 21st. 1960. The stone pillar outside the library was nearer the main road before the alterations

after Alderman Major Joseph Brooksbank, who lived in Grove Road.
Major Brooksbank was born in 1894 and from 1931 lived in Halton. The family had their roots in the Tadcaster area and settled in Leeds during the 19th. century. He enlisted in the Royal Marines and served his country for nearly 40 years. He saw First World War action at Jutland and the raids on Zeebrugge and Ostend and was wounded on six occasions. He was awarded the Belgian Croix de Guerre for gallantry. He served on HMS London and the Renown and between wars his duties took him on royal tours. He visited India and Japan with the Prince of Wales and went to Canada with Princess Elizabeth and Margaret. Major Brooksbank served his country during the Second World War in the Pacific, Australia, North Africa and in the Normandy landings.
In his retirement he became a Halton councillor and was a City Alderman. He was foremost in the development of St. Kevin's School but it was in 1934 that Major Brooksbank supported the Council in the purchase of Soldier's Field for a new school. He became a governor of Temple Moor School and in 1964 chaired the Area Board: Major Brooksbank died in October 1972.
On the corner of Chapel Street and Selby Road is Halton Institute - now Chapel Street Social Club - with the foundation stone laid by the Hon. Mrs.George Lane Fox and was the 18th. century milestone for the turnpike road: Milestone Yard took its name from this stone.
There was a row of shops including Harold Bower's Halton Fishery, Charles Henry Frame's butchers and Vamplew's cycles. The original row of four houses later included William Bedford's bakery and grocers F. W. White & Co.
The junction of the High Street Selby Road and Chapel Street Halton was the first terminus for the trams from Leeds. This was opened on April 30th. 1915 and a newspaper report on May 3rd. 1915 states that "the tram extension to Halton from the York Road terminus is now open with a regular 20 min service". This line from Halton Hill was abandoned in November 1936, with the introduction of a central reserved track up Halton Hill. The trams to Temple Newsam started on April 18th./21st. 1924 with the initial opening to Beech Walk. The tram service from Killingbeck to Cross Gates terminus also opened in that same year. The last trams from Temple Newsam, Halton and Cross Gates ran on November 7th. 1959 - the last tram in London had run on July 4th. 1952.
The row at the end of Chapel Street included James Schofield's newsagents, Alice Speight's drapery, Arnold Bedford's office and Helena Marsland's hairdressers. The row was demolished in May 1967 to make room for redevelopment - it is now a grassy patch. Graveley Square was once a complex of housing behind Dial House and was demolished: the £134,000 Brooksbank Home was opened on the site. The Home was started in March 1972 and officially opened in late June 1974 by Dr. Hugo Droller the Senior Geriatrician at St. James Hospital; the home was named

on January 21st. 1904. This lady had local connections as she was the Hon. Mary Agnes Emily Wood, daughter of Charles Wood 2nd. Viscount Halifax and Lady Agnes Elizabeth Courtnay - they married in 1869. The 2nd. Viscount Halifax was born on June 7th. 1839 and died at Hickleton Hall Doncaster on January 19th. 1934. Their daughter married George Lane-Fox of Bramham Park who inherited the property in 1906. Her husband was created Lord Bingley in 1933 for political services: he died on December llth. 1947. The brother of the Hon. Mrs.Lane-Fox was Edward Frederick LindleyWood who became the 3rd. Viscount Halifax and created Viscount Irwin in 1925 and in 1926 was Viceroy of India: he sold Temple Newsam in 1922 and died in 1959.
The architect for Halton Institute was Sydney Kitson and the cost of building was £1323 14s.9d. The accounts show that on January 26th. 1904 the architect charged £25 for the preliminary designs and £30.19s 6d for the commission on the accepted contract.
Halton Institute and the private car park occupy the site of the orchard that was once part of Dial House: there were a few apple trees remaining a few years ago between the Institute and Ernest Morris Chemist, now Chippy's DIY.
Dial House on Chapel Street was built in 1720 and altered in 1755. This house became a listed building in 1951 and still has the original timbers in the roof,which may have been from a sailing ship. In the 19th. century Dial House was home to the Graveley family of builders. The house was a dental surgery from the 1950's run by J. R. Stuart White, who came to Halton from Cross Gates about 1921 to live at Holme Lea, next to the chapel. His surgery was once next to Palmer's clothing shop, which was on the corner of Woodman Street. He lived in Thorner from 1961 and then moved to Barwick in Elmet.
There were large concrete blocks placed on Chapel Street outside Dial House at the beginning of the last War.
Holme Lea with an extensive paddock and- tennis court was once the home and surgery of Dr. Frederick William Pogson and could have been a farmhouse as it had a mistal and stables. They were converted to a garage and workshop and were to serve as the first headquarters for the 18th. N E Leeds Scouts founded by J. R. Stuart White in 1921. Dr.Pogson had a surgery at Rose Terrace on the High Street prior to moving to Holme Lea - the Pogsons were in Halton in the 1870's. Dr. Fred Pogson was the son of Dr. William Pogson of Seacroft Grange and he died on February 4th. 1913 aged 45, a year after his father. His widow continued to live at Holme Lea for a few years.

Chapel Street was named after the opening of Halton Methodist Chapel on September 25th.1840.The previous chapel was opened in October 1810 in two cottages on the same site.A new schoolroom opened in October 1877 and new porch was added in 1908.The whole complex of Christ Church Halton was demolished in 1991 and the new £600,000 Christ Church Halton opened on May 9th.1993.The Halton Congregational Chapel was opened on January 3rd.1931 having cost £5000.The United Reform Church was demolished in January 1992 and the land was sold for housing development.

Charles Carroll and son John of Holly House Farm at first continued the farm and milk business,with cows grazing on nearby rented land.In the late 1920's they changed to a haulage business and the property was demolished after the death of Walter Carroll in 1979.John's daughter Catherine married David Godson of Manston and have a large successful coaching business today.The site of the farm was opposite Woodman Street and was previously occupied by Nicholls and Pickersgill (Haulage) who had moved from a site behind Laurel Farm:this was home to the Daniels family.

Rose Cottage was once Dr.Pogson's surgery and then the home of funeral director Tom Shaw. Tom had his workshop - known as Banty Cock Hall - at one time behind the row of houses on the corner of Chapel Street and High Street in Graveley Square. Harry Cowell was a carpenter who once worked for Tommy Shaw and his elder brother Alec Cowell had a shop on the corner of Wilfred Avenue and Cross Green Lane.

East of Holly House was Miles Verity's Gilsyke Farm, demolished after Miles retired from farming due to ill health and now the site of a bungalow opposite the Woodman Inn.

The Woodman is probably the oldest public house in Halton being built for the turnpike and having top floor accomodation. It is often said that a ghost walks the top floor and the owner of the repair shop in the east of the building has also reported ghostly activity. The repair shop was once a sweet and cakes shop. The innkeeper of The Woodman in the mid-19th. century was William Smith who died on July 10th. 1869 aged only 29.

South of the main road is Field End Road with The Catholic Centre of St. John, administered as a chapel of ease by St. Theresa's Church Cross Gates. It was opened by the Bishop of Leeds on December 22nd. 1969 and stands near the site of some cottages and a piggery. The site was allocated to the RC church authority in 1967 through a compulsory purchase order. On the other corner of the road was a small shop run by Arthur Driver and the Hardwick family: now the garden of the first house on Field End Crescent.

North of Selby Road is the listed building of Temple Newsam-Halton Primary School, built with money raised by Rev. Arthur Martineau Vicar of Whitkirk. The building was opened on October 10th. 1842 and built of Colton sandstone, given by Lady William Gordon of Temple Newsam House. The school was first enlarged in 1851 and in 1862 Whitkirk Boy's School was dismantled to enlarge the churchyard and the materials were used to build an extension at Halton for 120 infants - opened on May 12th. 1863. The central schoolroom and two classrooms were destroyed by fire on January 13th. 1878 and children were taught from January 22nd. in the Methodist Church Sunday School. When the school was first built it was used on Sundays but in 1862 the Sunday School transferred to the tithe barn at Whitkirk, demolished in 1968 .In 1882 Sunday classes were held in the Halton Mission Room and were transferred to the Halton Parochial Hall when it opened on the site of the old pinfold in 1909. Extensions were carried out at the school from September 1893 until March 1894 while the school was in session. On July 30th. 1920 increasing numbers saw the use of an old army hut and in July 1926 the nearby field was bought as a playing area. In 1951 a new four classroom hut and a new infants department were in use. The huts were removed between March 14th. and March 18th. 1982, having been used for a few months in 1974/75 by Halton Middle School children waiting for their new school to be completed on Templegate Walk. In September 1967 the main hall and eight classrooms were built as a new block on Pinfold Lane and two classrooms near the old school. In the same year the four alms houses on School Lane were demolished.

In July 1992 Halton school celebrated their 150th. anniversary: the oldest attender at this event was the 89 year old daughter in law of the earlier headmaster Richard Thomas. The old school building was given a new roof in early 1994.

On April 1st. 1875 a ½ acre plot of land was bought for the headmaster's house and playground. The schoolhouse was once the home of Richard Thomas, who died aged 82 on April 26th. 1959: his wife Fanny had died in May 1938 aged 58. He was the headmaster of Halton Board School from 1917 until 1933 when he was appointed headmaster of Green Lane Council School: he retired from that post in 1937. Richard R. Thomas followed Joseph Owrid at Halton, who transferred from Colton School in 1883: Joseph Owrid resigned in 1916 and died in January 1922. In later years the occupant of the schoolhouse was deputy-headmaster Charles Dodgson until 1990/91: the property was sold in 1993 and is now renovated. Charles Dodgson retired from Halton School in

Temple Moor Coat of Arms

1980: for many years he was the Deputy to Eric Angood. Eric Angood was the Headmaster of Halton School from September 1956 until July 1978: he died in March 1992.

A report in 1938 stated that "Halton's new school is to be built on 16 acres - all allotment holders have received compulsory purchase orders". The holders, many of whom had left their plots, were dismayed when a delay in building was announced.

Temple Moor Grammar School opened on the site of old allotments - Soldier's Field - in September 1956 with the first headmaster David I. Breese. He was appointed from his previous post of Head of Science at Hatfield Technical College having a degree in Chemistry.

Building started on the 8 acre site in October 1954 and the architects were Yorke, Rosenberg and Mardall and the initial entry was 500 boys. It was a three form selective entry boys school and the £180,000 school was officially opened by Sir Edward Boyle Parliamentary Secretary to the Ministry of Education in May 1957. Lord Boyle revisited the school in May 1972 for the annual speech day.

Temple Moor was the first post War Grammar School to be built in Leeds and had additions of a swimming pool - opened in July 1966 - on the site of the old fives courts and new block on the northern playground opening in 1974. The school became a seven form entry comprehensive high school in 1972. David Breese retired in 1977, he died on October 4th 1994 and the second headmaster Roger Mainds was appointed from Foxwood School on September Ist.: he retired in December 1994. Temple Moor became coeducational and 11+ in September 1992. On October lst. 1993 the new west wing was officially opened by old boy and royal author Andrew Morton. The wing is used as a Sixth form centre and has rooms for art and music. The school has a swimming pool, new science and computer laboratories with a new library opened in September 1989 Temple Moor High School is a neighbourhood school for an eventual total of 1000 pupils.

To the south was built Halton Middle School opening in September 1974 for 9 to 13 year old children - the actual building was not occupied until early 1975. The first headmaster John Rex retired in April 1987 with Margaret Webb becoming the next head of Halton. Margaret Webb was appointed the first headteacher of Whitkirk Primary School when it opened in September 1992. Re-organisation of Leeds Schools meant the closure of Halton Middle School and the opening of Whitkirk Primary School in the same building.

On Wilfred Avenue was Barkston Ash Laundry, which was founded in 1910 and pulled down in the early 1980's. One of the managers was Ronald Wheater, who lived in the corner house on Selby Road - demolished in 1991 to make room for new housing. In the 1960's the laundry was run by the Initial Towel Co.

To the south was the Whitkirk Water Tower, demolished about 1921. This accepted water from The Crescent reservoir, which itself had received water from the bottom of Halton Hill. The house to the west of the site is called Tower Cottage but the tower stood on the site of the bungalow built about 1925 for the Townend family: Miss Florence Townend was a dressmaker. The retaining handmade brick wall of the tower precinct still has an archway to take the water pipes. There was a record that on September 21st. 1872 an unidentified man was drowned in the reservoir - now represented by the large grassy area of The Crescent.

The Halton Veteran's Shelter, once a feature of The Crescent field on Selby Road was demolished in 1972. In the later years the shelter had a temporary tenancy by the Halton Homing Association who could not maintain the damage caused by persistent vandalism.

In the 1920's Arthur Wilson was building houses in the area and the white limestone memorial cross was erected on land donated by Lord Halifax. This is a memorial to 73 local men who died in the First World War - the memorial to the dead in the Second World War is the church lychgate. This was restored and dedicated on Remembrance Sunday 1971. The iron gates of the Queensway memorial were presented by Nurse Elsie Dacre on her retirement as District Nurse. The plaque on the gatepost was unveiled in July 1959. Elsie and George Dacre lived for many years on Templegate before moving to the Field End estate.

Whitkirk cemetery was opened by the Bishop of Ripon on 17th. October 1874. There are two gates,west for the nonconformist burials and east for those who had been members of the Church of England - the two areas separated by six stones.

Whitkirk St. Mary's Cricket Club was formed in 1892, the year after the introduction of area competitive cricket and the Sagar - Musgrave Challenge Cup. The first ground was behind the timber framed Brown Cow public house on a field which became an auction market and then a supermarket.

In 1894 Whitkirk entered the newly formed Barkston Ash League and in 1899 the club's name was changed to Whitkirk Parish Church Cricket Club. In 1904 the club was ordered to leave the Brown Cow site for the building of the Bartle's Auction Market. A field was leased from the Hon. Edward Wood of Temple Newsam at 1/- a year: the ground and a new pavilion were opened on April 27th. 1907 and Lord Irwin was invited to be the first President. The league was suspended during the First World War and was reopened in May 1919: in 1922 the Hepworth Cup tie was played before 30,000 at the Selby Road ground in which Burmantofts defeated Allerton Bywater. The Whitkirk Club established tennis, bowling and a 9 hole golf course.

The ground was finally bought from the Temple Newsam estate in 1925 and became their outright property in 1959. In the same year the Earl of Halifax opened the changing room facilities. In May 1966 the sports sections agreed with a brewery to form a social club and a loan was obtained to build a clubhouse, completed a year later.

The large house on the corner of Knightsway and Selby Road was built in the 1920's and was the home of Herbert Morris in the 1930's. Herbert was a director of James Hare Ltd and his eldest daughter Jenny was married at Whitkirk Church in April 1933. Traquair was home to Ernest Armitage in the 1940's and from 1956 to 1970 was the home to Dr. & Mrs. Neville Shires and their sons Martin and Alan, following their removal from Main Street Scholes. For 31 years Dr. Shires was the Scholes and area GP and he retired in 1970 to live on the south coast. He died there in 1982 aged 76 and his widow Betty lives today near Southampton. Their Whitkirk home is known as "Traquair", after one of the oldest Scottish houses near Peebles.

In 1974 Traquair was sold to the Catholic Holy Family Convent, who now occupy the house. The Convent has seven nuns who have been teachers at Mount St. Mary's and St. Theresa's Schools or have been nurses.

Sunbeam Cottage was built in the mid-19th. century by Rev. Arthur Martineau (Vicar from 1838 to 1863) on Rawson's Close using stones from two old churchyard cottages. Arthur Martineau was financially concerned with the building of both Seacroft and Halton schools and with the refitting of the church in 1856. The area was Glebeland - as was the land of the "Brown Cow" inn. In 1855 Sunbeam Cottage was home to Robert Rollinson but between 1927 and 1931 the Vicar of Whitkirk lived at the house. During this short period the Rev. Walter Warburton (inducted September 1923) called Sunbeam Cottage "The Vicarage" and let the vicarage house as "The Old Hall". In the 1930's and 1940's the cottage was the home of traveller Harold Dawson. The cottage has been fully restored by the present owners.

The old air raid shelter east of Sunbeam Cottage is the meeting place of the Whitkirk Church Scouts,Cubs and Beavers. The Scout Group is the 5th. East Leeds (St.Mary's).

The 3rd.South East Leeds Scout Group was founded in 1958 and with two troops became the largest group in the area - members were boys of Temple Moor Grammar School. The school troop closed in 1969/70 and the equipment was redistributed to other troops in the area.

West of the church is Whitkirk Parish Hall which was opened on Saturday October 26th. 1968 by the Ven.Charles O.Ellison, Archdeacon of Leeds. The hall was designed by architect R. A. Wilde and built by Eric Bulmer. The £20,000 hall was officially opened on Sunday September 14th. 1969 by the Lady Mayoress Ald. Mrs. A. R. Bretherick, who unveiled a commemorative plaque. The cottage annexe to Ivy House, an unlisted Victorian addition and the 500 year old tithe barn were demolished by 1968 to make room for the new development. The tithe barn was behind the old vicarage and some of the stone was reused in the construction of the new parish hall. A Medieval stone fragment found when the tithe barn was demolished is set into the wall of the church hall on the east side of the main door: it depicts a cross with a two stepped base. There is another small piece of Medieval

stone built into the west wall of the church south porch. The new hall replaced the hall on Carter Terrace - the old Baptist Chapel - which became the hall of St. Theresa's Church, now to be sold.
The large old vicarage was to the south west of the church but replaced one that was on the north side. The old buildings were pulled down and the newer vicarage was completed in 1823 and was demolished in the early 1970's. The new vicarage for which approval was granted in 1971 was built to the south west of the new hall. The new vicarage gardens, used for the annual Summer Garden Party, were once partly designated as the cemetery: the present driveway once led to the old vicarage, now the site of houses on Pendil Close.
Ivy House was at one time a much larger dwelling, dating back to about 1730 retaining original wooden beams and stone flagging. It was the home of Robert Roadhouse in 1890 and later of the Piercy family.
Thomas Piercy was born on March 7th. 1851 and educated in York. He was articled to J. E. Jones Solicitors of York and then moved to their branch in Park Row Leeds: he was resident in Leeds from 1886. He became the President of the Incorporated Leeds Law Society in 1895 and was one of the oldest practising solicitors in Leeds. He was a supporter of St. Faith's Home in Leeds and was awarded the Freedom of York in 1872. He died on March 16th. 1939 and his wife Rose died aged 75 in 1934. The house became the home of the Martin family: daughter Carol married Dr. & Mrs. Shires' eldest son Martin. The church sold Ivy House in 1986 into private hands.
The "Brown Cow" public house was built on the glebe land and owned by the church. On Easter Monday 1810 the sum of 10/6 was paid by the church to the inn. In a terrier - a description of glebe land (terra = land) belonging to the church - in 1855 the inn had four rooms below and three on the top floor. There were stables to cater for up to 40 horses,a coach house and a brewhouse together with a mistal erected by Arthur Martineau (Vicar 1838-1863). In the mid-19th. century the licensee was John Darby, buried in the north section of Whitkirk Church graveyard and in the late 19th. century it was John Scatchard. During the Great War the manager of The Brown Cow was Frederick James Lole and the inn was a member of the Leeds Public House Trust Co. This public house was much smaller than the present building and by the roadside: it had additions built on the east side on the corner of Hollyshaw Lane. Mawson Movley was the licensee in more recent times: he died in 1958 aged 71. His son John Nelson was killed in Italy in February 1944 aged 24. Bertie Greaves followed as licensee and he died aged 72 in April 1961 having been at the inn for 11 years. The church sold the property in 1900. In earlier years the inn was the location for both Whitkirk and Temple Newsam Manor Courts. The Lordship of Temple Newsam had the two manors of Temple Newsam and Whitkirk. The former included Halton and Colton villages, while Whitkirk Manor

was spread westwards to the City. Lords of the Manor held their Courts by law, dealing with Manor misdemeanors and settling disputes of property. The houses of Whitkirk Manor tenants were distinguished by a Templar Cross placed on the outside of their dwellings. Tenants of Whitkirk Manor were exempt from the obligation of grinding their corn at the King's Soke Mill near Leeds Bridge. There were a few of these crosses in Leeds until recent years - "The Templar" inn on Vicar Lane remembers their properties in that area.
Whitkirk Manor Court or the Court of St. John was held every three years at the Manor House on Colton Road.Temple Newsam Court was held annually. In the latter part of the 19th. century the courts met at the "Brown Cow " inn. The Court Leet dealt with petty offences, while the Court Baron dealt with enforcing the Manor customs. It was involved with land administration, tenancies, uses of the commons and the rights of the Lord and his tenants. In 1733 the Manor of Temple Newsam held Court in October: Henry Milner was sworn as the Pinder in charge of the Pinfold of Halton and Thomas Morkill was fined 1/- for not rebuilding his fence on Colton Pit Field.
Planning application by Joshua Tetley Brewery to rebuild the Brown Cow Inn was approved on February 21st. 1939 and it opened on October 10th. 1941, designed by Sydney Kitson Architects, with the old inn being used for civil defence purposes before being pulled down in 1946. The new building was constructed on the site of the outbuildings of the old public house.
The traffic light system at the Selby Road/Hollyshaw Lane junction was opened in January 1983.
Selby Road at Whitkirk was the site of a Gothic style archway, with an 18' wide central section specially built for the visit of HRH The Prince of Wales, who became King Edward VII. The Prince arrived at Woodlesford Railway Station on May 18th. 1868 and stayed at Temple Newsam House. The next day he opened the National Art Exhibition in Leeds: there was also an archway at Halton and the Whitkirk School children were given a week holiday as the school was used as a temporary police station. There is a bust of the Prince of Wales in Leeds Town Hall foyer, presented in 1872 by James Kitson of Elmete Hall: there is also a bust of the Princess of Wales - he married Princess Alexandra of Denmark in 1863.
Hollyshaw Lane once included the length of road from Whitkirk to Seacroft: Station Road and Cross Gates Lane. Hollyshaw refers to a copse of Elder trees and has been known as Allerhagsik and Allershaw over the centuries. In 1639 it was recorded that "the King's highway between Whitkirk and Seacroft in a lane called Allershaw Lane is in great decay for lack of repair and the inhabitants of Whitkirk Parish ought to repair or else there is a penalty of £20." A mid 19th. century survey indicates the ownership of land on the east of Hollyshaw Lane was with William Heworth in the township of Austhorpe.

Land at Whitkirk was purchased by the Leeds Industrial Cooperative Society in October 1937: the foundation stone of the Whitkirk Co-operative store was laid on May 21st. 1938 by R. Marshall a director of the company. Although the store closed in 1964 the building is still owned by the LICS. There was a planning application in 1970 to open a hotel on the site and a year later another application for an 18 bedroom hotel was approved but did not mature.
Whitkirk Auction Market was opened in 1909 by John Clapham Bartle of Brookfield Garforth Bridge, having bought the land from the Temple Newsam estate. This land had been used as a cricket ground and was complete with seating, fences, water supply, wooden pavilion and practice facilities: Whitkirk Cricket Club used the site as their first ground. They were asked to leave in preparation for the building of the cattle market. The auctioneers opened an office at the Whitkirk premises in 1952 with cattle auctioned on Mondays and horses on Tuesdays. The Brown Cow inn had a market room and there was all day trading, when the auction market was in session - it was held on Thursdays in 1963. In September 1964 the auction market closed due to a shortage of stock and the "Queens" store opened run by two local brothers - there was another Queens supermarket at Knottingley. Whitkirk became the second ASDA superstore which opened on March 14th. 1966, retaining a dome that once stood over the old auction ring.
ASDA was founded in 1965 and is now the UK's 4th. largest retailer. There are over 200 stores nationwide with over 4 million customers weekly. The ASDA store at Whitkirk was sold to Tetley's Brewery and closed on March 12th. 1994. On April 7th. the tiles were removed in preparation for the demolition of the landmark, completed by mid-May.

The large house north of ASDA was the offices of the National Farmers Union from 1950 until 1989. They were opened by the NFU chairman H. W. Wood in premises built in the 1890's as a private dwelling. East of Hollyshaw Lane are new flats built on the site of Church View cottages, demolished in 1987. The cottages served the Prince Arthur Pit, with one being the house of the pit manager.
There is still slag heap evidence on Hollyshaw Lane of this pit, which opened about 1850 and named after the 7th. child of Queen Victoria born in that year. As Prince Arthur he came to Leeds on September 1872 to open Roundhay Park. Prince Arthur Pit closed by 1896, having had the winding engine removed to Dewsbury in 1880. The pithead gear was still in place in 1905. It was on the old pit site that many red shale fossil plants were found: including ferns from millions of years ago.
The row of tall houses on the west side of Hollyshaw Lane was built by Stevenson and Murgatroyd in 1898 with the end shop run by the Briggs family bakery and afterwards becoming Moxon's Shop. In 1905 it was reported that there was "rapid development of Whitkirk and Halton in the last four years and 300 houses had been

built on glebe land north of Selby Road; the houses face north and east which will make Whitkirk and Halton among the most popular of Leeds suburbs."

On the east side half way down the Lane near Hollyshaw Crescent was a field called Hospital Close. In 1521 Sir Thomas Lord Darcy granted his land on Allershaw Close for the foundation of a hospital or college for 12 poor people and one master. The land was built upon in 1934, although traces of the foundations of the hospital were said to have been discovered in the late 19th. century. When the free grammar school at the hospital of "Maison Dieu" closed, children would have been sent to Leeds Grammar School. The origin of this school dates from the will of Sir William Sheafield on July 6th. 1552. The school was founded on a site in The Calls, although there probably was an earlier school here which can be traced back to 1341. By 1579 the New Chapel on Lady Lane was being used as a school room and in 1624 the school was moved by John Harrison to his estate on North Street - between the Grand Theatre and Vicar Lane. Godfrey Lawson built a library on this site in 1692 and the school was extended in 1820-23. The present school buildings on Moorland Road were opened on June 27th. 1859 during the time of headmaster Rev. Alfred Barry with his brother Edward as architect - their father was Sir Charles Barry architect of the Houses of Parliament.

THE ROAD FROM LEEDS TO SELBY

PART 2 FROM WHITKIRK TO GARFORTH BRIDGE

The parish church of St. Mary the Virgin Whitkirk is the oldest Medieval church in Leeds. There was written evidence of a church in the 1185 inquisition into the estates of the Knights Templars. It is likely that a wooden church was the first building, replaced by a stone or white church built after the Domesday Survey of 1086.When the Knights Templar order was abolished in 1312 Whitkirk became the property of the Order of St.John of Jerusalem who appointed the vicars from 1324 until 1540.In 1546 the advowson passed to Trinity College Cambridge until 1898.The right of appointment of vicars then passed to Hon. Mrs. Meynell-Ingram and is now vested with the Meynell Trustees.

The church was altered from a simple nave and short chancel in the 12th. century and in the late 13th. century the chancel was extended. The piscina niche in the present south chapel wall belongs to this early period. The new chancel was built around the old one and the two aisles were added to the nave. The south aisle was altered to accommodate the Scargill Chantry in 1448 and the aisles were widened in this century.

The west tower was built in the mid-15th. century and has seen many repairs over the centuries, there being a fine view of the local area from the top. The chancel was extended in 1901 with contributions to the cost by Mrs. Meynell Ingram and designs by George Frederick Bodley (1827-1907).The vestry built in 1901 was a replacement for the older structure and was the gift of J. W. Morkill of Austhorpe Lodge. John Morkill also provided a marble pavement for the chancel floor in 1888 but this was taken up in 1980.The sanctuary area was floored in Yorkshire stone and what is believed to be a Saxon font bowl was introduced. During the re-ordering the altar was brought forward with a sacristy being formed behind.

The truncated spiral steps in the north wall are the remains of the access to the rood screen or beam: there is evidence of a rood in the church in 1591.The latest Whitkirk rood dated from 1935 and was taken down in 1980 at the re-ordering. The oldest monument in the church and made of alabaster is that of Sir Robert Scargill and his wife Lady Jane: Robert died in 1531.The Scargills came originally from Scargill on the banks of the River Greta, which flows into the R. Tees near Barnard Castle in Co. Durham. In the early 14th. century Lead Hall and chapel, founded by the Tyas family, became the property of the Scargills of Thorp Stapleton Hall near Temple Newsam. In 1421 Joan Scargill asked to be buried at Lead Chapel and it is likely that when her husband died Lady Jane went to live at Lead Hall. She died in January 1547 and the Lead estate passed to the Gascoigne family, who had just bought the Parlington estate. It was the marriage between Sir William Scargill and Margaret

Gascoigne that proved the descent of the property. Sir Robert Scargill's daughter Mary married Sir Marmaduke Tunstall and his other daughter Margaret married Sir John Gascoigne.

Other memorials within the church include the lighthouse memorial on the south chancel wall to John Smeaton. Smeaton was born at Austhorpe Lodge in 1724 and married Ann Jenkinson in 1756. He rebuilt the Eddystone lighthouse which had burnt down in 1755. The fourth Eddystone lighthouse was opened in 1882, with Smeaton's tower being placed on Plymouth Hoe. John Smeaton died in October 1792.

The large monument in the south chapel is that of Edward 2nd. Viscount Irwin of Temple Newsam: using the chapel which became the burial place of the family in the 17th. century. Edward was the eldest son of Henry Ingram, who was the grandson of Sir Arthur Ingram, who bought Temple Newsam in 1622.Edward married Elizabeth Sherard in 1685 and died in 1688 with his brother Arthur becoming the 3rd. Viscount. Five of Arthur's sons became the Viscounts Irwin between 1702 and 1763. The monument, which originally stood on a box tomb, also commemorates Edward's wife Elizabeth who remarried and died in 1746.

Above the Scargill tomb is an Ingram shield and an inscription to Sir Arthur Ingram. The monument against the west wall of the south aisle remembers Charles 9th. and last Viscount Irwin (1727-1778) and sculpted by Joseph Nollekens (1737-1823).Nearby is a small tablet to Lord William Gordon, husband of Frances Ingram Shepheard. He died at his house in London in 1823 and was buried at Whitkirk.

There are memorials to Michael Scholefield of the Manor House, Colton Road and steward at Temple Newsam House - he died in 1842 aged 80; John Graveley of Hawthorn House Halton died 1909 aged 80; John Wilson of Seacroft Hall died 1836 aged 69; Elizabeth Lowther of Little Preston Hall died 1751.

Many alterations have been carried out at Whitkirk Church during restorations in 1855 and 1901, when the chancel was extended by 9 feet. The north chapel was the Waud Chapel, having been previously known as the Manston Quire. Edward Waud ran the Manston Colliery until his bankruptcy in 1866.He was buried in December 1885 in the Manston Chapel, which had been re-roofed and restored at his expense. He also provided some stained glass in 1843 in memory of his wife Mary who died in 1842: he presented additional stained glass to the church in 1856 to mark the striking of coal at his West Yorkshire Pit.

The coat of arms in the vestry are those of Morkill and Falshaw. Sir James Falshaw was born in Leeds in 1810 being the son of William Falshaw merchant of Leeds (1775-1860). He worked on the Leeds/Selby railway for Hamer & Pratt in 1831 and was to have his own office in Leeds in 1874. He moved to Edinburgh in 1855 and in 1874 became Provost of Edinburgh and was created a baronet two years later when Queen Victoria visited the city. He had married his first wife Anne Morkill and she died in 1864 and was buried in Whitkirk's south graveyard. Sir James married Jane Gibbs who died in 1889: he died in Edinburgh on June 19th.1889 and was buried in Dean Cemetery Edinburgh. The Morkills were an old family in the area: John Morkill was Lord Irwin's park keeper and lived at Temple Newsam Lodge: he died in 1681.

In the south west corner of the graveyard is the large inscribed box tomb of Sir George Goodman. He was the first Leeds mayor under the Municipal Corporation Act of 1836.He was mayor again in 1846 and 1850 and 1851, when he resigned. He was the Leeds MP from 1852 to 1857 having been born in 1791 and died in 1859. His home was Goodmans House on Elmete Lane Roundhay, which became the home of the Lupton family and was the Beechwood Conference Centre until being put on sale in 1993.

Opposite the south doorway is an unusual inscription to an 18th. century John Atkinson which reads:"This world's a city full of crooked streets. Death is the market place where all men meet. If life was merchandise that men could buy: the rich would always live and the poor die."

In the north churchyard is the box tomb of William Porter, the eldest son of John Porter of Seacroft:"35 years the faithful and assiduous colliery agent to the late Sir Thomas Gascoigne and present Richard Oliver Gascoigne of Parlington Park." He died at Scarborough with poor health in 1818.

There are members of the Atkinson family of Austhorpe Lodge, Barrowby Hall and Manston Lodge Cross Gates (now the Manston Hotel).The Dawsons of Towton Hall owned land at Garforth Bridge; the Morkills of Killingbeck and Austhorpe are buried at Whitkirk and Catherine Wade of Halton, who was the last descendent of the family that produced the reformer John Wycliffe, is also buried at this church.

The large concrete rendered house by the north west churchyard is Glebe House built in 1825.This was the house for the Whitkirk schoolmaster: the school was opened in 1825 and cost £305.The house was enlarged in 1835 to accommodate a girl's Sunday School. There is a stone used as a back step inscribed "...DAY SCHOOL". In later years the boy's school was altered to accommodate girls and in 1862 the boy's school was demolished. The site became a part of the churchyard which was consecrated by the Bishop of Ripon in September 1864.

The Sunday School transferred to the historic tithe barn, which was demolished to make room for the new parish hall. The listed Glebe House has been tastefully restored by its present owners. The listed buildings form a group including the 19th. century churchyard stone wall and The Grange listed in 1951.

On the east side of Colton Road is a newsagents and general store, which started as an ale house called the "Salutation Inn" with Nathan Waddington as the licensee in the 1820's and 1860's. Waddington owned land north of Meynell Road (Colton

Street) near the site of the chapel. In the 1930's the shop was that of Fred Farrell grocer.
On Colton Road is the Manor House built in 1623 with the coach house from 1777.In the mid 19th. century the Manor House was the home of Abraham Horsfall, a solicitor and deputy coroner who gave a pair of brass candlesticks and some stained glass to Whitkirk Church - he died on October 16th.1873 and his widow continued to live in the house until Bessie Hick lived at the Manor House in 1887.Abraham Horsfall followed Michael Scholefield, who died in 1842.In this century it was the home of Christopher Scott (died 1903 aged 60) and Coun. Gertrude Bray. The Manor House and Keep have a late 18th. century wing and has an early 19th. century staircase.
The small house on Selby Road east of the old inn once belonged to Manor Farm and displays a Templar Cross with the inscription "1744 TW". On Colton Road is another Templar Cross "1732 TG":these crosses were placed on dwellings of the Manor of Whitkirk.
To the east is the large white house of The Grange: built in 1820 and once the home of the Chapman family, who later moved to Austhorpe Hall. William Chapman ran Grange Farm until 1939 and died in August 1990.The house is now three dwellings and the bell on the rooftop once summoned the coachman from the stables. Earlier inhabitants of The Grange were the Child family with Thomas Child living at the house and Henry Child at The Manor House. William Child lived at Ivy House in 1889: the family were maltsters.

In September 1964 the land east of Whitkirk Church was sold for £122,500 by the trustees of the Temple Newsam estate for the 18½ acre site of the Plandwell estate. The estate was started in August 1967.

Colton Lane is the main access to new Colton Village which developed by 1984 with 788 homes on the estate. In 1993/94 another 27 houses were built on farmland off School Lane; new housing was also completed on Meynell Road in 1994.The Colton housing plan of 1974 involved the council building 6000 homes with 60% under LCC control: this was reduced to 2000 houses with 20% council controlled. The 1981 housing plan for Colton involved 1100 houses with 80% private using 168 acres for building. The report stated that "the local centre retains in the plan shops, small supermarket, health centre, public house, library and a community centre". There was to be a new site for the Colton Centre as the former suggested area bounded by Colton Road East and School Lane was regarded as being not central. The development would incorporate the local field names: Kirkfield, Cranewells, Northwood, Stile Hill and Hollings with Chantry Fields and Ginpitt Wood.
Archaeological investigations revealed the Medieval village of Colton on Park Road

in 1980 with the sites of timber houses and their yards- Colton or Cola's tun was known as Coletun in the Domesday Book. The Colton Colliery near the junction of Meynell and Park Road was worked by Jeremiah Bourne Faviell in the mid-19th. century and this became a pumping station for Temple Newsam's Waterloo Colliery. The farm field which became the site of new housing in 1993/94 revealed a deep lined well, which was infilled for safety. The new houses built off Park Road were opened by the Lord Mayor of Leeds in September 1984.
The 420 acre Colton estate was sold by Lord Halifax in 1974 to the Leeds City Council and many homes were bought by the tenants, although the farms remained in council ownership. Park Farm was built about 1731 and was the probable site of Colton Hall which had been mentioned in 1322.
Many of the Colton houses are listed buildings as being of outstanding architectural interest and these include the late 18th. century Vine and Yew Tree cottages with the early 19th. century terrace of New Row.
The Colton lands were enclosed following the proclamation in Whitkirk Church on November 30th.1834.One of the first Methodist preachers prior to this event was William "Billy" Dawson, who was born at Barnbow in 1773 but spent most of his young life at Whitkirk. He travelled extensively as a preacher from 1801 and died at Colne in 1841.The first record of Colton Chapel was in January 1832 when a Trust Deed was made between a miner Thomas King and his wife Hannah - they occupied the corner site - the Trustees and Lady Hertford. The first wooden building was rebuilt and the new chapel opened on July 18th.1867.A hut was bought from Cross Gates Primary School in 1947 for extra accommodation and used as a Sunday School and Youth Club. The last service in Colton Methodist Chapel was held on June 26th.1988 and the building was demolished. The new chapel, built by Stocks Bros. of Garforth, was first used on July 9th.1989 and dedicated in September.

There was a post office run by Richard Fletcher and ale houses with an inn at Colton: the inn was the "Blue Bell", which changed to the "Drummers Arms", built in the mid-18th. century on Colton Road East near Bullerthorpe Lane. This is now a private house with 10' foundations and cellars with a game of skittles to be played outside. The stone with the space for the skittles is now part of the garden approach. In the mid 19th. century John Grubb was the innkeeper followed a few years later by William Sanderson. Ale House Cottage on Woodhall Court off Meynell Road also had cellars with beer being available in the front room. There was another ale house near the Colton Road East/Bullerthorpe Road junction, although now demolished. There was an application to build a new public house in Colton in 1980 but this has not matured.
Colton Institute was first mentioned in 1892 and used the village school for meetings. A new building completed in 1896 was used as a Sunday School. In 1922 a wooden

building was brought from Barnbow by horse and waggon to Colton and in 1951 ladies were admitted for the first time.

Colton Board School opened on September 25th. 1876 with Joseph Owrid as master. He left in 1883 to become headmaster of Halton Board School. The school was built on Common Side Lane - now School Lane - to designs by C. R. Chorley together with a master's house demolished in 1971.Colton ceased to be a board school in 1904 and the village pinfold disappeared at the time of opencasting in the 1940's. A wooden hut was built in 1957 and another was erected in 1965 but in November 1989 the school was forced to leave the old buildings. They were bussed to the old East Garforth Miners School until July 1990 and five portable units were placed on site for use until September 1992, when the new purpose built building was opened. Councillor William Hyde officially opened the school on July 5th.1993.The old building fell into disrepair and was sold.

Austhorpe was once dominated by TWO large houses: Austhorpe Hall and Austhorpe Lodge. The Hall stands on Austhorpe Lane and has been Chapman's Farm since 1939.It was built in 1694 by John More, whose name is intertwined in a plaque above the front door. In March 1695 the window tax was introduced into England and affected many large houses, who could not afford to pay this tax. Many windows were therefore blocked at Austhorpe Hall. This tax was repealed by Queen Victoria in 1851 when Crystal Palace was built for the Great Exhibition. John married Ruth Bretton in 1685 and he died in 1702.The last of the male line was their son Nicholas who was murdered in London in 1720.It was the home of Benjamin and Ann Atkinson in the 18th. century - John Atkinson married Miss Atkinson of Walls House Allerton Mauleverer in January 1793 (a newspaper report indicated that the young lady had a fortune) and Benjamin died in 1806.It became the home of the Appleyard family from 1843, who gave their name to "Appleyard's Hill" to Cross Gates. Henry Appleyard, farmer Joshua's son was married at Whitkirk Church in January 1885 to Mary Fallas. Henry Appleyard died aged 54 in 1905.The hall's contents were auctioned in April 1939 by Bartle & Sons of Garforth by order of John Appleyard. The hall became a listed building in 1963.
The area of Austhorpe Lane/Selby Road/Manston Lane was designated as a country park by Leeds City Council in June 1994, who reversed several decisions in the Leeds Unitary Development Plan for this Green Belt Land at Austhorpe. The plans for a small light industrial manufacturing estate and for a giant housing estate with thousands of properties were abandoned. Instead there will be a 110 acre country park acting as a buffer to a proposed 150 acre business park.
The Ring Road from Austhorpe to Cross Gates was completed in late 1931 and entailed a deep cutting to be excavated: the road was intended to divert increasing

traffic from the narrow Hollyshaw Lane to Whitkirk.
Whitkirk Lane End is now represented by the Austhorpe Ring Road roundabout - Whitkirk Lane once joined the Leeds/Selby turnpike at this point, where Gypsy Lane branches to Colton and used the old route of Leys Road. This old lane has been partially preserved as a track alongside Colton Lane - the lane was "stopped up" in 1968.The small Lane End School ceased to operate in January 1867 and the 60 children were moved to the old reading room at Whitkirk, used as a Sunday School. The Lane End School was established by John Wilkinson and his wife of Austhorpe Lodge - they maintained the school until they left Austhorpe.
A bungalow on the west corner of Detroit Drive/Selby Road is the only reminder of a large estate on the land between Whitkirk Lane and Austhorpe Lane. This was the lodge house to Austhorpe Lodge built in 1698 by John Smeaton, the grandfather of the famous engineer, who built the third Eddystone lighthouse. The first wooden lighthouse was built in 1696 by Henry Winstanley but a storm in November 1703 swept it away. John Rudyard built the next wooden lighthouse in 1706/09 but this caught fire in 1755.Smeaton made a 6 day journey to Plymouth in March 1756 and a few weeks later produced the plans and a model of the new stone built lighthouse. The centre was fixed on the rock on August 3rd.1756 and the 450 tons of Portland stone were prepared. The first stone was secured on the rock on June 12th.1757 and the light first shone from the new lighthouse on October 16th.1759.Smeaton's lighthouse was replaced in May 1882 by the fourth construction. John Smeaton concerned himself with navigation on the Aire & Calder canal, designed a water pumping engine for Lord Irwin at Temple Newsam and designed 43 water mills and numerous windmills.
The Lodge was John Smeaton's home and his family Ann, Mary and Hannah grew up in the house, after his marriage in 1756 to Ann Jenkinson. A square four storey tower south of the main house contained the engineer's forge and study. To commemorate the 250th. anniversary of John Smeaton's birth, there was a special service held at Whitkirk Church on June 9th.1974, attended by civic, industrial and educational representatives.
Austhorpe Lodge came into the Brooke family through John Smeaton's daughter: Ann's marriage to John Brooke of Killingbeck in 1780. Their daughter Frances married Major James Croft Brooke of Littlethorpe Ripon son of Richard Brooke of Scholes Hall - he was the brother of William Brooke who sold Killingbeck Hall to the Hanson family.
John and Ann's only son was John Croft Brooke of Clifton York (1789-1838) and he married Mary who died aged 83 on April 24th. 1884 at Tunbridge Wells. John and Mary's son John Croft Brooke died in infancy.
John Atkinson lived at Austhorpe Lodge with his wife Naomi Rosa in the early 19th. century. There is a stained glass window in the north aisle of Whitkirk Church given

in memory of the four daughters of John and Naomi - Isabella, Mary, Naomi and Anne all died under the age of 16 years.
Edward and John Wilkinson lived at Austhorpe Lodge in the 1860's, when John was listed as a "carpet manufacturer". While staying at the Lodge Ann Marshall, widow of William Marshall of Ely died on April 28th. 1861 aged 68 and was buried in Whitkirk's south east churchyard.
It was Ursula Wilkinson who was to sell Austhorpe Lodge estate on behalf of the trustees of the late Joshua Wilkinson. The estate was purchased by John William Morkill in June 1892 for £2170. Joshua Wilkinson died on June 19th.1873.
The estate and Lodge with modernised south porch was sold by Hollis and Webb at the Leeds Law Institute and was described as having "a ring fence enclosing 12 acres, which has 400 trees with a kitchen and fruit garden".
Austhorpe Lodge was the home of Sidney Batley during the Great War and was again sold at auction by Bartle's of Garforth in May 1932, having been the property of C. M. Atkinson, the "predecessor of the present stipendiary magistrate for Leeds."It was sold to a syndicate with prospects of development as a club and the land sold for housing. The plans fell through and the hall eventually demolished in 1936, with the tower pulled down in 1948.
The Austhorpe Lodge estate had orchards, fine trees, tennis court and two lodges. The main house entries were on the north side with the old courtyard and on the west side. There was stable accommodation, greenhouses with a vinery and peach house and a private carriageway through the grounds. The pond was changed into a Rhododendron bed in the early years of this century.
Austhorpe Primary School was opened in September 1968 near the site of Austhorpe Windmill and on land which had been compulsorily purchased in 1965.Thomas Steel was the miller in the mid-19th. century and he lived at Mill Cottage, which stands today.

Austhorpe was a productive area for good quality coal and the West Yorkshire Pit was sunk about 1850, Brown Moor in 1835 and Adelaide Pit near Austhorpe Hall. Edward Waud, the owner of the Manston Collieries, presented the east stained glass window at Whitkirk Church as a thanksgiving when coal was struck at the West Yorkshire Pit. Brown Moor Pit was on land owned by John Wilson of Seacroft Hall and was leased to the Gascoignes and then the Wauds of Manston Colliery, who built a side line in the 1840's from the main railway line. In January 1867 the Austhorpe coalfield was sold as part of the Manston and West Yorkshire Collieries: the sale also included 30 acres of land at Seacroft, a coalfield under Whinmoor and coal/ironstone in both Killingbeck and Seacroft. The smaller Ellen Pit - Ellen was one of Edward Waud's daughters - was on Barrowby Lane east of Brown Moor: the 210' deep disused pit shaft was finally filled in during 1965. In 1971 the Barrowby Lane pits

were landscaped with Mary Pit at Killingbeck - at a cost of £2500.
A large scale development on the north end of School Lane in the newly created Northwood Gardens is Colton Lodges Nursing Home. The project by Takare of Telford accommodates 120 in four bungalow style houses in landscaped gardens. Each house has 30 single rooms and have names as Garforth and Elmete. The home opened on December 20th.1993.Takare Group operate 42 homes in Britain including one in Hunslet Leeds.
The area east of School Lane/Selby Road was investigated as the Stile Hill/Colton Common Site by the West Yorkshire Archaeological Unit between November 1993 and February 1994.The initial discovery of this site was partially revealed through air surveys. Discoveries included post holes of early houses and earthworks which may well have been Roman. Numerous pieces of broken pottery have been dated to the 2nd. century. The investigations were funded by Trinity Investments Ltd.
In late January 1994 contractors were on this site to commence construction of a new Sainbury's superstore. The store is a part of the Colton Retail Park on a 12 acre site. The £15 million development includes a petrol station, non-food stores and a car park: Trinity Investments and the Royal London Mutual Insurance Society put up the funds for the scheme. The superstore opened in November 1994 having been designed by architects Seymour Harris Partnership of Aire Street Leeds.

Colton Mill stands on the corner of Bullerthorpe Lane/Selby Road with outbuildings and cottages and became a listed building in 1970.The mill was worked by sails until the mid 19th. century, when it was described as "Swillington Steam Corn Mill".The miller was Andrew Johnson who died in 1905 aged 75. The mill retains some internal machinery and was last worked in 1940 by the Barraclough family. For many years it was just "Barraclough's Mill" - John was at the mill in the 1880's and Frederick William Barraclough was born on July 14th.1867 and died on October llth.1929 and was buried at Whitkirk Church on October 14th: his wife Lilian had died aged 34 in 1903 and children Gertrude died in 1901 and Henry in 1899 in their early years. The mill chimney was demolished in the 1930's and an engine installed from the Palace Cinema Rothwell. The bricks from the chimney were used to surface a track at Newsam Green Farm. A plan to demolish the mill by the trustees of Lord Halifax's Temple Newsam Estate and develop the site was refused on October 12th.1970.The mill had been listed in March 1970 and the proposal had objections from the Victorian Society, Ancient Monuments Society, Yorkshire Archaeological Society and the Leeds Civic Trust.
Near Colton Mill the West Yorkshire Archaeological Unit investigated the site of an early brick works, with some of the bricks probably being used in Colton houses.
Selby Road crosses the line of the ancient earthwork known as Grim's Ditch, which runs on the west side of Bullerthorpe Lane and through Colton Mill. It is likely that

the ditch was man made in the 7th. century to defend the Leeds area from possible attack. The bank is still 9' high in places with a 40' wide ditch: it is probable that there would have been a wooden palisade on the top. The Whinmoor/Swillington Bridge 5 mile long east facing dyke would certainly have slowed down an invasion and allowed time for the defenders to be relocated to troublesome areas. The earliest known reference to Grim's Ditch is about 1257 and was then called "Grymisdyk". Grim refers to the pagan God Wodin, which was an alternative name. The ditch is a Scheduled Ancient Monument: excavated at Bullerthorpe Lane in 1983 during the layout of the car park and picnic area.
The proposed Al/Ml link motorway will cross Selby Road in this area en route from Belle Isle to Hook Moor. The £200 million 19 mile long road was approved in late 1993 with work starting in 1998. It was announced by the Leeds City Council in June 1994 that there will be a 150 acre Business Park of office type development. It is designed as a gateway to Leeds for traffic using the new motorway link.
The original proposal to opencast 600,000 tons of coal prior to the road construction was abandoned in October 1994 when the City Council announced that their plans to build the Business Park had been brought forward.
The opencast at Garforth's Barwick Road site started in late 1994 extracting 100,000 tons of coal lying underneath farmland.
Swillington Common is a small village mainly north of the main road, although the Methodist Chapel was on Swillington Lane. The village primary school was built in 1875 on the corner of the Lane and the main road. This school closed in 1965 and has now two bungalows on the site.
The Methodist Chapel on Swillington Common was opened in 1854 and closed in 1952.The chapel was converted into a private house known as "Four Winds Chase". The village north of the main road was mainly used by miners at the Waterloo, Mount Pleasant and Primrose collieries - Lowther Terrace indicates links with the Swillington pits. The area north of the houses and smithy was the brick yard. The smithy retains the wooden doors and was run by the Lawn family - the blacksmith's house was once an ale house. The smithy closed in the 1950's and the adjacent shop was also run by the Lawn family - it is now a private house. In 1917 Benjamin Hugh Lawn (1858-1924) was the smith, his sister Mary Lawn (1863-1868) the grocer, John Taylor the butcher and Sam Watson the village joiner. Benjamin and Mary Lawn were the children of Thomas and Elizabeth Ellen Lawn - they died in 1915 aged 82 and 1879 aged 54 and were buried at Swillington Church. The two sons of Benjamin and Martha Lawn: William died in 1904 aged 10 months and John died in 1985 aged 86.
Strike's Garden Centre was once the Llanberis Nursery but when the dual carriageway was being constructed in 1965/67 the land was cleared. William Strike started the business in Stockton in 1877 and they opened their first Leeds shop in the

Headrow in 1938.In 1946 the second Leeds shop opened in Albion Place and a third unit in Kirkgate Market in 1950.
In the 1960's the firm changed from high street shops to garden centres and they bought the Selby Road site in May 1967. They now have seven garden centres at Red Hall, Stokesley, Eaglescliffe, Darlington, Northallerton and Knaresborough.
Waterloo Manor was enlarged for the Sissons family of Garforth in 1908 - the front door has an inscription in stone "ES 1908".The family lived at Ashleigh House and Garforth House while William Sissons was living at the Manor in the 1920's prior to its sale to Leeds. The smaller house was known as Waterloo Villa and dated from the mid-19th. century: Mary Jackson was at the Villa in the 1880's.
The main house and lodge on the main road with extensive grounds, kitchen garden and greenhouse, which retains the original productive vine, became a local authority boy's home until 1987 when the Home Farm Trust bought the property. The Trust had its origins at St. Christopher's Special School Bristol who launched an appeal. They bought Frocester Manor Gloucestershire in September 1962.The Trust is a registered charity providing opportunities for the personal development of people with a mental handicap. This includes the provision of a wide range of activities catering for the residential training, work and social needs of people with learning difficulties.
Waterloo Manor was opened by Princess Anne in July 1987 as Patron of the Trust. Together with its satellite on Royds Lane Rothwell the Trust offers 27 places: Waterloo Manor in 7 acres of grounds, has thirteen places with a smaller house in the grounds providing another four places: there are 20 staff caring for the residents.
Brookfield House stands north of the main road near Garforth Bridge and Kippax (Sheffield) Beck. Brookfield was once part of the extensive Temple Newsam estate and was a small dower house probably built between 1520 and 1535.The old east wing was demolished in 1909/10 to build the present structure, leaving the west wing as the oldest part of the present house, together with the stables and barn.
David Bartle, who founded the firm of auctioneers and valuers in 1840, was a tenant of the estate and lived at Brookfield from about 1867 with his father Henry Bartle, an auctioneer. David Bartle died on June 10th.1895 aged 67 at Marak near Geiranger in Stranda Norway: he is buried at Vebluncsnaes: his wife Jane died in December 1906 aged 74.David Bartle was a regular worshipper at Swillington Church and was also a surveyor for the township of Temple Newsam.
David's son was John Clapham Bartle who was born in 1863 and lived at Brookfield from 1869 - Clapham was his mother's maiden name. He married Dorothy Fawcett of Barrowby Hall and Godfrey was born in 1912, who now lives near Ripon.
Brookfield was bought by John Bartle from the Temple Newsam estate on December 31st.1909 together with 56 acres of land. The family immediately undertook a programme of restoration and rebuilding, which was completed in 1910 - there is an

inscription over the north door "JCB DMB 1910" with the date repeated on the guttering. The architect for the alterations was Arthur Hartley of Castleford.
John Bartle set up an office of his firm in the east wing and became a churchwarden at Swillington Parish Church. There was a small farm set up by John Bartle with a few cows and pigs. The family soon extended their holdings with an eventual 83 acres of the Brookfield House Estate. The firm had offices at Leeds Corn Exchange - later in Merrion Street - Selby Auction Market and at Whitkirk Auction Market. Bartles opened an office at Whitkirk Auction Market in 1952, having closed the Brookfield office in 1946. John Bartle took John Robinson of Barwick in Elmet as his partner who remained with the firm for 40 years. John Bartle sold Brookfield on March 31st.1949, coinciding with his retirement from the firm. He went to live at Spofforth Hill Wetherby with his daughter Cathleen and he died in April 1954 aged 91.He had been an expert on tenant right valuation and had founded the Whitkirk Auction Market in 1909.
Brookfield was rented by John Wilson who worked the land until about 1960 when he bought the property. Some land to the south of the house was lost in 1965 for the formation of the dual carriageway from Austhorpe to Garforth Bridge.
The company continued with John's sons Godfrey and Ivor - there were four daughters - and today the company is based at Tadcaster as Bartle Residential, Chartered Surveyors, Valuers and Estate Agents. Godfrey retired in 1979 and his son Brian is now involved in the business with Ivor's son Philip Bartle - Ivor retired in 1976.
Brookfield became the home of the Edwards family for a about 20 years - they had a garage in Doncaster. Edwards was a composer and wrote the music "Wakey! Wakey!" for Billy Cotton while living at Brookfield. The present family has owned Brookfield from 1979.
On the northern horizon stands Barrowby Hall which was the home of the Ingram family from 1677 until 1742.It was during these years that architect William Etty remodelled the Hall in 1719: the estate had been bought from the Layton family by the Ingrams. At one time there was a squirrel's grave in the Hall grounds dated 1729. Barrowby Hall became tenanted by Charles Smith, son of Timothy,the entrepreneur who was working the Lowther's Astley pits with Thomas Fenton in 1773. Elizabeth Smith, the wife of Charles, died at Colton in 1865. During the 1830's to the 1860's Barrowby Hall was the home of William Simpson Atkinson and then the home of the Fawcett family of Maltsters. Eric Fawcett was born at the Hall about the turn of the century and Mary Fawcett married John Clapham Bartle about the same time.
In later years the Hall became the home of Bernard Hirst, agent for the Oulton Estate and then Stephenson's Riding School. The Hall and estate was Gascoigne property until September 1937 and is now a mixed arable farm run by the Barrowman family.
The "Old George" public house was established by 1822 serving the two turnpike

roads. It was bought by Bentley's Yorkshire Brewery of Woodlesford in 1880 and once had extensive stabling facilities. The present inn was built in the 1930's and became a Whitbread house in 1972 and is now a part of their Beefeater chain.
The main road dual carriageway of 1966/67 had a junction with traffic lights prior to construction of a roundabout Garforth Bridge crosses Sheffield Back, which becomes Kippax Beck having its origins in Spring Wood.
South of the main road was a large mill complex opened as a corn mill and operated by Horsefields. In 1897 it was the St. Helen's works of the Garforth Glue and Gelatine Co. having Charles Robshaw as the manager. It became a tannery and in 1908 possessed two chimneys, which were brought down in the 1930's. It became the Pilot Works of Naylor, Pollard & Co. Ltd., making cotton overalls and shirts and employing many Garforth girls. The houses of Hawthorn terrace were for the workers while the manager's house was on the site of the present Post Office building.
The Garforth Mercury Motel was built in 1974 on land that once belonged to nearby Well Green Farm. The farm was run by the Cramby family from the early 19th. century to the 1920's when George Bowman took the farm. William Cramby died aged 67 in 1868 and his wife Jane died in 1893 age 82.Thomas Cramby died in 1906 aged 80 and his wife Hannah had died in 1891 age 65. The Motel became a part of the Ladbroke Group and renamed the Hilton National in 1988.The hotel has a Leisure Centre with swimming pool and extensive conference facilities.
The garage at the Old George roundabout used to have an old hangar and in the 1920's the business was run by Charles E. Fitton, who also had a taxi hire service. In the 1930's the garage was run by Dennis N. Brook.

Old George, Garforth

THE ROAD FROM LEEDS TO SELBY

PART 3 GARFORTH BRIDGE TO MONK FRYSTON

The Leeds/Selby turnpike had a junction with the later Wakefield/Aberford turnpike dating from 1794. The roads were served by three inns in the area,of which two are remaining. The "Greyhound" inn was on the corner of Leeds Lane and Wakefield Road. When it lost its licence it became known as "The White House" and afterwards was demolished.

The "Old George" and "Gaping Goose" catered for the stabling needs of the turnpike traffic. The "Gaping Goose" was once known as "The White Swan" and it is probably the oldest surviving inn at Garforth. It originated in the early years of the 19th. century and in 1858 James and Samuel Ogle sold the property to John Butterfield and George Tindall. In November 1871 John Butterfield sold it to Richard Lumb of Leeds for £820 and when he died on June 17th. 1878 the property passed by will to his son George Denison Lumb (born October 27th. 1857). On January lst.1891 George D. Lumb sold The Gaping Goose to the Leeds & Wakefield Breweries for £930 - his wife Sarah had died in March 1884 and was buried at Burmantofts Cemetery. In April 1964 Joshua Tetley acquired the inn when they bought the Melbourne Brewery.

Gaping Goose Inn

The name possibly derived from a frieze which once was found in nearby Garforth Old Hall, featuring either a swan or goose. It has been suggested that the change of name from Swan to Goose was a result of the efforts of a rather drunken signwriter. There is some evidence that a nickname for the inn was The Cormorant, as the bird featured on the Witham coat of arms.

Garforth Old Hall was at one time the centre of West Garforth: it was suggested that the villagers had moved from Church Garforth during an outbreak of plague. The 600 year old Hall stood nearly opposite the "Gaping Goose" on the south side of the main road. There was a small paddock with stables and orchards. It was demolished to prepare the route for an intended dual carriageway in the 1960's.

In 1560 the patronage of Garforth Church was with the Witham family and in the mid-17th. century the Hall was the home of Cuthbert Witham. William Witham, one of his relations, was said to have been bewitched to death by Mary Pannal in 1593.

In 1662 Sir William Lowther (1639-1705) married the 16 year old Katherine Harrison and he lived with his family at "West Garforth Hall from 1672". While he was living at the Hall, he helped his father to run the estates and the collieries. The family left West Garforth in 1688 and moved to Great Preston Hall.

In 1927 Joshua Watson was living at the Old Hall and it remained a private home until 1958. Other residents have included the Hudson, Catley and Stanton families.

The site of the present petrol station was Crowther's Farm - Benjamin Albert Crowther in the 1920's.

At the top of the hill is the junction with Lidgett Lane, linking the two turnpike roads through Garforth and known as Coldwell's Corner. The word Lidgett refers to a swing gate which would have guarded the old route. Many of the present houses on Lidgett Lane were built between 1870 and the 1960's. Garforth Comprehensive School - now Community College was opened by the Rt. Hon. Barbara Castle in 1969.

Garforth House is a late 18th. century hall on the main Selby Road facing up Lidgett Lane. It had been the home of the Sissons family, prior to their removal to Waterloo Manor and to Henry Morton in the mid 19th. century. This century occupiers have included William Leigh and Hugh Smithson who was the general manager of the Airedale Collieries: he died in June 1937 aged 53. A few years ago there was a small zoo in the grounds and today the dwelling is divided into flats.

The main road crosses the railway bridge which served the old line between Garforth and Castleford. The line opened on August 12th. 1878 as the Leeds, Castleford and Pontefract Junction Railway. The company had been formed in 1873 to serve the Kippax & Ledston area coalfield. In 1876 it became a part of the London & North Eastern Railway and passenger services finished in June 1951.

When HM The Queen opened the Seacroft Centre on Thursday October 21st. 1965 the nine coach royal train spent the night before near the old Kippax Station. The

other station on the line was at Ledston, which stands derelict on the old platform west of the Castleford road in a builder's yard. Kippax Lane End is often known as Charlie Sweep's Corner passing across Kippax Hollins and the Moor Gate to enter the ancient village.
The "Crusader" public house on the corner of Ninelands Lane and Selby Road was opened in 1970. The signing displays a Knights Templar in his uniform with a red Templar cross on a white cloak. The Templars had their preceptory south of Temple Newsam House near the River Aire and the site was archaeologically investigated prior to being opencast. The street name "Ninelands" indicates nine parcels of land and was once called Dogcroft Lane.
St. Mary's Church Garforth was probably founded in Saxon times and there was an early 13th. century church on the site of the present Victorian church. Ilbert de Lacy had given the patronage of St. Mary's Church to St. Mary's Abbey York. Old St. Mary's Church was pulled down in 1844 and a part of the chancel was re-erected in Parlington Park as a folly. The new church was consecrated in November 1845 with the main cost borne by the Gascoigne family.
The Gascoigne family ran the Garforth Collieries: developing the area from the mid 17th. century. Isabella (Gascoigne) Pit opened in 1833 with Elizabeth Pit following soon afterwards; Sisters Pit opened in 1843 and they were connected to Aberford by the Fly Line railway opened in the 1830's and closing in 1924. Trench Pit on Ninelands Lane was opened in 1899 and closed in 1930: the site is now Stocks Bros.
Garforth Fire Station was opened on January 5th. 1985 by Coun. Cooper: before this date the area was served by the stations at Stanks, Gipton and Castleford.

Garforth Cliff marks the outcrop of the Magnesian Limestone or Dolomite, the composition varying from Nottingham to the Tyne. It is this limestone that outcrops at Knaresborough and Stutton Quarry. It has been widely used as good quality building stone both in the construction of York Minster and London's Houses of Parliament.
Garforth Cliff Water Tower was constructed in the 1950's to provide a head of water to many local homes. There is a 5 acre underground reservoir at Garforth Cliff which supplies the water to Kippax, Allerton Bywater, Garforth, Woodlesford and the Prestons. The water pipe passes through the area from Elvington to Sheffield as part of the Derwent Water Scheme. There is another pipe from Garforth to Kirkhamgate Wakefield via Swillington pumping station.
Cliff Top Park was once the site of the Isolation Hospital, built for the care of smallpox, diphtheria and scarlet fever patients. The Isolation Hospital with its original 28 beds was extended at a cost of £18,000 in 1937. After the closure about 1948 the huts were demolished and the old nurse's home was converted to a cottage.
Garforth Cliff Garden Centre is on a site bought in 1962 by Geoffrey and John

Saville. In 1964 the wholesale trade was supplied and the brothers went into the retail market in 1972. The Centre stands alongside Green or Gypsy Lane and has the attractions of a railway and cafe at a popular centre.
The site of Kippax moated castle and Norman church can be seen on the near south horizon from Garforth Cliff. Soon after the Norman Conquest Kippax became the the administration centre for the northern part of the de Lacy Honour of Pontefract. The centre moved to Barwick in Elmet in the 13th. century, although Kippax retained the meetings of the Manorial Court.
Roach Lime Hills are a few yards south of the main road and have a good variety of flora: the hills were once used to extract the rock for Peckfield lime kiln. Roach or Roche Grange is below the Cliff towards Kippax: Simon de la Roche granted Garforth land to Holy Trinity Priory between 1204 and 1209; St. Mary's Abbey York also held land at Garforth. In the 14th. century there is a record of John de la Roche being at Garforth and would have known this monastic grange.
The approach to Peckfield Bar and the junction with the Roman Ridge Road has Milestone Farm Cottages and Limekiln Farm to the south and the site of once extensive quarries, now grazing land. Sandgate Lane is a footpath to Kippax, with the houses once associated with the nursery. Goodcomb Place Fruit Gardens were run by the Goodall and later by the Sadler family: the nursery ceased operating in the 1960's.
The Roman Ridge Road was turnpiked in 1827 as the Haughton & Hook Moor Branch of the Leeds and Barnsdale Road. On the north part of the main road at the junction is Peckfield House dating from 1840. The house was originally built for the Gascoigne family and they rented the property out: in the mid 19th. century John Fawcett lived at Peckfield House - he died aged 39 in 1872. In 1887 John C. Fawcett was at Peckfield House: he was a farmer and maltster. The Farm became a pig unit and their accomodation is now the Peckfield House Farm Shop opened in 1980. The shop started as a roadside potato outlet and has now been developed by the Makin family who live in the house they restored from dereliction in 1979.
Peckfield turnpike barhouse was on the north side of the main road, east of the roundabout. The site of the bar was on the wide grassy strip by the roadside.
The name Ledston Luck derived from the expression used by Mrs. Granville Wheler, later Lady Wheler, of Ledston Hall when she dug the first sod for the new pit in 1909: "May we have luck in this place". The Number 1 shaft at Ledston Luck Pit was sunk in 1911 - the date is shown over the preserved winding shaft house. The Number 2 shaft was sunk in 1914 and both were run by the Micklefield Coal & Lime Co. before being taken over by Henry Briggs in 1937. The 450 tons of coal daily were taken by a 1½ mile endless ropeway to Peckfield Pit,where it was screened and washed.
The church was originally intended to be the village school but it was only used for

that purpose during the last War. The building was dedicated as a church by the Archbishop of York Dr. Cosmo Lang in 1923: the present church building dates from 1969.
Ledston Luck Pit closed in 1943 and was re-opened after the War as the first all-electric pit in England. The pit was the last to use pit ponies and closed in 1986. The Enterprise Park was opened on November 2nd. 1989 and now includes many small firms in the development. The area surrounding the pit has been landscaped by British Coal.

Ledston Luck Enterprise Park

Peckfield Pit was sunk in 1874 by Joseph Cliff & Sons of Wortley and had two shafts to the Beeston Bed and the Black Bed. Peckfield suffered a disastrous explosion at 7.20am on Thursday April 30th. 1896, caused by unprotected lights. Early Thursday morning 107 went down on the shift and the sudden explosion occurred in the 180 yard deep No. l shaft with the boom heard in both Garforth and Sherburn. The force of the explosion caused the cage to be blown from the pit mouth to the top of the head gear. Messages of sympathy poured in, one of the first from the Mayor of Leeds Rt. Hon William Jackson, who also sent £25 for the support fund. The Yorkshire Post started the fund which had reached £4000 a week later.Queen Victoria sent a message of sympathy for the bereaved: the pit was always regarded as one of the safest.
There is a memorial in Micklefield Church yard, erected in 1935, to the 63 men and boys who died in this accident. The miners had come from Aberford, Kippax, Sherburn and Garforth as well as from Micklefield. Most of those who died were buried in trenches on the north side of Micklefield Church and the funeral service was led by the Bishop of Beverley. Some of the killed are buried at Garforth Church,

including Edward Goodall aged 42. There were 21 pit ponies also killed in the disaster and there were 35 men who came out of the pit alive.
Micklefield Pit was opened by the Waud family of Manston Colliery in 1836 at New Micklefield - it closed in 1878 and was later used as a lime quarry. Joseph Cliff's Peckfield Colliery closed in 1981 having been given a facelift during 1974-77.
Micklefield New Town was built to accomodate the mining families who worked at Peckfield Pit. The Garden Village near the station and old school - now a derelict site - was built in 1920 and extended in 1931: the Churchville estate was started in 1948.

North of Warren House Farm, which is a part of the Ledston Estate, is the extensive site of the Micklefield Magnesian Limestone Quarry, opened by the firm in 1975 - permission was granted to operate in October. The quarry is upto 70' deep and provides crushed stone for fillings and for roads. Further quarrying to a deeper level is prevented by the water table.

Old Micklefield lies north of the railway with New Micklefield developing with the railway and pit, being south of the line. The village was known as Miclanfelds in 963AD meaning a large field, with possible foundation in 619AD. There could have been a Norman presence as indicated by "Castle Hills" and "Manor Garth" near the present A1. There was a small chapel in Chapel Garth in the 13th. century and in the late 14th. century some Micklefield land was taken by the Gascoigne family of Gawthorpe Hall.
Hall Farm in Old Micklefield is mostly late 17th. century and was possibly the manorial courthouse with undercroft. The stable block is probably early 18th. century with the barn and gin house from a later period.
In 1545 the Manor of Sherburn was exchanged by Archbishop Holgate and Micklefield reverted to the King. The land was granted to the local Foljambe family and it was in 1886 that the Bland family of Kippax Park obtained the advowson to appoint the vicars.
The Anglo-Catholic Church of St. Mary the Virgin is in the Deanery of Selby and was built in 1861: the new parish of Micklefield was created in 1886. The first marriage was in May 1886 by Rev. M. Vine who was to live in a new vicarage a year later. The patronage was changed from King's College Cambridge to the Archbishop in the 1940's. The church was built as a chapel of ease for £1100 and paid for by Thomas Davison Bland of Kippax Park, who owned the Micklefield Estate. The stone came from the Bessie Mason quarry on Jerry Lane, now Church Lane: there were several magnesian limestone workings including Galliard and Vandicourt quarries and the village Micklefield quarry.
The church contains an impressive locally carved rood screen and the altar and

reredos were specially commissioned from the Oberammergau school of carvers. There are several oil paintings of religious scenes in the church, bought at a London auction house by Thomas Davison Bland - they now adorn the walls of the nave. The processional cross is 15th. century and is reputed to have been used during the Battle of Towton in 1461. Some other church furnishings came from the Bland mansion of Kippax Park. The church has memorials to Cpt. Alleyne Bland (died 1891) and to Thomas Davison Bland's wife Susannah Emily who died in 1883. The benevolent Thomas Davison Bland died on January 10th. 1885 at Kippax Park and his son John Davison Bland inherited the estates. John had a sister Eleanor Frances and two brothers Thomas Edward and Arthur Davison Bland. John Davison Bland died in Torquay Devon on September 7th. 1928.
The aumbry in the church was presented in memory of the Tractarian Rev. Charles Druce Farrar the Vicar of Micklefield for 40 years from 1887: his son Ernest was a respected organist and composer with his music being performed in London and in Leeds. There is also a stained glass window in memory of William Forbes who for 20 years was the steward of the Micklefield Estate.
The war memorial in the churchyard was first dedicated in 1920 and was re-dedicated on Remembrance Sunday 1991: the memorial remembers 24 soldiers who lost their lives in the First World War and the four men who fell in the last War. The stones were restored by the local quarry owners.
The Great North Road through the village was by-passed in 1960. The old Great North Road was the Boroughbridge & Ferrybridge Turnpike Trust road from 1740/41 and on this road is the Hick Memorial School built near the forge, remembering Sam Hick the Micklefield blacksmith who set up in the village in 1779. Samuel Hick was born at Aberford, one of thirteen children, becoming an apprentice blacksmith at 14 years old. He was married at Spofforth in 1781 and after conversion to Methodism was a local preacher by 1803. He preached in London, Hull, Grassington, York and Huddersfield together with many other locations. He donated £20 to build a new Methodist Chapel at Aberford and he laid the first stone for this chapel. Samuel Hick was buried at St. Ricarius Church Aberford, he died aged 71 in 1829. Over 1000 people went to Sam Hick's funeral and within a few years a small chapel and the Memorial School were built at Micklefield. The old Hick Memorial Sunday school closed in recent years and is now used by a photographic firm.
A National School re-opened on October 4th. 1880 and in 1891 the Brigg School by the railway became an Infants School. On Sunday September 13th. 1981 the school caught fire although the infant department was unaffected. The 110 children were housed at first in Garforth and Kippax schools prior to temporary classrooms being obtained at Micklefield. A new £250,000 school was built on a site behind The Bland's Arms inn. The first children entered the new premises in September 1987

and the Micklefield Church of England Controlled Infant and Junior School was officially opened by Coun. G. Driver and was dedicated by the Rt. Rev. C. C. Barker Bishop of Selby.
The school retains the log books for 1880 and the entry on October 4th. reads: "This school after enlargement was opened this morning under my charge-Seth Wilkinson. A meeting of the managers was held at noon presided over by J. D. Bland Esq. and advantage was taken to formally declare the school open. This was done by Mr. Bland ringing the school bell and the children being admitted." The managers also agreed to provide a tea on October 22nd for the children to celebrate the school opening and to encourage them to attend.
The village pinfold was repaired in the 1900's, while water for housing was piped from St. Helen's Well from 1898 until 1821, when a water main connected the two parts of the village. The custom of "Joss's Wedding" was seen in Micklefield every year, when two sporting local men featured as bride and groom and toured the village by horse and trap. The Micklefield Co-op and Yorkshire Bank both closed in 1977. The "Bland's Arms" public house is named after the family who lived at Kippax Park from the 16th.century until 1756 and who held Micklefield as part of their estates. When Sir Hungerford Bland died heirless the estate passed to his two sisters Anne and Elizabeth who both died unmarried. The estate was devised to Thomas Davison of Blakiston Hall in the parish of Norton near Stockton on Tees, who added the Bland name to his own.
Alexander Davison a Newcastle merchant bought the Blakiston estate from Sir Thomas Blakiston in 1615. He was slain at the age of 80 with his son Joseph in the defence of Newcastle. His eldest son Thomas Davison married Elizabeth Lambton becoming the High Sheriff of Durham in 1661 - he died in 1667. His grandson Thomas Davison of Blakiston took Anne Bland, daughter of Sir John Bland of Kippax Park as his first wife. He was married again to Theophila Turner of Kirkleatham. His eldest son from his first marriage was Thomas Davison who married Martha Hoar of Limehouse: their son Thomas was born in January 1745 - it was this Thomas Davison who took the name Bland on succeeding to the Kippax estates. The old hall at Blakiston was demolished and the stone was sold at Stockton. The Manor of Blakiston was sold to William Russell of Brancepeth Castle.
Thomas Davison (Bland) died in 1794 and his son Thomas inherited the Kippax estate. He was born in 1783 and died in 1847 having married the daughter of Lord Stourton: one of their 12 children was Thomas Davison Bland who was born in 1812 and married the daughter of John Madocks. Their eldest son was John Davison Bland who died in 1928.
The Methodist Chapel was opened on November 22nd. 1837 for £171 with Thomas Davison Bland donating the stone. The first minister was Rev. J. Bate - the chapel was enlarged in 1869 and 1871 and was licensed for marriages in 1900. Meetings

of local Methodists were held at first at White Horse Farm and in the Ridge Barn. Micklefield Railway Station opened when the line from Leeds to Selby was built - the first passenger service was on September 22nd. 1834. The line linking Micklefield with Church Fenton and the main line to York was opened in 1869, in the same year that the line from Marsh Lane was extended to the new station in Leeds city centre.
The coat of arms of Micklefield was adopted in 1968 and features an anvil (Sam Hick), phaeons (Bland) and three sheaves, with the motto "Ut Prosim" meaning "That I may be of use".

South of the main Selby Road is the extensive Ledston Estate. Ledston Lodge is near the main road and features a ha-ha protection and the coat of arms on the house built by Sir John Lewis in the 17th. century.
The Selby Road now passes across the realigned AI on a fly-over but it once had a junction at a point called Hungate Nook. The 18th. century "Boot and Shoe" public house is nearer the main road than it used to be and is named after a cobbler who once plied his trade. The draymen collecting malt from Sherburn in Elmet had their breakfast at this inn on their return to the Leeds or Tadcaster breweries. It is said that the inn is haunted and once frequented by highwaymen. The inn was once a meeting place of the Bramham Moor Hunt. In the mid-19th. century the Boot & Shoe farm and inn were run by Edward and Esther Lodge - Edward died in July 1844 aged 62; Esther died in 1873. The inn was later held by William Hills and by John Dalby by 1897. The inn was also a farm until recent years with the Cawood family running the two parts of the business. It is probable that the inn was conveyed in 1883 from the Gascoigne estate.
The Selby turnpike followed a section of the Great North Road prior to the turning to Monk Fryston. The junction of the Sherburn Road was dominated by limestone quarries and once had the "Pointer Inn" catering for the trade to the south and east. The inn is presumed to be older than the Boot and Shoe and is now being converted into offices for a large company: it ceased to be a public house in the 1930's and became Pointer Farm. The low building to the south of the old inn, complete with beer cellars, was for use of the coaches where there was suitable accomodation. At the end of the last century farmer Edward Hills was at "Pointer House Peckfield".
Peckfield Lodge was first built as a wooden framed dwelling in the late 17th. century and became a coaching house. It has been rebuilt and this century was the home of Henry Briggs, the local colliery owner. This old manor house was then the home of Mr. Longdon,who was the Micklefield Colliery Manager in the 1940's. In later years it became an antiques outlet and now is a private home. Lodge Farm was a part of the complex, existing as a separate establishment from the Lodge.
The Leeds/Selby Forte Post House Hotel opened on March 18th. 1968 as the Ross

Motorway Services. The company was bought by Imperial Leisure and Brewing Co. and renamed the Selby Fork Motel. It was later bought by Anchor Hotels & Taverns in the 1970's and then bought by Lord Hanson, who sold out to Trust House Forte. In 1986 the hotel became part of the Forte Group and now has 105 bedrooms with a capacity for 200 residents. The hotel stands in 16 acres of grounds with the Happy Eater opening in 1982 and replacing a motorway cafe, which burnt out. The exit from the hotel and cafe uses part of the old Selby Road route, changed in 1968 with the opening of the AI motorway. In May 1994 revised plans were announced for the upgrading of the Al between Ferrybridge and Hook Moor costing £96 million. The plans include an abandonment of the motorway junction near the Boot and Shoe Inn and a new junction created with the A63 at Selby Fork east of the present junction. Complete plans will become available in 1995.

Lumby Garden Centre opened in 1981 in the present format although there had been a roadside nursery from 1908. The adjacent Leys House was built in 1904 and extended in 1960, Lumby Leys Lane links the area with Ledsham. Lumby village is north of the Selby Road on Butts Lane - Rawfield Lane is the route south to Fairburn.

Lumby is a small farming and residential village known in the 10th. century as Lundby - meaning a copse or grove. Lumby Hall is west of the main street and was originally a 17th. century farmhouse called Butts Hall, now separated from the main block. The old house became servant's quarters and retains the bell which once summoned the coaches to the house from the nearby stables. The farm was built on the site of a monastic grange run by the monks of Roche Abbey ,a Cistercian monastery east of Rotherham.

The main part of the stone hall was built about 1720 and the Victorians added on the brick built west wing: there are large cellars beneath the hall and at one time an underground passage to the property on the east side of the main street. In the early 19th. century Lumby Hall became the home of the Gouthwaite family, who built the steward's house dated 1868 RG. This refers to Richard Gouthwaite,a land agent and surveyor: there is a stone inset to the garden wall inscribed "JG 1817" referring to John Gouthwaite. By the 1880's the hall was the property of the Addinell family and in October 1902 Lumby Hall was bought by the Castleford maltster Edward Michael Fawcett. In November 1911 Lumby Hall was sold to William Percy Cliff, the Micklefield Colliery proprietor for £5000. In November 1919 the Cliff family sold the hall and Christopher Cadman from Newcastle on Tyne obtained a mortgage on the property. In October 1923 Major Clifford Harrison Stringer of Barton Seagrave Hall Kettering purchased the property. In 1927 the property was conveyed to a group of prominent businessmen, who were to form a Trust. Initially they included the surgeon Sir Berkeley Moynihan, Sir Harold Macintosh of Knaresborough and Sir George Martin of Leeds. The Trust was created in March 1951 and a sum was

provided by the Yorkshire Council of the British Empire Cancer Campaign with Lumby Hall being a Leeds University Experimental Cancer Research Station with accomodation provided for the director and staff: these included Prof. Richard Passey and later Professor Green. In 1961 members of the Trust changed and Sir Linton Andrews and Leeds solicitor James Booth were appointed to the board.
In September 1968 the Trust auctioned the property at Monk Fryston Hall to carpet dealer Roger Fell of Castleford, who formed a new entrance to the south replacing the gate by the old house - the pillars are still to be seen. He also sold some land and the old stables in 1968 to an architect who designed the conversion. The hall was sold in 1986 to the present owner. There are a few old buildings in Lumby including Forge House the old forge is now in a state of decay - and Hall Cottage. Hall Farm House is 18th. century and is one of three farms remaining in Lumby Village. These are contrasted with the recent development of Lumby Court. The village inn was adjacent to the farm but closed many years ago.
A Methodist meeting was licensed in 1799 to be held in a farm house of the Webster family. Some land was bought and a new chapel opened in 1871 but services ceased in 1912. The property was sold for £25 by 1941 - permission to sell was obtained in 1925. The building became used for agricultural purposes and has been demolished to provide a site for new housing. The old Chapel dated stone has been built into the roadside wall.

Monk Fryston Lodge - Frystone Lodge in 1850 - is south of the main road and was once the home of the Hemsworth family of Monk Fryston Hall. It was probably designed by John Carr in the mid 18th. century. The Lodge is set in extensive grounds and there were two lodge houses on the Selby (demolished) and Ferrybridge roads. David Hemsworth lived at the Lodge in the 19th. century: he was the son of Benjamin Hemsworth Snr and Ann Hanson of Wakefield and he lived from 1772 until 1840. In the 1930's the Lodge was the home of Henry Metcalf with George Lamb at Lodge Farm. Monk Fryston Lodge was bought by the C.E.G.B. in 1964 and was used as offices of the National Grid Company (Yorkshire) until recently: the lodge houses are now derelict.
The small wooded quarry to the north prior to the junction was opened in 1906 to supply stone for the restoration of Selby Abbey.
The main road has a roundabout junction with the Doncaster /Ferrybridge/ Tadcaster 1741 turnpike coaching route. Passengers from Leeds would have had to ride horseback to York or Ferrybridge when joining the 1683 service to Doncaster and London. In 1706 a 4 day coaching service opened from York to London, stopping at the "Red Bear" inn at Sherburn in Elmet, Brotherton and the "Angel Inn" at Ferrybridge.
The approach to Monk Fryston passes the old limestone quarry, now a land infill site and crosses the main railway line.

THE ROAD FROM LEEDS TO SELBY

PART 4 MONK FRYSTON

The magnesian limestone of Monk Fryston has been quarried for many centuries providing vital building material, as seen in the villages today. In 1381 Abbot Shireburn of Selby Abbey opened a Monk Fryston quarry to provide stone in order to carry out repair work at the abbey. In 1906 after a disastrous fire at Selby Abbey, the stone came again from Monk Fryston given by Benjamin Hemsworth. The quarry later provided lime, freestone and alabaster - a form of gypsum - to be made into Plaster of Paris. The Hillam Gypsum Quarry, Brick and Plaster Works were on Betteras Hill Road and were served by a rail track to the main line loading sidings. The mineral is used today to make plasterboard at Sherburn in Elmet. There is another old quarry at Betteras Hill which is now a landfill site and there are numerous other sites in the area.
The railway station at Monk Fryston was on the York/Normanton branch line of the North Eastern Railway. In 1917 Henry Raine is recorded as being the station master. The station served the Monk Fryston Hall Zoo and many excursion trains stopped at this station which closed in the 1960's.
There are two ownerships indicated by the village name: Fryston refers to Fripe or Frithi, an old Danish name, while the suffix tells of the link with Selby Abbey. In 963AD the village was known as Fryssetune. There are some thoughts that Fryston is derived from "free stone" referring to the local quarries.
In the pre Conquest years Fryston belonged to the Archbishop of York's estate at Sherburn in Elmet. Archbishop Thomas of Bayeux granted Fryston to the monks of the Benedictine abbey at Selby a year after its foundation in 1069. It was not for many years that the village acquired the Monk addition.
The most historic building in Monk Fryston is St. Wilfrid's Church which was built on the site of a pre-Conquest structure, when there was only a simple nave and short chancel.

In the early 13th. century the nave of Monk Fryston Church had the addition of narrow aisles and access was achieved by piercing the nave walls with arches. The nave still shows parts of the first wall, although the original round chancel arch has been replaced. The present chancel dates mainly from the 13th. century and includes a south wall piscina. This was the basin used for washing the Mass or Communion vessels with a drain, so that the water could be passed onto the consecrated ground of the churchyard. The font could be pre-Conquest although many have dated it to the 13th. century - it was brought back into use again following the restoration in 1891. In the 14th. century the aisles were widened and walls strengthened by adding strong buttresses. A few years later the aisle windows were inserted and two squints or hagioscopes were made to allow better views from the aisles of the high altar when Mass was being celebrated. During the 15th. century the tower arch was inserted and the tower itself was made higher and strengthened. The church was dedicated on May 12th. 1444.

The church of Monk Fryston once had a close link with Wistow, for in the 13th. century the Archbishop of York divided the old prebend of Sherburn in Elmet into those of (Church) Fenton and Wistow, which included Monk Fryston, Hillam, Fairburn and Burton Salmon. This meant that a priest was appointed at Monk Fryston by the Prebendary of Wistow. Prebends were the shares of church revenues allowed to an officiating clergyman, the word deriving from Latin "praebenda" meaning an allowance. They were abolished temporarily in 1649 and reinstated after the Restoration in 1660. The manor of Monk Fryston remained with the Wistow prebendary until 1840 when it was transferred to the Ecclesiastical Commissioners. In 1888-89 the Commissioners sold the Prebendary House at Monk Fryston to William Bentley, who died soon afterwards. This house would have been the home of the prebendary of Wistow, when he was in need of such accommodation. It is south west of the church with the original building mentioned in 1302 and the present restored house, with a wall 7' thick, dated to about 1400.

In common with most other churches Monk Fryston had much Victorian restoration, with most of the cost being borne by Benjamin Hemsworth of Monk Fryston Hall. This benevolent landowner died in 1923 and was buried in the family plot in the new Monk Fryston cemetery. The architect of the restorations of 1889-91 was Robert James Johnson from Newcastle on Tyne.

Johnson's improvements at Monk Fryston included renewing all the furniture and the floor being lowered two feet thus allowing access by steps from the south door, the foundations of the pillars strengthened with concrete and squints opened out. The roofs were all renewed and the tower archway was unblocked. Following these extensive and expensive restorations the church was re-opened on April 29th. 1891 with a service sung by the choir of York Minster.

In Monk Fryston church there is the grave of Tobias Swinden, prebendary of Wistow who died in 1661. There is also the grave of the son of Nicholas Mauleverer who died in 1678. In the 15th. century the Mauleverer family lived at Wothersome. When Sir William Mauleverer died in 1551 he owned a number of manors including both Thorner and Wothersome near Bramham. The coat of arms of the family featured three greyhounds and is seen both on the Monk Fryston grave and on a shield on the side of an old barn at the present Wothersome Grange Farm.

There is at Monk Fryston Church a stone armorial shield of the Hamond family, who were in this area during the 14th. century. Anthony Hamond bought the manor of

Scarthingwell from Baldewin Yong in 1542 and when he died in 1563 he was buried at Saxton Church, where his memorial plaque states that he had departed from "this miserable world".
The wooden reredos was erected in 1909 as a thanksgiving for the recovery from illness of young John Fawcett. The Lady Chapel was dedicated in December 1969. There is a small memorial by the door to Jane Bentley, who was the servant to the Hemsworth family at the Hall for 17 years - she died in 1840. On the west wall of the church is a framed list of vicars which commence in 1490 - the first known vicar was James Claughton, who served from 1490 until 1520 and was buried in the churchyard. Fragments of the 14th. century glass were reinserted in the west aisle window in 1891 and at the same time the Hemsworth family gave the other glass to the church designed by Charles Eamer Kempe (1837-1907). A new church hall was opened on September 11th. 1970 by the Archbishop of York Donald Coggan.

Monk Fryston Hall stands in its own grounds to the north of the Leeds-Selby turnpike, the area being "enclosed" in 1792; the neighbouring village of Hillam was enclosed in 1811. The road makes two bends at this central point, where there is a thatched cottage and village post office. It is thought that the thatched cottage dates from the reign of King George II.
The Hall is reached by a short drive after passing through the lodge gates. The western front of this large mansion is late 16th.century, although the windows have all been renewed. It is likely that the buttressed south west corner of the hall is a survival from the monastic days. A house was known here from 1070 but about 1740 most of the original manor house was pulled down and the rest was restored by David Hemsworth.
The Hall was the home of the Hemsworth family whose motto was "Manus haec inimica tyrannis" and their family tree has been traced back to the pre-Conquest Danish Earl Thorgils Sprakaleg, who came over to this country in 1014. The framed family tree was made in 1877 as a pedigree of Benjamin Hemsworth and is now on display inside the hall. After the Norman Conquest Siward became the Lord of Hemsworth holding this from Ilbert de Lacy of Pontefract Castle.
The family settled at Hemsworth and went to live at Swillington in 1487: they were Lords of Swillington Manor. The family then moved to Garforth and in 1562 were Lords of the Manor in that area. In 1649 Gabriel Hemsworth was a major in Charles 1st's Royalist army and was present at the siege of Pontefract Castle. There have been bullets found in the roof of Monk Fryston Hall having been fired by Cromwell's soldiers when passing through the village.
It was Gabriel's great-grandson David Hemsworth (1710-1788) who lived at Monk Fryston Hall; his father had bought the property in 1680. He was the son of David and Martha Hemsworth of Potter Newton near Leeds and he married Dorothy Sarah

Hudson from Stanley near Wakefield, whose family came from Hatfield Hall. Their son Benjamin (1747-1819) married Ann Hanson of Wakefield and son David Hemsworth (1772-1840) married Sarah Wild. Their son was Benjamin Hemsworth JP who was born in 1816 and died in 1886 aged 69. Daughter Mary Louisa Woodall died in 1913 aged 60. Benjamin's brother David was born in 1811 and died on July lst. 1866. In 1873 the wall, gates and railings of Monk Fryston cemetery east of the village were erected by Benjamin in memory of his brother. He married Elizabeth Bower and their son - another Benjamin - was born in 1848 and became the squire of Monk Fryston. He married Mary Constance Duke of Lake House Wiltshire on September 5th. 1894. He died in 1923 at the age of 75 having been the churchwarden of Monk Fryston for 30 years as a church wall memorial indicates. In the family plot at Monk Fryston are also buried Rev. Rashleigh Edward Hungerford Duke who died aged 75 in 1926 and Michael Duke died 1928 age 37. The date 1897 appears on a fallpipe at the Hall showing later restoration. When Rev. Benjamin died in 1923 death duties were so high that his widow could not continue with the pleasure park. When she died in 1940 the estate was left to a nephew who was killed in the War and in 1946 the properties were sold at auction. It was bought by S. W. Tinsdale a Yorkshire hotelier, who converted the hall into an hotel which he opened a year later. In 1954 the 34 year old Duke of Rutland bought the hall and took over the management in March of that year. A new wing was added in 1968 at a cost of £70,000 and this was opened by the Duke and Duchess of Rutland in September. The architect for this new wing was B. J. Minton of Nottingham and another extension was added in 1986. The Duke of Rutland estates also have Belvoir Castle, Izaak Walton Hotel Dovedale and Haddon Hall Derbyshire.
Over the old open fireplace in the Hall is the inscription "Far from Court - Far from Care". There is an ingle nook, an old creaking rocking chair coupled with fine food and service in this important historic mansion.
The 66 acres of grounds that surround the old Benedictine manor house of Monk Fryston feature an Italianate garden complete with lake - an extension of the monk's fish pond - and woodland walk. When it was the home of the Rev. Benjamin Hemsworth in the early years of this century it became known as one of the showplaces of the North. There was a large private zoo, which was open occasionally to the public including specimens of macaw, cockatoo, pheasants from China and a Golden Eagle - an aviary is all that remains of this venture. There were monkeys, baboons, fruit eating bats, opossums, mongoose, wallabies and armadillos together with chameleons and lizards. Boating was allowed on the lake, which has a replica of the recently fire damaged covered bridge in Lucerne, Switzerland. The paintings illustrate "The Ancient Mariner" and were the work of the Rev. Benjamin Hemsworth's wife Mary.
Although Benjamin was received into holy orders in 1875 he never held a church

living, although he was a curate at Halifax. When he opened his estate to the public, he was seen greeting the crowds dressed in clerical attire, spending most of his life at Monk Fryston Hall. His brother John David Hemsworth was three years his junior and was accepted by the Inner Temple in 1871 - he died in 1895 aged 44.

During the occupation of the Hemsworths there was a maze, a covered swimming pool of which only the filled in site and a few white tiles remain, cricket pitch, concert hall, fives court and alpine hall decorated with large paintings. There was a Scottish mountain ravine in an old quarry which is near the South Milford road junction and is now the site of newly built housing and in the orchard was a small lake with a waterfall which could be controlled. The ravine included large paintings by Mary Hemsworth and there are two smaller framed pictures by this lady in the church vestry - they depict the church and the prebendal house in their earlier days.

The Manor House stands adjacent to the main road and is complete with "1655 TC" on the lintel: it was a cafe in the early part of this century.

The school was founded on the Hillam road in 1857 by Benjamin Hemsworth and was built from high grade local limestone - the parish school dated from 1810.

On the same road stands the restored Methodist Chapel built in 1845 in hexagonal style, although it was squared off at one end in 1875. It was enlarged in 1876 at a cost of £600 and a schoolroom was added. Methodism had been active in the village from 1808 meeting in houses. Services were held in the schoolroom in the 1970's as the chapel decor was deteriorating. The Methodist congregation hold their services now in Monk Fryston Church hall. Along Old Vicarage Lane is the one time brick built home of the vicar, who now resides in Hillam.

There were at one time three inns in the village, although the "The Chequers" has now been converted. It is likely that the oldest of the two remaining turnpike inns is "The Crown" - at one time serving the traffic to Selby and Leeds. The "Blue Bell" inn had also stable accomodation and in 1838 the landlady was Grace Ramsden. At this time Joseph Fox was at "The Crown" and Ann Baxter at "The Chequers". The inns served at least four coach services on the turnpike: The "Accomodation" started in 1835 by John Turner of Selby using only one horse; the "Aire & Calder" from 1824 by John Hogg from The Rose & Crown inn at Leeds; The "Ebor" from 1843 from Leeds to connect with the steam packets and the "Union" started in 1823 daily through Garforth and Hambleton.

Monk Fryston was also complete with a reading room, institute and library - all supported by Benjamin Hemsworth! There were also at one time three mills in the village, the largest being at Mill Close, which had top and sails removed in 1922 and was demolished in 1953.

THE ROAD FROM LEEDS TO SELBY

PART 5 MONK FRYSTON TO SELBY

Hillam is a small village south of Monk Fryston, along the lane past both Methodist Chapel and School. The "Cross Keys" inn is at the village centre close by Hillam Hall. The Hall was remodelled from an older house and the two wings bear the dates of 1827 and 1875. The Hall was the property of Daniel Burton Mouncey in the mid-19th.century who married Mary Margaret Hemsworth, daughter of David Hemsworth of Monk Fryston Lodge. Mary died aged 82 in 1883. Although Daniel Mouncey was an Anglican he helped to build the new Methodist Chapel in 1846. The first Wesleyan Chapel at Hillam in 1816 became a joiner's shop. The new chapel closed in 1969 and was demolished in 1979 to allow for the extension to Kendal Cottage.

Hillam Hall has 19th. century stables and is now two separate dwellings. Henry Close rented the hall in the 1890's and Arthur Kirkness lived at the Hall in the early part of this century. In the 1930's the Hall had become the home of Harry Lyon JP. The Lyon family were shipbuilders of Knottingley and specialised in building barges. When Mrs. L. M. Lyon died her daughter Mrs. Bailey lived at the hall. The Hall was sold at an auction held on the premises on November 20th.1973 and the main hall was divided into two dwellings. The large stone built dog kennel by Coade and Sealy was also a feature of Hillam Hall but was sold. The west wing of the Hall was again sold in 1988 and the coach house was converted into a dwelling.

Rose Lea was run as a Ladies School by Fanny Mary Fox who died in 1935. The next owner was Mary Powell who retired in 1949. The school opened with six girls, initially to pay off her father's debts. The school closed in October 1961 with nearly 100 day and boarders, when the Meredith family, who were the new owners, went bankrupt. The premises facing the village centre have been converted into separate dwellings.

The Lord of the Manor of Hillam was once the Earl of Londesborough and the village possessed 12 farms. The few farms remaining today are owner-occupied. Hall Farm dates from the 18th. century, while nearby Chantries Cottage on Tom Lane was once an ale house and is probably one of the oldest houses in the village.

Hambleton was known as Hameltun in 1086 and refers to Hamela's village: after the Norman Conquest it was the property of the de Lacy family of Pontefract. The village was the scene of a Manorial Court and was where the tenants of the Selby Abbey lands worked their Penny Farms.

The last toll bar before Selby was at Hambleton and the barhouse was on the south side of the main road on the site of Bar Lane. In the 1830's the toll collector was

George Seymour. There was a chantry chapel at Hambleton mentioned in 1292 "the chapel of Hamelton ordain a chantry for ever to remain dedicated to the honour of the Blessed Virgin Mary". In 1536 there is also mentioned "a chantry of Our Lady at Hambleton," although the site of this chapel in unknown. The first priest was apppointed in 1292 and in February 1539 was suppressed by order of the King.
The new church of St. Mary Hambleton had the foundation stone laid on August 4th. 1881 and the church was consecrated on April 22nd. 1882 by the Archbishop of York. Prior to this church being built, Hambleton folk worshipped at St.Wilfrid's Church Brayton and at Gateforth Church from 1825.
There is an Oak pulpit within Hambleton Church whose bells were restored in 1982. There is a memorial to the organist and schoolmaster Matthew Cargill who died in 1917, having served the church from its opening. The organ was installed in March 1885 and was a gift of the Smith family of Hambleton House. The family is remembered in the west stained glass window to William Thomas Smith (January 10th 1810 - December 18th. 1882), whose memory is also remembered by the east window in the south chapel at Brayton Church. George H. Smith who died in 1925 aged 69 and Joseph Smith (died 1933) are buried in Hambleton Cemetery, together with Henrietta (died 1935) and Richard (died 1939).
On July 15th.1915 the church of St. Mary Hambleton became the parish church, thus replacing St. Mary's Church Gateforth, which was demolished in 1948.
Most folk at Hambleton worked on the many farms of the village - there were 14 in the early 1900's - and in Anson's Jam Factory on Station Road. The factory was burnt down in 1959 and is now the site of Campey's stores - Harry Campey died in 1970. The Anson family were at one time the largest employer in Hambleton, the family having two farms which grew much fruit that was used at the factory. The Ansons lived at the Manor House and were the first churchwardens of Hambleton.
The School-Church was dedicated in 1872 and was opened as a school in September 1872. Land had been donated for the building by the main landowner William Henry Denison Lord Londesborough. When the old school closed in 1973 the building became the Parish Hall and the new C. of E. Controlled School opened on Gateforth Lane. The school master's house belonged to the church and was sold in the late 1960's.
The Wesleyans built their chapel at Hambleton in 1816 and it was rebuilt in 1841. It contained a monument to Thomas Wade of Hambleton (1803-1862), a farmer's son who became a preacher. The chapel was again rebuilt in 1899/1900.
Owlet Hall, north west of Hambleton was used as a Medieval hunting lodge, while the old Hambleton Post Office dates from 1655: it was a PO from 1845. Hambleton railway station closed some years ago and the high speed line is now open between Hambleton and Thorpe Willoughby.
The two inns are the "Red Lion" and the "Wheatsheaf" and in the mid-19th. century

an alehouse was also trading. Hambleton corn windmill was on Mill Lane run by the Palframan family but it was demolished. The large parsonage on Gateforth Lane was provided in 1834 by Theodosia Brooke.
In the 1880's Lord Londesborough had become Lord of the Manor and one of the main landowners at Hambleton was William Thomas Smith JP of Hambleton House. The Smith family had built the House in 1801 and it was the home of Samuel Smith (died 1847 aged 81) and his wife Margaret (died 1840 aged 61). Their son was Samuel Wild Smith who died only 7 years old in 1813. William T. Smith had four daughters: Mary Veitch, Martha Kayll, Caroline Todd and the unmarried Ellen Smith, who died in 1932 aged 76.
The House was sold and became a roadhouse in the 1930's. Other owners included the Gill family, who had a ragmill at Selby and Scarths, cornmerchants. It later became a Country Club with major extensions. Having been used as an officer's mess during the last War it is now The Owl Hotel and Restaurant. The Hotel has a function room, conference facilities and nine bedrooms, in the ownership of the Widdop family from 1985.

South of Hambleton is Gateforth with an impressive Hall, now a Hotel. The village had a chantry chapel endowed in 1332 and on September 5th. 1825 the Gateforth Chapel of Ease to Brayton was consecrated, the costs being paid by Humphrey Osbaldeston, the owner of Gateforth Hall. The church was built close to the Hall on the slopes of Hambleton Hough at a cost of £5000 using Monk Fryston limestone. The church was left to decay when Gateforth Hall became a Sanatorium under Leeds Corporation. Prior to demolition many of the church contents went to Leeds Corporation with the organ to St. James Hospital and barrel organ to Leeds Museum. The site is now marked by a limestone plaque set into a ivy covered brick structure, inscribed with the members of the Osbaldeston family in the vault beneath: Church Lodge is the dwelling close by.
Gateforth Hall was built by Humphrey Brooke Osbaldeston in 1811/12 as a hunting lodge to his main residence of Hunmanby Hall near Filey. The limestone frontage of the brick built Hall was brought from Monk Fryston by cart. Humphrey was born in 1745 and became Sheriff of Yorkshire, he succeeded to the Hunmanby estate in 1770 under the will of his uncle Fountayne Wentworth Osbaldeston and assumed the Osbaldeston name. He married Catherine Pennington in 1772 and had two daughters Catherine and Theodosia. Catherine married and her daughter was Jane who married Richard Brooke. Theodosia inherited the Gateforth property on the death of her father but she died unmarried in 1851. Humphrey Osbaldeston died aged 90 in 1835 and was buried in the family vault in Gateforth Church. The vault was sealed in 1948 following the demolition of the church.
Jane, daughter of Lt. Col. Hutchinson of Wold Newton, married the Rev. Richard

Brooke in 1836 - he changed his name from Robson to Brooke on marriage. Richard was a magistrate and Lord of Askern Manor and was the great nephew of Humphrey Osbaldeston of Hunmanby and Gateforth and succeeded to the Brayton estates in 1850 - he died on June lst. 1871 aged 71. His wife was the grand daughter of Humphrey Osbaldeston and she died aged 77 in 1873: she left the "Gateforth Charity" and her tomb in Brayton churchyard describes the sums she left to various Yorkshire beneficiaries. There were donations to the Leeds General Infirmary of £30,000 and the same amount to the Royal Albert Asylum Lancaster; Cookridge Convalescent Home Leeds, York County Hospital, Christian Knowledge Society and the British & Foreign Bible Society received donations. There were legacies to the living at Gateforth and the poor of Brayton and Gateforth; to the living at Askern and to the founding of a Medical Dispensary for medecines and surgery for the poor of Selby. The Osbaldeston estates passed to Bertram Mitford who assumed the added Osbaldeston name and he was succeeded by his brother Robert Mitford RN. The heir was Humphrey Brooke Firman who died aged 34 in 1868.
It was Mary, the daughter of Sir Richard Osbaldeston of Hunmanby who had married Robert Mitford in the 17th. century. Their daughter was Philadelphia who married Rev. John Wickens and from this line was Squire George Osbaldeston (1786-1866) who lived at Hutton Buscel and Ebberston. His life was devoted to "pleasure" and in 1831 won a record for riding 200 miles on horseback in under 10 hours. This record was broken in 1993 by jockey Peter Scudamore. When the Squire died he was buried in Highgate Cemetery London.

Gateforth Hall was auctioned in 1896 when it was an estate of 2005 acres with 70 acres around the Hall and was bought in 1900 by Leeds Corporation for £85,635 to be used as a sewage treatment site. This was not carried out and during the First World War the Hall was used by the military - and it became a Sanatorium for TB patients and Convalescent Home belonging to the Health Authority. The Leeds TB Association held 21 acres of land at Gateforth. In 1920 the City Council sold a section of the Gateforth estate including 10 farms and 15 cottages: they retained the hall, gardens and parkland. The Hall became a Maternity Home until 1979 and was sold by Lane Fox & Co in January 1981 - at this time there were only 11 acres with the main Hall, three lodges, coach house, farm, a walled kitchen garden and a paddock. Gateforth Hall Hotel opened in 1981 with ten bedrooms and has good conference facilities. The property surrounding the Hall was developed into dwellings and new houses have been built on the land. There is a private road that links the properties on Hambleton Hough.

Thorp Willoughby derives the name from a thorp or farmstead with a 13th. century link with the Wilgheby family. In 1303 the village was known as Thorp Wyleby.

The Selby monks had their water mills, which caused land flooding, especially severe on Robert Wilgheby's lands. The ensuing dispute was settled with the monks granting Robert the enclosure of Thorp Park and Hall. The old hall was moated and developed, although returned to the monks by Robert's son. The mansion of Thorp Hall is north of Selby Dam and main village and was rebuilt in 1830. The present owner's son is TV presenter Barry Chambers, who was born at Thorp Hall.
Thorp Hall on Dam Lane also became the first meeting place of the local Methodists from 1818 until 1830, when the meetings took place in a farmhouse. In 1869 a chapel was built at Thorp Willoughby.
Thorp Willoughby has a new Primary School and a shared Anglican/ Methodist Church dedicated to St. Francis of Assisi. The new church was consecrated on September 30th. 1978 by the Bishop of Selby and the Chairman of the Methodist District.
The "Fox" inn once had a change of name to the "Londesborough Arms", after the new Lord of the Manor Rt. Hon.William Henry Forester Denison. The 1st. Lord Londesborough became Lord of the Manor in 1854 having purchased it from the Hon. Mrs. Petre. The Petre family took the title when Robert 7th. Lord Petre of Writtle married the daughter of Bartholomew Walmsley in 1711. In 1877 William Morley was the landlord of the Londesborough with Louis Ogley following by 1936.

Brayton is south of the Leeds/Selby turnpike road and is on the Doncaster/Selby turnpike with the junction of the two roads at Gowthorpe. Brayton toll bar was at Baffam Lane end and the old toll bar house is now a private cottage called "Bar House". Elias Senior was the toll collector in 1838.
Brayton was mentioned in the Domesday Book as Bretone meaning a broad farmstead and was part of the de Lacy lands. The district around Brayton was marshland and forest and communities became established on land reclaimed by the earlier Danes and Saxons. Although there is no evidence of a Saxon church at Brayton, there would probably have been a wooden building on the present site of St.Wilfrid's Church.
The present church was built in the 12th. century and modified in both the 14th. and 15th. centuries. The Normans would have used Monk Fryston stone taken along the Selby Dam to the church between 1100 and 1160. The original Norman phase included the west tower - without octagon and spire - an aisleless nave, south door, a short chancel with a wide arch and a short sanctuary. The south doorway is a good example of Norman architecture and shows beak heads together with human and animal figures with an inner order of zig-zag.
The 14th. century Decorated phase of Brayton Church covers the period, of the Black Death (1348-1350), which decimated the population: some villages ceased to exist. The chancel was remodelled and enlarged, aisles added and nave roof raised.

Between 1377 and 1547 the Perpendicular phase added the tower octagon and spire with alteration to the windows. The tomb of George Lord Darcy and Dorothy his wife dated 1558 is in the south chancel and is surrounded by coats of arms. He was the son of Thomas Lord Darcy who was beheaded on Tower Hill for his part in the Pilgrimage of Grace.
During the Reformation Brayton Church lost its stained glass, use of the side aisles and rood screen. A major restoration of the church was carried out between 1877 and 1878 at a cost of £2577. The reredos was given in memory of Mary Ann Elston, wife of William Elston of Bank House Selby.
On the chancel floor are the inscribed grave slabs to members of the Brooke family of Gateforth. Humphrey Brooke was the son of Humphrey of Gateforth and he died in 1688 aged 29; Gabriel Brooke died in 1797 age 71 and Theodosia his wife died July 1758 aged 38. Gabriel was descended from Humphrey Brooke of London who bought the Manor of Gateforth from Henry Lord Darcy and George his brother in 1564. There is another slab to Calisthenes Brooke and his wife Frances. She died aged 73 in 1737 and the slab also remembers Humphrey Brooke, son of Calisthenes who died aged 58 in 1754. Their family crest is shown on the slab together with their motto "Non Est Mortale Quod Opto".
The village of Brayton straddles the main turnpike road and both the "Swan" and "Grey Horse" inns are at the cross roads. In the 1830's the innkeeper at the Swan was John Settrington and at the Grey Horse was George Ream who was also the local shoemaker.
The village school was built in 1872 with the schoolmaster's house and has been supplemented with a recent Infant and Junior Schools to the east of the older building. The master in 1877 was Frederick Mould in 1881 and Robert Groves in the 1920's he died in 1924. In front of the school is the village green, which once had a pinfold and was the scene of Brayton Feast around the village pond.
Brayton Hall was the home of the Farrand family: John Farrand died aged 26 in 1825 and was buried at Brayton Church. William and John Farrand were at the hall in later years.
The domed building on the south of Brayton Barff is the Selby Water Works opened in April 1908: two boreholes were sunk to 400' to supply a resevoir with a capacity of 800,000 gallons. Brayton Barff is a natural hill rising to about 180' and the 80 acres support a mature Oak woodland. There is a good network of footpaths having good views from the top. A "barff" is an ancient British name for a barrow or burial place.

The first house on the north side of main road entering Selby is "Dial House" and the toll bar was at Gowthorpe. Selby High School occupies the Grade II listed Georgian Gowthorpe Lodge. It was founded as the Girl's Grammar School in 1908 and in

1968 it became a co-educational Grammar School and in 1979 became a 6 form entry Comprehensive High School.
St. Mary's Catholic Church is north of the main road and was opened in 1854/56 by the Hon. Mrs. Petre in memory of her husband. The new church was designed by Joseph Hansom (1803-1882), who designed St. Edward's Church at Clifford in 1845 and the Hansom Cab in 1834. The church replaced the first St. Mary's on its corner site, having been built in 1837 and becoming too small to accomodate the large number of Irish immigrants escaping the famine. The old church, extended in 1913, became a Primary School until 1977 when the new school opened on Doncaster Road. The building is now used as a Parish Hall and for the Employment Training Project which was started in 1980/81 by the Council for Churches.
Inside the new St. Mary's Church is the pulpit by a French carver as the First World War memorial, depicting scenes of the triumph of good over evil: St. George and the Dragon and Joan of Arc. The west end of the church has a replica of the Grotto at Lourdes: built in the 1920's as a reminder of Selby being the start of the Leeds Diocesan Pilgrimage to Lourdes.
In 1858 a peasant girl Bernadette claimed to have experienced visions of the Virgin Mary, besides a spring, which became credited with miraculous healing powers. An underground church was consecrated in 1958 to hold 20,000 people.
The road junction by St. Mary's Hall is the site of the Primitive Methodist Chapel opened in 1862. The chapel closed in 1956 and was used for commercial purposes.
The Methodist Chapel was on the south east corner of the Market Place. It was built in 1882 and demolished in 1983 for a shopping complex.
The impressive St. James Church is south of the road and was built by James Audus JP in 1886/87. On May 10th. 1944 an RAF Halifax Bomber on a training flight from Rufforth crashed into the spire of the church. The midnight tragedy claimed the lives of eight civilians, adults and children, and the seven man crew: five Australians and two British men aged 20 and 25. The plane crashed in flames onto the streets and nearby housing in which a baby was being born - Ann Field who now lives in Normanby Middlesborough. The church spire was reputed to be the highest in the county and it was replaced by a tower.
The Market Cross stands in the Market Place and was erected by Robert Edward 10th. Baron Petre in 1775. The weekly market is held on Mondays.

Selby is derived from Sele-by meaning a town with a willow copse and the willows are still grown today along the river banks.
Selby Abbey was founded by Benedict a monk from Auxerre Abbey: he arrived in Selby in 1069 following a vision he had in the Abbey, in which St. Germain gave him instructions to found an abbey at Selby.
Selby Abbey is dedicated to our Lord, St. Mary and St. Germain, a 5th. century

French nobleman-soldier who became Bishop of Auxerre. Benedict arrived with a dried finger of St. Germain and he knew the site from his vision, in which three swans landed on water (River Ouse). These swans appear today on the Selby Abbey coat of arms.
Benedict set up a wooden cross near the place where it was assumed that Matilda, William the Conqueror's wife gave birth to their first English born son later Henry 1st. In 1070 William granted the land at Selby to Benedict, who was made the first Abbot of Selby. The Abbey followed the rule of St. Benedict, the founder of Cistercian monasticism - St. Benedict died in 544AD. When Hugh from Durham took over as the Abbot of Selby, a decision was made to rebuild on a different site the original wooden abbey in stone from Monk Fryston. The stones would have been taken to Selby partly by means of a specially constructed eight mile long canal from Monk Fryston. In later years transport was by the Selby Dam (Mill Pond) from Hambleton and by the Hambleton Causeway, which only exists today as a land drain. The Mill Pond was built to store sufficient water to turn four mills in Selby. There were also mills at Brayton, Thorp and Monk Fryston.
Selby Abbey was completed in about 130 years and abbey life flourished with income from benefactors and the developing wool trade. Income included tolls from the ferry crossings and from house rents.
In 1539 Selby Abbey was dissolved and the last Abbot received an annual pension. Land was confiscated and many of the buildings became ruinous. In 1618 the abbey became Selby's Parish Church. In March 1690 part of the tower collapsed together with part of the choir and south transept areas. The damaged section was bricked off and worship continued in the choir, while the nave became a market storehouse. Restoration was completed under the direction of Sir Giles Gilbert Scott in 1871.
In the early hours of October 19th. 1906 disaster struck the Abbey when flames were seen coming from the windows and roof. Three fire brigades were in attendance from Selby, York and Leeds. A restoration fund was started and the architect John Olrid Scott was appointed: stone was obtained from Monk Fryston. The nave was re-dedicated in 1907 and two years later the tower and transepts were restored. In 1935 further restoration was completed under Charles Marriot Olrid Scott and in 1973 exterior cleaning was accomplished. Following an appeal the interior was cleaned and restored.
In 1969 HM The Queen handed out the annual Maundy Money in Selby Abbey and in 1976 HM Queen Elizabeth the Queen Mother attended a Thanksgiving for the completion of the Restoration. The west doorway is Norman and the eight round Norman arches on tall massive pillars are based upon those of Durham Cathedral. The second pillar from the east on the south side is called Abbot Hugh's Pillar and is a copy of one at Durham. The 14th. century east window or Jesse Window survived not only the great fire but also occupation by Cromwell's soldiers in 1643.

A window high up in the choir is the Washington Window: this 14th. century window displays the shield of the Washington family - three red stars above two bands - and became the model for the American flag the "Stars and Stripes".

Selby Abbey

At the north east corner of the aisle is Lord Darcy's tomb beneath the window which commemorates the Abbey's first abbot. John Lord Darcy died at Temple Hirst in 1411 and was the ancestor of Lord Darcy of Temple Newsam who was beheaded for his part in opposing King Henry VIII. Lord Darcy was the Abbey's High Steward and supervised the North on the King's behalf. The tomb of Hugh de Pickworth is found in the nave: he fought for King Edward IInd in Scotland and later served in his parliament. There are memorials to James Audus JP and Selby's Abbots John Barwick, Lawrence Selby and John de Shireburn.

Many of the Abbey's outbuildings have not survived including the great gateway, demolished in 1806 and which once faced the Londesborough Arms Hotel. All that remains of the huge tithe barn is part of a wall now built into an inn.

Selby is placed on turnpikes from Doncaster, created by a turnpike act of 1832 and Leeds, with onward roads to Hull, Beverley, York, Snaith and Tadcaster. The town has connections with the Aire & Calder Canal by the 5 mile Selby Canal from Haddlesey, proposed by John Smeaton. This canal opened in April 1778 and cost £20,000, although the original idea was to cut a 23½ mile long canal from Leeds to Selby adapting the course of Selby Dam for part of its route.

The crossing of the River Ouse was by ferry initially until the first bridge opened in 1791, paying tolls as compensation for the ferry owners. Tolls were removed on Thursday September 19th.1991.

Connections by rail started in 1834 with the opening of the line from Leeds, terminating at Selby station which was east of the present one. The line opened to Hull in 1840 using a river bridge, replaced in 1891. The York-Doncaster line via Selby opened in 1871 and a short branch line to Cawood opened in 1898 but closed in 1960; the Goole line opened in 1910 but closed in 1964.

THE ROAD FROM LEEDS TO WETHERBY

PART 1: SHEEPSCAR TO OAKWOOD CLOCK

The junction of Roundhay Road and Chapeltown Roads was also the separation of two turnpike roads to Harrogate and Roundhay. The Leeds/Harrogate turnpike dated from 1751/52 with the first toll bar on North Street. The second toll bar on the site of the old fire station/police station/library, served as the first payment for the Roundhay turnpike. The toll house was five sided and stone built. The Leeds/Roundhay turnpike was made in 1807/08: the route from Church Bar near St.John's Church Roundhay to Collingham was given the Royal Assent on May 28th. 1824. The tolls were removed on the Leeds/Roundhay turnpike in January 1867 at the same time as the removal of tolls on the Leeds/Harrogate turnpike. The last toll was removed from roads in the borough of Leeds in 1870. In July 1865 the Locomotives and Highways Act in Britain introduced a speed limit for road vehicles of 4mph in the country and 2mph in the towns.

Sheepscar Police Station opened in 1872 as the Divisional Headquarters. It was closed in 1930 and the HQ was moved to Chapeltown. The old station was sold in 1931 to the City Libraries Committee, who demolished the building. The foundation stone for the new library was laid on October 29th. 1936 by Councillor Eric Bullus, Chairman of the Libraries & Arts Committee: the architect was F.L.Charlton. The library was officially opened on April 26th. 1938 by Lord Mayor Ald. John Badley JP. The Leeds Central Lending Library opened in 1872 following the adoption of the Public Libraries Act in 1869.

The library became the home of the Archive Service in 1965, having been established in Leeds Reference Library in 1938: it became a part of the WYAS in 1982 and holds collections for Craven, Ripon, Harrogate and the whole of West Yorkshire. The records of Leeds Corporation form the backbone of the collections, with the archives of the Diocese of Ripon. The archives hold collections from businesses, social and cultural bodies together with family and estate records.

The area surrounding the Archives and old Post Office - now the home of the Ramgarhia Board - was altered in 1982/1983 with the opening of the Sheepscar Interchange in June 1983, which necessitated much demolition.

The Sheepscar Beck was once a navigable waterway from the River Aire and under Timble Bridge east of the Leeds Parish Church. Sheepscar Beck or Meanwood Beck accepts the waters from Gipton Beck, which is mainly enclosed in a pipe today: it flows by the old Gaiety Cinema/Public House.

The 19th. century "Victoria" public house is on the south side of the start of Roundhay Road: John Buck retailed beer and wine from the premises at the start of this century, followed by Lawrence Swallow in 1916.

The houses and streets between Roscoe Street and Boundary Place have been demolished to be developed partly as the new £2.5 million Thomas Danby College which opened in September 1977, transferring from premises on Sweet Street. The college opened in the old Little Holbeck School, which was built by John Marshall of Marshall's Mills for the education of his worker's children. The Leeds School Board bought the school in 1880 which closed in the 1930's. In the Second World War it became the Gas Board Offices and from the 1960's became the Thomas Danby College.
Work on the new building started in June 1973 and suffered some delays. It is the only College-based provider in Leeds of programmes in food, child care, hairdressing and beauty therapy. The college is named after the first Mayor of Leeds following the granting of a new charter by King Charles 2nd. in 1661. Thomas Danby was appointed on November 2nd 1661 and his crest featured three silver stars, which became part of the Leeds Coat of Arms.
The Roundhay Road branch of the Leeds Co-op opened between Preston Place and Terrace in August 1879: the foundation stone had been laid on January llth. by John Teasdill.
The "Prince Arthur" public house stands between Boundary Place and Street and once was a coaching house with stables and a brewhouse. Licencees included Joseph Fenwick in 1900 with Arthur Biggins and William Coates in later years. Prince Arthur was the Duke of Connaught and the second son of Queen Victoria: he came to Leeds in September 1872 to open Roundhay Park. The inn was conveyed in September 1926 by Elizabeth Sanderson to the Leeds City Brewery. The Prince Arthur became a Tetley's public house on February 12th. 1964.
The south side of Roundhay Road from Manor Street to Grant Avenue has been demolished. The shops once included the Singer Sewing Machine Co. Ltd. in the premises that once belonged to Thomas Flinton cycle agent and John Crockatt Ltd dyers. Isaac Merrit Singer (1811-1875) invented a sewing machine and patented the design in 1851. The company became the largest sewing machine manufacturer in the world, having entered the international market in 1855 with a first prize at the Paris World Fair. In 1910 the company started the mass production of electric domestic sewing machines: in 1970/80 the Singer Company started the manufacture of aerospace electronics. In 1986 the company spun off its sewing machine section to SSMC International. The Singer Company now makes flight simulators, navigation, defence and surveillance systems for the American Government.
The "Queen" public house was between Roundhay Street and Queen's Terrace and run by James Connell in the 1860's and then by the Wood and Grant families for many years.
The Roundhay Road Council School occupied the land between Enfield and Grant Streets. The school opened on November 25th. 1878 designed by R. L. Adams: by

1900 the school had 700 boys and girls with nearly 300 infants. The school closed and was demolished: the site is now a warehouse. Adams was appointed as architect to the Leeds School Board in 1873. The area now has the Albion House premises of Firth, Ray & Prosser and the Chel Centre - funded by the Government's Inner City Task Force and with private sponsorship through British Telecom.
Barrack Road is named after the extensive Cavalry and Infantry Barracks which were built in 1820 at a cost of £28,000 and covered 11 acres. There were soldier's quarters, officer's accommodation, canteen, stables, hospital and infirmary stables and a riding school. At one period the barracks would have looked over the Rosebud Gardens to the south.
The Leeds Rifles met at the old riding school and parade ground for 80 years before being transferred to Harewood Barracks in 1967. The Barracks were finally demolished in 1988: the car showrooms and garage of Reg Vardy opened in January 1995 following the takeover of PK Motors Street Lane by the Sunderland firm in June 1994. The Street Lane site was demolished and developed as a public house.
The large building on the corner of Barrack Road and Roundhay Road was built in 1925 as the Leeds Incorporated Institution for the Blind, Deaf and Dumb. It used a part of the barracks site, which the council bought for £16,000 and occupied 4 acres out of the 12 acres obtained. The architect was Frederick Broadbent and his designs included a warehouse, library, gymnasium and workshops to the rear of the courtyard. The development also included a new road through the estate. It is now the Leeds Social Services Department Roundhay Road Office and Leeds Equipment Service with the Roseville Enterprises in the courtyard. The Clifford Brooke Day Centre opened in 1966 on Barrack Road.
The development of Spencer Place was the grand plan in the creation of New Leeds in 1825. The development was bounded by Cowper Street, Spencer Place and Roundhay Road: it was once the area with the old farmstead of Squire's Pasture.
The new development was the inspiration of absentee landlord Peter 5th. Earl Cowper, who lived in Hertfordshire. A partnership paid Cowper £29,860 for 55 lots in Leeds New Town but was bankrupt by 1828. The Earl bought the empty lots back for £20,000 and his family Christian names Leopold, Reginald, Louis and Francis are remembered in the streets - Edward Spencer Cowper born in 1779 was his brother. There were only a few houses built on the estate by 1847 but some of the villas are still to be admired: these include Cowper Villa, Spencer House and Newton House, a Grade II listed building for the professional class. The sales of the land were dealt with by both the 6th. and 7th. Earl Cowper and were completed by 1873. In the 1930's Spencer Place was the home of Dr. Herbert Roper, Dr. James Gourlay and Dr. John Coleman.
Plans were announced in June 1994 for the Moslem community to build a £1 million community mosque: it would replace the overcrowded Islamic Centre and Leeds

Jamia Mosque. The new Mosque is to be built in Spencer Place for the city's 30,000 Muslims and will include a new prayer hall to accommodate 1000 people, library and senior citizens day room.
The building at the corner of Gledhow Road and Roundhay Road was the Yorkshire Penny Bank from December 10th. 1927 until July 1936. The opening hours were 10am to 3pm weekdays except Wednesday when the opening was from 10am to 12.30pm: the bank was open on Saturdays from 10am to lpm and from 6pm to 8pm. The bank buildings are now occupied by a firm of solicitors.
The United Methodist Free Church on Gathorne Terrace had the foundation stone laid on July 13th. 1878 and it was opened in May 1879 at a cost of £5000 with D. Dodgson as the architect. The building was built in the Italianate style with a frontage of pillars. All that remains of this church is a section of the boundary wall.

Gaiety Cinema

The Gaiety Cinema was opened on the adjacent area on July 6th. 1921 by the Lord Mayor Coun. Albert Braithwaite and had its own saloon orchestra. The architect was George F. Bowman who had an office in Greek Street Leeds; the design was one of his last undertakings as he died in the year of the opening. He lived at Park Lodge Roundhay which is now a residential Home: he was 61 years old when he died. One of the movies shown was "Gone with the Wind" (USA 1939) but the cinema closed in 1968 after showing "Woman in a Dressing Gown" directed by J. Lee Thompson in 1957 and starring Yvonne Mitchell and Anthony Quayle. The cinema was demolished and the foundation stone was laid for a new public house in April 1972. The pub opened in December 1972 and closed in November 1990 becoming derelict. A branch of the Leeds Co-op opened on Elford Grove on April 14th. 1892: the foundation stone had been laid on May 28th.1891 by S. Costigan. The store had both drapery and butchering sections and in February 1897 opened a boot and shoe store.

At the suggestion of the Vicar of Leeds a new parish was formed in June 1888 carved out from St. Clement's Sheepscar, St. Martin's Potternewton, St. Matthew's Chapel Allerton and the Parish Church. With the help of W. W. Clayton, the Rev. Samuel Taylor of St. John's Church created a congregation and raised funds for the new church. The first Mass was celebrated in a room over a stable in Frankland Place and in 1890 Earl Cowper gave some land in Elton Place for the site of the new church: built near the site of Murray's Nursery and Public Gardens. The foundation stone was laid in October 1891 and nine months later services were being held in the adjoining new Parish Room. The new church of St. Aidan was dedicated by Rt. Rev. John Pulleine the Lord Bishop of Richmond on October 13th. 1894. The church was built in memory of Rev. J. R. Woodford Vicar of Leeds and later Bishop of Ely at a cost of £15,000.
The brick built basilica Italian-Romanesque style church was designed by Robert James Johnson of Newcastle upon Tyne. He had set up his practice in that city in 1862 having trained with Gilbert Scott. Johnson died within a year of accepting the commission and A. Crawford-Hicks completed the project: the clerk of works was Henry Whiteley.
In 1908 Sir Frank Brangwyn was asked to decorate the interior of St. Aidan's Church, being the Parish Church of R. H. Kitson.
The Kitson family enriched artistic life in Leeds: Sydney Kitson lived at Hillside Gledhow and his sister Eva was married by the Rev. Arthur Swayne (Vicar St. Aidan's Church 1897-1911). Robert H. Kitson was Sydney and Eva's nephew and the son of Hawthorn Kitson of Elmete Hall as well as a friend of Frank Brangwyn. Kitson suggested to the Vicar that the eastern apse could be filled with a painting and that he would be willing to pay Brangwyn for the work. It was decided that the mural would feature four scenes from the life of St. Aidan. Over two years Brangwyn made many sketches and in December 1910 started to paint the apse wall, a job which engaged him irregularly for two years. His concern about the effect of the Leeds air on his painting led him to cease work and suggested that it be done in mosaic and marble. Brangwyn engaged J. B. Rust and Sylvester Sparrow in London who would paint the designs for the mosaic. The mosaic was set by a team of 50 girls from Battersea and sections sent to Leeds to be applied to the wall. The work of Frank Brangwyn is also displayed on the outside of the chancel surround, which includes the initials FB in mosaic. The Brangwyn mosaics were unveiled at a service

on October 13th. 1916 and the cartoons on which the mosaic was based were returned to Brangwyn, who presented them to St. Andre's Monastery near Bruges. The mosaics were presented with a new lighting system in 1992.
Sir Frank Brangwyn (1867-1956) was born in Bruges, where his father was a church architect. He became a Royal Academician in 1919 and was knighted in 1941 having produced a wide range of furniture, pottery, carpets and schemes for interior decoration. He gave 400 of his pictures to the Bruges Museum and he died aged 89 in June 1956 at his home in Ditchling Sussex. The interior of the church has an impressive rood beam installed in 1898 and font: this including a variety of semi-precious stones on a raised dais at the west end. In a large glass case are displayed the pastoral staff and mitres of Rev. Mumford Taylor who became the Bishop of Southwark and Kingston on Thames: he died in 1929. There is a marble plaque in memory of George Herbert Wilson, the senior curate at the turn of the century and a stained glass window in the Lady Chapel to Agnes Hayward who for 25 years was the People's Warden at the church: she died in October 1905. The brass lectern was presented in memory of James Ripley of Leeds, who died in June 1895.
One of the vicars of St. Aidan's Church this century was the Rev. Philip Lamb: he was appointed as the Principal of St. John's College York in 1945 and he retired in 1971. He became a Canon Emeritus of York Minster in 1976: he died on April 8th. 1994 aged 87.
The remodelled church halls were opened on a visit by HM The Queen on February 23rd. 1990. The Queen visited Chapeltown to open a new extension to the Home for the Elderly, set up by the United Caribbean Association in Hall Lane. At St. Aidan's Church the Queen saw an exhibition of the work of the Church Urban Fund and there was a service of dedication conducted by the Rt. Rev. David Young Bishop of Ripon. The new parsonage behind the halls replaced the large Victorian house on Roundhay Road.
The dedication of the church to St. Aidan is a reminder of this Celtic monk born in Ireland about 600AD. He lived for many years on Iona, where he was consecrated Bishop and sent to Northumbria in 634AD. St. Aidan made Lindisfarne his home and under his guidance St. Hild became the first Abbess ruling houses at Hartlepool and Whitby. St. Aidan died at Bamburgh in 651AD having been Bishop of Lindisfarne for 17 years.

Trinity Methodist Church was opened on January 10th. 1983 following the demolition of the 19th. century church and closure of two other Free Churches: United Reform on Harehills Road and Church of Christ on Gledhow Road. The new buildings include the Anchor Housing Trust's sheltered accommodation and a Day Centre for the elderly. The new Trinity Church is used by all three Free church congregations and take a part in the running of the Day Centre, together with the congregations from St. Aidan's Church and St. Augustine's R.C.Church.

Harehills Board School opened in 1890/91 on Roundhay Road/Shepherd's Lane to designs by architect William Landless: appointed the Leeds School Board architect in 1889 but left Leeds four years later. At the turn of the century there were 1108 boys and girls at this school together with nearly 400 infants. The school closed and it was demolished in 1986/87: a new building was erected on the site which opened in 1990 as a local community training centre.

The New Leeds Constitutional Club on the north side of Roundhay Road was opened in 1896: the foundation stone was laid by the Rt. Hon. W. L. Jackson in 1894, when the Director was Clifford Bowling. The Club was a Men's Snooker Club and used licenced premises. Although the club now accepts mixed membership, the original purpose still prevails as well as occasional dances on the upper floor.

On Harehills Corner and Karnac Road was The Picture House Harehills opened on Monday December 16th. 1912 by Harehills Amusements Co.Ltd. The building was designed by W. Peel Schofield of Park Row Leeds with 900 seats. The cinema was said to have been "luxuriously appointed with tapestried walls" and had a cafe from which the films could be viewed - a feature that was expected to be popular. The first movie shown was "The Mine Owner" and when it closed in October 1963 the film was "The Last Days of Pompeii". The following week saw the introduction of Bingo and the old cinema was finally demolished on July 24th. 1968: the site became part of a supermarket development.

The junction of Harehills Lane and Roundhay Road was also the site of the Gipton Wood Toll Bar and House. This low stone cottage was on the corner of the road and was demolished in October 1921 for road widening.
The Tetley Fforde Grene public house was opened in November 1938 by the Melbourne Brewery, named after the Ford family estate near Hanley in Staffordshire. The 13th. century hall was known as Fforde Grene and Edward Vyvyan Ford was the Managing Director of the brewery.

The branch of the Yorkshire Bank on the corner of Roundhay Road/Harehills Lane was opened on July 6th. 1936, replacing the branch near St. Aidan's Church.

Easterly Road was completed in 1927/28 and is now the main route to Wetherby avoiding Oakwood corner. There was a short tramway spur on Easterly Road and the trams to Oakwood cut through a roundabout at this junction. Trams from Sheepscar to Oakwood started in 1891 with extensions to Canal Gardens in 1897: in

1902 the service extended along Street Lane to Moortown Corner. The reserved track for trams from Harehills Lane to Oakwood opened on May 21st. 1922, with the extension along Princes Avenue to Roundhay a year later. The first section of this expressway was started in September 1921 and used 250 tons of rail from the Leeds Steel Works. The tram routes were closed on March 28th. 1959. In November 1935 an avenue of trees was planned for Easterly Road, in memory of Lord Brotherton who had died in 1931: one of his homes was Roundhay Hall, now a private hospital.

The Clock Cinema opened on Monday November 21st. 1938 with a showing of "The Hurricane" with Jon Hall and Dorothy Lamour. This American film was released in 1937 and was directed by John Ford. The film was shown at The Clock in Mirrophonic sound. The 1836 seater cinema was designed by Norman Fowler of Kitson, Parish, Ledgard and Pyman and built by C. H. & F. Lax: it was opened by Rowland Winn, Lord Mayor of Leeds with Donald Kaberry and Ald. C. V. Walker. The building included the use of terra cotta by the Middleton Fireclay Co. and had a 200 space car park. The name of the cinema came from the Clock Building which had been a feature of the corner for a few years.
The last film to be shown at The Clock was Walt Disney's "The Incredible Journey" (USA 1963) and closure came on Saturday February 28th. 1976. Conversion to a Bingo Hall followed a year later despite local opposition, including removal of many of the seats in a £200,000 scheme. The old cinema was auctioned in London in February 1992 and opened as the Empire Electrical Superstore on July 31st. 1993 after a complete refurbishment.

Gipton Beck includes the stream draining Gledhow Valley and area before the confluence with Sheepscar Beck. The stream once flowed across Harehills Lane by a ford but most is now culverted. Harehills Corn Mill used the waters of the stream north of Shepherd's Lane.
A small stone building set back east of Gledhow Valley Road is the "Gipton Spa" as a small metal plate indicates above the locked door. This once well frequented spa was known as "Waddington Bath" or Gipton Well. This springs were visited by Lord Irwin from Temple Newsam and by Leeds historian Ralph Thoresby in July 1708. The stone built bath house and sunken bath is surrounded with a high stone wall - the house has lost the slates and today is in a state of decay. The site was taken over by Leeds Corporation in 1926 following the purchase of nearby Well House Farm by the Hon. Hilda Kitson, daughter of the 1st. Baron Airedale. In 1888 Hilda Kitson gave an amount of money to Leeds for the preservation of this well house. The spring water was channelled into the bath area, where there was a small fireplace - the waters still flow today by the side of the bath house and are then piped under the houses and road. In more recent years the bath house, listed in 1951, was used as a

store for gardening tools for the Parks Department's Gledhow Valley depot.
There is a stone inside the bath house bearing the inscription:"Hoc faecit Edvardus Waddington de Gleadow annoquae domin 1671". In 1649 Edward Waddington bought the Chapel Allerton estate and this was inherited by his brother Benjamin Waddington: Edward Waddington is buried at Leeds Parish Church. Well House Farm was near the present valley road and Harehills Avenue - Well House exists today in the nearby street names. The construction of Gledhow Valley Road was proposed in January 1924 as a through route from Roundhay Road to Harrogate Road: the road was opened on July 14th. 1926.

The "Astoria" was opened in 1929 as the Harehills Palais de Dance and had a restaurant as well as the popular dance floor with two band evening dances until the 1950's. In the 1930's the manager was W. D. Metcalfe and in the 1940's the proprietor was Rowland Powell. The hall was bought by Associated Tower Cinemas in 1957 when the restaurant was described as having "gleaming silver, chandeliers and high class cuisine at reasonable prices". The Astoria was sold in 1985, 1987 by a Leeds Consortium and again in 1990. The last dance was held on July 17th. 1992 and the building became an electrical showroom in November of that year: the "Rendezvous" is on the western side of the building. On the corner of Harehills Avenue and Roundhay Road was the Kitson shelter, provided with money from Lord Airedale.
North East of the Clock complex was Gipton Lodge, being home to William Wikeley Clayton at the turn of the century. He was the son of the surgeon William Clayton and was educated at Leeds Grammar School and became the Managing Director of Hudswell, Clarke & Co. Ltd. of Leeds Engineers - he died in October 1901. The Lodge became the home of the Thomas family and the lodge house and gates were on Roundhay Road. The lodge house was demolished in 1921 to accommodate the reserved tram track from Harehills to Oakwood.
Gipton Wood, east of the main road to Oakwood, is an important archaeological site with the undated man made defences, measuring 45m by 65m. It is thought that King Penda's supporters under Aethelwald of Deira camped at Gipton Wood prior to the battle on the Whinmoor in November 655AD. It was the Brown trustees who dedicated the 18 acre Gipton Wood to Leeds: in 1925 they offered another gift of 1½ acres of woodland on top of the ridge between Gipton Wood and Harehills Lane.

The area north of Roundhay Road to Oakwood, now superstores, was the Blackburn Olympia Aeroplane and Motor Works/North Sea Aerial Navigation Company. Robert Blackburn OBE was born on March 26th. 1885, the son of George Blackburn, works manager of Thomas Green Lawn Mowers and Steam Roller Manufacturers. He was educated at Leeds Modern School and Leeds University. In 1908 Robert

opened a workshop under a clothing factory on Benson Street - it was demolished to make room for the Sheepscar/Regent Street road. In 1910 he formed Blackburn Aeroplanes of 18 Spencer Place and manufactured monoplanes for £500 each. In 1911 he was building the Mercury plane in premises off Balm Road - the stables belonging to the old Midland Railway Co.
The firm became known as the Blackburn Aeroplane Co. and in 1914 was made a limited company. In response to an order for 12 BE2c planes from the Admiralty, Robert Blackburn acquired the old Olympia roller skating rink on Roundhay Road and started to build the popular B type L Biplanes and the BE2c. The Sopwith Baby seaplane was made at the Olympia Works and tested by Reginald W. Kenworthy who lived at Castle Mona Scarcroft: he was the chief test pilot following the death of Rowland Ding in a disaster on Saturday evening May 12th. 1917.
The planes were taken to Soldier's Field at Roundhay Park for testing, where there was a small wooden hangar and it was on a flight from this field that Ding crashed. A propeller was erected on the site of the crash on Oakwood land - today the garden of 2 Tatham Way - owned by William Penrose-Green. The propeller was erected as a memorial on the site - the present Tatham Way - and a memorial plaque placed on the gates of the factory. The gate plaque was presented in 1946 to Mrs. Burley who sent it to Rowland Ding's old school. The propeller was removed in 1935 to the Nag's Head Inn on Vicar Lane Leeds where it was used as a toilet indicator; it was taken from the inn by Mrs. Burley, Rowland Ding's daughter and restored and placed into the care of the Armley Mills Museum.
The crash was caused by the failure of an interplane strut while looping a new BE2c: the air speed indicator stuck at 150 knots. The plane was a 2 seater trainer of wood and fabric, having the first flight in 1914 using a 70hp engine. Rowland Ding had a White Falcon monoplane made for his personal use in 1912 when he was on the staff of Grahame-White Aviation Co and had tested a land-sea monoplane on Lake Windermere in October 1915. He flew passengers from The Stray Harrogate for 5 guineas a time in a Handley-Page biplane: he crashed this at Northallerton Carnival. Rowland Ding was the son of a Cheshire clergyman and when he was killed at 31 years old he left a wife and two children including his daughter Aphra. He was cremated at Lawnswood and his ashes were interred at Papworth Church in Cambridgeshire on May 16th. 1917. Rowland's son Denys flew in the last War and Mrs.Burley's son is also a pilot.
Soldier's Field was used by the military as well as for plane testing: in June 1915 the Leeds Volunteer Battalions paraded to be inspected by Lord Harewood. There were three Leeds battalions under the West Riding Volunteer Force patrolling the city, guarding the waterworks and rail routes. The Military Field was known as Soldier's Field by the 1890's with many parades from Chapeltown Barracks.
Following the change of use of Soldier's Field after the War, Blackburn could not test

flight the aeroplanes on the site and they moved part of the factory to their already established works at Brough in 1929. The inspection department, machine room, airscrew and wing assembly shops remained in the Olympia Works until 1932. Much of the Leeds workforce were then taken by rail to Brough: the works reopened for a short period in 1936 but closed totally in 1946. The factory had manufactured a variety of aeroplanes including the Swift, Dart, Ripon, Shark and Swordfish. There also was built a motor launch to service the flying boats at Brough: they took the pattern from a launch that sailed on Waterloo Lake but on launching the new boat on the River Humber, they found that the flat bottom was unsuitable to ride the waves. The new launch was given to Leeds and named "Adelaide", after Robert Blackburn's wife.

A Blackburn Skua fighter bomber destroyed the first enemy aircraft in World War 2 on September 26th. 1939 and a Skua sank the "Koenigsberg" at Bergen Norway in April 1940.

Robert Blackburn was made a Fellow of the Royal Aeronautical Society in 1918 and he drove one of the first cars to be introduced to Leeds.

Robert Blackburn died on 12th. September 1955 aged 70 at Bowcliffe near Boston Spa, having spent some time at his other residence Hawthorn Farm Coal Road.

The "Roundhay" public house was the "Gipton" and "Gipton Wood" until it was renamed on June 12th. 1990. The inn is one of 350 Sherwood Inns, which are a part of the 1600 British inns that belong to Whitbread's Brewery. The inn once had a popular bowling green by The Woodland.

The Oakwood Fish Bar is a Grade II listed building in the late 19th. century parade. This shop was converted in the 1930's in the Art Deco style and included vitrolite, bakelite and neon. In July 1993 Leeds had 1856 listed buildings, of which those in Grade I make up 2% of the total. This shop was listed in 1986 and two shops lower down Oakwood Parade are dated 1898 and also are listed properties.

The detached building near the corner of the parade and Oakwood Lane was opened as Lloyds Bank in 1962, the bank having bought the freehold from the Main family. The bank closed in 1990 - the building was sold on July 1st. 1991 and became an estate agent's office. The bank transferred to newly built premises below Safeways on land that once was the telephone exchange. Lloyds Bank Moortown Branch on Harrogate Road was opened on August 6th. 1976.

Safeways store opened in 1972 in the building that was built for the greengrocer/butchery departments of the Co-op. The Co-op store foundation stone was laid by Miss L. Mottram-Playfoot on October 9th. 1926 and the store opened on October lst. 1927. The intention was to demolish the Co-op building but as this was not passed by the planners, extensive restoration work was needed by the Safeway (Argyll) Group.

The Oakwood branch of the Leeds & Holbeck Building Society was opened in 1960 in the same year as the Harehills branch: this was closed in 1991 and relocated to Harehills Road.

Oakwood Clock was restored in 1977 and was originally made for Kirkgate Market in Leeds being designed by John and Joseph Leeming for the new Leeds Borough Market Hall: the clock was made by Potts & Sons for £150. The Leeming brother's practice in London designed the markets at Oldham and Halifax and were responsible for the building of Kinloch Castle on the Isle of Rhum. The Market Hall was opened on July 1st. 1904 but the traders were concerned about the absence of a central Vicar Lane entrance. This was provided with the resiting of stalls and the removal of the central clock. In July 1912 the clock was removed by the Parks Department to Oakwood, close by the large Roundhay Park Entry Lodge complex. This was built in 1872 in the Italianate style complete with waiting rooms, toilets and offices. The plot for this large building was bought at a cost of £20,000 and included Hartley's Farm (Richard Hartley was the tenant), five Horseshoe Cottages, the Smithy, and the residence of Joseph Hobson with its outbuildings and gardens. In early 1914 the Police Station opened in this building, which was used as Parks department offices. The Lodge was demolished following an agreement in the Leeds Council in January 1937. The demolition was accompanied with a proposed layout of a games area and sports pavilion on the Military Field.

The tramway from Oakwood to Canal Gardens was officially opened on July 21st. 1923 by the Lord Mayor of Leeds Ald. Frank Fountain - he opened the Temple Newsam Golf Course in the afternoon.

Oakwood Clock

THE ROAD FROM LEEDS TO WETHERBY

PART 2: OAKWOOD TO THE RING ROAD

Oakwood Lane/Roundhay Road corner at the east end of the parade of shops was once the site of the local pinfold. In the mid 19th. century the route to Roundhay and Street Lane was by Old Park Road: Princes Avenue was only made after the sale of Roundhay Park to Leeds in 1871.
Oakwood Lane was originally Horseshoe Lane with Great Quarry Close near the turnpike. The street name came from Horseshoe Cottages and the village smithy nearby: the land was sold in 1871 with the Roundhay Park estate.
Roundhay Post Office had been on the corner of Oakwood Lane and Roundhay Road for over 100 years but closed in June 1962 transferring to premises on Oakwood Parade. The office was a wooden hut at first and stood adjacent to two semi-detached cottages which were converted into the Post Office. It is one of the oldest district Post Offices in Leeds.
The present Oakwood branch library was once also the Oakwood Police Station: the station opened in 1955 and closed in 1961. The development of the land between North Lane and Oakwood Lane started in 1810, following the sale of Samuel Elam's part of the Roundhay estate. Elam had bought the Roundhay estate with Thomas Nicholson in 1803 from Lord Stourton but had entered a period of financial difficulty - his bank founded about 1800 with his fellow Quaker merchant William Thompson had failed - and his part of the estate was sold at auction: he died in 1811. The Elam family were Quaker cloth export merchants and involved with shipowning, land speculation and banking from 1780 to 1810. Samuel lived at Portland House on Woodhouse Lane and Joseph Elam lived at Claremont in Little Woodhouse.
Gervaise Elam (1679-1771) was a Quaker clothier and he had four sons: John was a tobacconist and became a pioneer of the cloth trade with America; Emmanuel (died 1796) bought an estate near Malton with Samuel; Joseph was a merchant but went bankrupt in 1769; Samuel was a grocer and became a merchant in 1770 - he married William Greenwood's daughter and inherited a fortune. Their son was Samuel Elam who was a partner with Thomas Nicholson in the purchase of Roundhay Park.

By the mid-19th. century the development included Lady Well House, Oakwood House, Roundhay Villa and Roundhay Grove. Lady Well House was later known as Newton Lodge and was built for corn and seed merchant Edward Hudson; the house was altered in the 1880's for Jonathan Routh and has been demolished for housing development. Oakwood House was the home of woollen merchant Robert Hudson and is now a private nursing home. Later mansions included Oakwood Grange, once the home of Sir Edwin Airey, inventor of the concrete houses which

bear his name and Lord Mayor of Leeds in 1923. It was in the gardens of Oakwood Grange in 1888 that Louis le Prince photographed the family with a one lens cine camera which he had invented. Louis le Prince was born in 1842 and married the sister of his college friend John Whitley, whose father Joseph lived at Oakwood Grange. The Grange was originally known as Roundhay Cottage. The house was demolished about 1972 and the site re-developed.
Oakwood Hall was the home of Darnton Lupton, Mayor of Leeds in 1844: he died in December 1873 aged 67 at Harehills House and was buried with other members of this great Leeds family at St. John's Church. This family of woollen merchants were concerned in the civic life of Leeds: Charles Lupton was Lord Mayor in 1915 and Hugh Lupton followed in 1926. Oakwood Hall was reopened as a Mental Health Unit in November 1993, following a period as an Aged Person's Home.
North Hill was built in the 1820's for Stephen Nicholson but was demolished to make way for North Hill Close.
The sale of the Park in 1871 was followed by George Corson's plan for development. Corson had won the first prize of 200 Guineas in January 1874 and his work included the large houses on the north side of Wetherby Road and Springwood Road laid out in the 1870's.
George Corson was born in 1829 in Dumfries and in 1849 joined his brother at his Leeds architectural practice. In 1860 he took the practice over and retired about 1901: he was the architect for Foxhill in Weetwood, St. Clement's Church Sheepscar, Newton Hall estate, the layout of Lawnswood Cemetery, Leeds Grand Theatre, Leeds Municipal Buildings and School Board offices on Calverley Street together with many houses and industrial premises. Corson died in 1910 having been President of the Leeds & Yorkshire Architectural Society in 1897.
Many of the large houses to the north of Wetherby Road have now acquired other uses: these include Southlands, home to William Hemingway (1866-1925) which is now a private nursing home and the White House, once the home of William Macpherson, which has been converted into a public house and restaurant.

Roundhay was a part of the lands given to Ilbert de Lacy after the Norman Conquest. A charter was granted to Robert de Lacy giving rights to the timber and pasture in the Park to the monks of Kirkstall Abbey. Roundhay returned to the de Lacy family and the manor went to Henry's daughter Alice who married the Duke of Lancaster: the property then became a part of the Duchy of Lancaster. The Duke was beheaded in 1321 and the Duchy passed to his nephew Henry who died in 1362. Roundhay was inherited by his daughters Maude and Blanche - Blanche married John of Gaunt. Roundhay became a Royal Park when John of Gaunt's son King Henry IV inherited the property. About 1503 in the reign of King Henry VI a steward was appointed by the King to run Roundhay Manor. In 1512 the Manor and the Park of Roundhay were separated and Thomas Lord Darcy of Temple Newsam received the parks at Roundhay from King Henry VIII. Thomas was beheaded in 1538 for his part in the ill fated Pilgrimage of Grace.

In 1599 Sir John Darcy was granted the rights of hunting in Roundhay Park - the word means a round enclosure. Sir John Saville inherited the property and it became the property of the Duke of Norfolk and then through marriage to Baron Stourton. It was Philip Lord Stourton who sold Roundhay Park to Thomas Nicholson and Samuel Elam on August 4th. 1803.

Thomas Nicholson, the son of William who died in 1812, was a London shipping magnate and he engaged architect John Clark to build him a new mansion at Roundhay, which was altered by Thomas Taylor. This was completed in 1826 as were two lakes created from old quarry workings and a castle folly built by George Nettleton. Waterloo Lake was named after the famous battle fought on June 18th. 1815, at which the combined forces led by the Duke of Wellington and Field Marshall Blucher defeated Napoleon. In 1817 London's Waterloo Bridge was opened: originally called Strand Bridge but renamed on the anniversary of the battle in June.

Thomas Nicholson was the son of William Nicholson by his first wife Hannah and he died on January 14th. 1821 and the estate passed to his step-brother Stephen Nicholson: he was the son of William and his second wife Grace Whitaker. Stephen died in 1858 aged 79 and was buried in St.John's Church which he had built by 1826. William's third child was Mary who married Thomas Phillips and their son was William Nicholson Phillips MA JP; he assumed the Nicholson name on October 13th. 1827. He died in September 1868 having helped to develop the estate and create the Canal Gardens around a lake in the old kitchen gardens. He had married Martha Rhodes who died in August 1871. The estate was sold at auction on October 4th. 1871 to John Barran for £139,000. The main lot included the Mansion, lakes, park, canal garden with its fruit walls, Rhododendrons and flower beds with kitchen garden there was a vinery 100' long. The City of Leeds bought the estate from John Barran through the Act of Improvement of July 1872. The same auction offered the Manor and Lordship of Roundhay and Seacroft, which was bought by John Sagar-Musgrave of Red Hall. The lot included Seacroft Green, Mill Green, Stocks Hill and some land at Cross Gates: this was sold with the relevant mineral rights. HRH Prince Arthur officially opened Roundhay Park on September 19th. 1872.

Initially the new public park was difficult to reach and the Leeds Roundhay Park/Osmondthorpe Junction Railway was suggested in 1874 but was not developed. Another transport scheme using an overhead railway collapsed due to the expense involved. The solution was to extend the tram line from Sheepscar and this opened in October 1891. Difficulties with the electric system caused the brief introduction of steam trams until August 1897.

The amenities of the Park improved with the opening of the Barran Drinking Fountain in April 1882 with new park roads constructed in 1885/86. In May 1873 the Mansion House received a licence and was let for 10 years to Mr. Brayshaw of the Junction Inn: in 1884 William Gilpin took over and in 1894 his son Craven Gilpin was at the Mansion. The Gilpin family still run this important and popular facility.
A highlight of 1896 was when the 72 year old Charles Blondin crossed the upper lake on a wire and even cooked an omelette. Blondin died in February 1897 - he was the first man to cross the Niagara Falls on a three inch rope.
A zoo was proposed for the Park in 1906 and again in 1924, when the site in front of the castle folly was considered suitable. It was the Canal Gardens area that was to develop and become one of Britain's top tourist attractions: it was the top UK garden in 1992. The Coronation House was built in 1911 and modernised in 1939. The terrace and water feature was opened on April 13th. 1981 by Sir Richard O'Brien followed by the aquarium in December 1981.The John Dunstan Tropical House opened on April 17th. 1984 - Dunstan had been Director of Parks from 1974 to 1981. There had been a £30,000 grant from Wade's Charity for this work. The Tropical House was opened on May 6th. 1988 by Coun. Elizabeth Nash: the feature was provided through the generosity of Arnold Ziff. The Botanical Gardens were opened on December 22nd. 1993 by Arnold Ziff with assistance from Wade's Charity. The complex is known as the Marjorie Ziff Rainforest, Cacti and Orchid House.

The early 19th. century lodge houses are now derelict but once graced the entrance to the Carriage Way approach to the Mansion. In 1912 the lodge was the home of gatekeeper Christopher Curtis and in 1936 was home to PC James Dobbs.

The corner of North Lane and Wetherby Road was the site of the Roundhay Electric Light Co., a power station run by a generator with a storage battery house nearby. Adjacent was the entrance lodgehouse to "The Grove" east of Ladywood Chapel, once the home to the woolstapler Burton family of Leeds - John Burton lived there in the mid-19th.century. The mansion on North Lane is now converted into flats.

The spillway from Waterloo Lake carries the waters of Wyke Beck and was built in 1988/1990. The open air swimming pool opened on June 19th. 1907 and was rebuilt by May 1937. The pool finally closed in 1981 and was filled in.
Church Stream Cottage on the south side of the main road is on an old golf course site dates from the mid-19th. century and is a listed building.

St. John's Church was built by Stephen Nicholson in 1826 through property bequeathed by Thomas Nicholson, to designs by architect Thomas Taylor. Taylor

was born in 1778 and served eight years apprenticeship with James Wyatt. He came north from London about 1805 and the Leeds Court House was his first main commission in 1811. He was engaged to illustrate Whitaker's "Loidis and Elmete" and the a new edition of Thoresby's "Ducatus Leodiensis".
Thomas Taylor was appointed to restore Leeds Parish Church in 1809/1812 and built churches at Liversedge, Dewsbury, Pudsey, Bradford and St. Mary's Church Quarry Hill Leeds amongst many other works. Roundhay St. John's Church was Thomas Taylor's last design that he personally supervised. Originally Roundhay was in the parish of Barwick in Elmet but it was announced in April 1824 that Stephen Nicholson was to build a new church. Taylor had built the Union Bank in Leeds in 1812/13 and was a partner in this bank with Stephen Nicholson.
The first stone for St. John's Church was laid on September 22nd. 1824 by the Rev. William Bathurst Rector of Barwick in Elmet. The church was consecrated in January 1826 and opened in March, two weeks after Taylor's death.
The patronage of the church passed to James Kitson of Elmete Hall about 1885, when the church chancel was lengthened and another vestry was added. In 1888 the reredos was provided as a gift of Hawthorn Kitson: it probably came from Italy. Hawthorn Kitson sold the advowson of the church and this was paid off in 1926. In 1925 it was recommended that the Woodlands Estate be bought to build the Parochial Hall at Oakwood. The foundation stone was laid by Sir Edward Allen Brotherton in August 1927. There are three memorial plaques on the north wall inside the church to Thomas (died 1821), Stephen (died 1858) and William Nicholson Nicholson (died 1868) and the family vault lies below the church nave. The plaques also remember Thomas' wife Elizabeth who died in 1833 aged 66; Stephen's wife Sarah who died in 1862 aged 74 and William's wife died 1871 age 61. The churchyard contains graves of many prominent local citizens as well as other members of a large community. William Hodgson was Lord Mayor of Leeds in 1921; architect George Bowman of Park Lodge, now a nursing home; Edgar Smith of Parcmont; Sir William Clarke JP of Lady Well House who died in 1930.

James Kitson lst. Baron Airedale who died March 16th. 1911 aged 75 in a Paris hotel was Mayor of Leeds in 1896 and created Lord Mayor a year later: his tomb is north of the church with an inscribed plate. He was the President of the National Liberal Federation and an MP. Sir James was made an Honorary Freeman of Leeds on May 23rd. 1906. There is a bust in the foyer of Leeds Civic Hall by Leeds sculptor E. Caldwell Spruce completed from photographs. Caldwell Spruce once worked at the Burmantofts Pottery: his studio was in Cowper Street.
The Kitson family traced their ancestors in the Leeds area over four centuries: there was a James Kitson who died in 1551 and the succeeding generations had a James, John or William as the head of the Kitson family.

James Kitson Snr. was born in 1807 in Leeds, he was the son of Thomas Kitson a licensed victualler of the Brunswick Tavern on Camp Road. James received an elementary school education and was apprenticed in a dye works and worked in his father's inn. In 1828 he married Ann Newton, the daughter of a local decorator and moved to Hunslet in 1835 to found a small engineering business. His partners were David Laird, who supplied the financial backing and Charles Todd, who had been apprenticed to Matthew Murray at the Round Foundry. In 1839 it was known as Messrs.Todd, Kitson & Laird of the Railway Foundry Hunslet. This Airedale Foundry under James Kitson built the first locomotive in 1838, when it was delivered to the Liverpool & Manchester Railway Co. The engine had been seen by pioneer George Stephenson in Leeds, having been built in an old cloth mill the engine proved too large to move through the mill doors and Kitson simply demolished the wall. The firm lost money in the 1840-42 slump and a new partnership was formed of Kitson, Thompson and Hewitson and both the firm and the family prospered: it became Kitson & Co. in 1875. Kitson's Airedale Foundry became a major industry in Leeds producing 150 locomotives and 50 tramway engines annually.

The Monkbridge Iron & Steel Co. was started in 1851 and owned by Stephen Whitham of Kirkstall Forge: it was bought by James Kitson Snr.(1807-1885) in 1854 for his sons James and Frederick (died 1877). Kitson was elected Mayor of Leeds for two years in 1860/1861. His sons James and Hawthorn Kitson (died May 21st. 1899) carried on at the foundry. The Airedale works employed 1400 and the Monkbridge works employed 700. The iron used in Kitson's works was mainly local - it came from the York Road Coal & Iron Co. and the iron was taken to the works in rough pigs to be smelted.

James Kitson Snr. became an opponent of the Trades Unions, a leading local Liberal,an opponent of the Corn Laws, a patron of the Mechanics Institute and a Unitarian. He laid the first stone for the new Leeds Infirmary on March 29th.1864 and was an alderman in 1858 when the Town Hall was opened in Leeds by Queen Victoria and Prince Albert. James became very ill in 1864 but rallied: he died in 1885. There were over 1000 members from the Airedale Foundry and 300 from the Monkbridge works at his funeral. All the mourners walked from Elmete Hall to St. John's Church as the Leeds Town Hall bell tolled: the coffin was carried by servants from the two foundries.

The Foundry became a public limited company following the death of Sir James Kitson in 1911. During the First World War the firm came under government control and made forgings for guns. The Airedale Foundry closed in 1934 and was demolished a year later. The Monkbridge works were bought by Daniel Doncasters of Sheffield in 1953, who transferred their turbine blade forging development from Sheffield to Leeds. They built up the largest turbine compressor blade manufacturing unit in Europe with Rolls Royce and the Ministry of Aircraft

Production. The firm supplied the turbine parts for the Concorde planes in 1972 but the ensuing years saw redundancy at the company. In 1983 Doncasters occupied the 10 acre site on Whitehall Road with about 700 workers and was the largest consumer of Titanium and Super Alloy Bar in Western Europe. In 1980 there was a £1.2 million "factory within a factory"; Doncasters Monkbridge were bought out in 1987 by IEP (Inco Engineered Products) who continue to manufacture turbine blades for both commercial and services planes on their 15 acre site.
Sir James Kitson Jnr. of Gledhow Hall was a senior partner at the Monkbridge and at the Airedale foundry, having been educated at Wakefield Proprietory School and University College London: at the age of 19 years he started work with his elder brother Frederick William at the Monkbridge works, which came to specialise in steel. He was raised to the peerage as Lord Airedale in 1907 and was buried at St. John's Church on Wednesday March 22nd. 1911: a memorial service was held at St. Margaret's Church in London.
James Kitson Snr. married twice: first to Anne Newton having six sons and three daughters; secondly to Elizabeth Hutchinson with four children. Elizabeth was a Nottinghamshire Vicar's daughter who died in 1913 aged 80. The third son of the first marriage was James Lord Airedale: Albert Lord Airedale was the eldest son by James' first wife Emily (died 1876). The Hon. Albert Ernest Kitson became Lord Airedale on the death of his father in 1911: he was born in 1865 and married Florence Schunck, daughter of the woollen merchant Edward Schunck of Gledhow Wood. Their 6th. daughter was the Hon. Thelma Kitson and she married Dr.Noel Harris in London on July 24th. 1823. Albert and Florence lived at Cober Hall Cloughton near Scarborough. Roland and James Oliver were later Lord Airedales through his second wife Laura Smith. The baronetcy has now been dissolved with the last Lord Airedale having lived in Stamford.
Frederick James Kitson was Frederick William's son and Sir James Kitson's nephew and became Lord Mayor of Leeds in 1908. His niece was Jessie Beatrice Kitson who became the first woman Lord Mayor elected November 18th. 1942, following the death of Arthur Clarke. It was the Hon. Hilda Kitson who gave Gledhow Valley to Leeds and who was a promoter of the Flowers for Leeds scheme. She flew over the Victoria Falls prior to her death in 1944. The grandson of Sir James Kitson was Col. Geoffrey Kitson, who became the Pro-Vice Chancellor of Leeds University and was a Past President of the Leeds Chamber of Commerce - he served for eight years on the Leeds City Council and in earlier days was a director of the London & North Eastern Railway.
At the turn of the century Sir James Kitson was living at Gledhow Hall, which was bought for £17,000 in 1921 by the City Council for use as a proposed secondary school. Gledhow Hall was the scene of Lord Airedale's entertainment of Lord Roseberry and Gladstone and many other important figures of the period. Hawthorn

Kitson was living at Elmete Hall and Frederick James was at Gledhow Grove - he died on November 19th. 1935 aged 74; Hilda Kitson lived at Gledhow Grange.
There is a memorial plaque in St.John's Church to Francis Kitson, the eldest son of James Kitson Snr and his second wife Elizabeth. He was born at Elmete Hall and died in January 1895. His younger brother was Sidney Decimus Kitson, who married Winifred Tetley.

There are many graves of the Lupton family who were cloth and wool merchants in Leeds. Arthur's elder brother was Darnton (1806-1873) who became head of William Lupton of Wellington Street. He founded the Leeds Working Men's Institute and became the Leeds Mayor. Francis Lupton (1848-1921) was a senior partner in the firm and his sons were Frank, Arthur, Charles and Hugh. The graves are seen on the south side of the church. Lupton Avenue from York Road is named after Francis and Charles (died 1935) who were instrumental in clearing Leeds slums and in creating The Headrow in Leeds. There is a brass plate in the church to Margaret Lupton, daughter of Hugh - she died aged 84 in 1974. The Luptons lived at Beechwood, Springwood Oakwood Lane, The Acacias (Oakwood Hall) and Mount Pleasant Harehills Lane.

The large memorial west of the church featuring a lady with broken pillars remembers the Penrose Green family. Sarah Anne was the widow of William Penrose and Thomas Green of Oak Lea Adel: she died at her son's home of "Towerhurst" on Springwood Road. The family were the owners of Thomas Green & Son Ltd. Engineers and Machinists of North Street. The firm was established in North Street in 1835 with one of their variety of products being the lawnmower. The firm made locomotives and vehicles for street cleaning - the company was sold to Atkinson's of Clitheroe in 1975 and the Leeds firm closed down the Smithfield works. The fine frontage with the clock is still admired. Sarah's son was Alderman W. Penrose-Green, born in 1860 and educated at Harrogate, who took the name Penrose-Green in 1886 when he married Pattie Green. He became Deputy Lord Mayor of Leeds in 1914 having been elected Lord Mayor in 1909 there is a large painting of him in Leeds Civic Hall. He died aged 82 on November 16th.1941. He lived at both "Rosenheim" on Springwood Road and at "Towerhurst" and was a keen golfer: he was President of the Leeds Golf Club.
The monument in St. John's churchyard also remembers Vera Penrose-May who died in August 1977 and Leonard, William's infant son who died in 1887 aged 3 months. The inscription reads: "Life's work well done; Life's race well run; Life's crown well won - now cometh rest."
The almshouses and school were founded in 1837 by Stephen Nicholson. The six almshouses were provided for the retired servants of the Nicholson family or for folk

living in the local area. The dwellers in the houses had to attend the church twice on Sundays and not attend services in other churches during the hours of service at Roundhay. The almshouses and school house were upgraded in the 1960's.
The almshouses and school were conveyed by Stephen Nicholson to the trustees in November 1837 to educate poor children trustees and teachers to be Church of England members.
With the extension of the city boundary in 1912 the school came under the control of the City Council: it was extended and modernised but finally closed in July 1992. A new Primary School opened in September 1992 on North Lane.
The old Vicarage east of the school/almshouses was ready for occupation in 1841 - the first vicar lived in rooms made available at The Mansion prior to moving into his new house. At the start of this century the vicar lived at "Belmont" on the corner of Elmete Avenue and North Lane and the vicarage was let. The Roundhay vicarage then moved to Oakwood Grove and in 1992 the vicar of St. John's Church took over The Leeds Vicarage on Ryder Gardens. This had been the home of the Vicar of Leeds in the 1980's until he moved to the Leeds City Rectory Vicarage View Kirkstall. The Rector of the Leeds City Team Ministry is the Rev. Stephen Oliver who was appointed in 1991.
Braim Wood School opened on September 6th. 1960 as a County Secondary School for girls. The school was the second post War girl's secondary school. It became a mixed Middle School in the early 1970's. The school became the only state run boy's high school in Leeds in September 1992. With its motto "Esteem Thy Precious Time" the school is set in eight acres of land including mature woodlands, green fields, sports fields and tennis courts.
The land to the south of the almshouses and school was once Roundhay Golf Club from 1893 - 1896. Golf in Leeds was first played on the Soldier's Field, which was tenanted by a Leeds butcher. The farmer at Cobble Hall allowed his land to be used for golf at 30/- a year on a nine hole course. The club house on the Asket Hill site was moved to Cobble Hall in April 1896 and three years later the Leeds and Roundhay Clubs amalgamated. The grounds of Cobble Hall became an 18 hole course on a 188 acre site. The Leeds Golf Club was instituted on April 29th. 1896 at a meeting at "Leighton Villa". The new club house was opened on October 2nd. 1909 designed by architect Carby Hall: the old hut was bought by Baildon Club having originally cost £3. The Club President was Ald. William Penrose-Green when he was Mayor Elect: he also donated the trophy which was inscribed with his coat of arms.

North of Braim Wood School is Elmete Hall. In early days the site was a hunting lodge to Roundhay Park and the Hall was built by the Nicholson family as Roundhay Lodge after the Napoleonic Wars: one of the first tenants was Thomas Benyon of

Benyon & Co, flax spinners. James Kitson of Hyde House bought the property from the Nicholsons for £17,000 in 1863 and it was rebuilt: his coat of arms complete with three fish and motto "Palmam qui meruit ferat" - "Let the man who deserves a prize win it", is accompanied by the date 1865 carved in stone over the west door. He also brought an ancient stone coffin from the site of York Station to be a feature of the grounds. John Hawthorn Kitson JP (1843-1899), one of Lord Airedale's younger brothers, was living at Elmete Hall after his father's death: after Hawthorn's death his widow Jessie continued to live at the Hall until she died in 1920. Hawthorn and Jessie's son Robert was born at Elmete Hall and was to live at his house at Taormina Sicily built in 1905. Robert's younger sister was Jessie Beatrice who became the first woman Lord Mayor in 1942.
Elmete Hall was bought in 1921 by Bertram Redman, a Leeds furnisher and it was during the Redman occupancy that central heating was installed and it was furnished as a showplace. Sir Edwin Airey bought the estate from Redman in 1922 with plans to build 700 houses and no interest in using the hall as a residence. The housing scheme was withdrawn and Edwin Airey offered to sell the estate for £23,000 - the same price he paid Redman. The Leeds City Council bought the estate in 1926 and proposed in June 1937 that the hall became a home for Basque refugees accomodating 100 children. In 1939 it was suggested that it should be sold as a private residence. This never came about and the maintenance and interest charges were costing the Council £16,000. In 1950 it was proposed that a £30,000 plan be implemented to convert Elmete Hall into a school for deaf children. There had already been other plans for conversion into a hospital, sanatorium, nurses home, rehabilitation home for miners and the grounds to be used for a cemetery, zoo and for private housing.
In 1960 the school for deaf children opened in the grounds of the Hall, as Elmete Wood Special School with the hall used as a residence. Elmete Hall still retains the original wooden cantilever staircase, marble fireplace and an impressive stained glass dome, together with an excellent vista across the surrounding area: the domestic east wing has been demolished. The school closed in 1987 with the children entering mainstream schools - the school buildings became the Leeds Professional Development Centre from November 11th. 1987, with the Hall becoming empty from July 1993. The nearby Hammond Hall hostel also closed, while Elmete Wood Special School opened on Elmete Lane in 1970 - it changed its name on reorganisation to Elmete Wood School in September 1990. The extended Elmete Hall north lodge stands on Elmete Lane and the original gate pillars to the Hall are now the entry to Braim Wood School. This entry in 1893 was described as being on The High Road.
In May 1881 a Roman altar was found in the grounds of Elmete Hall: a single stone once used for incense burning and sacrifices. This stone is displayed in a case at

Leeds City Museum.
Cobble Hall is on the north end of Elmete Lane and was built about 1820 by the Nicholson family in a Gothic Revival style - the castellations were placed there by Thomas Nicholson in order to enhance the view from The Mansion. The Gilpin family live in one of the three dwellings of Cobble Hall Farm, which provides much of the food for use at their restaurants. The listed farm is complete with old byre, tack room and stables. Elmete Lane was also the site of the area Pinfold for strayed cattle.
"Netherleigh" is east of Cobble Hall adjacent to Roundhay Grange and was the home of William Samuel Sykes. He was the founder of the Leeds Golf Club and a flax spinner. He died aged 80 on November lst. 1930 following his retirement to Harrogate. Beechwood is the large house set back east of Elmete Lane and guarded by a lodge house and having a long drive. This was built as Goodman's House about 1840 for John Goodman - he later lived at Gledhow House and died in December 1869 - and his brother George, a wool stapler of Leeds and Bradford. George Goodman was born on November 17th. 1791, the son of Benjamin Goodman, whose portrait in Leeds Civic Hall was painted by C. H. Schwanfelder (1773-1837). Benjamin died on June 10th. 1848 aged 84 and was buried with his wife Ann, who died in January 1830 aged 63, at Whitkirk Church. Benjamin and Ann Goodman's daughters were Elizabeth and Ann, both of whom died in the 1820's.
George Goodman was four times Mayor of Leeds and his portrait is also hanging in the Civic Hall painted by T. Simpson in 1836 and presented by the burgesses on October 23rd. 1837: on April 30th. 1836 a chain of pure gold costing £197 was presented to him. He became the first Leeds Mayor after the passing of the Municipal Corporation Act of September 1835, from January lst. until November 9th. 1836, when the position was taken by James Williamson. George Goodman took over as Mayor from Charles Gascoigne Maclea in January 1847 until Francis Carbutt was elected later that year. George Goodman was elected Mayor of Leeds again for two terms in 1850 - 1852 but he resigned in March 1852, with his term being completed by John Hope Shaw. The resignation was due to his election as an MP from July 1852 until 1857 for the Borough of Leeds.
George Goodman was knighted on February 26th. 1852 as a result of his activities in connection with the Great Industrial London Exhibition of 1851 - he had been recommended by his friend the Earl of Carlisle. Goodman was a Liberal and a Baptist and when he died aged 67 at his residence on October 13th. 1859 he was buried at Whitkirk Church, where his box tomb is found in the south west corner of the churchyard. The inscription describes him as a "JP for the borough of Leeds, a magistrate and deputy lieutenant for the West Riding - a friend to liberty and a friend to all".
It is likely that the landscape designer Joshua Major drew up the plans for

Beechwood estate - George Goodman had subscribed to Major's "Theory and Practice of Landscape Gardening" published in 1852.
Goodman's House estate was bought by Francis Lupton in 1860 who renamed the Hall "Beechwood" and engaged architect George Corson to design the lodgehouse. Francis was born in 1813 and had married Frances Greenhow in 1847 and their family lived at this Hall which became the centre for both cultural and civic activities.
During the 18th.century the Luptons were involved in marketing cloth in Europe and a Lupton survived the Lisbon earthquake of 1755, having been in the city on business. Much of their trade would have been by barter - a shipment of cloth was paid for by cases of wine.
Arthur Lupton (1748-1807) was a schoolfellow of the German poet Goethe in Frankfurt. Frank Lupton (1848-1901) was involved with slum clearance while holding office on Leeds City Council and he promoted the Industrial Dwellings in modernising houses at a moderate rent. Frank Lupton's three sons died in the First World War.
It was Charles Lupton (1855-1935) who was the inspiration for The Headrow in Leeds giving 50 years service to the Leeds General Infirmary. He was made a Freeman of the City on October 6th. 1926 on the same day as the Leeds surgeon Sir Berkeley Moynihan and eleven years after having been Lord Mayor.
It was the Lupton family who gave the name "Merrion" to Leeds, when they sold the land to the City Council and obtained the name from Merrion Square in Dublin: it was in Dublin that the Victorian members of the family stayed while they were trading in the country.
Arthur Greenhow Lupton (1850-1930) was the first Pro-Vice Chancellor of Leeds University from 1904 to 1920 and was a pioneer in the supply of electricity to the City. He was a senior partner in William Lupton & Co. and he died on February 8th. 1930 and was buried at St. John's Church three days later. A memorial service was held at Mill Hill Chapel Leeds. He left £83,010 in his will to his two daughters: his son Michael had died after a hunting accident in November 1929 - he was aged 44. His brother Hugh Lupton (1861-1947) served many years on the Council and also had a special interest in the development of electricity.
Miss M. Lupton who died in September 1954 was the eldest daughter of Charles, the former Lord Mayor of Leeds. Miss Elizabeth Lupton was involved with the "land grab" of an eight acre field on Elmete Lane. This had been seized by the Land Commission in 1970 and Elizabeth fought a four year battle to get her land back again. She was finally forced to accept compensation from the Government and the land was earmarked for residential development. Nine years after her death in September 1977, it was agreed that the land would never be developed.
Beechwood was leased to the Industrial Common Ownership Movement as a

Conference Centre until 1993 when this function ceased. The Beechwood estate was then placed on sale by the Lupton family who still owned the property.

The junction of Asket Hill and Wetherby Road was the site of the "Church" toll bar serving the Roundhay/Collingham turnpike road from 1825 - three of the trustees or commissioners to execute this act for making and maintaining a turnpike road from Roundhay Bridge to Collingham were John Rhodes of Potternewton, Francis Lupton and George Buckton. The Royal Assent to make the turnpike from Roundhay Bridge to Collingham was granted on May 28th. 1824.
The house is on an old route from Shadwell to Seacroft - at one time it continued across the present Ring Road. The police station was opened in 1912 by Leeds City Police after the extension of the city boundary on the site of the former toll bar: the station was formerly a West Riding Constabulary station. The station was replaced by the Police Box system in 1931.

Wetherby Road joins the more modern Easterly Road and on the east were Grange Farm and the demolished Ash Bank House was north of Low Wood and a sandstone quarry. Beyond were the Lime Pits and Ash Bank Limestone Quarry, once worked by the monks of Kirkstall Abbey - Limepits Wood is now surrounded by a housing estate. On an 1856 map there is a note that several Roman coins had been found near Limepits Wood.
Set back north of the main road is Roundhay Grange Farm, one of the many granges run by the Cistercian monks of Kirkstall Abbey. A 12th.century charter of Robert de Lacy states that he "gave to the abbey of Kirkstall the cow pasture - vaccarium by Roundhay ... and the pasture of Roundhay to be used for the monk's purposes at the Grange as well as for building and making fences."
The Cistercian monks appointed a steward and bailiff for Roundhay Grange and at Braim Farm as well as being in charge of the nearby lime pits and the Seacroft forge. In 1287 the abbey was hampered by debt and Henry de Lacy Earl of Lincoln accepted the abbey lands in exchange for an annual charge of 80 marks and free warren was granted by the King.
The Grange was probably the manor house outside the deer park with the two other granges being Grange Farm between Ash Bank House and Pigeon Cote Farm - both now demolished - and another of unknown location. In 1292 Roundhay became a part of the Duchy of Lancaster and in 1361 it was inherited by John of Gaunt's wife: it became a royal manor when their son Henry IV succeeded to the throne. Roundhay manor was granted to the City of London in 1628 with the grant making mention of both the coalpits and the marlpits. In 1629 the manor was bought by Stephen Tempest but after the Civil War was confiscated. In 1653 the manor was held by William Lowther and in 1657 was conveyed to John Savile of Methley Hall -

it remained with the Savile family until 1811.
The manor was bought by the Nicholson family and in 1872 Roundhay Grange was sold to Thomas Coultate. The Lordship of Roundhay Manor was sold to J. M. Sagar-Musgrave of Red Hall.
Roundhay Grange Farm is an ancient site having an early 17th. century barn and buildings dating from 1669, with 17th and 18th. century additions. Some of the rooms are panelled in Oak and in the basement is a vaulted room with stone seats that could have been used as a chapel or a prison. It has been suggested that the chapel may have been connected with the re-establishment of the Roman Catholics in Leeds. In 1871 when the Grange was sold at auction, it was occupied by Francis Cookson. It has been suggested that Roundhay Grange was the site of the lost Domesday village of Watecroft, although there is no evidence to support this idea.
Roundhay Grange was in the Thorner parish and in 1844 it became part of Shadwell parish: in 1885 it was transferred to the parish of Seacroft.
Wetherby Road has a roundabout junction with the Leeds Outer Ring Road. By 1924 the Leeds outer ring road was developing with sections complete from Tongue Lane/Harrogate Road and from Shadwell Lane to Roundhay Park Lane. A few years later the Ring Road project was completed. A planning application was received in 1987 from Thistle Hotels for a hotel on Wellington Hill: this was not approved and there were suggestions that the hotel be transferred to the Colton development.

THE ROAD FROM LEEDS TO WETHERBY

PART 3 FROM THE LEEDS RING ROAD TO BARDSEY

The Red Hall Lane Garden Centre of William Strike Ltd. was opened on June 3rd. 1965 and was followed two years later by the other Leeds branch at Swillington Common.

The area is known as Wellington Hill, remembering the success at the Battle of Waterloo when Arthur Wellesley Duke of Wellington defeated Napoleon on June 18th. 1815.

Red Hall is set back from the main road and was built about 1630/50 for the Leeds merchant Richard Lodge. His widow Sarah and her five children lived at this house: in 1658 she married John Whelpdale but he died six years later and Sarah remained at Red Hall.

The next family to occupy Red Hall was Sir John Savile of Copley near Halifax (born 1640) and he lived with his wife Mary Paston until he died in 1677: their home became the centre for Catholic life in this area. Lady Mary Savile lived at Red Hall for another 33 years. Their memorial is well preserved on the south wall of Thorner Church: they were listed as recusants in the 1670's. Their daughter Elizabeth married Lord Thomas Howard of Worksop when she was only 18 years old and Thomas their eldest son became the 8th. Duke of Norfolk - born at Red Hall in 1683. It was his younger brother Edward who became the 9th. Duke of Norfolk.

Dame Mary Savile started proceedings to sell Red Hall in 1710 but died before completion: this was done by her daughter Lady Mary Howard to James Ibbetson, the wool merchant and he enlarged the property by adding the rear stable block - seven years later James Ibbetson bought Denton Hall. He died in October 1739 and was buried at Leeds Parish Church, where he is buried with his wife Elizabeth who died on November 4th. 1751: the gravestone is in the chancel. His sons were George who died on March 15th. 1732 and was buried at Leeds Parish Church and Henry Ibbetson lived at Red Hall until 1761: he was Mayor of Leeds in 1753 and a High Sheriff of Yorkshire. Henry was raised to a baronetcy on May 12th.1748 as he raised a corps of 100 men at his own expense, when a threat of the 1745 rebellion was looming. His first wife was Catherine Foljambe who died in 1740 and with his second wife Isabella Carr of Durham Sir Henry Ibbetson also managed to raise a large family of 10 children in 16 years - his wife died in June 1757 and was buried at Leeds Parish Church. Sir Henry Ibbetson died in 1761 and was succeeded by his eldest son who was himself succeeded by Sir Henry Carr Ibbetson, who married Alice Mary Fenton-Scott. Henry's son was Sir James Ibbetson, who inherited the Red Hall property when he was only 15 years old - his guardians included his uncle Samuel Ibbetson of Denton. James decided to live at Denton Hall when his uncle died in 1768 and he died aged 49 in 1795: he sold Red Hall to John Simpson of Roundhay Grange. His son was William Simpson who died in February 1738: Thomas Simpson of Red Hall died in 1787 and his wife Ann died in 1797. In 1821 William Simpson sold Red Hall to his brother-in-law Benjamin Atkinson of Manston Lodge Cross Gates. Benjamin's son William Simpson Atkinson inherited Red Hall when he was 18 years old but lived at Barrowby Hall, although he showed continued interest in the Red Hall property until his death in 1886. It was William Simpson Atkinson who restored the neglected Red Hall.

It was during this period that the Wetherby turnpike was constructed: prior to this access to Leeds was via Foundry Approach, Dib Lane, Asket Hill and Elmete Lane. It was William's nephews who inherited Red Hall and in 1928 the Hall became the property of Frederick Benjamin Atkinson until 1936. It was during the days when the Atkinson family "let" the Hall that the Stow family and then the Sagar-Musgraves lived there from 1865 until 1937.

John Sagar-Musgrave was a maltster, who owned about 1000 acres of land: in 1872 he bought the Lordship of Roundhay at auction, a title becoming extinct in 1935. John Sagar was born in 1835 as the only son of Richard Sagar a Bramley solicitor and Margaret Musgrave, daughter of John and Susanna Musgrave of Bramley. His uncle was Simeon Musgrave (1795-1874) manager of a malting business; his great-uncle was Abraham Musgrave (1778-1862) who left his fortune to John Sagar on condition that he added the Musgrave name to his own - this was done by royal licence in April 1863. There is a brass plaque to John Sagar-Musgrave on the south wall of St. Paul's Church at Shadwell - he died on April 13th. 1906 aged 71 and was buried at Bramley.

The Sagar family lived at Allerton Grange near Bradford in 1605 and it was James Sagar who founded the Sagar Charity in 1665 for the "benefit of the chapelry of Thornton and the town of Horton". It was his grandson Thomas Sagar who came to live in Leeds and when he died in 1702 he was buried at St. John's Church Briggate. Thomas's grandson was Henry Sagar who reverted to the home at Allerton Grange having been baptised at Leeds Parish Church. Henry's grandson was Richard Hartley Sagar the Bramley solicitor who married Margaret Musgrave in 1832.

Clara Kate nee Brooksbank was John Sagar Musgrave's widow they married in 1860 - and she lived at Red Hall, where her sons Abraham Musgrave Sagar-Musgrave and Robert Malcolm Sagar-Musgrave made their home. Robert was born in December 1871 and joined the family firm of brewers and maltsters - Musgrave and Sagar. The firm started in their Marlborough Street premises in 1857 and 30 years later the brewery employed 20 people.

The Red Hall estate was sold on November 18th.1937 for £14,000 by the trustees of the late Frederick Benjamin Atkinson to the Leeds City Council. During the war years Red Hall was used by the transport department and it then became a local

authority residential home for elderly ladies, which closed in 1992. In late 1992 the Hall became a Development and Training Centre for the employees of the City Council. In July 1994 it was announced that Red Hall would be the new Rugby League headquarters.
In July 1956 the New Central Nursery was opened by the City Council in the kitchen garden area of Red Hall. In 1957 there were 15 aluminium greenhouses built by the Parks department: in 1983 the 127' long greenhouse was damaged by high winds. The first greenhouse in Britain was erected at Oxford on June 15th. 1621 in preparation for a severe winter: a gardener tended a charcoal fire throughout the night.
Red Hall Services have their office in the old farmhouse and they are concerned with the maintenance of grounds and nursery facilities providing flowers on the many city wide locations often sponsored by local firms. The north east Leeds team which cares for thousands of trees in the city and its 2000 acres of woodlands received an award for their commitment to quality and service at Easter 1994. Red Hall Services have the responsibility for the trees planted on city streets, in schools and residential areas.
The Pigeoncote was fully restored in 1977/78 and now stands in the Services compound, although the ice house and fish pond have disappeared. In the 18th. century there could have been 30,000 dovecotes in England: the Egyptians and Persians were rearing pigeons 5000 years ago and used their droppings for fertiliser and gunpowder. The meat was a source of protein and because of the importance of rearing, the early dovecotes were large. After the Norman Conquest the Lord of the Manor or the clergy were allowed to build dovecotes. The 17th. century brought wider ownership and varying architecture. The archway at Temple Newsam is one of the largest in the country holding over 1000 breeding pairs. There have been 200 surviving dovecotes recorded in Yorkshire from at least 700 Medieval sites.

Wellington Inn was built for serving the new turnpike in the 1820's but was rebuilt in the 1870's. There have been suggestions that the inn is dated to the 16th. century. A few years before the 19th. century rebuilding the innkeeper was John Derrick. It became a Tetley Good Food House in August 1989 after a £300,000 refurbishment. There is an extensive car park and children's play area.
Winn Moor Lane on the north side of the inn was once known as Wellington Lane. In the mid-19th. century the area opposite the inn to the east was known as the Brick Field, represented by "Lake Side" in the late 19th. century.
Hobberley House is the large building on Hobberley Lane to Shadwell and it was once the home of the Earl of Mexborough's land agent: in the 1860's it was William Wray. The numerous sandstone quarries on Hobberley Lane have all ceased production: the stone was used to build St.John's Church Roundhay as well as many

local houses.
The Coal Road from Seacroft to Harewood via Wyke crosses the Wetherby Road and was once the main access to Scarcroft prior to the opening of the turnpike in 1837. The Coal Road once had the Bay Horse Inn which was built in 1779 and closed about 1890, now a private house.
Birkby Hill lies east of the main road and north of the Coal Road - known as Bretebi in the Domesday Book. The area remained a detached part of Shadwell until 1882. Following the Norman Conquest Ilbert de Lacy granted Birkby to Robert de Somerville and in 1308 it was granted to Jordan de l'Isle - Kirkstall Abbey also had a small part of Birkby. There have been suggestions that Birkby was once a village and the two farms of Birkby Grange and Birkby Hall today are the only survivors. The farms on the Earl of Mexborough's estates are dairy at the larger Hall farm and beef cattle and hens at the Grange. There is evidence in a field between the farm houses and the Coal Road of supposed Anglian farming strips or lynchets - these narrow strips on rising ground are seen more frequently in the limestone Yorkshire Dales.
North of Carr Lane to Thorner is Eltofts, the home of the Catholic Bishop of Leeds from 1966. In the 1920's Eltofts, part of the Earl of Mexborough's estate, was tenanted by Thomas Mylchreest, chairman of Fairbairn Lawson Barbour Ltd. of Leeds. The Mylchreest family rented Manor Farm and the shooting rights from the Earl of Mexborough: he also bought land and houses in Thorner in 1900 for £5000. He was later to sell the houses, which he upgraded in 1923. He was responsible for the bringing of piped water to Thorner - the pipe ran through Scarcroft Lodge across the main road. Thomas Mylchreest sponsored the Eltofts Cricket Club, which ended during the 1920's - the cricket field is now part of the farmland. The Mylchreest family left Eltofts in 1938 prior to the outbreak of War. The House became the temporary home of evacuees for a part of the Second World War - opened on October 12th. 1944 for 19 evacuees. Eltofts became the home of the Leeds physician and surgeon Dr. Norman Frederick Winder, who moved to Eltofts from Gledhow Wood Road: when he lived at Eltofts his surgery was on Springwood Road Oakwood. Dr. Winder's occupancy was followed by purchase by the Diocese of Leeds from the Earl of Mexborough in 1966, including a wood and immediate fields. The period during which Eltofts was the Bishop's House with the Rt. Rev. Gordon Wheeler as Bishop of Leeds was an active one with many visitors and occasions. Gordon Wheeler was enthroned as Bishop of Leeds on June 27th. 1966 at the age of 56 and soon went to live at Eltofts. His chauffeur was Charles Walker, who lived at a cottage on the site - the Bishop retired on September 10th. 1985 after his 75th. birthday. The new Bishop of Leeds David Konstant came to Eltofts before moving to the Bishop's House on North Grange Road off Headingley Lane in 1988. David Konstant was installed as the 8th. Bishop of Leeds on September 25th. 1985

following his appointment on July 23rd. Eltofts was sold in 1988 to a developer, who created three separate dwellings, although the outbuildings of coach houses and stables - part converted into cottages - have been left to decay. The sale included 16½ acres of parkland grounds with the 10 bedroom house having planning consent for conversion into seven separate dwellings. The views from Eltofts are memorable with Scarcroft Beck and the rolling hills of Elmet.
Eltofts Farm is a mid 18th. century development on the Earl of Mexborough's estate and tenanted by the Goodall family from 1970. The old farm building is not the main dwelling today and there is the evidence of a horse drawn wheel to grind the flour in the outbuildings. The farm is now managed together with Beech Grove on the main Wetherby Road.

Shadwell was mentioned in 1086 as Scadewell, meaning a boundary stream. It was held by Herbert de Arches who confirmed the grant of some of the Shadwell land to Kirkstall Abbey. Following the dissolution of the monasteries, there were changes of land ownership and the Gascoigne and Mauleverer families obtained some of the land. In later times both Lady Elizabeth Hastings of Ledston Hall and the Earls of Mexborough of Methley Hall were land owners. Lady Betty had much property in Shadwell as well as inheriting property at Bardsey, Rigton, Wike, Collingham and many other locations. Rents from her Shadwell farms were used to maintain her almshouses at Ledsham. Much of her property at Shadwell has been sold by the Trustees over the years since her death in 1739.
The Red Lion Inn was first mentioned in 1836 and the Dexter Inn at Slaid Hill remembers the Tetley family breeding Dexters at Shadwell Grange Farm.
There was a chapel at Shadwell in Medieval times and St. Paul's Church was consecrated in July 1842 having been designed by Robert Chantrell, who was the architect of the new Leeds Parish Church. Prior to the church being built the parish church for Shadwell was at Thorner.
Shadwell Methodist Chapel was consecrated in July 1814 with a new chapel opened in October 1892. The old chapel became the Sunday School and a branch library.
Although there was an earlier small school, the first National School opened in 1848 on a field donated by Stephen Nicholson of Roundhay Park. The second school opened in 1874 on land bought from the Lady Betty Hastings Trustees. The school closed in 1959 and in November 1962 the old school was bought as the village hall. The new Shadwell Primary School opened in 1967 and has recently been fully restored.

Scarcroft Beck flows under the main Wetherby Road north of Carr Lane and there is Providence House Farm - now Beech Grove - on the north side of the road. The row of houses on the east side were part of the Ryder estate of Scarcroft Grange.

Scarcroft Grange stands to the east behind a high wall with the original gateway now blocked. The mansion was built about 1840 and in the 1860's was the home of Samuel and William T. Miers, a Methodist family linked through marriage with the Gray family of Morwick Hall. In the 1890's John Samuel Miers lived at nearby Grove House. John Miers of Scarcroft was born in 1904 and died in 1977 - he is buried at Thorner Church.

The Grange became the home of Charles Foster Ryder who was a partner in Tetley's Brewery in Leeds: he initially lived at "Woodlands", which became the home of the YEB management. "Woodlands" is the large restored house on the west of the gateway to Scarcroft Lodge and was once the "William IV" public house and later home to the Watson family.

Charles Foster Ryder was the son of Charles Ryder who was a partner with Francis William Tetley in 1858. Charles started work at Tetley's brewery in 1881 at the age of 25 and he became a partner in 1883 when Francis died. In 1890 Charles Foster was placed in charge of the buying of suitable public houses: Tetleys bought 15 public houses a year later. When the firm became a private limited company in 1897 Charles Foster was one of the three directors. He was an expert in property and land purchase and he died aged 86 on February 28th. 1942 at Thurlow Hall in Suffolk, where he had lived for 12 years. He lived at "Woodlands" and then at Scarcroft Grange when on business in Leeds and was closely linked with the Bramham Moor Hunt. His interest in land acquisition enabled him to buy 20,000 acres in Suffolk and 5000 acres in Yorkshire.

Charles Foster Ryder married twice and one of his large family at Scarcroft Grange was Sue Ryder who was born at a Leeds nursing home in 1923 - when she was young Sue was to leave Scarcroft Grange to live in the south.

Sue was educated at Benenden School in Kent and later joined the First Aid Nursing Yeomanry in the Second World War. She worked with the Polish section of the Special Operations Executive in occupied Europe. She started the Sue Ryder Foundation for residential care of the sick and disabled at Cavendish near Sudbury in 1953 - this centre links 80 centres worldwide. Sue became the second wife of Group Captain Geoffrey Leonard Cheshire in 1959. He was born in 1917 and educated at Stowe School and Oxford University: in 1948 he founded the Cheshire Homes, which number 85 in Britain and 185 in 48 other countries including Russia. He was awarded a life peerage in 1991 and died in July 1992 aged 74.

Margaret Susan Ryder CMG OBE was awarded a life peerage in the Queen's Birthday Honours in June 1978, becoming Baroness Ryder of Warsaw.

Scarcroft Grange became a Ukrainian POW camp with the officers living in the mansion. There are the foundations of the huts in the grounds which once housed the men. After a period of dereliction the mansion was converted into six flats about 1953. The conversions of The Granary and Coach House into separate dwellings

followed and the long low Scarcroft Cottage in the grounds of the hall dating from the 17th. century was altered and converted by the Wilkinson Building Co. of Leeds in the summers of 1954 and 1955.
The Roman Road from Ilkley to York crosses the main road north of Scarcroft Grange. This old road divides at Scarcroft: the older south route is by the footpath to Thorner while the north route passes north of Scarcroft through Wothersome to Bramham. Ashfield House was once the stables to Scarcroft Grove Manor, once the residence of Leeds clothier Clifford Hare. The footpath continues by the Grove to Tennant Lake - after Robert Tennant of Scarcroft Lodge. Originally the pond served as a storage pond for Scarcroft Mill.
The row of cottages west of the main road were the wash houses to Scarcroft Grange and the cottage on the east side was once the village post office. Ling Lane crosses the Black Moor and is a product of the enclosures. The lane links the main road with Tarn Lane and the road to Wike and is known for its attractive gardens.
Scarcroft Lodge was built by Leeds Quaker merchant Newman Cash between 1826 and 1831: Cash was born in 1793 and was a "stuff merchant" with a warehouse on the site of the present Queen's Hotel in Leeds City Square. He had a good shipping trade with the United States and was a director of the North Eastern Railway Co., advancing a policy of a reduced rail traffic on Sundays: he died in 1866. In 1851 he sold Scarcroft Lodge to Robert Tennant, a former Leeds MP who was the son of John Tennant (died 1830) and his second wife Anne Shaw. Robert was born on November 14th.1828 and married Henrietta Garrett in 1850: their children were John Robert, Robert Hugh and Frederick William Tennant.
In later years Scarcroft Lodge became the home of the Savile family: in the early part of this century Lady Mary Louisa Savile lived at the house: she was the sister of the Rt. Hon John Henry Savile 6th. Earl of Mexborough.
In 1929/30 Scarcroft Lodge became the home of Albert Braithwaite, Lord Mayor of Leeds in 1920/21. During his mayoralty he lived at "Springwood" in Roundhay and later at Oaklands Manor Scarcroft, when O. J. Philipson lived at the Lodge in the mid-1930's.
Albert Braithwaite was born in 1868 at Horsforth and had a job at a local quarrying company. In 1918 Braithwaite and William Penrose-Green acquired control of B. Whitaker & Son Ltd forming a syndicate which took over several Leeds brickyards: they were contracted to supply 40 million bricks to the Government. The two men were involved in a lawsuit in 1924 and were fined £10, which was taken to the Court of Appeal where the decision was reversed. As a consequence Braithwaite and Penrose-Green resigned their seats on Leeds City Council. Albert Braithwaite had been a pigeon fancier for 50 years and became a Unionist MP for the Buckrose Division until 1945. He died at Ilkley on February 4th.1946.
It was Albert Braithwaite's son Albert who is regarded as the "father" of opencasting

in the Leeds area. The first site at Beechwood Temple Newsam was opened in 1941 after he persuaded the Government to tackle the problem of falling coal production by allowing shallow seams to be excavated. Beechwood closed in 1943 and left derelict: it is now the site of the sports arena. Albert Braithwaite Jnr. married the daughter of an American railways director and he travelled widely in his private train. He was an MP and a director of Sir Lindsay Parkinson: the Dunstan Hill opencast site at Temple Newsam Park was opened by the company. In the 1950's there were 14 opencast sites in South Leeds and in 1987 Skelton Opencast was opened and was to destroy the ancient site of the Knights Templars preceptory, which was surveyed prior to opencasting.
Extraction of coal ended in April 1994 and over a five year period about 866,000 tons of coal were taken from the Skelton site. The site will be completely restored and landscaped by the end of 1995.
Scarcroft Lodge was bought for use as their headquarters in 1945 by the Yorkshire Electric Power Company from the owner O. J. Philipson. On April 1st. 1948 the Yorkshire Electricity Board was formed after nationalisation and the buildings now employ about 500 staff. There were extensions built in both 1952 and 1956 with a temporary annexe. In November 1974 there was an application to demolish Scarcroft Lodge with the exception of the clock tower but this never matured. In 1975 there was a £2.5 million programme of conservation and alteration and in the same year the Lodge became a Grade II listed building, with the area surrounding the Lodge becoming a Conservation Area. The YEB occupied the new buildings in October 1976. A new YEB administration building designed by Huddersfield architects was opened in 1977. In 1985 there was a programme of major structural repairs and conservation work on both the Lodge and the gate lodgehouses.
Yorkshire Electricity is one of 12 regional electricity companies in England Wales, with 5300 employees and 2 million customers. The system has 30,000 sub-stations using 37,99km of underground cables and 15,000km of overhead lines.
The National Grid Co. operates the transmission system and co-ordinates the running of the main power stations. Coal and nuclear power stations are run by National Power, PowerGen and Nuclear Electric.

Scarcroft Village Hall was built in 1923 with the fundraising by local folk. The two castellated houses on the main road beyond the village hall are lodges built in 1830. They guarded the entrance to Castle Mona - now High Gables - built by the Mann family from the Isle of Wight. The house name derives from the Manx for Man = Mona. The house was often known as "Mann's Folly" and is a Grade II listed building. The foundation stone was laid for the House on January 12th.1830 and the builders were J.& T. Utley: the house was once the home of Blackburn's chief test pilot Reginald W. Kenworthy.

The New Inn dates from the 1930's and the previous inn operated its own brewhouse and was sited nearer the main road - the innkeeper at the turn of the century was Henry Rathbone. The inn today is one of the Harvester chain of inn-restaurants, called The Malthouse.
The row of cottages on Syke Lane west of the New Inn is called Maltkiln Cottages and earlier this century was used as a meeting hall prior to the completion of the Village Hall. One of the maltsters was John Titchmarsh, who lived in one of the cottages on a track that once led to a sand quarry. He died aged 84 in 1933 and was buried at Thorner Church.
The small stone toll bar house was built in 1826 and became a listed building in 1976: in 1984 a conservation programme was undertaken and the metal plaque was unveiled on April 14th.1986. The tolls were collected from all traffic for 50 years from the turnpike opening: one of the toll collectors was Marmaduke Dickinson at the "Scarcroft Bar" in 1841. There were several folk who avoided the charge of ½d. a hoof by taking the detour along Syke Lane.
The turnpike closed as a result of the Trust's bankruptcy in 1878. This was mainly due to the competition from the Cross Gates - Wetherby railway which had opened in 1876. Scarcroft residents would have used either Bardsey or Thorner stations, which closed with the other stations on this once popular line in January 1964.
Scarcroft Hall is on Thorner Lane, although there is little evidence of early building on the present modern farm. Joshua Hall who lived at Scarcroft Hall died aged 74 in 1895: he was followed by farmer Albert Rhodes.
Oaklands Manor was the home of Albert Braithwaite for a short period and the waters of Scarcroft Beck flow through the manor grounds. The manor was originally known as Scarcroft Hill House and was a large villa built by Ard Walker Jnr. in 1844 - he was a retired Leeds wine and spirit merchant.
Scarcroft Corn Mill once stood on Scarcroft Beck with its crushing stones turned by water controlled by a sluice, which is still in working condition. In February 1745 Scarcroft Mill was available "to let" as a good water cornmill with 20 acres of arable, meadow and pasture. In October 1791 the mill was again for sale with 537 acres including houses, farms and woods, occupied by serving tenants. In the same year the Scarcroft home of Wade Preston was on sale as " a hunting seat of a new brick house". The last miller was John Revis who produced good quality wholegrain flour: he was eventually bought out by Allinson's of Castleford and the mill became redundant before the last War. The old mill was demolished in 1982 following a local preservation campaign: in more recent years the stone has been taken away. The archway through which passed the waterwheel shaft is the only reminder of this once active mill. The mill race for Scarcroft Mill dam is now used for fish ponds: the fish are held in here from the breeding farms before transfer to the rivers.
The Revis family included John Snr. who died aged 60 in 1909: his sons and

daughters included Percy, who died in New Zealand in 1921 and John who died aged 71 in 1947. Henry Revis died aged 72 in 1963-the family are buried in Thorner Churchyard.
Scarcroft was not mentioned in the 1086 survey and the name of the community means "Scarthi's Croft", where a croft was an enclosure used for tillage. In the 14th. century Scarcroft was an independent township with the Brus family as Lords from the 12th. century. The Vavasours of Hazlewood were the mesne-lords by the early 13th. century and were replaced as an under-tenancy of the Ryther family by the end of that century. The manor was granted to John de Ros of Helmsley in 1280, who reverted the property to William Ryther. In 1491 Scarcroft was held by Robert Ryther from Henry Vavasour.
The original centre of Scarcroft was on Thorner Lane, although the pinfold and village pond were on the corner site of the present Post Office. The centre had the hall and mill together with Moat Hall, although the moat was filled in with material from a road widening scheme and the old hall was rebuilt.
Wetherby Road east of the New Inn crossroads passes the site of Rowley Grange Farm to the south. This was once a busy farm complete with a horse powered gin wheel - few buildings now remain intact. Rowley Grange was farmed by William Ridsdale, died 1858 aged 63; Charles Carr died 1881 and John Gaunt (1889-1931). Alfred Elam farmed Rowley Grange at the turn of the century prior to the family moving to Halton farms. The footpath from Rowley Grange to Hetchell Woods is a part of an original Roman Road, which crosses Bardsey Beck and passes the site of Pompocali.
The fortified hill top site of Pompocali was once part of Crow Wood and there are thoughts that the site was created by the after effects of sand quarrying. It was suggested that the name Pompocali is a form of Campodunum, being a Celtic name mentioned by the Venerable Bede in the early 8th. century. It could have been a corruption of "campo" meaning a field and "Calcaria" being the Roman name for Tadcaster. In 1867 reference was made to "Pampycallo - the remains of a British-Danish fort."
Hetchell Woods Nature Reserve is one of 60 nature reserves administered by the Yorkshire Wildlife Trust. Their first reserve was at Askham Bog near York in 1946 and there are now 6000 acres of Trust land in Yorkshire. The Trust has nearly 9000 members who enjoy access to outstanding areas of countryside. Hetchell Woods comprises 29 acres of land on the edge of the Permian Magnesian Limestone, which overlays the East Carlton Grits which themselves form the popular Hetchell Crags. The reserve was set up in 1967 when 21 acres were leased from Lt. Col. George Lane-Fox of Bramham Park. A further 8 acres are leased from Hon. Mrs. M. A. M. Lane-Fox. The highest point of this reserve is 300 feet above sea level on which there has been much alteration of landscape including limestone quarrying.

The reserve is divided ecologically into Aldercarr, marshland, scrub, Oak and Beech woodland and limestone grassland. It is on this sloping land that some interesting protected flowers are found including Rock Rose, Salad Burnet and Dyer's Greenweed.
The access to the Hetchell Woods Nature Reserve is from the Thorner/ Bardsey road, where there is a limited car parking space or from the main Wetherby Road near the site of the old railway bridge. The route of the old railway line is also open as a footpath and Hetchell Woods is approached across the stepping stones of Bardsey Beck.

The Cross Gates/Wetherby railway crossed the main Wetherby Road by a girder skew-bridge prior to the station at Bardsey - the site by the main road is now covered with housing. The station house has been converted into a modern dwelling. The steps to the platform from the roadside are now overgrown but there is still the old gate and track from the road. The single track line opened to Wetherby in 1876 with the track doubling in 1902. The stations were at Scholes, Thorner, Bardsey and Collingham Bridge, with the later Penda's Way officially opening on Monday June 5th. 1939. The railway was closed in January 1964 and the rails were taken up.
The waters of Bardsey Beck cross under the main road from the site of Bardsey Mill upper dam. The remains of the dam and sluice can be seen from either the old railway line - from where can be seen the brick tunnel under the embankment - or from the track to Hetchell Woods Nature Reserve. The dam acted as a storage pond to maintain the flow to the lower pond. This lower mill pond was on the site of The Dell and the waters flowed to Bardsey Mill by a goit, thus using both Bardsey Beck and Gill Beck waters to turn the millwheel.
Bardsey was known as Bereleseie or Berdesei in the 1086 Domesday Survey. It means Beornred's island which could refer to Castle Hill. It was perhaps on this site that the Saxon farmers, which included Ligulf, would have made their home and defended it from possible incursion.
The tower and its porch of All Hallow's Church dates from 850AD/ 950AD. The outline of the porch is clearly seen on the west tower wall and the south tower wall shows the late Saxon period windows: the tower was heightened a few years before the Norman Conquest.
Inside this ancient church there are outlines of blocked up Saxon windows on the north arcade walls, dating from the rebuilding of the church in Norman times. The church was rebuilt between 1100 and 1125 to include the south doorway together with the north arcade. There are deep splayed Norman windows on the west walls and the two aisles were widened between 1375 and 1400. The tower was given a battlemented top and new windows were inserted. There is a list of incumbents from 1312 when Adam de Lund was the vicar.

The large slab set against the west wall of the nave/tower is probably dated from the late 13th. century. It is incised with a chalice left of the cross and a book on the right. The slab was reused during the Civil War for the tomb of the Vicar Alexander Holden (1597-1644) and bears the initials AH.

The south arcade was built between 1175 and 1200 to balance the north arcade. The arches are pointed on the south side and round on the north side. In 1300 - 1325 the original short chancel was widened and extended. In the 15th. century the sedilia and piscina were placed in the chancel and in 1521 the north chapel was built. This was a chantry chapel which had been endowed by Edmund Mauleverer of Wothersome - some members of this family are buried at Bardsey Church.

The south aisle chapel was endowed in 1724 and known as the Bingley Chapel; the estate was bought in 1720 by Lord Bingley. The small chapel, with the private pews of the family now serves as the choir vestry. In this vestry is a 1867 copy of a 1731 benefactions board. The board is inscribed to "the poor of the parish of Bardsey in the eighth year of Queen Elizabeth 1st.(1541) £1 to be paid every Michaelmas for ever out of the rectory of Thorp Arch. The Rt. Hon. Earl of Strafford with an annual sum of 3/4d every Michaelmas and Mrs. Lister of Rigton, by will, a sum of £2 a year to the poor of Bardsey and Rigton - she died on January 27th. 1720". The chapel also has a large Royal coat of arms from 1819 - the reign of King George III and a year before George IV acceeded to the throne.

The tomb of Baron Francis Thorpe who died at Bardsey in June 1663 was removed during the 19th. century restorations, which included the removal of the early 19th. century west gallery. His wife Elizabeth Oglethorpe is remembered in a plaque on the south chancel wall. Baron Thorpe was the Sergeant of Laws and a Baron of the Public Exchequer.

The funereal hatchments to the Lane-Fox family of Bramham Park are no longer displayed within the south west corner, which was refurbished in 1986 to create a display area. The church was restored by architect Charles Chorley in 1909: he died in Herefordshire in November 1912.

The reredos was placed in memory of Edith Davidson (1885-1931) and there are two brass plaques on the north wall of the chancel: William Harold Ryder of the Yorkshire Hussars and RFC was the 3rd. son of Charles Foster and Anna Ryder of Scarcroft Grange who was killed in France on July 6th. 1917 aged 20 and was buried abroad; the other plaque describes the new chancel floor as being in memory of Anna Ryder. The carved Oak crucifix on one of the south nave pillars was also donated by the Ryder family. The church electric lighting was installed in 1930 in memory of Louisa Ryder. The church clock and chimes was placed in the tower in 1909.

The gnomon-less sundial south of the church porch is initialled JM and JB with J SAUL 1761 - Saul was the local schoolmaster and the initials are those of churchwardens Jonathan Midgley and John Butterfield.

The church registers record the baptism of William Congreve of Bardsey Grange. The cottage in which he was born stands on the hill top near Bardsey Grange Farm, which has been redeveloped for residential purposes: included are the old tithe barn, stables and the house. Bardsey Grange is a listed building and dated 1717, having a 17th. century inner core. There were extensions in the mid/late 18th. century with windows altered in the late 18th. century: the barn and cart shed also date from the late 18th. century and cowhouse and granary from about 1800. At the bottom of the slope on Cornmill Close are the restored "Old Forge" and the 18th. century Corn Mill, complete with grinding stones: the mill was linked with both the Midgley and Mawson families and in 1900 the mill was run by Alan J. Mawson. This water corn mill was last used in 1940 and was provided with the waters of two becks and two mill ponds.

William Congreve was born at Bardsey Grange in 1670 when his mother was visiting her uncle Francis Thorpe. His father was commissioned and sent to Ireland where William attended a school at Kilkenny. Congreve became one of England's foremost poets and dramatists and was known as the "Moliere of England". He died on January 19th. 1729 and was buried in the south west aisle of Westminster Abbey.

Bardsey Church

His tomb was set up by Henrietta Duchess of Marlborough and the inscription says that "she remembers the happiness and honour she enjoyed in the sincere friendship of so worthy and honest a man, whose virtue candour and wit gained him the love and esteem of the present age and whose writings will be the admiration of the future".

Bardsey has an important and ancient castle site north of the church and old vicarage. The keep was surrounded by a moat and it was probably built between 1184 and 1200 by Adam or Peter de Brus. Excavations have revealed a square stone structure and pottery from the 12th and 13th. centuries. Adam de Brus had been granted a small estate and Bardsey Castle was built as his residence to administer the area. There is no access across the site, although there is a footpath through a gate to the north of Callister Hall on Woodacre Lane, where a good view of the castle site can be obtained.

It was Sir Henry Carey who obtained the Bardsey estates in 1558 and in 1620 he sold them to Sir Thomas Wentworth: his descendent was Sir Thomas Earl of Strafford who died in 1641. In 1654 Bardsey went to Sir John Lewis of Ledston Hall and in 1671 Mary married Robert Leake Earl of Scarsdale. In 1720 Bardsey came to Robert Benson of Bramham Park.

There are three vicarages in Bardsey: the Old Vicarage is south of the "Bingley Arms" along The Ginnel; the second vicarage was built in 1849 as a gift of James Lane-Fox and bears the date and inscription "Deo Laus". From 1930 there was a succession of private owners and in 1985 the Castle Hill Nursing Home opened. The home is set amidst attractive secluded gardens and has been modernised to accommodate 26 elderly patients. The grounds of this old vicarage now have six dwellings on Castle Grove. The old entrance on Woodacre Lane is now blocked up but retains the gate pillars. The third vicarage on Woodacre Lane was built in 1929/30.

The first school was probably set up by the villagers and then was endowed from William Ermystead, Queen's Chaplain in the mid 16th. century. The old village school was endowed in 1726 by the bequest of Robert Lord Bingley. This became the Callister Hall in 1954 in memory of Frank Callister (Vicar 1944-1953) when the new school was opened in 1954.

The nearby Village or Trustees Hall was built in 1927 and now is administered by the Parochial Council.

The "Bingley Arms" inn was mentioned in the Domesday Book as The Priests Inn, the name from 953AD until the name was changed in 1780 to The Bingley Arms - the oldest part of the inn is the central section as the two ends were added in 1738. It is recorded as England's oldest inhabited inn with records of brewers and innkeepers from AID. Samson Ellis was the first member of the family to brew here

in 953AD: the brewhouse was demolished in 1942 in an ARP exercise. The inn was connected with Kirkstall Abbey and used as a rest house for the monks travelling to St. Mary's Abbey York. The links with Kirkstall were made in 1160 when Roger de Mowbray granted land at Bardsey to the abbey during the time of the first abbot. The Bardsey estates remained with Kirkstall Abbey to the dissolution of the monasteries. The monks would have used a road that passed north of the inn and south of the church. The inn was later used by stage coach passengers and the adjoining buildings were used as stables. There was a cellar now blocked up which was once considered to be a passage to the church.
The local court was held here from 1000AD and any offenders were taken to the pillory sited near the church: this custom was abolished in 1837.
The descendants of the Ellis family between 1600 and 1780 raised the height of the inn by 4'6" to allow for window fittings. The chimney contains two priest's holes made in 1539 for the sanctuary of Catholic priests following the dissolution of the monasteries.
The Cistercian monks would have brought their sheep through Bardsey and the animals were washed in Gill Beck before sale at the Wool Market in Leeds. The drovers were often inconvenienced with flooding of the beck and a bridge was completed in 1820 to ease this problem. The Dutch Oven inside the inn dates from 1738 and is one of the few in its original position in England. In 1900 the innkeeper and brewer was Charles Brown.
Inside the Bingley Arms there is on display Nathaniel Buck's prospect of Leeds in 1745 and a print of the Shire Oak in Headingley from 1829. There is a framed plan of Leeds coaching inns and a print of Ralph Thoresby's house in Kirkgate Leeds. The Bingley Arms is now a Tetley Heritage Inn with a new manager's house built in sympathy with the old building. This brewery took over from Russell's Brewery Malton in the 1960's. Oak Tree Cottage is a half-timbered house opposite The Bingley Arms and dates from the late 16th. century: there were alterations in the early 19th. century. The house was originally thatched and in the 19th. century it was a tobacconists shop there was once a sign which stated: "Here lives Nathaniel Clough, Seller of Tobacco and very fine snuff". Other listed cottages in Bardsey include Ghyll Cottage from the mid/late 17th. century showing few remains of the original timber framed house and Smallfield Cottage dating from about 1800 which was once a tailors and drapers shop.
Old Bardsey or Bardsey Hill is south west of the Church and is complete with farms and the village pond, although the old tithe barn in this part has been demolished. Bardsey Lodge on Tithe Barn Lane is dated 1729 SA, which indicates the dwelling of Samuel Abbott. The barns attached to Hill Top farmhouse possibly date from the late 16th. century.
East Rigton lies south of the main Wetherby Road on top of Rigton Bank and there

were eight farmers listed in the village in 1901. The hamlet had both a smithy and an inn at one period. The old smithy stands restored with a new sign on Rigton Green close by a horse mounting block. The present farmhouse is a listed building dating from about 1780 and having the roof raised in the early 19th. century. In the garden is a stone from the house dated 1781. Mizpah Cottage on Rigton Green dates from the early 19th. century and is a result of a squatter's encroachment on the village green.

Scarcroft Toll House

THE ROAD FROM LEEDS TO WETHERBY

PART 4: EAST KESWICK TO WETHERBY

The entry into East Keswick from the main road or via Bardsey passes Rigton Grange Farm: George Ridsdale of this farm died in 1862 aged 40.The Ridsdale family were later involved in the village trades of market gardening and boot & shoe dealing.

East Keswick is a Domesday Village known as Chesuic becoming Chesewich in about 1130: it is a Scandinavian form of the Old English for a "Cheese-Farm".

The village was the site of a moated mansion of the Gascoigne family, who came into the property. The mansion was demolished about the mid-17th. century and the stone used at Old Hall farm and at Moat Hall. The site is south of Moat Hall in the centre of a field, where the outline of a raised mound is visible. The water filled moat was once a skating rink in winter periods,although it was drained about 1953. The Moat House is 18th. century and once a farm: the adjoining building was converted into a surgery.

The village was part of the Harewood estate from its purchase by Henry Lascelles in 1739 for over two centuries: much land was sold in 1950 to meet death duties.

The Church of St.Magdalene on Moor Lane was built of local stone in 1857 to designs by Mallinson & Healey of Bradford at a cost of £1500 as a chapel of ease to Harewood - East Keswick is now in the parish of Bardsey. The site was donated by the Earl of Harewood and cash raised by the Harewood vicar Rev. Miles Atkinson. This small but beautiful church contains an abundance of Robert Thompson's Mouseman furniture. The church contains a brass plaque to George Vincent Roberts who died aged 29 in 1930 and was buried in Ceylon (Sri Lanka). The stained glass window in the north nave is a memorial to Harold, the son of George and Sarah Rushforth who died in 1919. The church porch was erected in memory of the local men who died in the two World Wars.

The Old Parsonage on Main Street was a former farmhouse and dates from the mid-18th.century with later extensions.

The first Methodist Chapel was built in 1792 - it was later used as a mill, now a private house on School Lane - and the present chapel on the Main Street was opened in 1891 in memory of Joseph Lawrence. The village Methodists had first met in Thomas Wright's house in the village in 1779. The Quakers or Society of Friends had a burial ground in East Keswick from the 17th. century.

The school was opened in 1851 with a schoolhouse attached and moved to larger premises by the church in 1914.The old school is converted into a cottage and retains the inscription "BOYS" over the door. The school closed in 1990 and village children now attend Bardsey or Harewood schools. The private East Keswick

College was once run by Helen and Mary Lawrence, following the running of the college by their father Joseph Lawrence as a training for young men into the Methodist ministry.
The village hall was officially opened by the Earl and Countess of Harewood on June 7th. 1987.
"City Square" is the local name for the junction of Moor Lane and Main Street, once the site of the smithy and the village Post Office.
There are two inns in the village: "The Old Star" and the "Duke of Wellington" with "The Traveller's Rest" on Harewood Avenue north of the village. The Old Star originated as a farmhouse and was altered to an inn by 1822 and in the 1830's the innkeeper at the Star was Abraham Barrett: at The Wellington was Thomas Watson. At this period there were three lime burners - lime was first quarried in the village in 1700 - and 15 farmers in the village area. Today there are eight farms in the parish including arable, sheep and dairy. The War Memorial on Whitegate Top remembers the fallen of the First World War.
The approach to Collingham on Wetherby Road passes the site of the old "Beck Toll Bar" near the milestone before entering the village. There were other toll bars on Harewood Avenue east of the Linton Road and the "Side" toll bar at the end of Jewitt Lane near "The Barleycorn" - a joiner's shop - controlling the traffic to York and Tadcaster. The Barleycorn public house,once the property of the Gunter family, had a six day licence for many years as decreed by the owning family.
Traffic entering Wetherby approached the toll bar at Micklethwaite near the main bridge.

In the 7th. century the Venerable Bede referred to Collingham as "Ingaethlingum" assuming this to be the site of a monastery founded by Aenfled in 651AD. Aenfled was the wife of King Oswy of Bernicia who had slain the Christian King Oswini of Deira possibly at Collingham in 650AD.When Oswy defeated Penda of Mercia on Whinmoor in 655AD Aenfled was sent to Whitby Abbey. The Oswini cross, probably dated from the 9th. century,on display in the church is inscribed with Runic letters: "Aenfled this set up in memory of her cousin Oswy and Oswini King - Pray for their souls". The other cross showing Christ and the Apostles is dated to the early 9th. century.
In 1167 the village was known as Collingeham, referring to the enclosure of Colals people. Collingham was held by the de Mowbray family and in later years passed to the de Stutevilles and to Kirkstall Abbey. Following the dissolution of the monasteries there was a succession of owners from Sir Henry Carey and Lord Hunsdon to the sale of Collingham lands to Sir Robert Gunter of Wetherby Grange in the late 19th. century.
The church has the core of an Anglo-Saxon building with a nave a short chancel.

There are Saxon stones to be found in the walls on the south side. The north aisle was added about 1200 and widened in the 14th. century:the chancel was extended in the 13th. century and the tower dates form the 15th. century: the tower was restored in 1907 by Sir Nevill Gunter in memory of his parents Sir Robert & Lady Gunter of Wetherby Grange. The architect for this restoration was Hodgson Fowler and the contractor was Wharton Thirlwall of Boston Spa. Sir Nevill also gave the peal of 8 bells, made by John Taylor & Sons Loughborough. There was an extensive restoration in 1840/41 for £700 raised by subscription. There was another restoration in 1870 by the London architect J.P.St.Aubyn, when the chancel was re-roofed. The clock was a gift of Sir Robert and Lady Gunter in 1891.Sir Robert Gunter (1831-1905) served in the Crimea and was a Colonel of Alexandra Princess of Wales's Own (Yorkshire Regiment). He represented Knaresborough in Parliament 1884/85 and for the Barkston Ash Division 1885 - 1905. Sir Robert Gunter was also a JP for the West Riding.

In the north churchyard at Collingham is the grave of Major General James Gunter (1833-1908) who served in the Crimea in the 1st. and 4th.Dragoon Guards.

It was during the Victorian restoration that the Saxon crosses were discovered in the old south wall and were at first displayed in the vicarage garden. There are fragments of three Medieval slabs, now forming parts of window sill and the internal vestry wall.

Set onto the wall of the south nave are large grave slabs: one is dated 1665 and remembers the Bielby Family of Micklethwaite Grange. There is also a Royal Coat of Arms of 1706 - the reign of Queen Anne (1702-1714).

The church also displays one of the rare Cresset stones, now mounted on a stand and having a central hollow surrounded by seven outer hollows for the melted fat and a cotton wick. The central hollow was for the Sanctuary light and from the outer flames the villagers would have lit their tapers for the cottage fires. The Cresset fire burned mainly at night and often one hollow was lit each day - the Collingham stone has seven daily hollows. Usually the Cresset stones were kept on the nave floor and care was taken not to ignite the rushes and bracken which was strewn over the church floor. The Collingham Cresset is made from Magnesian Limestone and is 5" thick. There are other Cresset stones to be found at Nun Monkton Church, Furness Abbey and probably the finest in England at Lewannick Cornwall, south west of Launceston.

In the churchyard are the 19th. century graves of the Eamonson and Medhurst families - Benjamin Eamonson was the Collingham Vicar for 29 years and died in 1867. In the south west churchyard area is a small stone which traditionally is the burial place of a man's thumb and arm!

The 19th. century vicarage on Church Lane is now a private house and the new vicarage was built in 1970. The Dower House was once in the Vicarage grounds and

was the first vicarage before the Victorian building was completed. On Church Lane is the Manor House, home to the Marshall family for many years: N.Marshall was a builder and contractor.
A small Wesleyan Chapel was built in 1827 on School Lane and the building was used for a few years as an annexe to the nearby school. The chapel was demolished and developed for new housing. The foundation stones were laid for the new Methodist Church on Harewood Road on July 4th.1925 - this Rambler's Church opened a year later.
The ginnel connecting Church Lane and Wetherby Road passes the Tennis Courts and three old stone milestones set against the wall of the public garden. One milestone reads "To Harewood 3 miles; Tadcaster 8 miles": another milestone indicates that Wetherby is 3¾ miles away. Many of the cast iron/gritstone milestones seen today along the roads are listed structures and were made by Brayshaw & Booth of Liversedge.
The picturesque neat garden was created and maintained by past and present members of the village and especially the late Mr.& Mrs.F.Bearder - as a stone indicates. The Collingham Memorial Hall was opened in 1920, being the first in the West Riding after the First World War. Hughenden House opposite the gardens was named after Benjamin Disraeli's home of Hughenden Manor now a National Trust property and home to the Disraeli Museum since 1949. The Manor is north west of Beaconsfield and Benjamin Disraeli (1804-1881) became the Earl of Beaconsfield in 1876. Disraeli's nephew had the Collingham house built in 1882.Nearby Primrose Cottage is named from the Primrose League, an association for political propaganda formed in memory of Lord Beaconsfield in 1883 and named from his supposed favourite flower.
It seems likely that Oliver Cromwell probably stayed the night after the battle of Marston Moor at the original "Half Moon Inn" - the new building dates from about 1900 and at one time the two buildings were adjacent until the original inn was demolished and the site became the car park..
Smithy Court is a 1992 development on the site of the old blacksmith's shop,which became the Chamber's Joinery Works the firm removed to larger premises at Tockwith.
Inside Collingham Church is a a metal board inscribed with the instructions to the living from Lady Elizabeth Hastings, who was Lady of the Manor and Patron of the Church. There is much property in the village which is now administered by the Lady Betty Hastings Trustees, including the 18th.century houses on Church Lane - once the main street before the turnpike - called Hastings and Holmstone Cottages. The Old Star Inn is a Trustee property - it is said that Dick Turpin stayed two nights here and posted out notices for his own arrest. The Old Mill became a Garden Centre in the mid-1960's. The mill still retains the 5' diameter wooden undershot water

wheel, complete with blades, iron extension and cogwheel. The mill buildings retain some original beams and many reminders of the corn milling. There are sections of the grinding stones displayed, which became redundant when the mill finally closed by the end of the last World War. The old millpond was along the north side of the main road and the Millgreen estate was built close to the beck and millpond site. The modern Millbeck House has attractive landscaped gardens down to the beck. On the north west side of the bridge on Harewood Road is the old toll house.

The village school was founded by Lady Betty Hastings in 1738 with £17 a year for free instruction of 20 children. This building on School Lane is now used as the Collingham Youth Centre and retains the playground:the building is leased to the Leeds Education Committee by the Lady Betty Hastings Trustees. The new school opened on Harewood Road in 1968.

The present 2200 population live in a variety of old, converted and new houses in an expanding village: the shopping centre of Hastings Court and the restored and converted housing on School Lane is typical of Collingham development.

The last railway station on the Wetherby line from Cross Gates was at Collingham Bridge, opening in 1876 and closing in 1964. The site of the station has now been covered with housing but the position of the girder bridge can still be seen from an attractive path on the east side of the road to Linton.

In 1086 the Domesday Book mentions Linton and it became part of the vast Percy estates. In 1175 Linton became part of the Earl of Warwick's estates but reverted to the Percy family.

The Linton township is made up from two hamlets: Linton and Whitwell. Whitwell House Farm is on the riverside road to Wood Hall Hotel: the route to the hotel is by Trip Lane.

Linton means a Flax enclosure, although it has been suggested that the name originates from the Old English "hlinc-tun" meaning a hill side enclosure. The long history of the village is shown by the presence of a Medieval priory and the site is now occupied by a house called Chapel Stile: by the roadside green and opposite the church.

In 1859 a Chapel-of-Ease to Spofforth was built by George, Lord Leconfield costing him £300: it served as a National School until 1924. On July 15th.1887 the boundary of St.James Church Wetherby was altered to include Linton: Wetherby became a separate parish from Spofforth in 1869. The building was conveyed to the Diocese of Ripon in 1940 and used for Wetherby services.

Linton Church was sold in 1979 and was converted into a dwelling, retaining the central doorway, bellcote and cross. There are many other conversions from old buildings in this village including the Granary, Old Barn and Smithy.

Linton Memorial Hall was designed by W.A.Jones of architects Jones & Stocks of

Leeds: it was opened as a memorial to the seven young men of Linton who lost their lives in the War.
The Windmill Inn is an ancient building and one of the attractions of a delightful village. Golf had been played on Linton Common and in 1910 a new nine hole course was constructed on the old Linton Ings racecourse. The club house was erected a year later. Lord Leconfield sold his Linton estate in 1921 and the land, with the golf course, was bought by Henry Crossley and Joseph Hudson, who sold it again in 1930.
Linton Ings was the site of the Wetherby Steeplechase on a course laid out in 1842-43 with the permission of Lord Leconfield. There is a record of 30,000 people attending the Linton Ings Steeplechase in March 1865. The Guardian's Steeplechase was run over the Workhouse Course on Linton Ings on April 7th.1887.
Linton Ings course was used until 1890 and in 1891 the race was held on the York Road, part of the Montagu estate. A race course railway station opened on October 31st.1924, as in previous years racegoers were conveyed by taxis from the Linton Road station.
Wood Hall Hotel on Trip Lane opened in 1989 and is set in 100 acres of parkland and bounded by a mile of the River Wharfe. William the Conqueror gave the Linton lands to Percy family: the Vavasours were the lords of the manor, whose seat was at Hazlewood. The first mansion nearer the river banks was destroyed by Cromwell's soldiers in the Civil War and the property became derelict. The two stone shields depicting the coat of arms of York are displayed in the hotel entrance foyer and were discovered in the river nearby.
The present Wood Hall was built in 1750 when the property passed to the Scott family, descendents of the Scotts of Scott Hall Leeds. William Lister Fenton Scott Snr died on March 27th.1813 and his wife Mary died in October 1815 aged 59. In 1817 their son William Fenton Lister Scott formed a trust for the Woodhall estate and he became Lord of the Manor of Sicklinghall and Woodhall. He was concerned with the Leeds Commercial Bank, which was founded in 1792 and ceased trading in 1812. William Lister Fenton Scott died on October 8th.1842 following serving 16 years as the Registrar General for the West Riding. His wife founded Sicklinghall School about 1850: the building is now a private house.
By the 1860's Woodhall was tenanted by the Hon.John Charles Dundas and soon afterwards the Scott family returned - in 1881 Henry Richard Johnstone Scott was at Wood Hall and laid the foundation stone for St.Peter's Church Sicklinghall on September 12th. Henry was the second son of Sir John Johnstone. Sir John Vanden Bempde Johnstone was born at Hackness Hall on August 28th.1799, succeeded to the title in 1807 and died on February 25th.1869.
Henry Richard Johnstone Scott married Cressida who was the founder and supporter of Sicklinghall Church from 1881 until 1926. Henry Richard died aged 82 on

January 29th.1910: Cressida died aged 96 in 1937, when she lived at nearby Banks House - now Sicklinghall House. Their son Egerton died in 1910 aged 37. The eight graves at St.Peter's Church Sicklinghall are all members of this Johnstone-Scott family and include the children of Henry Richard and Cressida: Henry Lister Johnstone Scott was the grandson of Sir John Johnstone: he was born October 18th.1869 and died at Scarborough February 14th.1946 - he was a magistrate and had been born disabled with no arms; Maynie Johnstone Scott (1876-1948); Ronald Johnstone Scott died aged 56 in 1967; Charles (1870-1948) and Elizabeth Irvine Johnstone Scott (1883-1957).
Sicklinghall Church was dedicated on September 20th.1882 and it remained in the care of the Wood Hall families until 1946. The villagers raised £3000 for the endowment and a service of consecration was held on June 24th.1957. The church was a chapel of ease to Kirkby Overblow until 1981 when it became part of the new united parish.
The Roman Catholic Church of Mary Immaculate was opened on August 30th.1854; it was designed by architect C.Hansom and the benefactor was Peter Middleton of Stockeld Park. In the churchyard is a tall cross in memory of the first Catholic Bishop of Leeds Dr.Robert Cornthwaite: he was the Bishop of Beverley from 1861 to 1878 and took over at Leeds in that year until 1890, when he died in office.The Diocese of Leeds was created from the Diocese of Beverley in 1889 and St.Anne's Church became St.Anne's Cathedral.
By the turn of the century Wood Hall was the seat of the Dawson family: plans were prepared in August 1910 by the Leeds firm of Connon and Chorley of Park Place for alterations at Wood Hall. John Wreghitt Connon was the son of a clergyman and was in partnership with Charles Chorley from 1885. In 1897 Harry Chorley entered the firm and John Connon died in 1921, having written the history of Bardsey cum Rigton in 1909.
In 1911 Joseph Watson the lst.Lord Manton bought Wood Hall but later moved to Linton Springs. Joseph Watson was born at his parent's house on Monkbridge Road Headingley Leeds in 1873 and was the son of George Watson, who inherited the Whitehall Soap Works from his father. He was educated at Repton School and Clare College Cambridge and "Soapy Joe" Watson was the 3rd.generation at the successful works in Leeds. In 1918 Watson sold out to Lever Brothers and also disposed of his shares in the Olympia Oil Works at Selby. He had a great interest in horse racing and received a peerage in the 1922 New Year Honours, while he was resident at Linton Springs. He bought the estate at Compton Verney in Warwickshire and also purchased estates at Manton, Offchurch, Thorney near Peterborough, Barlby near Selby and the 18th.century Sudbourne Hall in Suffolk this was the old home of the Marquess of Hertford. The estates totalled about 12,000 acres: he developed an agricultural research station at Offchurch with the director Dr.Charles Crowther.

Joseph Watson became the Chairman of the Directing Board, which was in charge of the No.l Shell Filling Factory at Barnbow: he attended the factory every day from August 1915 until the Armistice was signed. He was a member of the Leeds General Infirmary Board and donated £50,000 to the Infirmary in 1921. He was also a director of the Lancashire & Yorkshire Railway and of the North Western Group. In 1873 he married the daughter of Harold Nickols and they had four sons Miles, Robert, Alastair and Mark.
Lord Manton died as a result of a hunting accident at the 18th.century mansion of Compton Verney in Warwickshire, which he had bought from Lord de Broke. Linton Springs was bought by Major the Hon.Edward C.Lascelles, brother of Viscount Lascelles. Lord Manton was buried at Offchurch near Leamington on March 17th.1922 and there were memorial services held at both Leeds Parish Church and at St.James Church Wetherby, attended by all the servants at Linton Springs. His coffin carried the inscription:"Joseph Watson lst.Baron Manton of Compton Verney born 10th.February 1873; died 13th.March 1922". The title was inherited by his eldest son the Hon.Miles Watson at the age of 20. His will was dated January 9th.1914 and the estate was valued at £1 million.
By 1927 Wood Hall was bought by Lt.Commander Norman Whitehead OBE RN (ret), who leased the mansion for use as a school in 1935. The hall was empty in 1932 as Lt.Commander Whitehead moved to Harrogate. The founder of the Wood Hall School for Boys was John Watson Catlow FRGS, who bought the estate for his school in 1946 - the estate was sold on the death of Henry Lister Johnstone-Scott. He closed the school in 1965 and moved to be headmaster of St.Ives & Shire Oak School Headingley Leeds, where he stayed for 20 years. A Cambridge graduate and

Wood Hall Hotel

keen alpine climber John Catlow died in Harrogate aged 85 in January 1993, the main lounge of the present hotel was the headmaster's study.
Wood Hall was bought together with 190 acres of land in 1966 by the Roman Catholic Diocese of Leeds. The first Pastoral and Ecumenical Centre in Britain was opened on March lst.1967: the first warden was Monsignor Michael Buckley and he was at Wood Hall until 1977. In 1970 Wood Hall hosted the first national gathering of priests of England and Wales. Wood Hall became the temporary home to a group of Vietnamese boat people in 1979/80. There is a convent of Carmelite Nuns in the monastery of the Good Shepherd and they occupy a range of more recent buildings to the rear of the hotel: the Carmel Chapel is open to visitors. The Oak Bar in the Wood Hall Hotel was once the chapel of the Carmelite Centre. Some of the cottages were built in the reign of King James lst and the present dining room in the Jacobean Wing was formerly part of the out houses of the Vavasour estate.
The Ecumenical Centre was closed in 1985 and the property was placed on sale. In 1986 the estate was bought by John Wix, for more than £400,000 and he spent over £1.3 million on restoration as a hotel. He opened the hotel in April 1988 - he had sold Linton Springs for £5 million. In August 1988 Wix sold the hotel to Select Hotels.
The present Wood Hall Hotel has 43 luxury bedrooms, most with views over the Wharfe valley. The hotel is part of the Country Mansion Hotels chain, a part of Robin Howard's Equity Leisure Group. The £2 million investment resulted in the opening of the Leisure Centre in November 1992, which is available to residents and there is a Leisure Club. A new General Manager was appointed at Wood Hall in early 1994 and the present chef once served King Hussein of Jordan.

Wattle Syke is a small community on the corner of Wetherby Road, Collingham and the turnpike to Tadcaster: a name plate displays the identity. There are two buildings, one with three dwellings and the other with two cottages: the latter was bought from the Lady Betty Hastings Trustees. It was at Wattle Syke in 1874 that a local man Jeremiah Swales was seen to strike a pony. Farmer Groves retaliated by striking swales: the fine was 10/-.
A field east of Wattle Syke, threatened by widening of the Al was investigated by the WY Archaeological Unit, who proved that that the site had Iron Age origins with a small farmstead enclosed by ditches. An Iron Age roundhouse was at the centre of the site with three graves discovered with single skeletons. The 2000 animal bones discovered on the site were investigated: animals such as cattle, goats, pigs, horse, dog with small mammals and birds were identified. The site is now under the A1 road.
Dalton Parlours is an Iron Age/Roman site on Moor Lane/Dalton Lane near the Al, based on the Magnesian Limestone. There are sites of four Roman villas in West

Yorkshire including Dalton Parlours. Remains of the walls of the villa were above ground until 1806, when the stones were removed. The site was excavated in 1854 revealing a pavement and remains of hypocausts. In 1975/76 there were amounts of tesserae, roof tiles, wall plaster and coins discovered. In 1976 an intensive archaeological investigation was started at Dalton Parlours with the permission of the field's owners Lady Betty Hastings Estate Charity.
Initially the site was an Iron Age farmstead but was later Romanised. The excavations were continued until June 1979 and in 1988 the ownership of Dalton Parlours transferred to Leeds City Council and the Charity gave the finds to Leeds Museum.
Discoveries and research indicate that the site was first used about 300BC, as the axes and arrowheads date from that period. The settlement was composed of eight round houses with their boundary ditches. Occupation of the villa in the Roman period probably started about 200AD and ended about 370AD. Evidence for the dates is from the discovery of Roman coins and pottery from the period.
The Roman site was of a set of rooms with hypocausts: raised floors on sets of pillars allowing hot air to circulate providing a primitive but effective heating system.
There was a baths building with related agricultural outhouses with ovens, kilns and flues. Two wells were discovered in which was found a wealth of material from Roman occupation, providing the evidence of an orderly abandonment of this settlement. Analysis of the bones revealed that cattle were kept for market and sheep for their wool, possible for sale to the inhabitants of Eboracum at York. Other artefacts unearthed during the Dalton Parlours excavations include quernstones, glassware, ceramics, worked bones, tiles and mosaics. The later occupation of the site was proved by the discovery of a late Anglo-Saxon crouched burial, with an annular brooch. The site has now reverted to agricultural land.
Leeds City Museum displays the Roman plaster ceiling from Dalton Parlours with sections of the frieze from the 3rd.century bath house. This is one of five Roman ceilings from Britain from which the complicated pattern can be reconstructed. These Roman artefacts came to Leeds Museum and are displayed together with the Wolf and Twins mosaic pavement from Isurium at Aldborough - donated to the Museum in 1863.

The approach to Wetherby is past the Wetherby Resort Hotel and Conference Centre. The hotel first opened in 1972 as the privately owned Turnpike Hotel, which was taken by Ladbroke Mercury Hotels and then Penguin Hotels. This small Gloucester company was followed by Resort Hotels of Brighton in 1991, who have 46 hotels through England and Wales. The Wetherby Hotel has 72 bedrooms together with the Wharfedale Suite and the Doves restaurant. The Penguin Pool at the Harewood Bird Garden is sponsored by the hotel: the Abbey Park Hotel at The Mount York is also

a group hotel.
The Wetherby by-pass was opened on October 29th.1959 by Ernest Marples taking in some Grange Park land.
Entry into Wetherby is by the hamlet of Micklethwaite, where the Drover's Inn was in business until about 1870. The former inn was converted into three dwellings, originally built in the mid 18th.century with additions in the following century. The houses are Grade II listed together with the nearby gateway. The large gateway, now isolated from the park, was the north lodge to Beilby Grange: the south lodge is at the junction of the Al and Tadcaster Road on Grange Moor. This lodge is also isolated from the park and is at the centre of the roundabout with the flyover. The avenue of trees once leading into Grange Park is still to be admired from the roadside.
Beilby Grange was situated by the River Wharfe and as Micklethwaite Grange was the home of the Beilby family by 1612. Richard Beilby's daughter received the Grange estate - so called from the Kirkstall Abbey grange in the 12th.century and Thomas Beilby inherited and lived in the mid 17th.century. The Beilby coat of arms dated 1660 was once displayed over the entrance to the mansion and a grave slab from 1665 is in Collingham Church. At the beginning of the 18th.century John Beilby's sons died young and his daughter married Henry Thompson MP of York. In 1730 the Grange passed to Beilby Thompson and his daughter Jane on her marriage to Sir Robert Lawley took the name Thompson. Sir Robert died in 1793 and his youngest son Sir Paul Beilby Lawley-Thompson was raised to the peerage as Lord Wenlock of Escrick Park in 1839. A year later the estate was sold to William Brown of Liverpool and then tenanted by Christopher Wilson, known as the "Father of the Turf" who died in 1849. It was Christopher Wilson who bought the manorial rights of Wetherby at the 1824 auction. His son Alexander Brown lived at Wetherby Grange until his death in 1849 aged 32 and in 1856 the trustees of Robert Gunter bought Wetherby Grange as a home for Col.Sir Robert Gunter who was serving in the Crimea until the war ended in 1856. The Gunter family was of ancient lineage and traced the ancestors to the times of William the Conqueror, when Sir Peter Gunter was an aide-de-camp to the King.
Col.Sir Robert Gunter was born on November 2nd.1831 and was educuated at Rugby: when he was 31 years old he married Jane Benyon daughter of Thomas Benyon of Gledhow Hall Leeds and he settled at Wetherby Grange. The land that Sir Robert Gunter owned included all of Micklethwaite, most of Collingham with other land at Wetherby and in Middlesex. He was a breeder of short horn cattle and became President of Wetherby Agricultural Society: he became the Conservative MP for Barkston Ash in 1885 having been MP for Knaresborough the year before. He died in 1905 aged 74.
His son Sir Robert Benyon Nevill Gunter followed his parents at the Grange and was

the elder brother of Sir George Gunter. Sir Nevill succeeded on the death of his father in 1905: he had married Clara Barrett in 1902 and their son Ronald Vernon was born in 1904. The Gunter fortunes were based on a London catering business and an involvement in real estate. Sir Nevill was born on August 4th.1871 and died in France in August 1917. Sir Nevill was a cricketer and he provided the Cricket Club with a new ground in his parkland. At his death Sir Nevill left an estate of £14,759: his son was the racing car connoisseur bachelor Sir Ronald Gunter who was the last member of this old family at The Grange.

Grange Park was the home of the Wetherby Show, an event starting in 1840 but the mansion was demolished in 1962. The 201 acre Grange Park was auctioned in 1984 and bought by David Hudson, who was elected Chairman of the Agricultural Society. The graves of the Gunter family are at Collingham Church, as Micklethwaite was in that parish.

The road approaching Wetherby Bridge passes the Police Station and Court House to the east built in 1962 and the Barracks used as racing stables - to the west. The barracks date from about 1800 and are part of Micklethwaite Farm, being the front range of a set of limestone farm buildings. The Fire Station was also on this site from 1877, until a new station was opened in 1958.

There was mention of a bridge at Wetherby in 1233 being rebuilt in the 17th.century. After flooding in 1767 the bridge was widened in 1773. In 1823/24 the six arched bridge was built into the old arches to a design by Bernard Hartley. The bridge once had a small chapel of ease to Spofforth Church dedicated to St.Mary.

The War Memorial was dedicated on April 22nd.1922 and stands on a stone rampart: the bronze angel holds a wreath of laurel and points a sword to earth. The memorial was designed by E.F.Roslyn.

The weir was repaired in 1871 and was reconstructed in 1982 by the Weir Preservation Trust and close by is the site of the water powered corn mill, where only the wheel house remains. There was mention of a mill in 1238, when it was taken over by the Knights Templars.

The Domesday Book mentions Wetherby as Wedrebi meaning a wether or ram farm - another meaning could be a settlement where the river bends. Wetherby became a part of the Percy estates after the Norman Conquest and in 1238 they granted Wetherby mill and much land to the Knights Templars. They had already been granted a weekly market at nearby Walshford and in November 1240 King Henry III granted the Knights Templars a weekly market at Wetherby on Thursdays: a feature preserved in the town. When the Knights Templars were dissolved in 1312 they had 740 acres of land at Wetherby, two water mills, a preceptory and granges at nearby Ribston together with their fair and chapel at Walshford.

Wetherby has a castle site with few remains standing high above the river at Castle Garth House. It was possibly completed by the mid-12th.century by the Percy family

to guard the river crossing. The Templars would have used the castle and about 1220 had acquired the Percy mill. The castle was destroyed during the Scots raids of 1312/19 and Wetherby's population was decimated by the Black Death in 1349.
In 1845 the old court house, complete with prison and stocks was demolished. The foundation stone for the new £1300 Town Hall was laid on June 11th.1845. The building had many uses including the county court, assembly room, prison, church school and a reading room. The schoolroom was also used for the Statute Fair, when farm servants were hired - an occasion that was both festive and a local holiday.
In the 16th.century Wetherby had passed to the Crown and in August 1602 the Manor was granted to the Countess of Shrewsbury or Bess of Hardwick, who then conveyed Wetherby lands to the Cavendish family. The Devonshire family sold Wetherby in October 1824 to finance work at Chatsworth. The sale took four days and included the sale of the Manor of Wetherby with the courts, tolls of fairs and rents of shops in the Shambles. This was the last of 170 lots and was sold for £5010 to the Wilson family. Other lots on offer were the late 18th.century Angel Inn (£2010), the George and Dragon ((£640), the White Hart (£1220) and the Black Bull (£730). The manor was inherited by Andrew Fountayne Wilson Montagu of Ingmanthorpe Hall, who became Lord of the Manor and died in 1895 - he was buried near his family residence of Melton Park. In the 1820's Ingmanthorpe was owned by Richard Fountayne-Wilson of Melton on the Hill, near Sprotbrough west of Doncaster. The Wetherby York Road racecourse was built on Montagu land south of Ingmanthorpe Hall.
Wetherby was once part of Spofforth parish and was served by a number of chapels. In 1760 an old chapel in the market square was demolished and a new thatched chapel was built. This was rebuilt in 1763 and was demolished in 1845. The foundation stone for a new church was laid by Wharfedale Brewery owner Quentin Rhodes in April 1839. St.James Church was consecrated on February 1st.1842 by the Bishop of Ripon and cost £4000 to complete. The chancel was lengthened in 1877 and the tower arch dates from 1887/8 during restorations by Chorley & Connon of Leeds. There were further alterations in 1910 and in 1939 when the tower pinnacles were removed: the church was reordered in 1981. The first clock in the tower was from the old Town Hall. It was bought by the Duke of York in 1789, when he left Allerton Mauleverer Hall, where the clock had been in the stable yard tower. It was installed at Wetherby Church in 1845 and in 1920 the present Potts clock was placed on the church.
In St.James churchyard are buried Benjamin Barstow an ironmonger and James Craven Hudson a watchmaker and silversmith (1812-1869): together with James Swithenbank of Raby Park (died 1899) and Henry Crossley (1865-1929). They were all important parts of Wetherby's past.
Wetherby Methodist Chapel was built in 1829 at a cost of £720 and opened on

October 30th: it is a listed building.
There have been many changes in Wetherby through the centuries: the site of Quentin Rhodes' Wharfedale Brewery became Braimes (Tadcaster) Brewery and then Oxley's mineral water factory demolished in 1959. The bus station opened in 1960 and was demolished for the offices and shops development in 1992. Recent changes in Wetherby include the opening of a small £200,000 bus station in March 1994.
In the market square is the Grade II listed Shambles built in 1811 by the Duke of Devonshire as butcher's shops. In 1888 it was converted into an open market for dairy products and poultry: in 1914 it was used for miniature rifle practice. The facade was added in 1911 to mark the coronation of King George V.
The Conservative Club was built on the site of the second Devonshire Hotel at the end of the last century. St.James Church School was built by subscription in 1894/95 using Potternewton and Killinghall stone. The Parish Room opened in 1893 when Rev.G.A.Durrant was the vicar is adjacent to the school.
The High Street was at one time mainly inns and stables: the early 18th.century "Swan & Talbot" and "The Angel" were the two main coaching inns and were already established when the "White Hart" was built in 1700. When coaching traffic was at a peak Wetherby had about 40 inns and ale houses. The White Hart has been demolished and The Angel was placed on sale: even in the 1840's coaching was being eclipsed and by 1857 only the Wetherby-Leeds coach was being run on a twice weekly service. The first Wetherby railway station opened on the Church Fenton/Harrogate line on August 10th.1847. The line from Cross Gates via Scholes, Thorner, Bardsey and Collingham Bridge opened in May 1876 and in July 1900 a curved line was built forming a triangle: the Leeds line was made into a double track in 1902. Linton Road station opened on July 1st.1902, as the first station was closed. The line closed to passengers in 1964 and to goods in 1966.

Wetherby Town Hall

THE ROAD FROM LEEDS TO YORK

PART 1 QUARRY HILL TO HALTON DIAL

Quarry Hill has the reputation of being one of the most ancient sites of Leeds. In the times of Ralph Thoresby (1658-1725) there were detected traces of embankments. It has been suggested that Quarry Hill was the site of the Roman camp of Cambodunum, meaning a fort on a crooked hill or hill-range. Thoresby said that on ascending Walflat on Quarry Hill are the vestiges of a very large camp with deep trenches, which could be Roman or Saxon.

Quarry Hill was once called Quarrel Hill and is the starting point of the route to York by a thoroughfare called York Lane, although it was the starting point of the Leeds and Selby turnpike road: the Tadcaster turnpike started at Halton Dial. It is surprising that the area was once noted for its medicinal spa waters but it acquired a notoriety for some of the worst slums in Leeds.

There were three wells on Quarry Hill: St. Peter's Well, Lady Well and Quarry Hill Spa. Baths were built on the site of St. Peter's Well, which were still flourishing until the early 20th. century. In 1847 an advertisement stated that the sulphur baths of St. Peter's Well included a Turkish Bath with supplies from a 66' deep well. The baths were demolished in 1908, as part of a slum clearance started in the area in 1895.

The so-called Building Clubs developed Quarry Hill between 1786 and 1789.Thomas Whitaker mentioned in 1816 that the area was "occupied by buildings". By 1851 the whole area was built over except for "the course of the western agger about 6' deep". The unhealthy nature of the area was made worse by the cholera outbreak in 1832 spread by drinking water infected by sewage. It was declared to be an "Unhealthy area" and with the York Street area, there were 53 public houses serving nearly 3000 houses. These were demolished in the 1930's and on the 26 acres was built one of the most impressive blocks of council flats, with only 14% of the available space being used.

There were 938 flats in which were living 3280 people in this well appointed area. The Quarry Hill flats were built between April 1936 - building started in August - and 1941 and the Lord Mayor opened the first flat on March 30th. 1938. The structural system was by Eugene Mopin and the architect was R. A. H. Livett.

In 1944 the Ministry of Health announced that the child mortality rate in Quarry Hill flats was only 10.9 per thousand compared with 13.4 for the rest of Leeds.

One of the complexes was known as Oastler House, remembering Richard Oastler who was born in Leeds in 1789.It was his battle that freed many thousands of factory children from slavery. The 10 hour factory bill became law in 1847 and there is a memorial tablet in Leeds Parish Church to "The Factory King" who is buried at Kirkstall Parish Church.

The thirteen houses at Quarry Hill flats were mainly called after well known Leeds people including James Kitson, Sir Charles Lupton Lord Mayor 1915, Lord Moynihan LGI surgeon, Joseph Priestley minister at Mill Hill Chapel from 1767 for 6 years and discoverer of Oxygen in 1774, Joseph Rhodes founder of Leeds school of art, Sir John Savile Leeds first Alderman, Ralph Thoresby Leeds historian and Griffith Wright the founder of the Leeds Intelligencer.
The expense of continuous repairs - £2 million was spent in 1961 - poor waste disposal and structural deterioration meant that the flats were doomed. Demolition was completed by June 1978, taking two years to complete the levelling. The last tenant had left the flats in 1977 and the area was cleared and redeveloped.

The £13 million West Yorkshire Playhouse theatres opened in March 1990, having transferred from part of the University Sports Hall. The Quarry and Courthouse theatres offer numerous productions with wide appeal and it has already established for itself an enviable reputation. The creation of Playhouse Square was started in October 1993.
Excavations on the Quarry Hill area in 1991 revealed an old cemetery: the bones were removed and reinterred at Harehills Cemetery. When the area was cleared to build the flats hundreds of cellared dwellings were brought down, two burial places were removed. A brewery, factories and the foundations of two gasometers were all cleared. It was reported that seven 14th. century coal workings were discovered and filled and that there were 3 miles of disused sewers.

The skyline of Leeds from the approach from York Road is dominated by Quarry House: the headquarters of the Department of Health and Social Security. The eight storey block took two years to build and was topped out in April 1992. The project cost £55 million, transferring the entire operation from London. The complex, including a swimming pool and extensive leisure facilities opened in 1993 with nearly 2000 workers. There was accommodation for 1200 staff of the National Health Service Management Executive and 800 working in the Benefits Agency. The first phase opened in July 1992 and it was announced in October 1993 that from April 1996 the 14 Regional Health Authorities would be replaced by Regional Offices reporting via a director to the NHS Management Executive based at Quarry House, making Leeds the centre for NHS operations.

St. Mary's Church was consecrated in October 1826 costing about £12,500.Built under a Parliamentary sanction it took three years to complete being designed by architect Thomas Taylor. Taylor made his reputation with Christ Church Liversedge in 1812 and in 1818 the Church Building "Million" Act provided a number of commissions in Yorkshire. The commission set up in response to the Act worked for

ten years and reported on the state of parishes and recommended the building of new churches, being able to make a full grant to the cost of building. St. Mary's Quarry Hill was one of three "Million" churches allotted to Leeds.
Taylor was announced as the church architect in February 1822 with contracts for stone and carpentry sought in October. The foundation stone was laid on January 29th. 1823, although delays due to strikes affected the attainment of the expected completion date. The church was consecrated after the two other "Million" churches at Meadow Lane and Woodhouse, on October 12th.1826.The stone for this Gothic style design came from Bramley Fall and New Lathes quarries. Thomas Taylor designed the churches of Pudsey St. Lawrence (1821) and St. John Roundhay in 1826 for Stephen Nicholson. He died after catching a cold while in St. Mary's Church a few months prior to its consecration and was buried in the crypt at Liversedge.
One of the early vicars of St. Mary's Church was the Rev. William Studdert Kennedy who was born in 1825 and died in 1914: he was the vicar from 1879.His son was Geoffrey Studdert Kennedy who was born on June 27th. 1883 and educated at Leeds Grammar School. He entered the ministry as curate of Leeds Parish Church in 1908 and in 1914 became a curate at St. Mary's Church where he was married in that year to Emily Catlow, sister of a Leeds solicitor. At the outbreak of war he became a padre to the forces and was stationed at Rouen. He became known for handing out cigarettes to the troops, which earned him the nickname "Woodbine Willie".He was an inspiration to the troops and a respected preacher. He gained the MC in 1917 and after the War the King made him an honorary chaplain: in 1922 he became rector of St. Edmund King & Martyr Church in London.
The schoolroom, built soon after consecration was used for services following the demolition of the church. The building caught fire in May 1994 and the congregation hold their services in the new St. Peter's School. It is a part of the team ministry of the parish of Leeds City. St. Mary's Church was demolished in 1979 and the Ripon Diocesan Office was built in St. Mary's Street on the site of the nave. The foundation stone for the office was laid by the Bishop of Ripon in November 1980 and it was officially opened on October 8th. 1981 by the Archbishop of York the Most Rev. & Rt. Hon. S. Y. Blanch.
There are only a few gravestones to remind one of St. Mary's church Quarry Hill. Hundreds of corpses of 19th. century cholera victims, due to the epidemics in the 1830's and 1840's, were buried in St. Mary's churchyard.

The first Catholic chapel in Leeds was on Lady Lane opened in 1793.The York Road chapel was opened by Bishop Penswick on July 12th. 1831. In 1899 this building was converted into St. Patrick's school.
St. Patrick's Chapel on York Road was designed by John Child and built by the

Leeds Dominicans. John Child who died in 1868 had a practice on Boar Lane and later on Guildford Street. He was responsible for the first St. Anne's Cathedral at the top of Park Row, built in 1837-38 and demolished in 1904 to be replaced by the present Cathedral.
The foundation stone of St. Patrick's Roman Catholic Church was laid on September 29th. 1889 by Bishop Wilkinson and this new church was officially opened on April 30th. 1891 by Bishop Gordon. The architect was John Kelly (1894-1904) who was in partnership with Richard Adams in their Park Row offices. When Adams died in 1883 Kelly took Edward Birchall as a partner. In 1873 the firm was appointed architects to the Leeds School Board with many of their schools still remaining in the city. The church cost £7000 to build and in 1897 the chancel was decorated with the Crucifixion Scene by Belgian artists. The white marble altar and chancel were a response to Vatican 2: the large west stained glass windows were destroyed by the bomb that fell in August 1941 and replaced by plain glass.
There are a few memorial plaques from the old York Road chapel now in St.Patrick's Church. They include the memorial to the Rev. Albert Underhill Pastor of the Catholic Congregation Leeds who died on October 22nd. 1814 aged 70; two plaques in the west porch remember Bernard and Lydia Peacock who died in September 1840 aged 80 and January 1827 aged 68 respectively - the memorial also includes Elizabeth (died 1821) and John (died 1834) and the plaque was erected by the then surviving members of the Peacock family.
The other memorial plaque remembers Antonio de Macedo who died on July 12th. 1863 interred at Sicklinghall. His wife Anne died in 1880 and their son Joao de Macedo died at Lisbon in October 1857.Anne's sister Mary Peacock is also remembered in this plaque: she was interred at Dublin when she died in August 1873. There is a large statue of St.Patrick at the west end of the north aisle, adjacent to the altar which remembers the many priests who ministered to the population of The Bank during the 19th. century epidemic. The south aisle has a memorial to the Polish Community who used St. Patrick's Church after the last War: the large coloured wall cross is dedicated to Our Lady of Czestochowa Queen of Poland. The south west corner of the church contains the Grotto of Lourdes built by a former parishioner from Yorkshire limestone.
The Rev. Austin Joseph Collingwood was the parish priest at St. Patrick's Church for 40 years: he was born on May 6th. 1841 and died on July 27th. 1928.He was buried at Killingbeck Cemetery.
A Roman Catholic school was opened on Charles Street, Quarry Hill in 1873 by Rev. Browne, at a cost of £2500. St. Charles Catholic Primary School occupied buildings on the site adjacent to the busy main road, being assisted by the nuns from the adjacent convent. In 1987 the premises were occupied by St. Peter's Church of England Primary School following the fire on November 5th. This school moved

into new buildings in September 1993, having been designed by architects Jones & Stocks. This firm designed the Leeds Permanent Building Society Corporate HQ which opened in 1993 and have been appointed as the architects of the Alwoodley Gates site for Leeds Grammar School.
The St.Patrick's Picture Palace was a cinema in church buildings, opening in December 1910 and closing in November 1924: the manager in 1918 was C. P. Parkinson.
Agnes Stewart Church of England High School was the second C of E High School to be opened in Leeds - Abbey Grange School opened in 1962 - on September 7th. 1965 having been built at a cost of £300,000.The school was officially opened by Princess Margaret on June 24th. 1966. It was Mother Agnes Logan Stewart (1820-1886) who bought three old houses at Knostrop in 1871 and converted them into a girl's orphanage opened a year later. In 1880 Agnes Stewart built St. Hilda's Boys School at her own expense and was instrumental in the building of St. Hilda's Church. This opened as an iron church in 1873 and the permanent building to designs by John Thomas Micklethwaite was opened on September 18th. 1882. This good lady was buried at St. James Church Seacroft on May 5th. 1886, although she had requested that St. Saviour's Churchyard was used for her interment: this had closed in 1856.

Burmantofts is derived from "burgher-men's tofts" and had a 17th. century hall, once the home of Sir William Neville High Sheriff of Yorkshire. There is a memorial plaque in Holy Trinity Church Boar Lane to Hannah wife of Richard Strother of Burmantofts Hall - she died aged 61 on December 16th. 1799.The old hall had been a boarding school before demolition.
The foundation stone for St. Agnes Church was laid on July 9th. 1887 and the church was consecrated on May 20th. 1889. The church was designed by John Kelly and Edward Birchall in 1886/87: Birchall had designed the Quaker Meeting House in Woodhouse Lane in 1866 - it is now the BBC.
There is a large memorial tablet on the west wall to James Holroyd the founder of the Burmantofts Faience Works, who was born on January 10th. 1839 and died on April 8th.1890: the tablet was erected by his employees. There is a plaque in the chancel to the Rev. Willard H. Stansfield first vicar of the church and parish: he was born on April 12th. 1853 and died on August 8th.1927.The east stained glass window remembers his vicariate from 1889-1927 and there is a framed address. The address was given to the Rev. and Mrs. Stansfield on the occasion of their silver wedding on December 12th. 1906: it mentions that he received a purse of gold and that in his time the vicarage was built, the organ placed in the church and there was the erection of the mission church of St. Cyprians and the Sunday School. The brass lectern was given in 1931 and the marble font was a gift of the Sunday School Scholars on

Consecration Day.

The "Regent" Cinema on Torre Road was designed by Fred Mitchell and opened on May lst. 1916. It closed as a cinema on May 29th. 1971 with a showing of "The Bounty Killers".The cinema is now a leisure centre and amusements with a tombola club.
The raised motorway of the Leeds Inner Ring Road, completed in 1992, now takes a large volume of traffic westwards. The eastbound Woodpecker flyover was opened on February 4th. 1973. The junction of Marsh Lane, Burmantofts Street and York Road were once the site of the "Woodpecker Inn". The first inn dated back to the early 19th. century and was bought by Leeds Corporation in 1938 for £6000.Planning application for the new inn was approved on April 12th.1938.The inn closed down in 1939 and was demolished. The new "Woodpecker Inn" opened on the opposite side of the road on October 14th. 1939.This new inn was destroyed by a bomb which fell on the pavement outside the inn on August 31st. 1941. The building was later re-erected on the same site. The inn was finally demolished after closure in January 1990 to make way for the £7.5 million road development scheme, being stage 5 of the Leeds Inner Ring Road.
The August 1941 bomb also shattered thousands of windows in the Quarry Hill flats, there was severe damage to St. Patrick's Church and Presbytery and Stephenson's drapers was destroyed: the attack left one dead and 33 injured. An air raid on September Ist. 1940 hit the Marsh Lane railway depot and also damaged many houses on Easterly Road. There were 87 alerts in Leeds during the War between September 4th. 1939 and March 17th. 1944 - there being only 9 bombings on Leeds: the first city raid was on August 25th. 1940 and the last raid was on August 28th. 1942. In the City there were 197 buildings destroyed and 7623 were damaged by enemy action.

The "Woodpecker" was not the only public house in the area, as the "Fleece" Inn once stood between Plaid Row and Elm Street south of the main road; the "Shoulder of Mutton" was near "The Woodpecker" but was demolished and the site redeveloped. There were also "The Stag" and "The Greyhound" inns. It was at "The Greyhound", situated by the York Road Baths between Bath Street and Woodman Terrace, that horse drawn trams terminated in May 1890.The inn closed in 1938/39 and the licence was transferred to the Wykebeck Hotel on Halton Hill. In 1897 the tram service was extended to Victoria Avenue. Steam trams travelled to Easy Road in 1902, while in 1900 an electric service travelled from "The Woodpecker" inn to Victoria Road.
The north side of York Road from the "Woodpecker" junction was occupied mainly by back to back terrace housing, which was replaced by the present council flats. At

one time there were street names such as Bean, Acorn, Cranberry, Wheat, Bread and Apple. There was a linen factory near Accommodation Road in the mid-19th. century.
York Road/Edgar Street Boy's Board School between Plato Street and Accommodation Road was opened in 1876 to designs by the Leeds School Board architect Richard Adams. The building was demolished to make room for redevelopment. In this area was the Riding School, a plain quadrangular building of the Leeds Cavalry Volunteers. At the start of the 19th. century, it was one of the only buildings on this part of the road.

A few yards off York Road on Accommodation Road was the Miner's Institute, whose licence as a cinema was granted in July 1910.The name was changed to "The Cosy" in February 1932 but it was to close finally in April 1938 and the building was eventually demolished. The area was redeveloped in post war years as the Ebor Gardens estate: a £33 million Government grant is allowing improvements to be made at Ebor Gardens in 1994.In the early days the Miner's Institute was used as a public meeting hall and there was an occasion when James Keir Hardie spoke to a large audience. He became the first Socialist to win a seat in the British Parliament at Holytown Lanarkshire on July 4th. 1892. Hardie died in 1915 having been a champion of socialism and the unemployed.
South of York Road is the "Hope Inn",which replaced the original public house in 1970.The inn was built in 1825 for Joseph Lassey and once possessed a brewhouse, malt chamber, sheep sheds and stabling facilities. The brewhouse was bought in 1918 by the Leeds & Wakefield Brewery Co. - which in 1889 became the Melbourne Brewery. Melbourne started as Dickinson & Co. in 1840 and with buyouts became Melbourne in 1958.The Hope Inn became a Tetley House in 1960 and the new building was built by Kiernan's of Leeds.

The building now occupied by a funeral director started as a blacksmith's shop and still retains the cobbled floor. It became Roberts joiners and then concentrated on a funeral service. The family sold in the mid-1960's to Williams, who in turn sold to the Co-op in August 1986.
Further east was John W. Hemingway's Brewery, which had been founded in Regent Street Leeds in 1866.Under Albert Hemingway they moved to Beckett Street and with William they opened on the York Road site in 1923. In 1967 Hemingways had 5 public houses with 26 employees and was taken over by Tetleys in August: it had been a private company from 1949 and suffered a disastrous fire in May 1958. The site became a car showroom and a Co-op supermarket. In February 1987 the site was rebuilt as "Great Clothes".

All Saint's Church was designed by architects James Mallinson and Thomas Healey of Bradford. They had a large ecclesiastical practice and other churches included St. Peter Thorner in 1855 and St. Mary's Church East Keswick in 1856. The foundation stone was laid in October 1846 by Dr. Walter Hook, Vicar of Leeds from 1837. The church was consecrated on All Saints Day 1850, the parish having already been created in 1847, with 7000 people living in 1200 back to back houses. In 1872 the district of St. Edmund was formed and in 1875 the foundation stone of the new church was laid in Providence Street and opened in 1876 with Dumfries born George Corson as the architect. Corson (1829-1910) was also responsible for many public buildings including the Leeds Grand Theatre in 1876 and Foxhill Weetwood for Francis Tetley in 1862. St. Edmund's Church was closed in 1935.
In 1969 All Saints Church vicarage was demolished, and the parish of Richmond Hill was created in 1979. Peter Hill was appointed architect and in October 1978 the foundations of the new All Saints church were laid with the new building opening a year later. The low stone built church was consecrated on February 19th. 1980 by the Bishop of Ripon, when the old church was demolished.
In July 1847 All Saints School opened in a small building and was completely rebuilt in 1896. In 1969 money was made available from the Agnes Stewart Trust to rebuild the school which opened as a new Middle School in 1970.

In the area of Pontefract Lane was Black Bank: described in the early 18th. century as the seat of Henry Iveson, Lord of the manor of Bilton. Iveson had been Mayor of Leeds in 1695 and 1709 as well as being JP and High Sheriff. Edward Iveson was an Alderman in 1715 and the Leeds Mayor in 1716 and 1728.Lancelot Iveson died aged 72 in May 1803: his wife Martha died in October 1810 aged 77. In the early 18th. century William Broadbent (1676-1730) was the overlooker and steward at Iveson's Black Bank Colliery. William Broadbent married Ann Smeaton, the daughter of John and Hannah Smeaton of Austhorpe, the grandparents of the famous Austhorpe engineer.
Three churches east of the area are Mount St. Mary's Roman Catholic Church, St. Saviour's Church and St. Hilda's Church. Mount St. Mary's Church was started possibly as a challenge to St. Saviour's Church in 1852. The church was designed by Joseph Hansom and W. Wardell and is now in a derelict condition. St. Saviour's Church Ellerby Road was built in 1842/45 by John Macduff Derick for Dr. Pusey, who as Mr. Z paid for this church. The designs of the stained glass executed by O'Connor were by Augustus Welby Northmore Pugin: he was born in 1812 and when he was 15 years old designed furniture for Windsor Castle. He designed or part designed over 100 buildings, he wrote books, designed religious objects, wallpaper, tiles and this Catholic convert became known for his Gothic style. The Victoria and Albert Museum London held an exhibition in 1994 called "Pugin: A Gothic Passion"

- Pugin died in 1852.
St. Hilda's Church was designed by John Thomas Micklethwaite in 1876/1881. He was not only an able architect but a distinguished archaeologist. There is a plaque on the floor of the cloisters of Westminster Abbey London to this architect which describes him as the "Surveyor of the Fabric": he was born on May 3rd. 1843 and died on October 28th. 1906.

On the north side of the main road between Searl's Yard and Blossom Street was the York Road Police Station. The station opened in 1867 and closed in 1945. It was sold for £400 to the Town Improvement Committee and later demolished.
York Road Baptist Chapel and Sunday School was north of the main road on Ainsty Road. The foundation stone was laid on July 10th. 1872. The architect W. H. Harris built the chapel in classic style with accommodation for 700, at a cost of £5500. The minister from 1926 to 1935 was the Rev. John Dow but the last service was held on July 4th. 1959.The chapel was demolished to allow for redevelopment of the area and the new chapel opened in Ebor Gardens in July 1959.This new Baptist Church was closed in 1986 and became the Community Centre.
The area north of the old chapel was once the Burmantofts Brick Works with the terracotta works north of Torre Road. These extensive works produced a glazed coloured earthenware known as faience and were on a 150 acre site. A 180' deep shaft extracted red clay and coal, both being used to make the faience which had a universal appeal. In September 1993 a large collection of pottery from Burmantofts, Woodlesford and Leeds Art Pottery was auctioned in Leeds: they were the property of collector James Fox.

A branch of the Leeds Industrial Cooperative Society opened on York Road between Ainsty Road and Bickerdike Road in November 1877. The corner stone was laid on May 5th by Thomas Wilberforce.
The LICS started as the Leeds Flour Society as a result of the scarcity, cost and quality of flour in 1846. A group of folk at Benyon's corn mill in Holbeck decided to organise a cooperative and called a meeting in March 1847. The first Co-op corn was ground at the Britannia Mills on Wellington Street and shopkeepers were appointed as the flour sellers. In 1853 the name was changed from The Leeds and District Flour Society to The Leeds Co-operative Flour and Provision Society with the Leeds "People's Mill" destroyed by fire in October 1881.Stores had been opened in 1859 at The Bank, Bramley, Hunslet, Pudsey with the Marshall Street store having opened in 1856.Stores on Marsh Lane and in Armley were opened in 1860.The main Leeds stores in Albion Street were opened between 1873 and 1894.
The Co-operative Movement started at a small shop in Toad Lane Rochdale opened on August llth. 1844 by the Rochdale Equitable Pioneers Society. The movement

today now has 700 million members in over 100 countries. It is Britain's most comprehensive retail organisation, commercial farmer, funeral director; one of the main travel agencies, food manufacturer and supplier and is provider of financial services through the Bank and Insurance Society.

On the south side of the main road is the listed Grade II public library opened in October 1904 and designed by H. Ascouch Chapman. The top floor is now being used as the library bookbinding department. The new brick built library opened on May 13th.1983.York Road Baths were once a part of the same building as the old library. They were opened by the Lord Mayor Robert Armitage on April 4th. 1905: the baths were closed in the 1970's and demolished.

On the same side of the road are the premises of John Curtis, shopfitters. The firm was established in 1852 and the York Road site was taken over in 1925: there was also a factory on East Street.

On Berking Street were the premises of Marsh, Jones and Cribb: the firm was founded in 1760 as Messrs. Kendall & Co and this was taken by Edward Jones and Henry Cribb in 1850. Their premises were on Boar Lane/Basinghall Street and they were cabinet makers, artists, decorators and upholsterers. The firm were the painting contractors for many royal palaces in St. Petersburg, Russia. They made good quality furniture and during the First World War manufactured 75 Sopwith Camel aeroplanes. The firm closed down in 1991.

The Primitive Methodist Chapel was on Temple View Road/York Road corner and was built in 1879: it was demolished for redevelopment.

The Leeds Irish Centre east of the Curtis factory was opened in January 1970 and officially in June of that year.

St. Alban's Church was on the north side of the main road on County Street. It was consecrated on March 31st.1876 being a design of architects Walford and Pollard of Bradford, at a cost of £5100.A new parish was created on May lst. 1877, out of St. Stephen's Church on Accomodation Road Burmantofts which had opened in 1854. St.Alban's Church closed after the Harvest Festival service on October 9th. 1939 and the parish was united with that of All Saints. The authority to demolish the church came in February 1941 but waited until the 1950's for eventual demolition. It had been proposed to build a new St. Alban's Church on Lupton Avenue to be shared with the wooden church of St. Cyprian's on Coldcotes Avenue. This did not come about and a new St. Cyprian's Church was completed in 1949.

The area was once known as Gallows Hill - Ralph Thoresby suggested that this place was used for executions.

Saville Green was not only the site of the board school opened in 1874 but St. Patrick's School south of the church in the building that once was the Catholic

Chapel: in the 1940's the Sisters of St. Paul were in charge at the school. St. Patrick's Chapel was founded on March 1st. 1831 and opened on July 12th. 1832 to designs by architect John Child. It was built in the pointed style of the 14th. century and ornamented with turrets and crosses; there was a small lantern tower. In the chapel was a monument to Dr. Underhill who for 30 years was a priest in Leeds: there is a memorial in the new St. Patrick's Church. In the churchyard was erected a stone cross raised over the graves of five Catholic priests who laid down their lives ministering to the victims of cholera and typhus: there is now a memorial in St. Patrick's Church Quarry Hill. In 1832 cholera killed 702 people in Leeds. The disease reappeared in 1848 and between June and October killed about 2000 people mainly in the slums of Marsh Lane, Quarry Hill, Newtown and The Leylands. The origin of the cholera outbreak were traced to a house in Blue Bell Fold on The Bank, a small cul-de-sac containing about 20 houses and inhabited by poor families, many of them Irish.

In 1847 there was an outbreak of typhus and was virulent amongst the Irish population of The Bank and the lower part of York Road. Inside St. Patrick's Chapel was a memorial slab: "On your charity pray for the souls of Reverends Henry Walmsley, Richard Wilson, Edward Metcalf, Joseph Curr and James Coppinger, who fell victims to fever in the discharge of their sacred duties in 1847. Requiescat in Pace".

The chapel and school were both demolished to allow the Ebor Gardens housing estate to develop. The burial ground was also closed by the Burial Grounds Committee :this resulted in there being many Catholic burials at Beckett Street cemetery until the opening of Killingbeck in 1895. The so-called Guinea Graves at Beckett Street date from the 1890's and are in Recusants Row and list many Irish familes including the Rileys, O'Mahoneys and Murphys.

Ebor Gardens, named after York Road, was a 51 acre site with more than 1150 dwellings with school, shops, church and social amenities. The scheme was prepared in 1954 and in 1965 the Ebor Gardens scheme was near completion. A major restoration scheme took place in 1993/1994, including the complete refurbishment of 109 flats/maisonettes.

The "Victoria" hotel originated in pre-war years with a new building replacing the original inn. In 1991 this freehouse was renamed "The Trotters".

The "Victoria Picture Hall" opened on York Road and Glenthorpe Crescent in 1912 - the original site of Coach Hall Farm - and was replaced further back from the main road by "The Star" Super Cinema. The plans for the new cinema were approved in November 1935 and it opened on February 21st. 1938, while the old Victoria had been already demolished a year before. Goldstone Cinemas had bought the land to the north to allow for possible main road widening and opened a cinema with 1300 seats. The first film to be shown was "Lost Horizon" with Ronald Colman, released

in the USA in 1937 - James Hilton's novel was directed by Frank Capra and was nominated for an Oscar.
The Star Cinema closed in November 1961 showing "The Secret Ways" with Richard Widmark and "Posse from Hell" with Audie Murphy. The cinema was converted into a Bingo centre, which later became both a snooker and a social centre from 1985. It is now privately owned but still retains the balcony and projection box of the old cinema. The balcony seats were only removed in 1992.

The Yorkshire Bank opened their premises at 194 York Road on June lst. 1931 and the bank is still open for business. The pioneer work for the founding of a bank came from Col. Edward Akroyd of Halifax in 1856, having heard a sermon at Whitehall Chapel London preached by Rev. Charles Kingsley. He believed that the poorer classes needed a means of saving with security, through a Penny Savings Bank. He suggested that the bank would operate alongside a Working Man's Provident Society providing burial funds, insurances, endowments, pensions and sick payments. The Colonel advocated the setting up of a Guarantee Fund and a meeting was convened on November 17th. 1856. The official opening of the bank was at 2 East Parade on May Ist. 1859, the house of Dr. Heaton, as the West Riding of Yorkshire Provident Society and Penny Savings Bank. By the year end the bank had 24 branches with nearly 10,000 depositors. The name was changed to the West Riding of Yorkshire Penny Savings Bank as the Provident Society was trimmed off. On January 23rd. 1871 the name was changed to the Yorkshire Penny Bank and it became a limited company in 1911.
It was 40 years later that expansion was essential and the old Leeds Infirmary was bought in 1890, which was demolished to build a new head office on the eastern part of the site. The official opening by the Duke of Devonshire took place on August 17th .1894. In 1959 the Bank centenary was marked with the change of name to Yorkshire Bank Ltd. and a new purpose built head office was opened on Merrion Way in 1980. This was followed by expansion at Brunswick Point, within sight of the head office building. The bank became known as Yorkshire Bank PLC in February 1982.

Victoria School on the south side of the main York Road opened on October 31st. 1904 having been built at a cost of £18,000. It was originally a Junior and Secondary School and in 1923 Boys and Girls departments were created with separate headteachers. In 1964 a Junior School was opened and in 1972 a new Middle School was formed in the old buildings. This closed in July 1992 and became the temporary home of St .Mary's Catholic Primary School Richmond Hill. The Victoria Junior School was opened in new buildings on Ivy Avenue adjacent to the York Road sports field in 1983.

East of the school was Ivy Lodge or House. This was established in 1868 at Bank Lodge Pontefract Lane and the home moved to Ivy Lodge in 1872 as a fever convalescent home accommodating 30 people, supported by private means. The lodge was demolished to make room for development.

On the corner of Torre Road and York Road is the bus depot,opened for trams and buses in April 1937 by Lord Stamp of the LMS Railway Co. The tram shed had enough space to house 80 trams and was equipped with wiring for the bow collectors. The bus shed had 112 vehicles transferred from Donisthorpe Street, which was to become a bus repair centre. The Swinegate depot in Leeds held nearly 200 trams and was demolished after a period of use as an exhibition hall.

The 1971 flyover and road alterations obscure one of the original entries to East End Park on the south side of York Road. It was opened in 1897 having been bought by Leeds in 1886, for the use of the "working people of East Leeds". It was known as Jubilee Park, marking the diamond jubilee of Queen Victoria's reign and was developed from the former Osmondthorpe Hall estate. There are gates at both north and south ends, although the wrought iron work was taken away for the munitions effort in the last war. Victoria Avenue is lined with trees specially planted as the park entry, although through access for traffic is now denied. The Avenue once had a high iron work arch as entry to an area that once had coal pit hills and barren fields. There are many leisure activities including tennis and bowls with walks across the landscaped old coal workings. There was a bandstand ,shelter and teas were available on the 42 acre site. The small lake with its iron fountain was filled in and made into a play area. A 1926 guide commented: "The black refuse heaps were mercifully covered with a carpet of green turf, shrubs and trees appeared to clothe the arid slopes and the place is now one of beauty ,recreation and repose".
The "Ivy House" branch of the Leeds Industrial Co-operative Society opened in 1890, although the foundation stones have now been obscured. There was a butcher's section at this store, where there are reminders of this trade. The ceiling hooks are still in place: the original entrance is now blocked.

St .Brigid's Senior School opened on Torre Road in 1935 and this became a Middle School in 1978. Following the reorganisation of Leeds Catholic schools,it became St. Patrick's RC Primary in 1989 absorbing children from St. Charles RC School. Torre Road was also the site of the Burmantofts works of the Leeds Fire Clay Co. making sanitary tubes and bricks.
The corner of Lupton Avenue - named after the great Leeds family who lived at Beechwood Roundhay - and Torre Road was once the site of the 19th. century Victoria Spice Mills. In 1924 Percy Dalton and H. H. Stokes opened their mills on

Victoria Road. The factory transferred to York Road in 1932 and became well known for "Sagion": a sage and onion stuffing. The firm made rusks, cornflakes and sausage making machines having 150 workers in 1956.
Between Stokes & Dalton and Sumrie's factory were the White Horse building works of Dunhills,who built many houses at the bottom of Halton Hill in the early 1930's. The "White Horse "inn on the opposite side of the main road is one of the oldest public houses of Leeds being first licensed in 1677. The public house was refaced in 1938/39.
On the corner of Skelton Terrace were the works of Stocks Bros. In 1928 Fred Stocks set up a block making business on sites at Easy Road and later on York Road. The hand made blocks used coke breeze - "breeze" was the name given to the waste from coke ovens. The small plant produced 450 breeze blocks daily and land was acquired at Thorpe Lane Robin Hood for increased production. In 1952 the Stourton site was acquired and the company moved from Robin Hood to Ninelands Lane Garforth in 1963: the site of the old Gascoigne Trench Pit. The Trench Pit opened in 1899 to work the Middleton Main coal seam and closed in 1930: the engine house was pulled down in 1964.
The first concrete blocks were made in Britain by Joseph Gibbs in 1850 and it was from 1910 that the concrete block industry became established with growth between 1918 and 1939. Stocks made Insulite blocks for the Harrogate Conference Centre and Lytag blocks for the St.John's Centre Leeds and Coppergate Centre York. Hi-Thermal blocks were used to build the International Hotel Harrogate and for many supermarkets.
Stocks Bros. (Buildings) was founded in 1955 by Stanley Stocks making precast concrete garages for homes in the North of England. It developed into building car showrooms and in the 1970's started building churches. The firm celebrated the Golden Jubilee in 1988 and now have an extensive market for over 100,000 blocks made daily.

Once the site of the extensive works of the York Road Iron and Coal Co., the land between Lupton Avenue and Harehills Lane is still scarred with reminders of its industrial past, although some landscaping has been completed.
Sumrie's clothing business was founded by S. Harris in 1896 in Worth Place. In 1919 his three sons joined their father in works on Cross Stamford Street and started the wholesale ready-to-wear trade. Plans were approved for a new factory in September 1932 and it was opened in 1934 on York Road employing 1500. The factory was a great success, despite the strikes of 1958 and 1970. The firm closed down in February 1989 and the building fell into serious disrepair. The premises were demolished in 1993 becoming the site of the York Road Shopping Centre.
The premises once occupied by Jacob's biscuit makers are east of the Sumrie site,

displaying the mosaic "By Royal Appointment" coat of arms and Jacob's trade mark. This brick built building has been the premises of I. J. Dewhirst manufacturers of uniforms for the police and armed services since 1977.
Isaac Dewhirst started his business at 32 Kirkgate Leeds with Norman Backhouse in the 1870's and became licensed to supply hawkers with buttons, wools and pins etc at wholesale prices. The building on the corner of Kirkgate and Harper Street still bears the Dewhirst "Wholesale" sign.
It was Isaac Dewhirst who met Michael Marks in Kirkgate and lent him £5, with which Marks bought some goods from Dewhirsts for sale on his rounds. By 1884 Marks had a stall in Leeds Market with the popular slogan "Don't ask the price - it's a penny". While Marks visited other northern towns with his wares, the Leeds market stall was being looked after by Charlie Backhouse and some of the girls from the Dewhirst warehouse.
Marks was born in Russian Poland in 1863 and arrived in Leeds from London looking for a job with Barran's clothiers. His Leeds stall with cotton reels bought from Dewhirsts at 11 shillings a gross, sold at a penny. In 1886 Marks married Hannah Cohen in Leeds Belgrave Synagogue and two years later Simon was born Rebecca was born in 1890. In 1894 Marks asked Isaac Dewhirst to be his partner but he was too involved in his own business. Instead he suggested a partnership with Dewhirst's cashier Tom Spencer, who was a good bookkeeper; Marks offered Spencer a half share and on September 28th. 1894 Marks & Spencer was born. There are now 700 branches of Marks & Spencers worldwide with about 300,000 shareholders and a annual turnover of £6 billion.
Simon Marks married Miriam Sieff in 1915 and became Lord Marks and Chairman of Marks & Spencers for 48 years.
I. J. Dewhirst now have 31 branches throughout Britain making military uniforms, general clothes, coathangers and toiletries. The firm is based at Driffield supplying many goods to Marks & Spencer - the store group takes 85% of clothing and 45% toiletries from the Dewhirst group. The present chairman is Tim Dewhirst and the group took over the Ashington based Van Dyke ladies clothing and now have a 7000 workforce. Their branch at Stevenage is the only firm making the guard's bearskins, made with the skins of culled bears. Chairman Tim Dewhirst said in June 1994 that "The business is in robust health, stronger and better balanced than ever before". There had been substantial growth in the core businesses of menswear, ladies-wear and toiletries.
Hepton's factory was to the east and manufactured Heptex raincoats. The House of Hepton was founded by Harold Epstone, who used his name for the firm. The firm closed in the 1980's and the premises were demolished in 1989-90. Redevelopment followed in 1991-93 with Hepton Court office accommodation.

South of the main York Road from the Leeds Co-op on the corner of Victoria Avenue to Osmondthorpe Lane were built rows of terrace houses. One of these (No.310) was a home for girls run by Miss G. Joy in 1940. In the 1920's this was the Board of Guardian's Home for Boys and Girls with Louisa Gledhill as matron

Part of the sports field was once the property of the Low Moor Company (founded 1788) of the Osmondthorpe Collieries. Low Moor operated the Park Pit Beeston, which closed in 1928/29. The Osmondthorpe pits were linked to the coal staithe and weighing machine on York Road by a tramway. The pits were once owned by Sir Charles Ibbetson of Osmondthorpe Hall. The line of the tramway is still visible with its bridges and access to the south side of the railway. The coal was taken from the pits to the York Road on a line that was still being used as a narrow guage tramway in the 1920's. Ibbetson's coal travelled by road due to a dispute with the railway company.

Sir Charles Ibbetson was descended from the family who lived at Red Hall Shadwell and at Denton Park near Otley. Sir Charles Ibbetson had married Charlotte Houghton and their son was Sir Charles Henry Ibbetson (1814-1861).

The Ibbetson family bought the Osmondthorpe Hall estate from the Skeltons and a new Hall was built in 1814: this was also demolished with some of the land being restored as East End Park.

The ceremony of Breaking the Ground for the new St. Philip's Church took place on Saturday August 13th. 1932 and was conducted by the Bishop of Knaresborough. St.Philip's Church on Osmondthorpe Lane was founded on October 1st. 1932 and the stone was laid by the Princess Royal of Harewood House: the Bishop of Ripon was Edward Arthur Burroughs and the Vicar was the Rev. Arthur Hoskins. The architect was F. C. Charlton and consecration took place on July 22nd. 1933. The church has a wealth of Robert Thompson's Mouseman work including the altar which was carved from a magnificent piece of Oak which Robert Thompson had kept for years for a suitable occasion. The choir stalls, now at the rear of the church, were a memorial to the Rev. Hoskins who died aged 46 on December 9th. 1941. The church was awarded a plaque by the ARIBA in 1935, which is displayed on the east front.

The Co-op on the corner of Osmondthorpe Lane and York Road was built in 1929 - the foundation stone was laid on June 22nd. by director W. Whitworth. The site was originally a farm run by Charles Jakeman in the early 1920's and there was a shop run by J. Brayshaw on this site. The store was a DIY establishment until February 1981 when a motor cycle store took over the building.The Co-op Dairy Department was on the site until May 1987 where the milk floats were serviced.

In 1926 a report stated that: "The streets become fewer and with the appearance of Harehills Lane, open country is reached with a prospect of leafy Roundhay and historic Temple Newsam ahead of us. Signs are abundant that the main road is undergoing a gradual change from a narrow country road to a wide thoroughfare and probably in time the tramway will be transferred to a sleeper laid track beside the road as at Roundhay. These changes are especially conspicuous about the old turnpike at Killingbeck".

On the corner of Harehills Lane and the main road was the Shaftesbury Cinema, built near the old Broom Hill Farm, once run by the Elam family. The cinema was opened on October 20th. 1928 by Sir Charles Wilson MP and was followed with a performance by the Black Dyke band and a showing of "Beau Geste" with Ronald Coleman.

Sir Charles Wilson was the Leader of Leeds City Council and was an accountant in Park Row Leeds. He was born on January 13th. 1859 and lived on Louis Street - he died at Osgodby in December 1930 aged 71: he was buried at Skipwith Church. He received his knighthood on July 25th. 1923 and the Freedom of the City of Leeds in March the same year: he also received an honorary Doctor of Law from Leeds University bestowed by Sir Michael Sadler.

The film at The Shaftesbury Cinema the week after opening was "Ben Hur" which had been released in 1925 starring Ramon Novarro. This three hour film was regarded as America's biggest silent film epic. The ballroom opened on February 12th. 1929.

The cinema was built by Thompson & Co of Stoney Rock Lane to designs by J. P. Crawford of Leeds: there was a black cat in residence from the opening. On the opening night there were photographs shown of Sir Charles Wilson and his wedding and a display of Holophane colour illumination. This prompted the comment that "colour may play a part in cinema entertainment". In November 1928 the film "Dangers of Ignorance" was shown to ladies and gentlemen at separate performances with "mixed" houses allowed on Saturday night.

There was a large 25' by 26' stage at the Shaftesbury and shows included a troupe of performing elephants and Mantovani and his orchestra. In June 1931 appeared Al Wright's Comedy Circus starring performing ponies and dogs: later that same year there were even performing crows. The "Best in Vaudeville" was the boast of the Shaftesbury.

The troupe of four elephants appeared for the week commencing March 30th. 1936 and was the first visit to Leeds of Power's New York Hippodrome Dancing Elephants. The company had been at the NY Hippodrome for 18 years and had toured 20 countries in 8 years. They performed at the Shaftesbury each evening with two matinees, playing baseball, cricket, fencing, military and acrobatics. These shows on stage were performed between films: the elephants were stabled at Elam's Farm on Halton Hill. In 1962 the ballroom was converted into a casino and the cinema reopened in October 1964 with "Tom Jones" and Cliff Richard appeared on

stage.
There was a short period for bingo but films were again shown for a few more years until eventual closure on June 28th. 1975 with the film "Death Wish" with Charles Bronson. Most of the old cinema was demolished, leaving the facade and the Harehills Lane shops. The site became Southern House for the Benefits Agency of the Department of Social Security. Staff moved into the building in October 1986 and it was officially opened on December 3rd. by the Permanent Secretary Christopher France and Ald. Arthur Vollans Deputy Lord Mayor of Leeds (Lord Mayor 1988/89).

On the east corner of Harehills Lane is the Shaftesbury Hotel, built as the vicarage of St. Alban's Church. The land on which the vicarage was to be built was sold in February 1884 by Earl Cowper to the Ecclesiastical Commissioners for England. In 1854 an indenture or contract was signed between George Augustus Earl Cowper and the Rt. Hon Francis Thomas de Grey his eldest son regarding the land on the site. Two years later another indenture was signed between four people including the Rt. Hon. Anne Florence Countess Cowper and the Rt. Hon. Anthony Ashley, the Earl of Shaftesbury as an estate of inheritance.
Plans for the new parsonage were completed in March 1885 and building commenced. In May 1898 the Council sold some land west of the vicarage as a result of straightening Harehills Lane at its junction with York Road. In 1900 the vicarage grounds were enclosed with a wall and shrubbery was planted and walks made through the grounds. In 1923 the vicarage was the home of Rev. Samuel Porritt. On October 28th. 1927 the Rev. Edmund Beabey signed the bill of sale to the Leeds & Wakefield Breweries and in 1929 the Council transferred the licence from the Commercial Hotel in Albion Street to The Shaftesbury Hotel. In April 1964 Tetley's acquired the Melbourne Brewery.
The Shaftesbury cinema and hotel were named after the 7th. Earl of Shaftesbury (1801-1885) who did so much to improve working conditions in both factories and mines. The public house was closed for refurbishment for a short period and re-opened on May 12th. 1994 with new facilities.
The Weigh House Garage opened in 1928 by John Edwin Waite, who was the last owner of the Weigh House Toll Bar shop at Halton Dial.
The Police Station opened in 1937 and was built as a section station. It was later extended and in 1958 became a divisional headquarters. In 1968 Gipton station became a sub-divisional HQ of B Division and was closed in May 1993.
The fire station designed by W. H. Thorp FRIBA was officially opened by the Lord Mayor Tom Coombs in the afternoon of October 7th. 1937 - work was in progress on the building in September 1936 - the total cost was £27,000. The Watch Committee decided to erect a Gipton sub-station in 1934 to ease the pressure on

machines and men at the Park Street Central Fire Station. Gipton was one of the most advanced fire stations in the country and included the Fire Station Houses built on the square. The personnel was an inspector, sergeant and ten constables: originally the fire service was part of the police force with staff known as "Fire Bobbies". During the last War changes were made in administration and on August 18th. 1941 the fire brigades were embodied in the National Fire Service. This was based on 12 Civil Defence regions with a Chief Regional Fire Officer in charge in each region. After the War the fire fighting functions of the National Fire Service passed to local authority control. On April lst. 1948 the Leeds City Fire Brigade resumed responsibility for the city's fire protection operating as a separate command and not as previously as part of the Police Force.
In September 1948 a Collective Training Centre was established at Gipton by the Leeds Fire Brigade: it trained recruits belonging to the 13 local authority fire brigades who participated in the scheme. Gipton Fire Station now has 5000 calls a year working on four shifts of 15 officers and is one of the busiest in the North of England.
Ald. Rowland Winn who was the Chairman of the Watch Committee and later Lord Mayor, said that Gipton Fire Station was the first to be built out of the four stations planned for the outskirts of Leeds. Prior to the opening an official lunch was held at The Mansion Hotel Roundhay Park. In 1987 a brass railway name" Gipton" was presented to the station on the Golden Jubilee which is now on display.
The Gipton estate commenced in 1934 on 359 acres building a total of 3534 dwellings. It was announced in March 1994 that £12 million was to be spent on a facelift in an area bounded by Coldcotes Drive, South Farm Road, Gipton Approach and Wykebeck Valley Road.

Gipton Approach is a wide route leading to Wykebeck Valley Road, allowing for the building of a tram line from York Road to Seacroft which never materialised. The short line to the valley road was opened on September llth. 1936 using a central reservation and a cutting to make the gradient easier for the trams. Tram route no.21 was the first and in 1946 this route was changed to become no.ll. It was intended to continue to Seacroft by South and North Parkway and form a loop at the terminus. The route closed on April 23rd. 1955.

The area was once the site of Gipton coal pit, sited near St.Wilfrid's Circus with Amberton Court standing on the site of the old pit heaps. The pit was run by the Low Moor Company, who built a tramway to take coal from the pit to a coal staithe at the Hovingham Avenue/Harehills Lane junction to join with the main tram route on Roundhay Road. Workings in the "Black Bed" ceased in 1896 and the other seams of coal were extracted until 1919 and August 1921. The pit sent coal to the

Farnley Iron Works via tram.
The 18th. century part of the " Dog and Gun Inn" on York Road is represented by the eastern part with the lower roof. The western section was added in 1936, to serve the developing Gipton estate. The mock-Tudor exterior was added in the late 1980's but the form of the Inn in the 1960's can be seen in a framed aerial photograph on display in the bar area. The "Dog and Gun" once had W. Green as licensee in 1817 and John Rhodes in 1834.
The inn originally served the increasing traffic on the turnpike and once had stables and outhouses. A 1922 photograph advertises afternoon teas and a charabanc park available at the "Dog and Gun" inn. The inn's bowling green was also once a popular venue. There were alterations carried out in 1935 with the addition of a pavilion.
The Albion cricket ground and the pavilion behind the Inn was a popular sports site for many years. The Inn possesses an advertisement and ticket for a Bowler's Benefit Cricket Match on Saturday July 7th. 1877 - the admission was 2d.
The introduction of the reserved tram track on York Road from Harehills Lane to Halton Dial was on April 24th. 1932. The tram routes were opened to High Street Halton in 1915 and to both Cross Gates and Temple Newsam in 1924.
Halton Dial is the junction of the Leeds and Selby turnpike with the Halton Dial to Tadcaster turnpike.Tadcaster turnpike charges were collected at a toll bar west of Killingbeck Bridge near the entrance to the old hall.
The small 18th. century stone built Halton Dial Weigh House cottage,with its central doorway between two windows was last maintained by John Edwin Waite as a sweet shop. The weigh house would have calculated payment for the many loads of coal using the road between Garforth and Leeds.
Halton Dial could refer to a new turnpike road or originate from the Latin word "dialis" meaning daily, as the toll house was open all hours. This century has seen many changes in the road system at Halton Dial. In the early years York Road ran by the old toll house and by the side of the present "City Lights" public house. The road crossed Wyke Beck by old Killingbeck Bridge, which still remains, although the carved stone parapets have been removed. The alteration in the alignment in 1931 removed the bend: the new road used the site of a weir and Killingbeck Pond, which was infilled. The trams to Killingbeck and Cross Gates used the old route until 1933, when the old road was abandoned and later used by the Highways Department.
Alterations in 1972 at the junction at Halton Dial created a mini-roundabout although this system was the scene of many accidents. Finally, in 1991-93 a new traffic light system was introduced with one way passage for traffic under the 19th. century Selby Road railway bridge.

THE ROAD FROM LEEDS TO YORK

PART TWO: HALTON DIAL TO SEACROFT

Wykebeck Valley Road was the first area to be completed on the Gipton Garden Estate and there is a bronze plaque on the wall of No. 15 recording "the completion of the first municipal house erected since the formation of the housing committee in November 1933, was unveiled on the 1st. January 1935 by the Lord Mayor Alderman W. Hemingway JP". William Hemingway was the Leeds Lord Mayor prior to the appointment of Percival Leigh.

On Wykebeck Valley Road are the tall flats and recently refurbished housing, together with the Wykebeck Day Centre. The Catholic Church of St. Nicholas was the inspiration of Father J. Holdright, who held the parish for 13 years. Masses were held in a new church hall until the opening of the new church with its 70' high campanile in 1961. A year later the adjoining Junior and Infant School was opened with children transferring to St. Brigid's School on Torre Road and St. Kevin's School on Barwick Road.

Epiphany Church on the Foundry Lane roundabout was designed by architect N. F. Cachemaille-Day, based on a church at Coutances in France, which the architect had visited on holiday in 1936. The ceremony of Breaking the Ground took place on March 20th. 1937 and the foundation stone was laid on July 12th. 1937 by Elsie Burroughs, the sister of Edward Arthur Burroughs, Bishop of Ripon 1926 - 1934: the builder was Armitage Hodgson of Leeds. The foundation stone is set into the east end of the church.

Epiphany church was consecrated on May 14th. 1938 as a memorial to Dr. Burroughs who became Bishop on the Feast of the Epiphany in 1926.The consecration was performed by Dr. Lunt Bishop of Ripon and was attended by the Princess Royal and the Earl of Harewood. The church hall opened in 1962, replacing one destroyed by fire in 1959.

The Halton Dial-Tadcaster turnpike road had the first toll bar north of the Wyke Beck near the drive to Killingbeck Hall. It was recorded in October 1750 that "at a meeting of several gentlemen and merchants of this Town, upon the Bill intended to be preferred the next session of Parliament, for erecting turnpikes between a certain place called Halton Dyal near Leedes and Tadcaster in the West Riding of the County of York". Wyke Beck originates as Great Heads Beck and flows through Roundhay Park and Waterloo Lake. The beck flows under Easterly Road at Asket Hill and under Foundry Lane, near Monkey Bridge. Wyke Beck then flows around Killingbeck Hill and at one time formed a lake or pool near the main road. This pool was drained and the beck continues under the railway and York Road, past the Wykebeck Arms Hotel on Halton Hill. The waters flow through Halton Moor and west of Skelton Moor Farm and then uses a man made diversion round the sewage works. Wyke Beck drains into the River Aire near the site of the Scargill family mansion of Thorpe Stapleton Hall.

On the route of the old York Road once stood Whitebridge House. This was a 16th./17th. century building in Tudor Style and was one of the oldest houses in Leeds. It was the home of William Thompson in 1638 and the letters "WT" were carved over one of the interior doorways. In 1722 the cottage was advertised for letting and included 30 acres of pasture. In later years the Green and Stead family occupied the building and Mrs. Meynell-Ingram was the owner in the late19th. century. This old house was finally demolished in 1949.

South of the York Road is the Killingbeck Sutton Housing Trust estate. The building of this estate started in 1926 with H. S. Chorley as the architect. There were plans for 220 dwellings and they were handed over to the Trust a year later. The estate was complete by 1929 and now has 246 dwellings with resident staff.

On the north side of the main road is the Killingbeck Science Park, where the large ASDA Superstore opened in 1990.

Killingbeck Hall estate once covered the land between Wykebeck Valley Road and Foundry Lane with the main York Road. The hall stood on the top of a hill, which is supposed to have been the early defences of ancient Celts. The area is named after an early farmer called Cylla who obtained his living from the area by the Wyke Beck. Thoresby suggested that the name originates from the Celtic "cylle" meaning recluse or Kil(n) - a Saxon word for corn drying. The arms of the Killingbeck family included three unicorn heads and three rings on a chevron: they were tenants of Allerton Grange. William de Killingbeck is referred to in 1335: John Killingbeck married Isabella in the 17th. century. Edward Killingbeck lived from 1599 until 1644 and John Killingbeck became Mayor of Leeds in 1677 and Vicar of Leeds in 1712.

Killingbeck Hall was built in 50 acres of land in the early 18th. century by the Brooke family. The family built it close by an earlier hall, ruins of which were still seen in 1860.This had been built in the 17th.century for Richard Greggs and when he died in 1638 the estate passed to his son in law Edward Brooke. It was Edward Brooke's great-great-grandson who sold Killingbeck to the Hanson family of Osmondthorpe in 1788.

John Hanson was born in 1759 and married Mary Isabella Oliver in 1784, making the hall their eventual home. Their son was John Oliver Hanson and was one of 16 children: he was born at Killingbeck Hall in May 1791 and died 1861. John's elder brothers were William (1788-1813) and Henry who was born in 1792 and was drowned in China in 1809.The family were descended from the 13th. century Hansons of Rastrick and were to sell their properties at Killingbeck and Osmondthorpe to buy the manor of Great Bromley near Colchester.

The Brooke family had land and property in Rothwell and lived at Royds Hall from 1724. Their other properties were Hollin Hall and Iveridge Hall. In 1788 the family objected to a turnpike road being built through Royds Hall parkland.
Richard Brooke (1630-1709), Edward's son, was a great benefactor of Whitkirk parish giving money to educate the poor. He willed the Killingbeck estate to his nephew William (1677-1728),who willed it to his son James (1712-1766).It was HIS son William who sold the Killingbeck estate. He was one of a family of 12 children and younger brother Robert was born at the Hall in 1739 - he was buried at Whitkirk Church in 1802.
James Croft Brooke, who has a memorial in Barwick in Elmet Church, was one of the sons of Richard Brook - another of Richard's brothers.
In the late 18th. century the Hanson family sold the Killingbeck estate to William Walker, who lived at the hall with his son George, who remodelled the hall. On his father's death George lived at Killingbeck Lodge. George died in August 1856 and had been the author of "Costume of Yorkshire" in 1814.Thomas Walker was living at Killingbeck Hall in 1837.
At the turn of the 19th. century the Hall became the property of Samuel Wilkes Waud, a member of the local coal mining family.
A succession of people followed the Walkers at Killingbeck Hall from 1812 including Leeds merchant G. Bischoff, F. H. Salvin in the 1850's and Arthur Kirk. From 1881 the hall was unoccupied for 17 years and on December 7th.1898 the hall and 144 acre estate was sold to Leeds Corporation for £21,000 by the owner Mrs.Meynell-Ingram.
The main hall became the administration unit of the smallpox hospital, officially opened in September 1904 by the Leeds Lord Mayor Arthur Currer-Briggs. After the decline of smallpox the wards were used for general infectious diseases after 1904.From 1913 Killingbeck Hospital specialised in TB cases, although the outbreak of the last war saw in revert to a general hospital. There was a new ward block opened in 1936 and a nurse's home followed in 1942.An application to demolish the Hall was made in 1976 and demolition started in April 1978, having been last used as a hospital staff/social centre. There has been much debate in recent years about the future of Killingbeck Hospital, with suggestions for closure and centralisation of hospital amenities in Leeds.
Seacroft Hospital on the eastern side of York Road has had a history dating back to 1846 when Edward Waud built his new hall on the site and called it Manston New Hall: on a map of 1849 it was called Bush Hall.
The Waud family owned the Manston Collieries and lived at Old Manston Hall, which following conversion into cottages was being demolished in April 1938. When Samuel Wilkes Waud started extracting coal at Manston, he was in direct competition with the Gascoigne pits at Garforth. In 1811 Samuel opened the pits near

Shippen Hall and in 1836 he opened a pit at Micklefield. Samuel was the grandson of Samuel Waud who was born in 1688 and married Katherine Horsfield in 1725.It was their son Samuel who was born in 1729 who married Alice Wilkes of Blackbank. Their son was Samuel Wilkes Waud who married Ellen Hodgson and had two children: Samuel Wilkes Waud born in 1801 who became a priest and Edward born on April 10th. 1806 and who soon joined the rapidly expanding business.
Edward ran the Manston Collieries but was declared bankrupt in 1866 - a sale of the Manston and West Yorkshire Collieries together with land in Seacroft was held in that year - and the colliery was sold in January 1867. Edward had married Mary Dorothy Sayle, daughter of Thomas Sayle of Wentbridge on July 30th. 1833 and they had two sons: Edward Wilkes Waud born on September 30th. 1834 and Brian Wilkes Waud born on June 4th. 1837.They had four daughters Ellen, Mary, Kathleen and Margaret. Manston Colliery was closed in 1883 and Edward Waud died in 1885 and was buried at Whitkirk Church. Two of the Waud pits were named after their children: Mary Pit and Brian Pit.
In 1891 Leeds was seeking a site for a new hospital and in June 1892 the Manston Hall estate of 97 acres was bought for £10,000 from Edward Simpson and the trustees of Ald. Edmund Stead - he died in September 1881 aged 78 and was buried at St. James Church Seacroft. In 1903 five more acres of adjoining land was bought from Darcy Bruce Wilson of Seacroft Hall for £2000.
In 1898 a start was made on new buildings to form the Manston Infectious Diseases Hospital, opened by the Lord Mayor Ald. Charles Francis Tetley on October lst. 1898, in the last month of his mayoralty. Manston Hall was used at first as the administration block and servant's quarters. The foundations of the new hospital were laid in 1900 and the complex opened at the same time as Killingbeck in September 1904.The old hall was demolished and the listed 110' clock tower designed by E. T. Hall in 1903 was built to hold 28,000 gallons of water for hospital use.
TB cases were admitted to Seacroft in 1912 but a year later they were transferred to Killingbeck. In the First World War Seacroft continued as an infectious diseases hospital but in the last war it was the base of the Emergency Hospital Services, with infectious cases at Killingbeck.

The Catholic Cemetery is east of Killingbeck Hall and was officially opened in its 11 acre grounds on July 14th. 1895, although the first burial had been in March of that year. The cemetery, which is nearly full, lost some ground when York Road was widened in May 1956 and some burials were reinterred. There are many Catholic priests buried in a circle within the cemetery and two Bishops of Leeds are interred near the chapel. This recently refurbished chapel, built in 1900, was once a chapel of ease to St. Patrick's Church York Road. Some services were also held in the chapel prior to the opening of St. Theresa's School Cross Gates in 1930 and the church in 1953. There is a stone cross from the gable end of old St.Patrick's Church in memory of all the priests who worked in that parish from 1831 until 1922.There is also the grave of Mgr. Austin Joseph Collingwood (1841-1928) who for 40 years was the parish priest of St. Patrick's Church. Killingbeck is the burial place of Dr. William Gordon 2nd Bishop of Leeds who died on June 7th. 1911: he was born in 1831 and succeeded Dr.Cornthwaite as Bishop in February 1890. The third Bishop of Leeds is also buried at Killingbeck in the centre of the priest's circle: Rt. Rev. Joseph Cowgill was born in 1860 and died in 1936. A cross which once stood over the sanctuary of old St. Anne's Cathedral Leeds is a feature of a memorial to the priests who laboured in that parish from 1838 until 1904. In that year the old church at the top of Park Row was demolished. There is also the large marble seated grave to Agnes - the "Duchess" who died aged 85 - and Vincent Savile, parents of Sir Jimmy Savile.

Killingbeck Lodge was a late 18th. century house demolished early this century. It stood on the present Lyme Chase and was home to the Morkill family, closely linked with Whitkirk Church. Thomas Morkill of Halton (1739-1810) was a churchwarden at Whitkirk: his daughter Anne married Sir James Falshaw (1810-1889) and his son William died in February 1808 aged 39. John Morkill lived at Killingbeck Lodge and he died in April 1881 aged 64: his wife Mary moved with her son to Newfield Hall Malhamdale where she died in July 1904 aged 82. John William Morkill bought Austhorpe Lodge estate in 1892, in the same year publishing "Records of the Parish of Whitkirk" with the vicar Rev. George Moreton Platt, who died at the vicarage in May 1898.

John William Morkill moved from East Leeds to live at Newfield Hall, now a Holiday Fellowship Guest House. He lived in the Dales from 1901 until he died on April 27th. 1932 having become a respected landowner in the Craven area.

The roundabout at the York Road/Foundry Lane junction was once the site of the "Melbourne Hotel". This was demolished in 1988 and the site redeveloped. The garage between York Road and Cross Gates Road was established in 1932.

Seacroft Iron Foundry was near Wyke Beck, west of Seacroft Grange Primary School, which opened in 1974. On the north side of Foundry Lane was a row of cottages and these were demolished along with nearby Seacroft Lodge. The Lodge,near the old corn mill, was sold in 1931 as part of the Seacroft Hall estate. In the early part of this century Seacroft Lodge was home to poultry dealer William Askham. The corn mill,on the site of the old manorial mills, was in evidence in the 1920's near Corkett's farm.

Christopher Mather is recorded as having altered and extended Seacroft Mill in 1577 and he made a mile long water conduit from a point at Asket Hill to the mill. The

corn mills in 1701 passed to the Nelthorpe family and thence to the Wilsons.
Close to the corn mills was Seacroft Colliery, having an opening above the mills and it was Mather who "drained the colliery and cleared the water course".
Ironstone had been worked in this area for many centuries, as there is a record of William de Somerville - a surname remembered in local streets - owning and mining ironstone in the late 12th. century.
In 1779/80 John Smeaton designed a steam engine and wheel for a coke furnace at the colliery. The overshot wheel was 28' in diameter and used at the pit at the time that the iron foundry was being redeveloped. The wheel drove the furnace and there was an auxiliary engine that would pump water from the mill ponds to the wheel in dry weather. Smeaton was also consulted on the provision of a fire engine in order to supply air to the colliery blast furnace. In 1781 there was an advertisement in a newspaper for the appointment of "experienced moulders at Seacroft Iron Foundry". There is now no trace of this industry except in the street names.
The nearby corn mills were active until about 1912 and the 30' wooden wheel, designed by John Smeaton in 1783 was in use until that period. This wheel was enclosed in a brick built housing with a stone roof. The water supply was from Wyke Beck and used a hatch about 20 yards from the mill. The hatch worked a lever and the system was in working order in the early 1930's. When the hatch was raised the water raced along the channel, over an artificial fall and turned the blades of the wheel. Part of this creation was a large pond east of the mill, drained within living memory but had been used for ice skating in winter periods.
The mill stones turned by Smeaton's wheel produced a coarse brown flour but there is no trace now of the remains of this corn mill, once the home of the Green and Bowes families. The mill wheel was abandoned when the water carrying culverts collapsed and repairs proved to be too expensive. The Green family originally farmed at Coach Hall Farm on York Road - the site of the Star Cinema - and after the years at Foundry Mill lived at Pidgeon Cote Farm Seacroft from 1902 until 1941.
There was an attempt in 1938 to preserve the wheel in a museum and although there was an offer of £1000 by Lord Mayor Ald. Rowland Winn, the suggestion proved impracticable. The housing committee decided to demolish both the farm and the wheel in 1939, as the proposed housing development and supply roads would cover the site.

The Killingbeck Divisional Police Headquarters opened to the public on May 18th.1993 at the Melbourne roundabout. The £5.2 million building accommodating up to 300 staff replaced Gipton Police Station. It was officially opened by Lord Merlyn Rees on September 30th. 1993: he had been the MP for South Leeds and was Home Secretary in 1976. He was awarded the Freedom of Leeds in February 1993.
The continuation of York Road from the roundabout passes between the sites of the

short lived Brian Pit and Seacroft Colliery. Brian Pit was linked to the Mary Pit which opened in 1863 and closed in 1929 due to flooding. An application for £181,000 to make the dual carriageway from Foundry Lane to Barwick Road was made in 1962 and the road was completed.
Seacroft Colliery had been bought by Sir Thomas Gascoigne in 1778 but had been in existence in the early 17th. century.Seacroft coal pits were mentioned in 1603 and 1638, although the position varied throughout the period 1701 to 1837 about the time it closed.
William Porter was the colliery agent to Sir Thomas Gascoigne with responsibilities for all his pits and particular interest in the Seacroft Colliery on purchase from Mrs. Ann Porter, the wife of John who worked for Sir Thomas at Sturton Colliery. John died in 1774 after a fall from his horse and Anne advertised the Seacroft pit for sale in 1775 - the coal itself was a part of the will of James Nelthorpe. In the north graveyard at Whitkirk Church are the tombs of William Porter and Lucy Nelthorpe. William is described as being "the eldest son of John Porter of Seacroft 35 years the faithful and assidious colliery agent to the late Sir Thomas Gascoigne and the present Richard Oliver Gascoigne of Parlington. He died at Scarborough with poor health 29th. August 1813 - and Elizabeth his wife died aged 59 1829".
Lucy Nelthorpe was the wife of James Nelthorpe of Seacroft the Nelthorpe family lived at Seacroft Hall from 1656 and James was the grandson of James Nelthorpe who bought Seacroft from Lady Hansby. James jnr. married Lucy Wilmer at York Minster in 1744 and she was buried at Whitkirk in December 1756 - her husband died in October 1767.

The present "Lion and Lamb" inn is on the site of Townend's Park Farm, demolished in 1940 to become in later years the new public house and car park. The building of the inn caused the demolition of Wright's Cottages (White Houses), once a part of the Wilson Seacroft estate and sold in 1931.
William Townend of Seacroft died on March 12th. 1809 aged 70 with his wife Elizabeth having died on February 2nd. 1797: they are buried at Whitkirk Church. There is also the grave of John Townend, late of Garforth and a blacksmith who died on May 3rd. 1826. The Townend family were active in the life of Seacroft: William was a churchwarden on the opening of St. James Church and his son John Townend was born on November 24th. 1842.His wife Mildred was born on March 6th. 1850 and their daughter Sarah married Dr.William Pogson of Seacroft Grange. Mildred died in June 1906 and John died in August 1916. The old "Lion and Lamb" inn closed on September 4th. 1958 and the key is preserved in the new "Lion and Lamb" public house. This inn opened in 1958 as the "Seacroft" and was changed in 1983 to the new name following a ballot of customers. The last landlady of the old inn was Mrs. Morrison and she became the first at the new Davenport's inn. In 1983 the

Mansfield Brewery took over the licence.
On the opposite corner was Poplar House, which was the home of the store-owning Dobson family at the start of this century. The original Lion and Lamb inn is now known as the Old Lamb Guest House. When the "Lion and Lamb" was sold in 1931 to a Birmingham brewery, the inn was described as doing "a heavy summer trade in home brewed beer - the tenant being licensed for home brewing": the inn ceased brewing its own beer in 1939. This stone built inn had the brewhouse at the rear and this has been converted into two cottages - the new owners having spent two years renovating the building. The tenants of the inn were Thomas Sowden who died in 1848, Mary Sowden in 1853 (she died in 1863) and R. S. McNeill in 1931, who transferred to a Barwick in Elmet inn. The old Lion and Lamb ceased to be an inn in the 1950's and it became the home of the Spence family, who were specialists in wrought iron work. The listed old inn, complete with cellars, became a guest house in July 1992.
This part of Seacroft High Street was once lined with stone walls, which were made with material from the quarry that occupied the site of Waterloo Lake in Roundhay Park. Sections of this wall are still visible on the main street.
Stock's Hill or Green is still evidence of the rural charm of Old Seacroft, opposite the entrance lodge and gates to Seacroft Hall. The old hall entrance now gives access to a builder's merchant yard.
In the years following the Norman Conquest Seacroft was held by the Somerville family as tenants of de Lacy of Pontefract. They continued at Seacroft until the mid-13th. century. In 1285 the Earl of Lincoln held Seacroft and by 1316 it was held by Thomas Earl of Lancaster, executed in 1321. The Crown granted Seacroft estates to the son of John of Gaunt, who became Henry IV, who inherited the de Lacy estates in 1399. Until 1603 Seacroft was part of the Duchy of Lancaster and in that year the King granted Seacroft to the 8th. Baron Mountjoy, who became the Earl of Devon. The Earl granted Seacroft to George Shillito and after his death the family conveyed Seacroft to James Nelthorpe in 1656. It remained with the Nelthorpe family until about 1811 when Seacroft was sold to John Wilson of Camp Hall Leeds - this was a two storey building in Water Lane near to Water Hall and it remained with this family until John's great grandson Darcy Bruce Wilson died unmarried in January 1931.
Seacroft Hall was probably built in the 17th. century by the Shillito family, although there are references to the "site of a manor, hall, chamber, granges" in 1341. The hall once had a large ornamental pond, which was filled in to form Parklands High School sports fields.
Parklands with 160 girls under the headmistress Mrs. A. C. Newell opened as a Girl's Grammar School on September 9th. 1958 and stands to the north of the site that once was Seacroft Hall, demolished in 1953. The first Parklands Speech Day was held on

November 13th. 1963.
Foxwood School occupied the buildings of Parklands School for two years, prior to opening as the first comprehensive school school in Leeds in September 1959. Foxwood School on the 37 acre campus was officially opened on February 5th. 1960 by Hugh Gaitskell MP.
Seacroft Hall was the home of both John Wilson (1808-1891) and his sister Constance Eade. Constance married the Rev. Charles Eade Vicar of Aycliffe in 1887 and she died widowed at Seacroft Grange in December 1938 - her will published in 1939 left about £5000. Her son Aylmer was killed in the First World War in 1917. Seacroft Hall was finally demolished in July 1953 after 20 years of being unoccupied. In 1934 it was suggested in Council that Seacroft Hall and the 50 acre park may become one of the major Leeds City parklands, similar to Temple Newsam and Roundhay. In 1937 the Council suggested that the Hall park, woodlands, footpaths and open spaces will be "preserved in the development of the Seacroft estate". The Council retained many of the hall's contents, including a fireplace which was placed in Temple Newsam House about 1939 and when the House reorganised the carved wooden mantle piece and surround of a Georgian fireplace was removed to the Leeds City Museum. In March 1994 the fireplace was placed on permanent loan in the Tetley's Brewery Wharf Museum, where it is a major feature of the Georgian dining room. The fireplace is the only item from Seacroft Hall in the City's collections.
Near the entrance to Taylor's Yard the new housing of Taylor's Close now stand in this area was the "New Inn", at which James Granger was the landlord in the mid-19th. century.
The inn was the end house of a row occupied by Seacroft estate workers. This was also the site of the Seacroft Post Office which closed in November 1967, when the Crown Post Office opened in the new Centre: prior to Taylor's Yard it was housed next to the Thrift Stores on the west side of the main road. On the same south side of the main street (York Road) was once James H. Gibbon's wheelwright premises. The Gibbon family lived at Jasmine House on Taylor's Yard: the last member of the family was Tom Gibbon.
Marshall's stores east of the main road were owned by the Shoesmith family and stocked a wide variety of goods. The Darcy Bruce Wilson Institute was opened on January 6th. 1934 by Col. C. Eade. He was the nephew of Darcy Bruce Wilson, who left £1000 in his will for the land and new hall. The hall was designed by F. L. Charlton and built by J. W. Shippon of York Road, replacing the original institute demolished in 1934. There is an oak memorial board to local men who died in the last War made by Mouseman Robert Thompson on the wall of the Institute. Adjacent to this building is St. George's Garden with its attractive iron gates.
On the west side of the road is Seacroft Methodist Church: the first meeting of

Seacroft Methodists took place in William England's house. The first Wesleyan Chapel was built in 1751 with part of the original walls remaining. The chapel was rebuilt in 1821 and enlarged in 1840 and 1874: the last date appears over the frontage. The chapel was enlarged mainly to accommodate increased membership in Cross Gates - their chapel opened on Austhorpe Road in 1882.
The new wing to the north was opened on Saturday May 24th. 1980 by Paul Long and dedicated by the Rev. Stanley Rose, Chairman of the Leeds District. The chapel has an impressive interior with the balcony and organ dating from 1910: electric power came in 1927. Charles Wesley came to Seacroft in October 1756 followed by his brother John Wesley on July 25th. 1761.
John Wesley was born on June 17th. 1703 as the 15th. of 19 children of a clergyman at Epworth Lincolnshire. John Wesley was the founder of Methodism and first attended evensong at St. Paul's Cathedral on May 24th. 1738: he went on to a meeting at Aldersgate, where he experienced his conversion.
Seacroft Methodist Church is one of the ten constituent churches of the Leeds (Richmond Hill Circuit) which also includes the churches at Cross Gates, Halton, Colton, Garforth and Gipton. The Leeds Circuit was formed in 1755 and in 1892 Richmond Hill was the head circuit church.
The only wall memorial in the church is to those Seacroft men who were killed in action during the Great War.
The Methodist Conference opened in Leeds on June 25th. 1994: the first conference on June 25th. 1744 in London was attended by ten people including John and his brother Charles Wesley. The Leeds Conference was attended by more than 600 ministers and lay people representing the ½ million active Methodists who make up Britain's largest Free Church. The first time the Conference was held in Leeds was at Boggard House Quarry Hill on May 22nd. 1753 with about 50 people attending.
The area south of the parish church was once the National School opened in February 1840 and later extended in 1859, 1871 and 1880. On closure in 1950 the children moved into Seacroft Grange and the old school was demolished, becoming the site for the new rectory - there has been a Rector at Seacroft from 1970 when the five churches were formed into a team ministry. The old vicarage was built west of the church near Laburnum Farm in 1847 and was eventually demolished, after renovations in 1953.
The idea of a church at Seacroft was promoted by John Wilson of the Hall and the Vicar of Whitkirk: Seacroft was in this parish. Land was granted by Stephen Nicholson of Roundhay Seacroft being part of his manor. The foundation stone of the new St. James Church was laid on July 22nd. 1844 by John Wilson JP and the architect was Thomas Hellyer of Ryde Isle of Wight. The church was consecrated by Dr. C. T. Longley Bishop of Ripon on November 28th. 1845 and a year later it acquired its own parish. The church was built of Roundhay stone by Benjamin

Russell of Leeds and the cost of £3174 was covered by John Wilson, the Vicar of Whitkirk, the Diocesan Building Society and Trinity College Cambridge. The spire is 94' high and the three bells were donated by Martha Wilson in 1865: she died aged 92 on February 18th. 1869.
There are two Oak plaques to John Wilson (1808-1891) and to his son Darcy Bruce Wilson. A brass plate on the north wall indicates that the east window was placed in memory of Sarah Wilson, daughter of John and Martha in June 1868 and erected by friends and neighbours. The family vault lies beneath the church containing six coffins or ashes including Isabella Wilson (died 1867 aged 5), Roderic (1847-1881), Louisa (1862-1948) as well as John, Martha and Darcy Bruce Wilson.
The original stone font now lies outside the south side of the church but the present font dates from 1878 and is made from alabaster. The small columns are made from Derbyshire Blue John and the whole font was paid for by John Wilson, in memory of his daughter Ann. The west window was placed in memory of George Walker of Killingbeck Lodge who died in 1856 and whose father bought Killingbeck Hall from John Hanson: the south nave window remembers Martha Wilson.
The reredos is carved from Caen stone and is dated 1868: it was designed by Thomas Hellyer and commemorates Sarah Wilson, daughter of John and Martha Wilsom, who died in 1867. The reredos is now covered with curtaining.
There is a board in the church which states that the church was erected in 1845 and contains 400 sittings: 323 of these sittings are to be free for ever made possible by a grant from the Incorporated Society for promoting the enlargement, building and repairing of churches and chapels. The boards bears the names of the first vicar Rev. R. H. Blanshard and churchwardens W. S. Townend and John Hirst. The tile dado featuring a trailing vine and pelicans was in memory of Mary Wilson, wife of Major General Bush who died at Bath on May 25th. 1883 - the inscription is now in the vestry. The dado was erected by John Wilson in 1884 and made by Dalton & Co London. The chancel pavement was given by the Rev. and Mrs. Henry John Longsdon (Vicar 1854-1877) as a thanksgiving for his benefice.
The St. James Community Room was opened by Mrs. Jane Young and dedicated by the Bishop of Ripon Rt. Rev. David Young on July 3rd. 1988.

John Wilson was born in January 1808 and educated at Rugby and Cambridge University, graduating in 1830-33. He became a JP for the West Riding and was Captain of the 2nd. W. Y. Militia. He married Anna Macleod in April 1846 and had children including Roderic, Darcy, Arthur, Constance and Louisa. John Wilson died in January 1891 and was buried at Seacroft.
Both his grandfather and father were also John Wilson: grandfather John was born in 1731 and bought Camp Hall, Water Lane, Leeds. He married Sarah Lucas in 1762 and had nine children. He died aged 90 in 1821 having bought Seacroft Hall about

1811.
His eldest son John was born at Camp Hall in 1767 and he married Martha Bassett having eight children. Their other property at Cliffe Hall at Piercebridge near Manfield became the home of the eldest son Richard Bassett Wilson and his wife Anne Fitzgerald, by whom he had eight children. Cliffe Hall was built in 1859 and has an older wing.
There is a wall memorial in Whitkirk Church to both John and Martha Wilson, who outlived her husband by 32 years. The Wilson coat of arms features a wolf's head and three lion's forelegs: their motto was "Perseverando".
The second son was John Wilson of Seacroft Hall, whose son Darcy Bruce Wilson lived at the hall. In 1912 Darcy was nominated for the post of Leeds Alderman in the new ward of Roundhay, Seacroft, Shadwell and Cross Gates. He was a J. P. for the West Riding, barrister at law and Captain in the Yorkshire Hussars. He died aged 79 on January 5th. 1931 and the estate was sold by auction in July at the Church Institute Albion Place in Leeds. The sale included properties in Cross Gates, Manston as well as the inns of Seacroft.
In the churchyard of St. James Church, which stands by the Green, once the scene of cricket matches, are many memorials including Agnes Stewart, Mother Superior of St. Saviour's Home at Knostrop who died on April 30th. 1886. The granite obelisk is the tomb of Alderman Edmund Stead of New Manston Hall, now Seacroft Hospital. Richard Stead, the alderman's grandson (died 1826) is also remembered with his wife Christine and daughter Joyce, who died in 1956. Other tombs include Jonathan Phillips of Foundry Mills; Joseph Burton who was killed at the Garforth Sisters Pit aged 55 in 1900 and the Sowden family of the old Lion and Lamb inn. There is the grave of James Fowler (1830-1899), who was the head gardener to the Earl of Harewood for 35 years. The grave of Isaac Chippindale (1826-1889) of Scholes brickworks and his wife Charlotte - she died aged 39 in 1865 - also remembers four of their children who all died in infancy.
North of the Green is Seacroft Grange, built in 1627 which became the home of the Tottie family. They came from Allerton Gledhow and John and Martha Tottie lived at "Tottie Hall" in the 18th. century. William Totty bought a property in Potter Newton from the Lindley family; Thomas Lindley died in 1543. John Totty married Elizabeth Shillitoe and his brother William Totty married Rebecca Shillitoe. John and Elizabeth's son John married Martha Shillitoe and they bought Seacroft Grange: their three children John, William and Sarah all died as infants. John Totty died in 1703 being buried at Wakefield, whereas Martha died on May 8th. 1735 aged 83 years and was buried at Whitkirk, where there is a brass memorial plaque on the centre nave floor. The inscription reads: "Esteemed by all for her piety and charity". A smaller adjacent grave cover is to the memory of Ruth Tottie. On the north wall of Whitkirk's chancel is a memorial to Elizabeth Lowther of Little Preston Hall, who

died in 1751 and wished to be buried close to her niece Mrs. Tottie of Seacroft. William and Rebecca Totty's son William was a Leeds draper and his descendents included Richard Totty born 1770 who married Sarah Walker of Killingbeck in 1800 and Richard's sister Margaret who married Thomas Bischoff a Leeds merchant. The Bischoff family, who were also tenants of Killingbeck Hall for a few years, had their home at Bischoff House, built as Sheepscar Hall in 1692. John Bischoff owned the hall from the end of the 18th. century and they had their clothier's business in Woodhouse Lane, where Thomas Bischoff was in residence. Bischoff House was demolished in 1968.

In 1837 Tottie Hall became known as Seacroft Grange after extensive remodelling and the property of John Wilson, being leased to tenants including Dr. William and Mrs. Sarah Pogson and Constance Eade, the sister of Darcy Bruce Wilson. The Wilson coat of arms is displayed in stone over the east door of the Grange. In 1931 the Grange estate became the property of the Leeds City Council on the death of Darcy Bruce Wilson and a listed building in 1951. It has been suggested that Seacroft Grange became the dower house to Seacroft Hall.

Dr. Pogson lived at the Grange at the turn of the century: he was a surgeon and medical officer, qualifying MRCS in 1864. William Pogson was born in Halifax in 1837 and when he came to Leeds became a close friend of John Wilson of Seacroft Hall. He occupied the Grange and professionally became a skin specialist with patients from all over Britain. He offered specialist advice to King Edward VII and developed a skin soap known as "Dr. Pogson's soap", sold in pink wrappers and popular at 1/6d a tablet. The soap was made for him by Joseph Watson's Whitehall Soap Works - the firm was manufacturing soap from 1848. William Pogson married

Seacroft Grange

Sarah Townend, daughter of John Townend of Park Farm Seacroft - he was a farmer and maltster, being overseer and estate agent to Darcy Bruce Wilson. William and Sarah had five children including Frederick William, Gertrude, Kate and Florence. Dr. Pogson was presented with a silver claret jug in 1885 by the sons and daughters of James Kitson Snr. following his death at Elmete Hall Roundhay. The letter accompanying the gift stated that it was "in recognition of valuable services to the late Mr. Kitson, in appreciation of your unwearied kindness and care as a testimonial of their regard for such faithful and devoted attention to him. He looked forward to your coming with pleasure when on the bed of sickness and pain." The letter was signed by H. Ellen Kitson, James Kitson, Mary Clarke, Emily Playfair and J. Hawthorn Kitson.
Dr.William Pogson became the Seacroft doctor in November 1872 until his death on Saturday November 9th. 1912 aged 75. He was the President of the Cross Gates Flower Show and left his widow Sarah who died on September lst. 1928.
William left much property including Pogson's Cottages or Pogson's Row at Whinmoor overlooking Mill Green and houses at Burmantofts, Normanton and Garforth. He owned the old almshouses, which were also popularity known as "Pogson's Cottages". He was buried at St. James Church, where he had been both People's Warden and Vicar's Warden during his active life. Sarah was still living at the Grange in the 1920's but the family later lived in Park Road Colton.
Seacroft Grange became the temporary home of the Primary School in 1941, which moved to new premises on Moresdale Lane in 1974. The Grange became an Adult Education Centre and became a derelict property: the listed Grade II property was boarded up and placed on sale through the Leeds Development Agency. The main house and outbuildings stand on a site of nearly an acre: the Grange still contains a magnificent Oak staircase removed from John More's 1694 Austhorpe Hall in 1836. The City Council suggested that the Grange be used as a Seacroft Old People's Centre but the idea was not developed.
West of the Green is the early 19th. century Cricketer's Arms public house, sold in 1931 with its own brewhouse as part of the Wilson estate. This one time coaching inn was complete with stables and served the turnpike: it contains a framed front page of the "Yorkshire Observer Budget" from 1912 and a painting of the inn as it looked in the early years of this century. The listed inn was enlarged in 1977 to include three adjacent cottages and was sold in October 1994.
Further to the west is the Aged Peoples Home with the Day Centre opening in January 1990.
Pidgeon Cote Farm,with its once familiar pigeon cote landmark,was once known as Seacroft Upper House and the home of the Eamonson family. The Eamonsons came to Seacroft in the mid 17th. century from Leeds - their coat of arms graced the fireplace at the farm until about 1880. The family spread in the area occupying the

Seacroft Lower House in the early 18th. century, Austhorpe Hall, Kiddal Hall in the 1750's - Benjamin Eamonson of Kiddal Hall was buried at Whitkirk Church in 1753 - and Bramham,where another Benjamin Eamonson died in 1800 - his sister Eleanor married John Gray of Morwick Hall. When this Benjamin died he devised his estates at Bramham to his son Benjamin, who became the Vicar of Collingham and those lands at Seacroft to his daughter Eleanor Ann who married the Vicar of Ferrybridge. On the north wall of Barwick in Elmet's chancel is a memorial stone to William Eamonson of Lazingcroft who died in 1781. The slab also remembers his daughters Elizabeth who died aged 17 in 1772 and Alice who died aged 18 in 1775 and was buried in Scarborough.

Pidgeon Cote Farm was the home of the Carter family before the Green family from Foundry Mill Farm came in 1902 and stayed at the Seacroft farm until 1941, when it was taken for a short while by John Goodall, before its eventual demolition.

On the south side of the main road facing Seacroft Green once stood Dixon's farm, demolished to make room for a garage. To the south of the farm were Seacroft Almshouses, demolished in 1935 and now the site of a house.

The ascent to the Windmill was called Pogson's Hill and now approaches the Centre, opened by The Queen on a foggy Thursday October 21st. 1965. The Queen arrived at Cross Gates railway station following an overnight stay for the 9 coach Royal train on the old line from Garforth to Kippax. The Centre was built on a 10 acre site and cost £1.5 million. The following day the Queen and the Duke of Edinburgh visited York University's Heslington Hall and opened two new colleges and a new science block.

Seacroft Branch Library opened on Seacroft Crescent on June 25th. 1964 and marked the event on June 24th. 1994 with a specially baked cake and a talk on Old Seacroft by John Gilleghan: attended by George Mudie MP.

In 1993 Leeds agreed to a multi-million pound redevelopment of the Seacroft Centre, serving an estate developed from 1947 initially with 7000 dwellings - in 1965 the population of the estate was 40,000.

THE ROAD FROM LEEDS TO YORK

PART 3: WHINMOOR TO BRAMHAM CROSS ROADS

The Leeds Stakis Windmill Hotel stands at the junction of the York Road and the Seacroft by-pass. The hotel was opened on May 14th. 1974, was extended in 1985 and refurbished in 1991. There are 100 rooms and the hotel has extensive conference facilities, based around the old Seacroft windmill. The history of the area is displayed inside the old mill.

The Seacroft Windmill was owned by the Wilson family of Seacroft Hall in the mid 19th. century and was rented to James Pearson. There have been suggestions that the mill could be the Flint Mill mentioned by John Smeaton in 1774 and was one of several local tower mills grinding corn from farms. In 1822 William Chippindale moved from Yeadon to Seacroft mill: he died in 1854 and was buried at Whitkirk. On the occasion of his 80th. birthday in 1842 William is said to have stood on his head on top of Seacroft Mill to show that his health was good. His son Isaac, who was born at the mill house in 1826 and started the Scholes brickworks in 1877, died in 1889 and was buried at Seacroft Church. In the early years of this century the farmhouse became known as Betty Barker's, although the mill had stopped working: the Robinson family later lived at the Mill.

The Ring Road Seacroft by-pass was opened in 1964 and provided easier access to the main York Road and Barwick Road - itself a result of a turnpike act of 1840 promoted by the Tadcaster and Halton Dial Trust to Scholes, thus avoiding crossing Whinmoor. The Coal Road was used by tenant farmers on the Harewood estate who delivered coal to Harewood House from the coal staithe of the Waterloo Colliery. The old Bay Horse Inn on the Coal Road was built in 1779 and brewed its own beer using water from Brandon Drain stream. The centre house has been converted into a private dwelling and the two adjoining houses were once outhouses of the farm. It lost its licence in about 1888 and ceased to be an inn.

Tolls on the turnpike at Whinmoor were paid at the Penny Toll, which was accepting payment for crossing Whinmoor prior to the turnpike act. The Lord of the Manor was allowed to charge "chiminage" or "moorage" on travellers across the moor who were provided with protection for their journey. In 1702 Thoresby recorded that he saw Sir Thomas Gascoigne's toll collectors: the charge was a penny per pair of wheels. The tolls were still being collected when the turnpike ended in 1873. The toll bar was finally removed in 1913 and the toll house was demolished in 1959.

The Old Red Lion Inn was the first inn after the toll bar and the present Berni Inn is a development of the 18th. century coaching inn. Stage coaches stopped and started at the Red Lion on a route via Thorner and Bramham to York. When the Whinmoor was enclosed in 1804 the present road line was fixed replacing an even older route

on the northern section of the moor to Red Hall and Elmete Lane. William Gascoigne was the farmer and innkeeper in the mid-19th. century: William died on July 14th. 1870 and was buried at Manston Church. His wife Martha died on March 29th. in the same year.
The Manor House, demolished in 1991 following a period of dereliction, stood by the roadside opposite the Old Red Lion. It was surrounded by a wall and iron fence, some of which still remains. It was once the house of Jos. M. Rayner, the Chairman of Craven Dairies: his partners were Noel Stockdale and Clifford Lister. Craven Dairies of Deighton Street amalgamated with Provincial Dairies in 1940, following the establishment of the Milk Marketing Board on October 3rd. 1933.
Provincial Dairies of 77 Park Lane was founded in 1874 and in June 1887 was selling milk at 3d a quart from their newly opened shop in Upper Headrow. Craven Dairies absorbed Bramham's shops to become Associated Dairies, the forerunner of Associated Fresh Foods. They opened the new plant on Kirkstall Road in 1959, with building on their 4 acre site starting in 1957. The area was bought in 1955 and the £½ million factory had an output of 30,000 gallons of milk a day. Jos Rayner ran Manor Farm,which was separated from the Manor House. Craven Dairies were also concerned with Flying Horse Farm on York Road and nearby Woodhouse Farm. When Jos Rayner moved from his farm at Gouthwaite near Pateley Bridge he walked with his cattle all the way to Whinmoor. The Manor was sold to Leeds City Council and for a few years was used as a nursery before it was abandoned.

Whinmoor Lodge was south of The Manor House and was demolished in 1991/92. The Lodge was the home of the Blakey family in the 19th. century. Thomas Blakey died on December 28th. 1907 aged 85 and his wife Mary Ann Blakey died aged 78 on November 24th. 1900. Their son Charles died aged 31 on August lst. 1875. The street past their home was once known as Blakey Lane. A few years later it was the home of Ald. Isaac Jowitt Dewhirst,who was born in Huddersfield on February 2nd. 1863. He came to Leeds in 1885 and established his Kirkgate business: warehouse signs are still seen on the Harper Street corner. In 1898 he became a member of Barwick in Elmet Parish Council and in 1904 a member of Tadcaster Rural Council. In 1910 he contested and won the Garforth Division on the WRCC held by Granville Wheler MP. He became a Leeds Alderman in 1923 and lived in Cross Gates and at Whinmoor Lodge. He married the daughter of George Backhouse of Cross Gates: Clara died on March 17th. 1934 aged 67. County Coun. Dewhirst died on Sunday May 16th. 1937 aged 74 and the funeral service was held at Cross Gates Methodist Church with interment at Manston Church. He had two sons Stanley and Harold together with daughters May and Elsie: his other daughter Ruth died as a child aged seven years on November 7th. 1907. On March 6th. 1915 Elsie married the son of Mr & Mrs S. Jackson of Moor Allerton: the grand reception was held at Whinmoor

Lodge. In the 1940's it was the home of Stanley Dewhirst, a descendent of Isaac Jowitt Dewhirst JP of the family firm of tailors. The remains of the gardens of the 19th. century house still contain a tall Monkey Puzzle tree together with Laurel, Silver Birch and Yew - only a few scattered bricks mark the site of the house.
The main road crosses Cock Beck and through Grimes Dyke: a system of man made defensive earthworks from Swillington Bridge. They were constructed by local folk as a defence against possible 7th. century Saxon incursions into the Kingdom of Elmet.
In July 1792 there was a notice "to let by the Trustees of the turnpike: the levelling of the hills on that part of the road called Grimes Dyke". Grimes Dyke Farm belonged to the Goodall family, who had their stock destroyed prior to the outbreak of the First World War, when anthrax was discovered on the farm. It later became the property of the Leake family and it was Selwyn Leake who bought Morwick Flats in 1976. The family now run Bramley Grange Farm on Skeltons Lane. Grimes Dyke farmhouse was sold in 1977 and became empty again in 1990: the house was demolished in 1992.
The Whinmoor was the scene of a battle between the forces of King Oswy of Northumbria and the aged King Penda of Mercia in 655 AD. This was the "Winwaedfield" of the Venerable Bede and the result was the defeat of Penda and his pagan principles: one of his objectives was the acquisition of more land. The victory is shown in a stained glass window in the north nave aisle at Barwick in Elmet church.
Penda's own army was strengthened by those of King Catgabail from Wales and of the forces led by the 19 year old Aethelwald. The day before the battle was November 14th. 655 AD and Penda was camped on the Hungerhills and Aethelwald in the defences of Gipton Wood. King Oswy had marched from York and camped at Morgan Cross near Potterton - there are only field marks of the Anglian encampment today. Catgabail withdrew his forces during the night before the battle, fought on the Whinmoor Sunday November 15th. Penda marched to Stanks to meet Aethelwald - the place is still known as Penda's Well - who withdrew his men from the rain sodden field to leave Penda fighting alone. Penda was killed and the victorious Oswy gave his daughter Aelfleda into the care of Hartlepool monastery. She was to become a nun and later abbess of Whitby Abbey. The abbey had been founded by St. Hilda the abbess of Hartlepool following a vow of King Oswy after this victory of Winwaed.
Morwick means a "fen dwelling" and was part of the de Lacy property. The hall was built by Edward Gray,when he demolished the old hall of the Vevers family in the late 18th.century. William Vevers was a lover of horseracing and two of his horses "Morwick Belle" and "Winnmoor Jenny" are said to be buried in the grounds of Morwick Hall.

Edward Gray, the son of William and Catherine Gray of Kippax, was twice Mayor of Leeds in 1749 and 1768. The family were descended from the Lords Rotherfield and included the 13th. century Archbishop Walter Grey of York. In the 16th. century the family were settled at Kippax. Edward's brother John Gray was the rector of Swillington,who married Mary Squire and they had six children including John who married Eleanor Eamonson of Roundhay. John was born at Ledsham in 1757 but the Morwick line continued with his younger brother Robert's son John Squire Gray (1794-1884). His grand-daughter was Betsy Hardy Gray who was born in 1879. The last members of this family at the hall were Herbert Miers Gray who died March 22nd. 1951 aged 82 and his wife Betsey Hardy Gray who died aged 85 on September 8th. 1964 and were buried at Barwick in Elmet church.
The family sold the property to seed merchants Kenneth Wilson who moved into Morwick Hall in 1965. The company moved out of the Hall in April 1993 and the 40 acre estate was placed on the market.
Leeds Agricultural Show took place during the War years in land belonging to the Grey family at Morwick Hall. This was in aid of the Red Cross and held during August/September.

Morwick Flats is the land north of Morwick Hall on the Whinmoor and was suggested by Sir Alan Cobham in 1930 as a suitable site for the Leeds Airport. In his report to the council Cobham stated that Whinmoor was "an ideal position from the flying point of view ... an absence of physical obstructions ... visibility on the plateau may be expected to be above average ... a valuable property as an aerodrome site ... Whinmoor is in my opinion the only area within a radius of 5 miles from Leeds which is suitable for development as a municipal airport." Cobham further said that "Whinmoor is so much better in every way than Yeadon and it would be a great mistake for Leeds to forego acquiring Whinmoor, a truly perfect site although Yeadon is the only site for Bradford airport."
During the First World War it was a night flying base for 33 Squadron between March and October 1916. The squadron was based at Headley Bar and also had bases at Middleton, the York Knavesmire and Copmanthorpe.
A giant RAF Handley Page Hyderabad aircraft made an emergency landing on the airfield on October 2nd. 1926 and the crew stayed on the field for 10 days until repairs were brought up from the home base at Newton in Norfolk. The crew ate and washed at the Old Red Lion Inn at Whinmoor and when repairs were completed the plane circled over the inn and dropped a lead weighted message to "Landlord Jimmy Crampton and Mrs. Crampton... from Fitter J. Barker and Pilot Flt/Sgt. J. Wood."
A British Hospitals Air Pageant took place on Thorner Aerodrome on May 28/29th. 1933 and T. Campbell Black brought his British Empire Air Display to Thorner field on June 21st. 1936.Admission was 1/- and flights were just 3/6d, with the land being

leased from the local farmer.The flying ace Amy Johnson also appeared on Morwick airfield but by the end of 1939 the rough field had been ploughed for crops. During the War there was a searchlight and anti-aircraft gun positioned on Morwick Flats, with the generator hidden in woodland. The land was part of the extensive Darcy Bruce Wilson estate of Seacroft Hall and was sold in 1976 by the Trust.
Sir Alan Cobham's Flying Circus came to Middleton Park on June 20th. 1932 as part of National Aviation Day displays by his team in 180 towns. They were also at both Yeadon Aerodrome and Sherburn in Elmet on the two previous days.
Cobham's second tour of towns with his Flying Circus brought him again to Middleton Park on June 11th. 1933. The display was marred by an accident with an aircraft, piloted by Flt. Lt. H. C. Johnson. When the Handley-Page aircraft was landing it hit an air pocket, descended suddenly and killed two boys watching the display from a hill overlooking the display area. They were Fred Smith (aged 12) and Leslie Taylor (aged 8) and three others had narrow escapes. The evening display was cancelled and an inquest a few days later in Leeds exonerated the pilot. Sir Alan described the accident as being the "first in 800 displays". Fred Smith is buried at Beckett Street cemetery and the inscription mentions the sad happenings of the boy's outing to Middleton Park.
The displays included inverted flying on a Tiger Moth, formation flying, wing walking and a display of aircraft including the Avro Lynx and the Autogyro - forerunner of the helicopter.
Cobham also gave flights to many children from Sherburn Aerodrome on July 6th. 1929 and gave a Flying Circus Display on Wood Lane, Wakefield Road, Rothwell on September 14/15th. 1935 displaying the Mignet's "Flying Flea".
There was another local air display on a field north of the Church Lane/Barwick Road junction in Swarcliffe.
Alan Cobham was born in 1894 and married in 1922. He joined de Havilland in 1921 and organised the National Aviation Day Ltd. which toured Britain in 1932-33. He arranged National Aviation Displays in 1934-36 and in the 1250 displays in 300 towns carried 900,000 people. Cobham was knighted in 1926 and died on October 21st. 1973.

The large house north of Skelton's Lane - once Occupation Lane - on the Whinmoor is Bramley Grange. Known as Whinfield House it was once the home of Henry Skelton and the Nussey family. Sisters Ethel and Hilda Nussey were the daughters of Mr & Mrs Thomas Nussey and sisters of Sir Willans Nussey, who was MP for Pontefract from 1893 to 1910. Ethel Beatrice Nussey was a generous benefactor of Thorner and was killed by a bus in London in 1933. The lychgate at Thorner Church was erected to her memory in 1935. The house was built about 1810 by Christopher Bramley, who held the land in 1807. The house became an educational college in

1968, following a period of occupation by the Padgett family.
York Road passes the end of the road to Scholes and the old railway station is the "Buffers" inn which opened in August 1979. The station was opened in May 1876 as the route from the junction at Cross Gates to Wetherby via stations at Penda's Way, Scholes, Bardsey and Collingham Bridge. The track was doubled in 1902 but the line closed in 1964, with Scholes station remaining open for goods traffic for a few months after the January 6th. line closure.
The station is near Arthursdale, a development of the Scholes brickworks opened in 1877 by Isaac Chippindale - the tall chimneys were demolished in 1981 - and named after Arthur Chippindale who built houses there between 1901 and 1914. Arthur was born on October 23rd. 1866 and died on January 8th. 1954: his wife Susan Lister Chippindale died on March 6th.1956. Barwick in Elmet churchyard has a large cross north east of the church to this Scholes family: Arthur's brother was William Chippindale, son of Isaac and Clara who died on June 22nd. 1921 from injuries received in France on service with the Royal Flying Corps. Isaac Murray Chippindale was another brother and he died in 1983 aged 100. Arthur and Susan Chippindale's son was Arthur Kenneth Chippindale who died in Peachland Canada on August 8th. 1993 aged 84, he leaves a widow Freda and son Nigel Kenneth who was born in 1939. The Barwick grave also remembers Arthur and Susan's sisters Miranda who died in 1926 and Kate who died in 1931.

Vevers was a family who lived in the Scholes area from the 16th. century and eventually held property in Morwick, Scholes and Potterton. They lived at Scholes Hall, Scholes Park and Morwick Hall, which they sold to the Gray family. It was William Vevers who was a lover of horse racing and buried two of his horses at Morwick Hall; William died in 1744. Scholes Hall was demolished in 1973 - the sheltered housing complex opened on the site in July 1976 - and was a Vevers home. In the 18th. century the hall was leased to Richard Brooke of Killingbeck Hall and was later bought by John Crosland and then to Edward Gray of Morwick Hall. Members of the Crosland, Vevers and Gray families are buried at Barwick in Elmet Church.
St.Philip's Church on Main Street was consecrated on November 27th. 1966 replacing the earlier small 1875 church, standing nearby and used for many functions.

Whinmoor Grange Farm to the north on the main road has been recently developed from the farm run by the Goodall family from 1925 until 1976 and well known for their Shire Horses. The farm was bought from a group of trustees by the Leeds City Council on May lst. 1939 for £5700 with the row of the four cottages on the main road and 130 acres of farmland covering a wide area to Thorner Lane. The first

mention of this farm was in 1867 when the owner was William T. Smith, who died in 1882.
Plantland Garden Centre was opened in the early 1970's as a development from a poultry farm. In July 1992 the garden centre was bought by Carr Gate Nurseries of Wakefield, who opened Plantland at Whinmoor in the following August.
White Tower or Whinmoor Garage was sited to the west of Plantland and the concrete paving is still to be seen. The garage and cafe were run by Mr. and Mrs. William Dobson from 1925. William bought a Blackburn "Dart" aeroplane used by the Naval Flying School at Brough in 1928. The plane was withdrawn in 1933 and sold in December to William Dobson. This was not the only plane he used for advertising purposes as he also bought a Bristol Scout and a Wren Monoplane, which is now at Biggleswade. He loaned this plane to the Shaftesbury Cinema on York Road to advertise the film "Hell's Angels"-the film was made by Howard Hughes in 1930 and starred Ben Lyon.
The Adams family ran the garage as Adams Motor Services, together with his other garage at Stoney Rock. He placed a white globe on the White Tower Garage and lit it with flourescent lighting.
Rose Dene Garage to the east of Plantland was run by the Atkinson family, who sold out to Jesse Lightfoot, who started a car auction in South Accomodation Road. Lightfoot sold to Myers and Franks: Charlie Franks opened an all night transport cafe at Whinmoor in the early 1950's. It was Franks who developed the car auction business and it became the present Central Motor Auctions of Pontefract Road Rothwell. Franks also developed a caravan business at Acaster Malbis; caravans are still a feature of this Ouse-side village.
On the north side of the road east of the railway bridge and Leeds Heliport based at Saw Wood House are the remains of a garage that was the first to sell petrol on this road. It was opened in 1923-24 by the Staples family, on a 10 acre farm and is now a derelict site.
The approach to the 600 acre plantation of Saw Wood is also the half way seven mile point on the Halton Dial-Tadcaster turnpike. Flying Horse Farm was once known as "Half Way House" and there are still the old coachman's house and stables at the present farm. This one-time inn was the mid/late 17th. century Osmondthick Hall, where a hoard of five bronze axes were discovered in 1709 and later auctioned. In a letter from Rev. George Plaxton - Vicar of Barwick in Elmet from 1703-1720 to his friend historian Ralph Thoresby he says that "Mr.Ellis's servants were ploughing in Osmondthick last week and found 5 brass implements of different shapes". There are only field marks that represent the lost village of Osmondthick or Osmerethyk to the south of the present farm. This Grade II listed building had additions in the mid-18th. century and again this century. The farm was run by Tom Bickerdyke in the 1930's and became a supplier of milk to the Leeds dairies.

The road crosses Potterton Bridge, with the beck having its source in Saw Wood being complemented with water from both Jacob's Well and Copple Syke Spring.
On the top of the rise above Potterton Beck stands Kiddal Hall, mentioned in the Domesday Book as Chidale - meaning cow valley. In the late 14th. century Sir John Elys held Kiddal, whose family built the hall and were associated with Kiddal for 400 years. The hall was enlarged in the early 16th. century by Sir John Elys or Ellis - he died in 1515 - who also built a decorated bay window on the west side. There were stained glass coats of arms in the window representing Thomas Ellis and Anne Calverley. It was John Ellis who supported the King in the Civil War and it is said that he was killed by Parliamentary forces on the doorstep or in a small room at Kiddal Hall. It has often been stated that occupiers can hear the sound of feet haunting the old hall.
The Hall was home to the Ellis family until 1729 and the property was mortgaged. It became the home of the Eamonson family. Benjamin Eamonson died at Kiddal in 1753 and his wife Elizabeth died in 1765 - their son John also lived at the hall and all three were buried at Whitkirk Church.
On the south wall of the Ellis chapel in Barwick in Elmet Church is a stone tablet to William Ellis of Kiddal Hall who died in 1771 - he had married Mary Bourne and was the last of the Ellis family to have lived at the Hall. He was a surgeon in London who inherited the hall from his brother in the 1740's and proceeded to pay off the mortgage.
In 1804 Kiddal Hall was bought by Edward Wilkinson, who had inherited Potterton Hall with his brother John in 1785 on the death of Robert Denison.
In the 1920's the hall was the residence of C. F. Ryder who in 1928/29 sold the Ellis mullioned oriel window dated 1501 and interior Oak panelling to an American buyer. The farmhouse was probably the early 17th. century kitchen to the old hall: the 16th. century barn has a timber frame and was encased in stone in the early 18th. century. In 1959 the hall was marketed together with 228 acres - it had been for sale in 1953 with 2 cottages and 327 acres but was withdrawn at £14,500.
In recent years there has been much conversion and conservation at Kiddal Hall, together with a new access drive. There are now four dwellings although retaining the old smithy, barn and gatehouse with its archway entry. The owners have had a Victorian post box installed,which although there are no collections helps to retain an atmosphere of history.

Kiddal Lane End was the site of two turnpike bars, in consequence of the alteration in the route of the road. The road originally past Bar House Farm on Kiddal Lane and curved around to link with the road to Bramham Cross Roads. In 1819 a new bar house was built for the straightened road - it was sited in the east garden of Kiddal Lane End Farm. A new turnpike Act was passed in June 1819 creating a new

Trust - the original Trust set up in 1750 was to cure the sad state of the highway between Tadcaster and Halton Dial because:"...from the heavy traffic it has become very deep and ruinous and in some seasons almost impassable and dangerous." The toll bar house at Kiddal Lane End was demolished in the summer of 1961 as it was said to provide a blind spot for motorists. The last inhabitants of the toll house were Mr. & Mrs. Charles Garrett and their son, who lived there for 18 years. Water was obtained from a pump and lighting was with oil lamps. In 1958 both power and water were introduced into the house - the well was on the south side of the labourer's cottage addition of the farmhouse. The old barn has been dated to 1691 and together with the stable block were converted in 1991 to a pine furniture business.

The turnpike "Fox" coaching inn on the south of the road and in the triangle created by the two road routes was established in the mid 18th. century together with stabling and accomodation. The name changed to the "Fox and Grapes" and it is now a Tetley inn and restaurant.

Potterton Hall lies south of the main road and the present mansion takes its origins from the Denison family in the late 18th. century. A house at Potterton had been mentioned in the 16th. century - in 1571 it was sold to Richard Gascoigne. In May 1675 the "manor house of Potterton with its lands" was sold to William Hodgson and five years later it was taken by William Ellis of Kiddal Hall. In 1743 Robert Fretwell bought both the hall and the Potterton Tannery that had been run by the Vevers family. Fretwell had financial problems and in 1762 sailed for India. In 1765 Potterton Hall was bought by Robert Denison of Leeds and six years later Denison had acquired the whole estate. He died unmarried in 1785 and built a new Potterton Hall on the 1740's original dwelling - the present west front. Robert had succeeded to the family estates in Leeds and Ossington when his father William Denison died in 1782 - he had been mayor of Leeds in 1758 and lived at Denison Hall in Hanover Square Leeds, built in 1786. When Robert died the estates passed to his nephews John and Edward Wilkinson. John received the Ossington property and assumed the Denison name, while Edward took Potterton Hall and built the south extension. Edward died in July 1836 and was succeeded by his son John Edward who married Catherine Bathurst. Their son Bathurst Edward married Jane Breary, who had 9 children. When Bathurst died in 1901 his eldest son inherited although never lived there as he was the Rector of Illington Norfolk. Potterton Hall became tenanted - the first being Sir Theophilus Peel. The hall was sold in 1970 and became three separate dwellings: the Grade II listed Potterton Hall West with seven bedrooms and vaulted cellar was placed on sale in March 1994 for £350,000.

The public footpath from Aberford and through Becca Park, avoiding the hall emerges on to York Road west of Whitewell Farm. In the mid-18th. century this track continued across the main road as the "Aberford-Thorner" road: the original line to the north of the main road was moved by the Bramham estate to Mangrill Lane near Park House Farm - the path joins the Thorner/ Bramham road passing Jenny Sober Plantation. There are two farms on the north of the main road towards Bramham Cross Roads and the A1. They are White Well and Windsor Farms and both date to the mid-19th. century, although some thought offers an earlier 18th. century date. Windsor farmhouse was built of local sandy Magnesian Limestone, obtained from a nearby quarry to the north west. In this quarry area there have been some pieces of Roman pottery discovered together with the site of an Iron Age village. At Windsor Farm there is a barn and stabling built with hand made bricks, together with a limestone horse mounting block.

On the south side of York Road before Bramham Crossroads is the North Lodge to Becca Hall. This Lodge was built after the 1823 enclosure award, which also moved the gatehouse towards the main road. The two gatepiers were to be seen on the driveway to Becca Hall until their removal in 1978 - the earlier gate was known as Cowthwaite Gate. This drive was the site of a venerable Beech tree felled in 1960 and the habitat of many rare plants, which have disappeared following landscaping.

Becca mansion is now owned by the National Grid and has a long history. To the east of the drive down to the hall - which is private - was the site of the vanished village of Cuford or Cuforth. One of the first owners of the land at Cufford were the Grammary family in the 13th. century,who sold their lands in 1348 to Sir Philip le Despenser. A few years later Becca became the property of Sir Roger Fulthorpe and in 1513 it was acquired by Thomas Lord Darcy, executed in 1537 for taking part in the Pilgrimage of Grace. In 1544 the Earl and Countess of Lennox held Becca and in 1624 Becca became church property, being confiscated in the Commonwealth period and sold to Colonel White.
In 1660 the church took over Becca again and Colonel White became a tenant of the church. Tenants included Lord Irwin in 1746, Sir Edward Gascoigne in 1756 and Sir Thomas Gascoigne in 1772. Becca became the property of the Markham family, when at the end of the 18th. century the hall was built by William Markham (1760-1815). William was the son of William Markham, Archbishop of York and was the private secretary to Warren Hastings, Governor of India. In about 1780 William used the money earned in India to build his new Becca Hall around the core of the earlier 17th. century house. When Warren Hastings died on August 22nd. 1818 he was buried in Westminster Abbey, where there is a memorial in the north transept. William Markham's son, another William, was born at Becca Hall and was to take the Grand Tour and settled to manage the Becca estate following his father's death in 1815. These two members of the Markham family are buried in Aberford churchyard: the graves have large inscribed stone slabs - there are other memorials

within the church to this family,who came from East or Great Markham in Nottinghamshire.
William Markham was Archbishop of York from 1777 until 1808 and during his period as Archbishop consecrated St. Paul's Church in Park Square Leeds on September 10th. 1793. The church on the south side of the Square had been designed by Leeds Architect William Johnson and was demolished in 1905, when the area was cleared. Archbishop Markham also consecrated St. James Church Leeds. This church was built in 1794 as the Zion Chapel of Lady Huntingdon's Connexion and was consecrated for the established church in September 1801. The church on the corner of York Street and Cross York Street, was closed in February 1949 and demolished in 1952.
On October 25th. 1894 Becca Hall was sold by Ronald Anthony Markham (1870-1914) and Arthur Thomas Schreiber lived at the hall until his death in 1902 - he gave the brass lectern to Aberford Church. His widow died at Becca in 1907 and it was sold to Mr. Lund a Bradford wool magnate, who held the estate until 1922. It was then bought by the Fawcett family and they lived at Becca until 1946 - the family live today at Cufforth House, built in 1910. In 1958 Beeca Hall and estate was bought by the CEGB from Mr. Thompson.
In March 1990 Becca became the Leeds Grid Control Centre of the National Grid Company and in October 1993 Becca Hall became the nerve centre for the electricity supply centre for the north of England. Lord Wakeham officially opened Becca, the new national centre at Wokingham and three regional centres at Birmingham, St.Albans and Bristol. The £79 million programme involves Becca taking in 35% of total generating capacity from 23 power stations and 90 sub stations. The electricity is then transmitted through the 2000 Km of power lines to the regional distributors.

The land north of the York Road and west of the A1 is Bramham Park, created by Robert Benson lst. Lord Bingley from 1700 until 1710. Robert Benson's daughter Harriet Benson inherited Bramham in 1731 and she married George Fox, who inherited the Lane estates of Viscount Lanesborough and in 1751 changed his name to George Fox-Lane. He became Lord Bingley in 1762 and died in 1771. His nephew James Fox inherited Bramham and lived there from 1792 as a married man, changing his name to Lane-Fox. He married Marcia Pitt, daughter of George, Lord Rivers in July 1789 by whom he had George Lane Fox; William Augustus Lane Fox who married a niece of the Earl of Harewood, Sackville Walter Lane Fox who married the daughter of the Duke of Leeds and Thomas Henry Lane Fox who took holy orders. James and Marcia's daughter was Marcia Bridget who married the Hon. Edward Stourton and who assumed the name and arms of Vavasour. Marcia died in June 1826 and was buried at St.Leonard's Chapel Hazlewood.

"Gambler " George Lane-Fox inherited when his father died aged 65 on April 7th. 1821. The mansion caught fire in 1828 and it was finally restored in 1907. Bramham passed to "Squire" George Lane-Fox who died in 1896: his son George signed over his right to Bramham to his brother James Lane-Fox. George had married Fanny Slade as his first wife and she was buried at Hazlewood Chapel when she died in Paris on April 28th. 1875 aged 30. It was his son George, created Lord Bingley in 1933, restored the great house: he married Agnes Wood daughter of Viscount Halifax. Their daughter Marcia inherited Bramham in 1947 and married Cpt. Ward Jackson in 1929 - he took the name Lane-Fox - and it is their son George who is the present owner of Bramham Park.
The gardens at Bramham are a delight, complete with ponds, fountains, canals and superb views. They were created in the early 18th. century and based on the gardens at Versailles and elsewhere in France. The 70 acre formal garden and woodlands remain today basically as they were created.
The two gatepiers visible to the north of the York Road stand on an old established route called Bramham Park Road, which once was connected to the A1 by Occupation Lane. The gatepiers were moved from the A1 in 1872 to a nearer position on the A64.

The A1 flyover at the Bramham Cross Roads was completed in July 1964. The many tons of limestone and slag that helped to build this flyover came from as far as Castleford and as near as Hazlewood Castle grounds and Headley.

THE ROAD FROM LEEDS TO YORK

PART 4: FROM BRAMHAM CROSS ROADS TO TADCASTER

Cross Roads Farm was also once a busy turnpike public house: it was called "Filbert Grove" and then became the popular "White Hart Inn" with stable accomodation and room for coaches. The coach houses have been converted into three houses and there are now two houses in the old stable block. The access to the cobbled courtyard was through an archway or through high gates: the hinges remain from the hanging. The inn became known as "Mrs.Barkers" as Mary Barker was the licensee in the 19th. century. The two storey building inn building is now disused and has a large arched cellar together with the beer drop from outside. The beer pumps were only removed in the 1970's.
The farm and inn were part of the Vavasour's Hazlewood estate and once paid an annual rent to a Bishop's Fund. When Sir Walter Vavasour died in 1802 he had agreed to sell the castle to the Church to be used as a seminary. The new baronet Sir Thomas Vavasour was interned in France but managed to come to England to persuade the bishops to waive their claim as the documents had not been signed. The seminary was built at Ushaw in Co. Durham but it was agreed that £60 a year was to be paid to the Bishop's Fund from the income of Cross Roads Farm as recompense. These payments only ceased in the early part of the 20th. century.

White Hart Inn, Bramham Cross Roads

Prior to the flyover there was a small filling station and workshop on the south side of the main road. It was well established before being bought by Frank Cooper in 1951 and was closed when the crossroads were abandoned in favour of the raised flyover in 1964. The premises became derelict and were eventually demolished. Frank Cooper started his garage business on Aberford Road Oulton in 1946 which was built on the site of one of Armitage quarries: Cooper's ran garages at Rothwell, Methley and at Bramham Cross Roads and entered the car sales market in 1947/48.
The main road follows a section of the Roman Road from Aberford and Nut Hill. It joins the present main road near the entrance to Hazlewood Castle and follows the line of Garnet Lane from Headley Bar: a branch of the Roman Road leaves the Tadcaster route, passes Manor Farm on the route north. Rudgate crosses the River Wharfe at St. Helen's ford, where there is a site of a Roman fort.
On the night of March 5th. 1945 No. 6 Group took off from their Royal Canadian Air Force base at Tholthorpe between Boroughbridge and Easingwold. The airfield had opened in August 1940 as a satellite for Linton-on-Ouse and it reopened in June 1943 as a base for the RCAF. The raid on Chemnitz in Saxony was part of Operation Thunderclap with 760 planes, of which 256 were Halifaxes. No. 1630 Halifax of the "Snowy Owl" squadron was affected by the bad weather and severe icing after take off. The plane had been in the air for 50 minutes when it lost height and nosed dived into Hayton Wood, Hazlewood - west of Hayton House. The plane caught fire and there was only one survivor, the rest of the crew were buried in Harrogate. The Tholthorpe airfield closed after the Canadians departed. A memorial to the RCAF squadrons was unveiled in June 1986.
The large estate of Hazlewood dominates the south side of the main road past the A1, opposite the Little Chef, opened in the late 1970's. The gateway leads by a long drive to the ancient seat of the Vavasour family at Hazlewood Castle.
In 1086 Malger de Vavasour held Hazlewood from his overlord William de Percy - a vavasour held lands from the lord and not the King. It was Robert le Vavasour who granted the use of his limestone to repair or rebuild York Minster about 1225: stone was given in 1829 to the Minster following a fire. During the Baron's Wars Malger le Vavasour of Denton attacked John Vavasour's Hazlewood and the original Norman manor house and chapel were destroyed. It was Sir William Vavasour who rebuilt Hazlewood between 1283 and 1286, when the chapel was rededicated. The founder of the chapel of St. Leonard died in 1313 and his tomb is within his chapel under an arch on the south east side.
The main castle structure is Medieval, although the west part is presumed to be the pele tower of the Norman house - the building was crenellated in 1290 and it thus became a fortified manor house or castle. There are remains of a 13th. century spiral staircase from the rotunda to the Lord's solar on the top floor. This floor was removed when the Great Hall was created by John Carr in the 18th. century. The

18th. century alterations obscured many Medieval features and added the north stable block, designed by John Paine about 1750.
In this century there were more alterations by both Edward Simpson and Donald Hart, including the addition of the south terrace and steps and the demolition of the north wing revealing the Tudor tower. The main entry today is on the north side formed in the 1960's by Donald Hart and leads into the Flemish hall, where 17th. panelling is from a Carmelite church in Ghent, bought by Donald Hart in 1964 and placed into position in 1966. The stone fireplace is from Heath Old Hall Wakefield. The library in the Tudor tower is a 1960's reconstruction using materials from the Bridge Inn Walshford Bridge and a Welsh castle. There is a passage hidden behind false bookshelves and leading into the orangery - based on a feature at Grimston Park and created by the Boroughbridge craftsman Mr.Apps.
The main hall is perhaps the most impressive room in the castle, designed by John Carr and having over fifty armorial bearings of members of the Vavasour family, including their marriages to the Gascoigne, Scrope and Fairfax families. Carr's false walls covered the Medieval windows, one of which was uncovered by Edward Simpson in 1910, who also introduced the Adam style decor. The main hall is now the chapel, having been transferred from the Carmel Chapel in the Tudor Tower in 1994. The present conference room was created by John Carr from a Medieval room

Hazlewood Castle

and the Adam influenced decorations were introduced in 1910. In the original pele tower on the first floor is the Victoria Room. It was Donald Hart who placed the armorial fireplace with the panelling from Eaton Hall in Cheshire: the metallic wallpaper once decorated a room prepared for Queen Victoria at the Great Exhibition. Excavations of the castle cellars in 1978/81 revealed the old kitchens and servants hall: the area is now used as a tea room. The bookshop at Hazlewood Castle was probably the dungeon of the pele tower. The fortunes of the Vavasours fluctuated over the centuries until Sir Thomas Vavasour 7th. baronet settled the estate on Edward Stourton, from another strong Catholic family. He took the Vavasour name and in 1828 was created the Hon. Edward Vavasour, a baronet of a new line. He married Marcia Bridget Lane-Fox of Bramham, who became a Roman Catholic and who died aged 36 on June 10th. 1826 and is buried in the small cemetery adjacent to the Clitherow cross. In 1847 his religious pilgrimage to Rome ended with his death at Chanceaux near Lyons on March 16th. 1847 aged 60. His remains were brought to Hazlewood from France in 1876 by his son Philip Canon Vavasour. It was Philip who was the builder of the Roman Catholic Church of St. Wilfrid's at Ripon the church was designed by architect Joseph Hansom in 1860/62.The Very Rev. Philip Vavasour died in London on April 19th. 1887 aged 61 and was buried at Hazlewood.
After the early death of his wife following the birth of their eighth child. Sir Edward asked his mother to live at Hazlewood and help with the estate management. Lady Stourton was the daughter of Baron Langdale who married Charles Stourton who became the 16th. Baron Stourton and she ran the Hazlewood estates until her death in 1841 aged 89: she had been widowed in 1816. In the cemetery of Hazlewood chapel is the grave of Sarah Winship who was the "faithful attendant as lady's maid of the Rt. Hon. Mary Dowager Lady Stourton": she died aged 52 on January lst. 1828.
Edward's grandson Sir William Vavasour inherited the estate in 1885 although by the turn of the century financial problems were great. In 1908 he placed the whole estate on sale and the purchaser was the solicitor Edward Overend Simpson. Edward died aged 61 on April 18th. 1927, while his widow lived at the castle until her death on March 30th. 1951. The Simpson graves are in the west cemetery at Aberford Church, including their son Cpt. Philip Overend Simpson who died on active service on January 22nd. 1945.
During the Simpson occupation of Hazlewood it became a maternity hospital and the family sold the estate to Eric Fawcett, when it had been a hospital for 14 years. His son Richard Fawcett - he had married Sir William Vavasour's granddaughter - lived at the castle with his family although they disliked the conditions in the castle and later moved out to live nearby.
In 1960 the Fawcett family sold Hazlewood to Donald Hart, who commenced a

programme of restoration and alteration: this included the Flemish Hall and taking down the north east section to leave the chapel separate. Donald Hart had a milliner's shop in Briggate/King Edward Street Leeds.
The Carmelite Friars bought Hazlewood from Donald Hart in 1967 and when he died in 1972 the Carmelite Community became established at Hazlewood Castle from St. Joseph's Tadcaster. In June 1967 an inaugural Mass was said at Hazlewood Chapel by the Bishop of Leeds Mgr. Gordon Wheeler, on the designation of the Shrine of Our Lady and the Forty Martyrs.
The Chapel was once separate from the castle until the early 18th. century connecting corridor was made from the first floor to the Vavasour family pews in the gallery: this was demolished during the 1960's alterations by Donald Hart.
The small cemetery at Hazlewood Chapel contains members of the Vavasour family together with John Briggs the Bishop of Beverley who died in January 1861. The tall cross,with the headless angels at the base, probably represents the burial place of York Catholic Martyr St. Margaret Clitherow. On March 17th. 1586 this good lady was crushed to death for allegedly hiding Jesuit priests in her Shambles home. The bells nearby came from Holy Trinity Church York - the church was demolished in 1937.
The worn inscription on the box tomb by the south door of the chapel is to the Hon. Elizabeth Stourton, the sister of Sir Edward Vavasour who died in March 1836. The tomb bearing the coloured ceramic coat of arms is that of William Vavasour the son of Sir Edward: the arms include the families of Stourton and Clifford of Chudleigh. The statue over the porch is that of St. Margaret of Antioch and may be dated to the early 15th. century: it was Sir Henry Vavasour whose wife was Margaret Skipwith who died in 1415.
The chapel porch seat has an inscribed game of Nine Men's Morris or Merils. This was a game for two people with the object being to get three counters in a row at the intersection of the lines joining the corners and the mid points of the sides. The game used nine counters as compared to Fivepenny Morris. The main inside door with its iron grille is dated to the 15th. century. The altar painting is by Adam Kossowski, who also designed the stations of the cross in the formal gardens of Hazlewood Castle. Sir Walter Vavasour and perhaps architect John Carr of York modernised the interior about 1770. The monuments were rearranged, walls raised, roof pitch altered and the Palladian style east end introduced.
On the north side of the sanctuary is an aumbry and a glass fronted case containing two skulls. Tradition says that the skulls are those of Ralph Grimston and Father Peter Snow, who were martyred at York's Knavesmire in June 1598. The skulls were placed on the top of Micklegate Bar and eventually taken to Hazlewood Chapel.
A large glass case behind the altar contains the wax image of a child St. Clara - an early Christian martyr, given to Sir William Vavasour by Pope Pius IX in 1867 as

Hazelwood Chapel

gratitude for his support in the campaign against Garibaldi. Sir William had taken a group of Catholics from Hazlewood to Italy to defend the Papal States as members of the Zouaves: it seems likely that the Hazlewood group were not involved in any fighting.

On the south chapel wall nearest the altar is the effigy of Sir William Vavasour, who founded this chapel in 1286. He was the son of Sir John and Alice Vavasour and he married Nichola Wallis: he died in 1313. Sir William's brother was Sir Mauger, who on his marriage to the daughter of William de Denton inherited the Denton estate. His son Sir John Vavasour married the daughter of Sir William Stopham of Weston near Otley. The Vavasours came to have estates at Copmanthorpe and Spaldington.

The stone coat of arms over the sacristy door was part of a monument to Sir Walter Vavasour 2nd. baronet and his wife Ursula Bellasis, daughter of Viscount Fauconberg.

The adjacent monument has been made from two separate monuments: Sir Thomas Vavasour, who died in 1632 and his wife Ursula and their nine children and includes two chrisom children in swaddling clothes. Their eldest son was Sir Walter, raised to the baronetcy by King Charles in 1628 and one of his brothers Thomas was killed at Marston Moor in 1644. The kneeling figures are perhaps William Vavasour and his wife Anne Manners: William died in 1637 and his wife died in 1611.

The adjacent large monument to the west is that of Sir Walter Vavasour and his wife Dame Jane with their three sons who died as children. Sir Walter died in 1712 and when Dame Jane died in 1731 she left an endowment to the chapel in trust for the Hazlewood mission.

The old effigy by the south door is that of Sir Walter Vavasour the son of the chapel founder, whose monument was once on the north side of the chapel.
The estate at Hazlewood has shrunk to about 70 acres and includes fine gardens, woodlands and a Rosary Way. The heated walled garden and maze have been lost but the rock garden has recently been renovated. The delights of the nature trail, established in May 1981, includes a walk through a "quarry" which was created during the extraction of limestone in 1962/64 for the Bramham Cross Roads flyover. There has been much work in managing the woodlands and tree planting is proceeding. There is a wide variety of wild flowers, birds and mammals to be seen through the seasons at Hazlewood Castle.
The grounds of Hazlewood Castle are now closed during times of retreats and the nature trail is open throughout the year.
Castle Farm to the north of the castle was bought from the Vavasour estate in 1908 and was again placed on sale in June 1989 for the second time in 700 years. The present farmhouse is Georgian but was formerly the presbytery to the castle. Paradise Lane leads from the main road to join with Chantry Lane from Stutton. The north east gateway leads into the Hazlewood Castle courtyard: the octagonal Gothic tower was built in the 18th. century as a folly from old stone.
An annual feature of life at Hazlewood is the Summer Fair which raises essential money to maintain and run the house and estate: in June 1994 the fair was opened by John Gilleghan.

Headley Bar was the last toll bar before Tadcaster and was demolished with the building of the by-pass. The plans for this route were approved in 1975 and construction lasted two years at a cost of 8½ million. The new by pass opened on May 24th. 1978: officially on August 22nd. The low brick built building on the south of Headley Bar was a short lived local jam factory between the two World Wars.
Headley Hall was the home of Lord Headley, who once owned more land in the parish of Bramham than the Lane-Fox family. The farmhouse, now used in part as offices of the National Institute of Agricultural Botany, dates from the mid-16th. century. It was built by Bishop Owen Oglethorpe, who was born about 1500 and became the Bishop of Carlisle in 1557.
In later years Headley Hall became the home of Sir George Winn, who in 1797 was created Lord Headley,Baron Allanson and Winn. He had succeeded to his cousin Mark Winn's estates in 1763 and in 1775 he obtained those of his cousin Charles Allanson of Bramham Biggin - he was MP for Ripon. In 1877 the 4th. Lord Headley succeeded his father, although the family were hardly ever at Headley Hall.
In 1825 the hall was divided into two houses, of which the eastern side is now a private residence. In the early 1900's the Headley estate was bought by the Bramham

estate. Leeds University Farms were the tenants of Headley Hall from 1951 until the mid 1980's when they bought the property and land. There are now three farms as part of the Headley Hall complex: Wise Warren, Spen and the Hall itself. NIAB,which has a seed testing station on Huntingdon Road Cambridge, carries out its trials for grasses, cereals, potatoes and sugar beet at Headley Hall.

In the grounds of Headley Hall is an aircraft hangar, which is one of two known First World War hangars of similar design and is a listed building. The hangar was part of the Headley Bar or Bramham Moor airfield, being the base for B Flight 33 Squadron of the Royal Flying Corps in April 1916. The BE2C planes were a part of the defence of Leeds and Sheffield. In December 1916 the No .46 Reserve Squadron was based at Tadcaster (Bramham Moor) until July 1917. The site was expanded in June/July 1918 and the hangars were erected. The field became the No. 38 Training Depot Station from July 1918 with 36 type SE5A and 36 Avro 504. The 94 Squadron arrived from Senlis France in November 1918 and were disbanded on June 30th. 1919. The Ripon based 76 Squadron Home Defence arrived at Headley in March 1919 to fly Bristol fighters: they were also disbanded in June 1919. The airfield was closed in 1919 and was handed over for sale.

In the early 12th. century Headley and Oglethorpe were given to the church of the Holy Trinity at York and a small monastery was founded at Headley. It was a small cell of the York church and in 1254 the monks held "free warren" in the Headley area.

North of Headley Hall is High Moor Quarry of the Tadcaster Building Limestone. Part of the Sam Smith's estates, the 20 year old quarry extracts and processes stone for building..

Stutton is hidden between the Tadcaster bypass and the Doncaster-Tadcaster turnpike. The village stands on Cock Beck and the Old London Road: this road fell into disuse after the completion of the turnpike with its toll bar at nearby Raw Lane End - where the railway crossed in later years at Towton Bridge.

There are a few magnesian limestone quarries in the area including Darrington Quarries' Jackdaw Crag, providing crushed stone for house foundations, car parks and for roads. This was once known as Thevesdale Quarry, which provided the stone for the south transept of York Minster in the early 13th. century and later building. A right of free passage was granted to the Minster Chapter by Robert le Vavasour to his Stutton quarry.

Wingate Hill was known as Windeyates in 1279 and means "windswept gap in the hills: a narrow ravine through which flows Cock Beck prior to the confluence with the River Wharfe.

Sugar Hill Farm is the only farm remaining today at Wingate Hill and the Sugar Hill Golf Club received planning assent in 1994. The new club will feature a full 18 hole golf course in this area. Wingate Hill Farm once stood adjacent to Sugar Hill but the

land was sold to Sam Smith Brewery estates: the Cundall family lived for many years at this farm and are buried at Tadcaster Cemetery.
The large house on the junction of the old London Road and Chantry Lane at Wingate Hill was a Roman Catholic day school founded in 1831 and supported by Sir Edward Vavasour. The school transferred to St. Joseph's Road Tadcaster: St. Joseph's Church was opened in 1861.
The large cross on an older base stands on Chantry Lane to Hazlewood: it has been assumed that the cross was used by pilgrims to pray on their way to St. Leonard's Chapel at Hazlewood or to York.
Stutton was known as Stouetun in 1086 and could be derived from the Old English for a hill (OE Stut=stumpy hillock): it could also be derived from the Old Norse personal name Stufr. There were three manors in Stutton held by the Percy - the Vavasours held the lands from the Percies - and de Arch families. There was a dispute with the Percy holding of Stutton and it was once asserted that William Haget had "all Stauton, three manors, three carucates of land and one mill."
St. Aidan's Church on Church Crescent was the inspiration of an archbishop who was journeying from Grimston to Stutton and learned of the lack of a church in the village. He managed to persuade some local folk to buy and donate a small piece of land and the church was dedicated on February 18th. 1900. The oak pulpit was

Stutton Windmill

carved in 1877 and came from Tadcaster Church soon after the rebuilding of that church in 1875. The altar cross was given in memory of George Ellerbeck in 1903. Stutton corn mill dated from the llth. century and was served by Cock Beck, whose waters turned the wheel. The mill was described as being for "corn and rape" in 1850 with William Clough as the miller. In later years it was run by the Copping family: Wright Copping died aged 59 in October 1880 and Mary Copping died aged 81 on July 29th. 1894. The rebuilt mill had stopped turning by the end of the century and was finally demolished by the Second World War. The mill was by the bridge and is marked today by a roadside stone wall and a marsh with an attractive flora. The mill race from Cock Beck has been filled in and landscaped: the frequent flooding of the Cock Beck bridge area is indicated by the presence of a water depth pole. There are memories of the villagers transporting washing water from the beck in barrels: drinking water came from the wells. The population in 1867 served by this mill was only 157, when Thomas Moverley was the village blacksmith and William Mortimer was the licensee at the "Greyhound" inn.

The inn, which once had a shop attached, is now known as the "Hare and Hounds" and displays a small plaque over the front door "MEE 1730". In the mid 18th. century the inn was run by the Stothard family. Thomas Stothard was the innkeeper and in 1754 moved to London where he became the innkeeper of The Black Horse in Long Acre: he died in 1760. His son Thomas was born in 1755 and was educated at Stutton village school remaining until his apprenticeship. He became a distinguished artist and was elected a member of the Royal Academy in 1794 - he died in 1834. Charles Alfred Stothard was his son and published the epic "Monumental Effigies of Great Britain".

There are a few old buildings in Stutton including the Manor House Farm on Manor Road and dated "JH 1697": indicating the home of the Heptonstall family.

Chapel Cottage on Green Lane was the late 18th. century Methodist Chapel. The chapel was closed in the 1920's and was converted to a private home with an extension. One of the last ministers was Rev. Wilkinson, who gave his name to the adjacent row of houses.

Stutton Grove on Garnet Lane - now reverted to the original name of Stutton Lodge - was the home of Captain Markham and later became William Stacey's boy's school from about 1852. The school had a large lawn and parkland with a cricket ground and gymnasium. By the end of the century the school had closed and it was converted to a private house. The house retains the cloakroom pegs and once had a small chapel.

The railway came to Stutton in August 1847 when the line from Church Fenton to Tadcaster was opened. The station closed in 1905 through lack of business although there were several special excursion trains which stopped at Stutton until closure in January 1964 with the Beeching Axe. Stutton railway station was converted into a

private dwelling and is known as "Station House", the last stationmaster being Mr. Hunter. The railway house for the goods yard is now Stutton Gates and was once the home of Mr. Parnaby.
Stutton village school closed in the 1920's and is now a restored private house. The last schoolmistress was Mrs. Grimston, who took a newsagents shop in Tadcaster on retiring.
The large area by Cock Beck is "The Willows", where willow was gathered and after treatment sold to basket weavers. Many local folk were engaged in this minor industry and still remember gathering the willows and stripping the bark: many willows still grow by the beck. The Brown family were one of the last to run this trade at Stutton: Joseph Brown died aged 71 on May 31st. 1892 and James Brown died aged 58 in September 1923.
The Wilson family provided a laundry service from their premises facing up Wilkinson Terrace. In the mid-1960's the field where the old pinfold was sited on the original oval village green was developed and modern houses have created a new atmosphere in this old village. One of the most recent is Manor House being a conversion and additions from an old barn. Stutton may have lost the smithy, malt kiln and laundry but is home to many commuters and new families.

Tadcaster Grammar School occupies Toulston Lodge, which the Riley-Smith family bought in 1890. It became the school annexe in 1952 and moved out of their older buildings in Tadcaster in the late 1950's: the school was on the corner of the Leeds and London roads from 1906. Tadcaster Grammar School was founded by Bishop Oglethorpe in 1556 - four years after the foundation of Leeds Grammar School. Bishop Oglethorpe was the only Catholic Bishop to officiate at the coronation of Queen Elizabeth lst. Owen Oglethorpe left some land in order to found a school for 12 poor boys and a hospital for 12 men, although only four almshouses were ever completed. The site of this first school was west of the church where the present Adult Education Centre and car park are situated. In 1884 a playground was made for the boys by Castle Hill.
Toulston was held by the Fairfax family in the 17th. century: in 1640 it was sold to Sir Robert Barwick and his widow Ursula died in 1682. Toulston was inherited by their daughter Frances Barwick who married the 4th. Lord Fairfax. The 10th. Lord Fairfax of Toulston died in 1869. Their old hall was demolished in the 19th. century.

Toulston Lodge was a Fairfax dower house and in the 18th. century became the home of Sir Frederick Milbank. It became a Ladies School and then a Boy's School when it was owned by the Brown family from Leeds. In 1890 the trustees of the Yorke-Scarlett family sold the Lodge to Herbert Riley-Smith, a principal of John Smith's Brewery.

Harry Riley-Smith was born in 1863 and educated at Leeds Grammar School joining his uncle William Smith (died 1882) in John Smith's Brewery. In 1886 he married Annie Heaton (died 1899) and he died on May 19th. 1911.
The west corner of Rudgate Lane on the main Tadcaster Road is the Manor House, although it was originally the "Beehive Inn". Inholmes Hall is north of the main road near the junction with Station Road and Garnet Lane. The Hall is now the home of the Riley-Smith family, who opened a Peace Centre from the old outbuildings of the hall in the 1980's. There is a seat in the stable courtyard inscribed to Tony Riley-Smith presented on his retirement as Director of John Smith's brewery in 1979. There are meeting and quiet rooms with facilities in beautiful surroundings.
The Tadcaster toll bar was sited on the south side of Station Road near the Beeches Day Centre opened in 1992, and not built until the mid-19th. century after objections to the previous position.
Edgerton Lodge once stood to the north of Station Road and was the home of local maltster Major Colley, who retained a clump of trees to hide the unsightly Skew Bridge. The Lodge was built in 1834 by Benjamin Maddock, who was the Vicar of Tadcaster from 1830 until 1869. Major Frank Colley DSO/Bar died aged 81 on April 14th. 1966: his wife Zillah died in 1983 aged 99. Edgerton Lodge was also the home of his father Francis Colley (died 1902). Major Frank's brother was William Ramsden Colley (March 23rd. 1891 - July 29th. 1933) whose wife Katherine died on October 14th. 1984. The Colley brothers purchased the Newton Kyme estate including the hall and farms which they held for a few years.
The old vicarage became a boarding school for young ladies run by Catherine and Mary Tasker and later as a boys school. Elsworth and Storer's vicarage school operated in 1849 and transferred to Toulston Lodge. The vicarage transferred to Highfield on Station Road in 1938 and the present vicarage was built in its grounds in 1964. The old vicarage became home to the British Legion until 1987, who have now opened premises near the Post Office and the old building is being conserved.
The Tadcaster Board School was built in 1877 and closed in 1985 - the Infants section is now the town library. The schoolmaster's house is now a private dwelling and the rest of the school is home to St. Joseph's R. C. School. The old Sunday School in Westgate was built in 1788 as probably the first purpose built Sunday School for girls. It was restored in 1985 and is now a curtain and carpet firm.
The turnpike entered Tadcaster to its junction with the turnpike to Otley, created in 1753. The first toll bar on this road was near the paper mill at Newton Kyme.
Tadcaster Railway Station opened on an 8.5 acre site between Station Road and the newer Leeds Road. The railway from Church Fenton to Harrogate was opened in August 1847 by the York & North Midland Railway. The first station to serve Tadcaster was at Bolton Percy opened in 1840 with a connecting coach service. The railway buildings were designed by G.T.Andrews but were demolished following

Tadcaster Railway Station

closure of the station in January 1964. The area was cleared to build the present Industrial Estate and the old level crossing on Station Road was covered. In 1846 a link line from Tadcaster to York and Leeds was to be built by George Hudson of York: the only part built was the railway bridge at Tadcaster across the River Wharfe, which remains today as a railway folly.

On the corner of Station Road and Leeds road was the Union Workhouse, demolished in March 1985. The building housed the poor people after its opening in 1872 as the new Tadcaster Workhouse. Following the 1834 poor Law Amendment Act parishes and townships were combined into Unions responsible for poor relief. The change in the areas to the north and east of Leeds was prevented by the Gilbert Unions set up by an earlier Act. They held up any reforms until the Tadcaster Union was created in 1862, from townships not in the Gilbert Union. Tadcaster used the older workhouse in St. Joseph Street which became too small and inconvenient. The new workhouse built on the corner - still called Union Corner - was one of the last to be built in the country. Workhouses finally came to an end in 1948 and the Tadcaster building became the Beeches Old Peoples Home - the land is owned by Samuel Smith's Brewery.

On the south side of Leeds Road is the public cemetery, opened in 1876, when the Parish Church graveyard became full. There were two chapels with one for Anglicans and the second for the other religions. Only one is used today - the other is a storehouse. The Skew railway bridge serving Tadcaster Station was demolished in 1967 and the houses to the north called Railway Terrace were brought down in 1974. Leeds Road meets the old London Road from Stutton near the junction with

the Tadcaster, Ferrybridge and Doncaster turnpike, formed in 1734.
John Smith's Brewery completed in 1883 dominates this part of Tadcaster. It was Stephen Hartley who sank a well, which is now part of Samuel Smith's Old Brewery and he brought in the Backhouse family. The 24 year old John Smith started his own brewing business in 1847, when the railway came to Tadcaster. John Smith died in 1879 and following over a century of acquisition and expansion the brewery became a public company in 1953. In the 1970's John Smith's Brewery joined the Courage Group and seven years later a new brewhouse was opened with another following in 1985. The firm was to be later taken over by Hansa and GrandMet and then by the Australian Elders IXL Group.
Samuel Smith's Old Tadcaster Brewery is adjacent to the larger complex and has a prize winning Shire House stable. It brews beer using the old Yorkshire Square Slate method. In the early 18th. century the Old Brewery belonged to the Beaumont family and in 1759 Stephen Hartley sunk the well in use today and built a brewing tower. In the 19th. century the Hartleys took the Backhouse family as partners but in 1847 they sold the near bankrupt brewery. It was bought by Samuel Smith for his eldest son John aged 24 and capital was injected into the firm. Sam Smith is buried at Newton Kyme Church. Until John's death there was only one Smith brewery. The Old Brewery was entailed to John's nephew, John Smith who was still a minor. John Smith's Brewery was built by John's brother William on land outside the entail for

John Smith's Brewery, Tadcaster

his sister's sons Henry Herbert and Frank Riley their father was Henry Riley. Sam Smith re-opened the Old Brewery in 1866 and it is still a family business.
The Tower Brewery was originally built on a one acre site bought from the North Eastern Railway near the Otley turnpike. The brewery was started in 1882 by the partners in Hotham & Co of York, founded in 1716. The investors were Hon. Frederick Milner of Nun Appleton Hall, Viscount John Lambert of Co. Durham and Hon. Reginald Parker, the son of the 6th. Earl of Macclesfield and the brewery acquired the tag "Snobs Brewery". Parker moved to Askham Bryan Hall in 1879 on lease from Colonel Preston. Building of the new brewery was completed by Autumn 1882 and in November Hothams were renamed Tadcaster Tower Brewery Co.
In the early 1900's branches were opened at Brigg, Sunderland, Grimsby and Wakefield. In 1946 Hammonds bought the company and renamed it Hammonds United Breweries Ltd. The later Northern Breweries of Great Britain were merged with the London Charringtons and Tadcaster. It became the new brewhouse for Charringtons United Brewery in 1966. A year later CUB merged with Bass Mitchells and Butler to become Bass-Charrington. Only the base remains today of the original tower, demolished in 1974. On Bridge Street are the offices of Samuel Smiths Brewery, being the old Londesborough Hotel. This was reopened by Lord Londesborough of Grimston Park in 1855 and it became offices in 1977. The next building to the offices was the old Tadcaster Town Hall, becoming the Cosy Cinema until 1938. In this year the new Regal Cinema opened in Westgate and closed in 1976.The building was demolished in 1986.
The Angel and White Horse Inn on Bridge Street - originally called The White Hart in about 1700 - is the frontage of Samuel Smith's Brewery and the Shire horses have their own stables and tack rooms. The Angel Inn was the present public house and the White Horse became the Londesborough Hotel - the archways into the yards of these inns still exist. These were Tadcaster's coaching inns and served about 50 coaches a day in the 1800's, which were exempt from paying tolls on the turnpikes. Horses were changed at Tadcaster by the majority of coaches and this service was also provided by the demolished Rose & Crown inn on Oxton Lane corner. The White Horse was the main inn of Tadcaster and was once kept by William Backhouse, who had a good posting trade. The post office also had good stabling facilities and was run by John Hartley in the mid-18th. century,where he serviced the mail coaches which started in 1786 from London to York via Tadcaster. Coaching services were available from Tadcaster to Hull, Leeds, Newcastle, Selby, Scarborough, Sheffield and Edinburgh. In 1870 Lord Londesborough bought the Manor of Tadcaster and erected a new Post Office in the High Street. The present office in Westgate was built in 1910. In 1837 Tadcaster had 24 inns and 11 beer houses and in 1851 the population of the town was 2520.
The small market square is at the end of Kirkgate. A market charter was obtained in

Angel and White Horse, Tadcaster

1270 from King Henry II and is now held on Thursdays on the car park.
On Kirkgate stand important buildings: the "Ark" has been conserved and refurbished following fear in 1959 of demolition. W. H. Riley-Smith decided the town's oldest building should be preserved and this was accomplished between 1962 and 1967. The building dates back to the late 15th. century with extensions a century later. In later years other rooms were built over and around the building, which was mainly the old "Falcon Inn". In the alterations the additions were removed revealing the original stones at the base of the Medieval posts and the timber construction. In the 17th. century it was called Morley Hall, with Robert Morley registered as a Tadcaster post master in 1653. His son Robert held Presbyterian meetings in the house from 1672 - it is supposed to be the house in which the Pilgrim Fathers met to plan their voyage to America. The nickname Ark derives from the two heads on corbels at the front, commonly known as Noah and his wife. The Ark became a Museum, which closed in 1983 and opened again in 1987. In 1991 the Tadcaster Council bought the property for use as offices and now hold their meetings in the large room.
On the north side of Church Lane is the house of the 6th. Duke of Somerset built

about 1700. Elizabeth Percy had married three times prior to her 16th. birthday - Lord Ogle, Thomas Thynne of Longleat and when she was 15 to the Proud Duke of Somerset. The house was built for his agent and perhaps for his family when he was in the North from his home in Sussex. The family had their own pew in Tadcaster Church and the Duke was Master of Horse to both Queen Anne and King George I. The Duke's daughter Elizabeth married the Earl of Thomond and they were given the manor and lands at Tadcaster. The Earl was created Viscount Tadcaster in 1714. The house was a doctor's surgery and is now the home to the investment and pensions company M. Newton & Co.
St. Mary's Church was built inside the old Roman fort of Calcaria, now the name of a nearby inn whose original name was The Old Fleece. Evidence of Roman occupation is scant but does include a coin dated 276AD. Although the Domesday Book does not mention "Tatecastre" church, there was probably a wooden church on the site. A fragment of a 10th. century cross is now in the west wall of the south aisle. The first stone church is dated to about 1150 and by the mid-12th. century the church had acquired both a north and south aisle. In 1318 the church was burnt by the Scots and was rebuilt about 1380. The present form of the church came by the end of the 15th. century.
In Norman times the church became the property of the Percy family and in 1189 the church and lands were given by this family to Sawley Abbey. The monks built their Grange in Oxton Lane to administer their estates. The restored Percy coat of arms displayed in the church was presented in memory of the 10th. Earl of Northumberland in the 17th. century. It shows the arms of the llth. Earl (1644-1670), who had married the daughter of the 4th. Earl of Southampton. The Duke of Somerset was the wife of Elizabeth Percy and the pew seen at the west end of the north aisle was once part of their private church seat.
In 1875 a meeting took place with regard to the frequent flooding of the church and it was agreed to take the church down and rebuild on the original foundations 5 feet higher. An idea of the height alteration can be seen on the capitals of the columns on the inside tower base, as the tower was untouched during the heightening. A re-dedication service was held on May 29th. 1877 and 20 years later the north aisle was widened by 8 feet. The 12th. century Norman archway was removed during the rebuilding and was positioned on the interior west wall. There are fragments of early stained glass rebuilt into the modern window. One part shows St. Catherine treading on the Emperor and part of her wheel can be seen.
The font in use today was presented by John Ramsden of Oxton Hall in 1877 - the hall is now the home of the Smith family. The pulpit was given in 1912 in memory of Isabella Oliver of Oxton Hall. The old pulpit was removed after the restoration to Stutton Church.
Victorian stained glass by William Morris is seen in the east window,which was

given in memory of Arthur Harris of Oxton Hall in 1876.
West of the church is the Norman motte and bailey castle site, represented by a tree covered mound. It was built by the Percy family as a watch tower and is now known as Castle Hills. The stones used came from the Roman fort nearby and these were taken in Medieval times to build the road bridge across the River Wharfe. A few Roman remains have been discovered in this area, including a wine jug found in 1893.
The present road bridge was built originally in 1698 and widened in the 19th. century. There is evidence to suggest that a chapel existed east of the bridge which was used when the main church was flooded. The piscina discovered in 1881 at the Manor House site could have originated from the manor house itself or the chapel, which was thought to have been dedicated in 1504.
The "Britannia Inn" east of the bridge was built as a private house for the Dyson family who were coal merchants and barge owners. The 90 ton keel barge "Britannia" was launched in 1870 and took the first cargo of John Smith's beer to Hull. It was exported to Amsterdam, where it won a gold medal in 1895. Opposite the Britannia Inn were Lancaster & Tindall's saw mills.
North of the bridge were the bonded warehouse, demolished in the early 1980's and Ingleby's Flour Mills, demolished in 1985. In 1883 a line was built across the viaduct bringing coal to the mill: the viaduct had been built in 1846-49 for the proposed Leeds-York extension. Work on the line stopped when financial hardship arose and Hudson fell from grace: one of the most expensive parts of the proposed line had already been completed. The viaduct was bought in 1980 by Tadcaster Council for £100.
The field mounds by the riverside west of Castle Hills are in an area called Applegarth which could have been the result of the extraction of gravel in the 19th. century.
Tadcaster Weir was made in 1611 and replaced in 1807 by the Earl of Egremont, who held the advowson of Tadcaster church from 1790 until 1869. The Roman crossing of the river was nearby to eventually become The Old Street to Copmanthorpe and York.
The road to Wighill leaves the main road at the hill top and once led to Healaugh Manor. It was built by Benjamin Brooksbank in the 1770's for his wife, who did not like living at the old house as it was dirty and damp. He also built Healaugh Manor bridge - made of wood with stone parapets - across the Wharfe in 1793 to connect with the deer park and link with the road to Wetherby near the Tadcaster one milestone. There was a fire at the Manor in July 1901 and restoration followed: when it was the home of Edward Brooksbank JP. Healaugh Manor was demolished in 1944 after failing to attract the reserve price at the auction on August 15th. Only the two gate posts now remain from this mansion.

The turnpike leaves Tadcaster by Gallows Hill to the toll bar at Islington. This house is the only bar house left at Tadcaster and stood opposite The Slip Inn, also operating as a farm. The old Roman Road continued in a straight line from Islington Bar - The Old Street joining for a few yards with the turnpike at Street Houses near The Wild Man Inn.

South of the Tadcaster by-pass stands Oxton Hall, now overlooking the main road. This white stuccoed hall was built in the 18th. century by the Dawson family and had an entrance front added in 1803. In the 19th. century the hall was the home of William Ramsden, born in 1789, after his marriage to Annabella the daughter of the Marquess of Winchester. His brother Captain Henry James Ramsden - his son John Ramsden presented the font to Tadcaster Church in 1877 - lived at Oxton Hall. His daughter Isabella married Richard Silver Oliver of Bolton Lodge near Ulleskelf in 1858. Isabella died in 1908 and the pulpit in Tadcaster Church was given in 1912 in her memory. In 1872 Oxton Hall was sold to Arthur Harris; his wife Anne died in 1876 and her husband gave the William Morris stained glass window in her memory in Tadcaster Church. It is now the home of Humphrey Smith, Chairman of Sam Smith's Brewery.

Tadcaster Church

THE ROAD FROM LEEDS TO YORK

PART 5: TADCASTER TO COLTON

The road to Wighill north of Tadcaster passes through the hamlet of Easedike (Esdyke), which on an 1850 map was described as being the site of "supposed ancient foundations" and on a recent OS map as "Medieval village of Easedike". The hamlet has been the home of the Thomlinson family, who include Matthew (1740-1817), John (1815-1900) and Matthew (1847-1927) - their graves are on the south side of Wighill Church. The family are estate agents in the local area. Easedike was a part of the Harewood estate until 1783 and was transferred to the Brooksbank family of Healaugh. In early times Easedike and Wighill were both possessions of the de Mowbray family.
Easedike was the site of the local manor house, which was the home for both the Fitz Alan and Stapleton families during the 13th. and 14th.centuries. It was occupied until the early 17th.century on its position between river and road.

The church of All Saints Wighill stands on the top of a drumlin - a mound of glacial clay - and was built in Norman times. It was administered by Healaugh Priory and built of Magnesian Limestone. There is a fine Norman south doorway with capitals showing carved scenes of the Crucifixion and Descent from the Cross; the outer arch has the Norman zig-zag with the middle arch showing beak heads; the inner arch has seventeen scenes and figures including an eagle, animals fighting and animal heads. The whole is protected by an 18th.century porch. There is a wide nave and north aisle dominated by the Norman chancel arch. The north "choir" was the Stapleton Chapel and once had the large tomb of Robert Stapleton, now resting at the west end of the church. He married Catherine Fairfax of Walton in 1622 and died in 1634 aged 33. His feet rest on a Saracen's head which is the crest of the Stapleton family. It is said that his ancestor Sir Bryan Stapleton slew a Saracen single handed. The side of the tomb shows the kneeling figures of three boys and three girls: one of the boys holds a skull indicating an infant death.
There are other tombs and memorials to this great local family, including Henry Stapleton of Wighill Park who died in 1779. His daughter Martha married Cpt.Granville Chetwynd and when she died in 1822 she ended the long family line at Wighill. Cpt.Chetwynd added the Stapleton name to his own and sold the Wighill estate to Fountayne Wilson MP in 1811. On the wall of the south chancel is a memorial to Miles Chetwynd Stapleton who died in 1933.
A brass plate in the chancel records that "In and about this north aisle, formerly the Chapel of the Virgin Mary, the eleven generations of the family of Stapleton, who purchased this manor AD 1376 are buried."

Near the ancient font are two 18th.century funereal hatchments of the Stapleton family, showing their coat of arms. The "achievement" has the arms in a black edged lozenge shaped frame and was formerly placed on the front of the owner's house. The royal coat of arms on display are those of King George III, who reigned from 1760 until 1820. During the period of the King's insanity from 1811-1820, the Prince of Wales acted as Prince Regent. The pulpit is an example of restored 17th.century Jacobean work and there is a Saxon cross shaft set into the south wall dated 900-950AD.

The church was restored by Walter H.Brierley of York in 1912/1913. Brierley was also concerned with the building of Thorpe Underwood Hall about 1906 and the restoration of Whixley Hall in 1907. In 1953 Wighill became part of the United Benefice of Healaugh with Wighill and Bilbrough.

Outside the church on the east side are two graves of the Hawke family. These are Edward Henry Julius Hawke 6th.Baron of Towton who was the Rector of Willingham Lincolnshire from 1854 until 1874. He was born in 1815 and died in 1887 - he lived at Wighill Park from 1874: Rev.Edward Hawke inherited the title on the death of his father. The other tomb is that of Edward Julian 8th.Baron Hawke (1873-1939) with his wife Frances who died in 1959.

At the east end of the church is the tomb of Maria Brook of Brook Hall (1788-1858), which is north of the church in its own grounds. The house was built in 1838 by Elizabeth Dawson (died 1900), who is buried with her husband John Miles Dawson JP and chief landowner (1826-1895) in Wighill churchyard.

The village of Wighill has the ancient "White Swan" inn, with Samuel Easterby being the victualler and smith in 1838 and John Whitehead in 1904. The Wesleyan Chapel was built in 1828 and now converted into a private house.

The Stapleton family bought Wighill in 1376 and built the first Hall. He gave the estate to his son Sir Miles and the property remained in this family for 450 years. The Elizabethan hall stood on the site of the present house by the park gates and was north of the 14th.century wood/stone building, which itself replaced the earlier pele tower of the Haget and Turet families. Sir Robert Stapleton built his house in 1580 following his Grand Tour to Italy: the entrance to the manor house is incorporated into the modern dwelling. There are two stone shields of the Stapleton family displaying the lion rampant the family crest.

In 1790 the Elizabethan Manor House was demolished and Wighill Hall was rebuilt on higher land within the vast park. Later tenants included the York family until 1871 and the Lords Hawke. In the 1830's Richard and his wife Lady Mary Ann - the daughter of the 1st.Earl of Harewood - York lived at Wighill Park and when he died in 1843, the East Window of Wighill Church was dedicated to his memory by his son Edward York.

The East Window and reredos in Healaugh Church are in memory of Edward

Brooksbank and his wife Lucy York of Wighill Park, who died in 1893.
In the 18th.century Edward Lord Hawke had Towton Hall, where he was Lord of the Manor. He was created Baron Hawke of Towton in 1776 - he had been Admiral of the Fleet from 1766 until 1771.
The cricketer Lord Martin Bladen Hawke inherited the title on the death of his father in 1887 and became the 7th.Baron Hawke. He was born at Willingham rectory south east of Gainsborough and educated at Slough Preparatory School and when he was 14 years old he went to Eton. Here he played for the school eleven in 1878/79. While at Magdalen College Cambridge University he played for the team in 1882/83 and in 1885 as Captain. He first appeared as Yorkshire CCC Captain on July 2nd. 1883 at Trent Bridge against Nottinghamshire. He captained the county until 1910 and scored 16794 runs in first class cricket with an average of 20.15 including 13 centuries. He was President of Yorkshire CCC from 1898 until 1938 and was responsible for introducing the county badge and colours.
Martin Bladen married the widow of Arthur Cross in 1916 at St.Paul's Church Knightsbridge London.
He became President of the MCC and often invited the Yorkshire team to his Wighill Park home, where he had one room devoted to hundreds of souvenirs of his cricket tours. Lord Hawke played 744 innings for Yorkshire scoring 13197 runs with 166 as his highest score. His average for Yorkshire was 20.20 with 10 centuries scored. Lord Hawke played five test matches for England between 1896 and 1899 scoring 55 runs. He was the 14th. cricketer to play for Yorkshire who was born outside the county boundary.
Lord Hawke left Wighill Park in 1924 to live at Huttons Ambo. In 1926 he became the President of the Scarborough Festival and was awarded the Freedom of Scarborough in 1930. He died on October 10th. 1938 in an Edinburgh nursing home after being taken ill at his holiday home at North Berwick. He was succeeded by his brother the 8th.Lord Hawke Hon.Edward Julian, who was a partner in the firm of Wyer and Hawke East India Merchants.
Scarthingwell Hall was also a Hawke property until 1848 and members of the family are remembered in a large monument on the north side of the chancel at Saxton Church.

South east of Wighill village is Healaugh Manor Farm, once Healaugh Priory. Between 1161 and 1184 Geoffrey Haget, Healaugh's Lord of the Manor, confirmed lands and woods to the Church of St.John and to Gilbert, monk of Marmoutier near Tours, to found a Hermitage in the woods. In 1218 an Augustinian Priory was endowed, with the generosity of Alice Haget of Wighill. This was dissolved on August 9th. 1535 (there was the prior, five canons and eight servants). It was granted to James Gage in 1549 and passed to Sir Arthur Darcy and was converted into Lord

Wharton's Manor House surrounded by a deep moat, some of which exists today. Much of the Priory was demolished as the stone was used to build the new Healaugh Manor near Tadcaster. There is a good example of both stone - in an outbuilding - and brick walls, showing a herringbone pattern, although the proportions of the buildings have been substantially reduced.
The two main houses at Healaugh Manor Farm are the west house built in 1830 and the east manor house which dates from the 16th.century and part of a post-suppression mansion which replaced the Priory. The old stones have also been reused in the building of the 19th.century farmhouse- the whole complex being Healaugh Farms: part of the Sam Smith's Brewery estates. In 1877 the farmer at Manor West was William Jackson and at Manor East was John Hutchinson.

The approach to Healaugh village from Wighill reveals the hilltop splendour of the Norman church of St.Helen and St.John the Baptist. St.Helen was the mother of Emperor Constantine who was proclaimed at York in 306AD. She lived from about 247AD to 327 and according to legend was the discoverer of the True Cross of Christ at Jerusalem.
Since the discovery in 1842 of an inscribed stone in Healaugh churchyard, there have been suggestions that the site was that of a convent founded by St.Heiu in the mid-7th.century, although it could have been nearer to Tadcaster.
Most of Healaugh Church is Norman, built about 1150, including the tower, nave, chancel and a splendid south doorway. There are three arches with the zig-zig motif, beak heads and figures. The church was given to the Priory of Healaugh by Sir John Depeden in 1398. When the priory was dissolved in 1535, Lord Wharton was given the property and divided his time between his home near Kirkby Stephen and Healaugh. He married Eleanor Stapleton of Wighill and later married Lady Ann Bray, the daughter of the 5th.Earl of Shrewsbury. The Wharton coat of arms in limestone is shown above Healaugh Church doorway.
In the church is the tomb of the Whartons bearing three effigies - Thomas 1st.Lord Wharton (1495-1568) and his two wives: there is a replica of this tomb in Kirkby Stephen Church. Thomas bought the manors of Healaugh and Catterton from the Percy family, Earls of Northumberland in 1531 and ten years later bought the rectory of Healaugh with the tithes and advowson.
Thomas and Philip the 3rd.Lord Wharton, who died in 1625, were buried at Healaugh. The 4th.Lord Wharton was born in 1613 and married three times having many children. He lived at Healaugh on occasions and is remembered for his great bible charity, founded in 1692 - the income from local lands was used to buy over 1000 bibles annually and given to children in certain towns, including York with 100 copies distributed. This good Lord Wharton died in 1696, leaving 463 acres of his lands at Sinningthwaite to provide the income for the provision of bibles and prayer

books. Sinningthwaite Priory for Cistercian nuns was founded by Bertram Haget in 1160 and was dissolved in 1535. The remains of this priory are now a farmhouse with a good 12th.century door. There are remains of Norman windows, mostly blocked up in the Medieval period: the Victorians added the present west wing. The church contains a Victorian pulpit and reading desk, using Jacobean chair backs from Healaugh Manor.

In 1715 Healaugh Manor was bought by Stamp Brooksbank of Hackney, from Thomas 5th.Lord Wharton and 1st.Marquis. Stamp Brooksbank was a governor of the Bank of England and the MP for Colchester and Saltash. It was Joseph Brooksbank of Elland who married Mary, who was the heir to her uncle Sir Thomas Stamp - Lord Mayor of London in 1692.

The Brooksbank family eventually lived at the Old Hall and the new Healaugh Manor, which the family built near Tadcaster. The old hall is by the church and has the remains of a village cross on the green. At the north end of the hall is an archway and seat, used by coachmen waiting for the family in poor weather. Parts of Healaugh Old Hall date from about 1680, although the building probably dates from the mid 17th.century. For a short period there was a small Puritan chapel in the hall. The Rev.Edward Hawke Brooksbank MA became Vicar of Healaugh in 1814 and was also the Squire, with his own pew in the church. Until about 1938 the Squire was the patron of the Healaugh living. Edward was born in 1789 and died in 1883; he resigned the living in 1863 and was followed by the Rev.Charles Voysey, who was deprived of the living through heresy in 1871. During the First World War the Brooksbank family lost their two sons Captain Stamp Brooksbank and Lieutenant Hugh Godfrey Brooksbank - he was an officer in the Yorkshire Regiment and died of wounds received at Ypres on December 16th.1914 aged 21. They are remembered in an inscription on the old village hall by the roadside - now converted into a cottage.

In the family plot on the north side of Healaugh Church are buried Benjamin of Healaugh Manor died age 85 in 1842; Edward who died in 1916 aged 90; Sir Edward Clitherow Brooksbank, who died in 1943 aged 85. He lived at the Old Hall with his wife and four children - all of whom died in their parents lifetime.

The long connection with the Brooksbank family at Healaugh ended in 1961 with the sale of the estate to Major H.J.Gillam. Major Gillam sold it in 1991 to the Sam Smith's brewery estate of Tadcaster. The Old Hall is now the home of Oliver Smith and Major Gillam lives in a new house in the village.

North of the church is the site of an ancient castle and it was described by John Leland in the reign of King Henry VIII: "..... I saw great ruins of an ancient manor of stone with a fair wooded park nearby, that belonged to the Earl of Northumberland."

A cottage on the Wighill Road is the traditional home of Darby and Joan. Edward

Darby was a blacksmith and Sam Hick, the well known Methodist preacher of Micklefield, was an apprentice to Edward at the age of 14.
Although Healaugh has now no school, village shop or public house, it was the "Bay Horse" which served the village in the 19th.century. In 1822 John Brown was the victualler and in 1838 his wife Hannah had taken over the licence. The old inn, with its window shutters, is by the present Post Office on the main street and is now a private house. There is some discussion of a possible new inn for the village.

South of Healaugh is the hamlet of Catterton and the site of a moated fortified hall, which would have belonged to the Whartons and is now a listed area. The site is a few hundred yards south of Middle Farm - originally Moat Farm - and the deep moat still contains water, although there are no stones remaining having finally disappeared about 50 years ago. Middle Farm is about 250 years old and has a cobble herringbone wall to the barn area. The stone coffin in the garden was once used as a pump, using water drawn from near Buckles Inn. In the 1877 directory there were five farmers at Catterton.
The Catterton Estate was sold by auction at the Royal Station Hotel York on December 5th.1946 to the Halifax-Ainsty Trust, of which one of the partners was Lord Halifax. On April 6th.1970 at the Brunswick Hotel Wetherby the estate was again sold to the Metcalfe landowning family, who live at Sharow near Ripon.
Catterton, which once had a small chapel of ease to Tadcaster, retains the estate cottages, now converted and an air of antiquity. Eastgarth Farm on the road from Catterton to Bilbrough was formerly known as Paradise Farm and was sold at auction on February 26th.1968.
There is another moated site north of Moor Farm, Catterton called White Hall. It was presumably a timber house and all trace vanished at about the same time as the adjacent village of Sandwith: the main road linking Healaugh and Askham Bryan was known as Sandwith Lane prior to now being York Road.
It has been suggested that the lost village of Sandwith was destroyed by Lancastrians during their flight from the Battle of Towton Moor in 1461. At one time the village of Sandwith would have been as large as Bilbrough.

The Tadcaster Bridge - Hob Moor Lane End turnpike opened in 1745, six years prior to the route from Tadcaster to Halton Dial. The new route only doubled with the old Roman Street for a few hundred yards near Street Houses. It branched from the old road at Islington toll bar and the meetings of the trustees were held at the 18th.century Wild Man Inn. In 1785 John Trees was convicted before the Trustees of the Tadcaster Road, assembled at the "Wild Man" inn," of riding in his master's wagon not having another person to guide the horse." The fine was 10/-.
The Roman road is now part of the Ebor Way and leaves the turnpike near Steeton

House en route for Copmanthorpe. The Roman road becomes Top Lane and joins the turnpike again at the new traffic lights to Dringhouses toll bar and Micklegate Bar at York.
In 1936 the turnpike road from Islington to Top Lane end was made into a dual carriageway. During this construction the well established "New Inn" was demolished as it stood on the intended carriageway north of the original road. The New Inn was run by the Buckle family for many years and when the new inn was built further to the north it was renamed "Buckles Inn". It is said that the ghost of Annie Buckle is still heard in the pub in which she died. In the early 20th.century Henry Buckle farmed Steeton Grange Farm on the south side of the main road. Askham Richard mill stands behind the Buckles Inn with the lower stone built half still to be seen. The top section now serves as a water tower supplying both Bilbrough village and part of Askham Bryan College. One of the last millers was George Ward.
Bilbrough is a village of two parallel streets and a large rebuilt Hall. In the Domesday Book Bilbrough is mentioned as Mileburg and by 1167 had become Billedburc. It has been suggested that the Romans would have had a look out station at Bilbrough, where some tiles of that period were discovered about 1900, while excavating the foundations for the new Bilbrough Manor.
The Normans built a church at Bilbrough and the lands were held by Ralph Paganel. The manor passed into the Norton family in the 15th.century. When John Norton died in 1464 he was buried in the church at Bilbrough and his tomb now lies in the south chapel with that of Thomas 3rd.Lord Fairfax, who died in 1671.
In 1537 Bilbrough Manor was granted to Sir Leonard Beckwith and in 1556 was granted to Sir William Fairfax. In 1716 Bilbrough was sold to Admiral Fairfax, who lived at the old manor house, demolished in 1900 to build the new hall: the present country house hotel. The old manor house had been rebuilt in the late 17th.century and became known as Bilbrough Hall in the late 18th.century. Thomas Fairfax was born at the hall in 1804 and the eldest of his seven children lived at the hall. Thomas Ferdinand married Evelyn Milner of Nun Appleton in 1869: the hall was demolished during the ownership of their son Guy Thomas Fairfax. Guy was born at Nun Appleton in 1870 and married Joan Wilson from Warter Priory in 1899. When he died in 1934 Guy was buried on the south side of Bilbrough Church. His son Ferdy was born in 1900 and died in 1974.
In the separate graveyard north west of the church is an enclosed area with some members of the local Fairfax family. Under the large cross bearing the family motto: "Fare Fax", is buried Albert Kirby of New York City and 12th.Baron Fairfax (1870-1939). He was the son of John Contee Fairfax of Northampton, Maryland USA, who married Mary Kirby, daughter of a Captain in the US army. In an act of piety Albert returned to England to document the career of Black Tom Fairfax. His efforts left

the largest and important private collection of 5000 papers of the Civil War outside the Bodleian and British Libraries. They record all aspects of a war that raged in England from 1642 until January 1649 when Charles 1st. was beheaded. The Fairfax collection was auctioned in London on December 14th.1993 for £441,582 and bought by private collectors from the Fairfax trustees.
The 13th.Baron Fairfax was Thomas Brian (1923-1964) who is also buried here.
"Black Tom" Fairfax was the 3rd.Lord Fairfax, Commander in Chief of the Parliamentary Armies 1645-1650. He was the MP for York in 1660 and when he died at Nun Appleton in 1671 he was buried at Bilbrough Church. The daughter of Thomas and Anne Fairfax was Mary, who married George Villiers the Duke of Buckingham in 1657.
Thomas or Black Tom because of his swarthy appearance, was born in 1612 and knighted by King Charles 1st. at York in 1641: he was a moderate and controversially opposed to King Charles 1st.'s trial. He defeated the King at Naseby in 1645. It was Tom who is said to have been responsible for the saving of the stained glass in York Minster during the Civil War. The tomb of Tom and Anne at Bilbrough was restored in 1984-1986 by York Minster stonemasons, after a successful appeal, to which members of the Fairfax family had contributed. Inscribed on the tomb of Black Tom, erected by their daughter Mary, in the south chapel of Bilbrough Church are the words: "Here lye the bodies of the Right Honble Thomas Lord Fairfax of Denton, Baron of Cameron, who died November XII 1671 in thr 60th yeare of his age; and of Anne his wife, daughter and co-heir of Horatio Lord Vere Baron of Tilbury. They had issue Mary Duchess of Buckingham and Elizabeth."
His son in law the Duke of Buckingham said of Sir Thomas: "He never knew what envy was nor hate, his soul was filled with worth and honesty and with anothyer thing besides quite out of date calld modesty".

Sir Thomas Fairfax took Leeds for the Parliamentarian forces on January 23rd.1643. The battle which was fought in the town centre resulted in about 40 killed but the battle of Adwalton Moor in June put Leeds again into Royalist hands. It was the battle of Marston Moor in 1644 that turned the tide against the King in the North.
Thomas 5th.Lord Fairfax married Catherine Culpepper, daughter of Lord Culpepper. She inherited Leeds Castle, Kent together with a vast estate in the Shenandoah Valley, Virginia west of Washington DC. Her son Thomas 6th.Lord Fairfax inherited his parents now enlarged estate of 5 million acres and founded Fairfax town and county. He was born at Denton near Otley and built the manor house of Greenaway Court in Virginia, where it is said the young George Washington often stayed with Fairfax becoming his first patron.
The Fairfax family held properties at Denton, Bolton Percy, Nun Appleton,

Bilbrough and Steeton. Today, the Fairfax family is represented in Australia, America and Nicholas the 14th.Lord Fairfax lives in London.
Bilbrough is noted for its links with the English poet Andrew Marvell (1621-1678). Black Tom Fairfax appointed Marvell tutor to his daughter Mary and he lived at Nun Appleton Hall from 1650 to 1653. His poem "Upon the hill and grove of Billborow" was dedicated to Lord Fairfax and he wrote "The Garden" and "Upon Appleton House" while at the hall. The hill is known as Ingrish Hill and was the site of a beacon during the Napoleonic Wars. Marvell became the assistant to John Milton, when the great poet was nearly blind. Milton became Latin Secretary to the Commonwealth in 1649 and carried on his duties with the help of assistants such as Andrew Marvell.
The Norman Church of St.James at Bilbrough once belonged to the Priory of Holy Trinity at York, was rebuilt in the 15th.century. The church was demolished in 1872 and the present building designed by George Fowler Jones was opened in 1873. It was paid for by Thomas Ferdinand Fairfax of Bilbrough Hall. The rebuilding did not include the main body of the south chantry chapel, which dates from the 15th.century. It is probable that some of the old stones from the demolished chapel at Steeton Hall were reused for the new church.
George Fowler Jones (1818-1905) built the almshouses at Aberford in 1844 and St.Mary's Church Garforth, also restoring All Saints Church Barwick in Elmet.
The chancel was re-ordered and dedicated by the Archbishop of York in 1971 and further restoration took place in 1984. This includes the Medieval altar stone and the reredos from the redundant church of St.Sampson at York.
The original Manor House was east of the church on the main street and there is a stone doorway remaining inscribed "TF 1670" - now a, part of the present house interior. There is a stone archway on the west side of the house dating from this early period. The manor house was the birthplace in 1560 of the 1st.Baron Fairfax of Cameron: when he died in 1640 he was buried at Otley Church.
The "Three Hares Inn", well known for its cuisine, absorbed the village smithy into the main building. Originally "The Hare Inn" in the early 1900's it was run by Charles Farndale and William Hartley was the village blacksmith.
Bilbrough Manor, built in 1901 to designs by Temple Moore (1856-1920), was converted into a exclusive Country House Hotel by the Bell family, who bought the house in 1986.
The Wesleyan Chapel was opened in 1838 and the 18th.century Bilbrough Grange was used by Guy Fairfax, while building his new Bilbrough Hall. The Grange lies behind a high brick wall on the west corner of the Back and Main Streets. In the mid 19th.century the Grange was home to John Fisher, one of the main landowners of this area, together with Rev.Robert Thompson, who lived at the Hall. On the death of the owner Bilbrough Grange was sold at an auction on the premises on May lst/May

2nd.1969. The village school was built in 1874 and had 60 children. It is now closed and converted into two cottages: the old playground was used to build new cottages.

West of Colton is the historic Steeton Hall and home of the Fairfax family. It is now a part of the estates belonging to Sam Smith's Brewery of Tadcaster.
At the entrance is a sign that reads: "Steeton Old Hall built by Sir Guy Fairfax 1477." This listed building built of limestone has brick chimneys and a new roof was provided in 1984. The hall was once a part of Steeton village, decimated by the plague and afterwards deserted.
In the 14th.century Steeton was owned by Sir John Chamont: in 1378 the hall lands were farmed by William Cerff. The lands became the property of the Fairfax family, who rebuilt the manor house. This was accomplished by Guy Fairfax, of the family branch from Walton, who escaped alive from the Battle of Towton Moor in 1461. By 1477 Guy Fairfax was a Judge of the King's Bench and he had married the grand-daughter of Lord Chief Justice Gascoigne - he is buried in Harewood Church.
Sir Guy also rebuilt the old chapel, consecrated by Archbishop Rotherham: the chapel was destroyed in 1873. There remains today an old archway into the south garden, presumably once a part of this chapel.
Gabriel, the second surviving son of Sir William Fairfax of Steeton - he is buried at Bolton Percy - succeeded to the manors of Steeton, Bilbrough and Bolton Percy. The Steeton property became home to his son Sir William and grandson Sir Philip. Sir Philip, who sold the Bolton Percy manor to the Denton branch, married the daughter of the Earl of Mulgrave. Their son Sir William of Steeton was a commander in the Parliamentarian army in the Civil War and was killed at Montgomery Castle in 1644. It was at Steeton that Ferdinando Lord Fairfax stayed the night, before fighting at the Battle of Marston Moor.
Steeton passed to Sir William's son William and his grandson Robert, who was an Admiral in the Royal Navy. Robert's brother William was the last of the Fairfax family to live at Steeton Hall - he died aged 30 in 1694. The Admiral lived at Ruswarp near Whitby - his father-in-law's house - and Robert built Newton Kyme Hall. It was from this time that Steeton Hall became unoccupied and partially dismantled. The paintings and tapestries went to Bilbrough Hall and the old hall was converted into a farmhouse, which it still remains.

The village of Colton is approached from the main road by Colton Lane, which was called Sansick Lane in the 19th.century. Colton Lodge, with the Westgate well and old pinfold to the south, was the home of the Lawson-Smith family. They gave the land on which was built St.Paul's Church: Mrs.E.M.Lawson-Smith laid the foundation stone for the church in 1897, the year of Queen Victoria's Diamond

Jubilee. The church was consecrated on June 16th.1899 - prior to the opening of the church services were held in the village schoolroom.
The Lord of the Manor early this century was Edward Maule Lawson-Smith JP. In the church is a memorial plaque with his coat of arms and motto: "Leve et Relius". He was born in October 1859 and died in November 1942, in his later years living opposite Dringhouses Church near York. The two sons were killed in the First World War: Lt.Thomas Edward of the 13th.Hussars was killed in action at Messines in October 1914 aged 25 and Lt.John Lawson-Smith was killed in action at Boisgreier a few days before aged 22. The East Window of Colton Church is a memorial to Ethel Mary Lawson-Smith who died on January 27th. 1906. The family were great village benefactors: the houses opposite the Church bear the inscription "E.M.L-S 1909".
During the last War the Grange was occupied by members of ENSA - Entertainments National Services Association.
Colton was sold at auction in 1919 and the farms and houses are both tenanted and privately owned.
At the east end of the main street, in a field by the inn, is Hall Garth, the site of an ancient moated house. This house would have been the property of Sir George Ratcliffe in the 17th.century. The Morritt family took over the manor and lived at the Lodge, which had replaced the earlier moated house. The Morritt family were property owners around Cawood and Sherburn in Elmet. They were later to hold Rokeby Park in Teesdale, purchased by John Morritt in 1769. William J.Morritt was Lord of the Manor in the 1860's, when Edward Brooksbank had the Lodge.
"Ye Old Sun Inn" was once known as The Star Inn in the mid 19th.century, when John Barnes was the innkeeper. In 1904 Thomas Blakey was the landlord of the inn dating from the 17th.century complete with resident ghost.
The Wesleyan Chapel closed in the early 1940's and now stands in disrepair, being without some windows and used as a farm store.
The Victorian school was enlarged in 1868 and eventually closed in 1949, with the village children being educated at Appleton Roebuck School. The old Colton School was partly demolished and this white painted house, west on the village street, was converted into a private house.

THE ROAD FROM LEEDS TO YORK

PART 6: ASKHAM RICHARD TO MICKLEGATE BAR

North of the turnpike is the village of Askham Richard, named after Richard Earl of Cornwall who had interests in this area. In 1291 the village was known as Askham Ricardi and could have been the original home of the Aske family - the name meaning "where the Ash trees grow".
It is sometimes known as West Askham, to distinguish it from its neighbour Askham Bryan. In the 12th.century it was held by Roger de Mowbray: there is a street near the school bearing this name today. He gave it to William de Tykhill who fought in the Crusades. It was William de Arches who gave Askham Richard Church to the priory at Nun Monkton - the priory had been founded by William de Arches in 1150. William's daughter Matilda became a nun at the Priory.
The church is of Norman foundation and there is the base of a Cross with a serpent design, in the church - the cross had been found in 1879. Evidence of an older church is in the Saxon doorway, which was moved from the North wall to become the entrance to the vestry on the north west side. There was also a narrow Saxon window discovered during the restoration, which was inserted above the east window for ventilation.
The church of St.Mary contains a few Norman remains including the south doorway, wall and parts of the North and East walls. The doorway displays two orders of colonettes and has an arch with zig-zag design and leaf markings.
The church was restored in 1879/80 at a cost of £1790, when the west end was moved by three feet to the east, the north nave was rebuilt and a new porch completed. The chancel received a panelled ceiling in 1890, designed by architect Temple Moore.
In 1838 the Roman stone coffin, now outside the south door of the church, was found used as a water trough in Ox-Close, Home Farm and the lid as a ditch bridge. In 1903 Major Wailes-Fairbairn paid for its removal to the church.
East of the church are the tombs of the Fairbairn and Swann families of Askham Hall and Grange. There is also a tall pillar and urn as a memorial to Elizabeth Berry, who died in 1770. Also buried at Askham Richard was Richard Vavasour, the son of Richard and Margaret Vavasour of Copmanthorpe. He lived at Askham Richard with his wife Dorothy, the daughter of John Clayton. They were both buried at Askham Richard when they died in 1563 and 1587. The church has a list of incumbents from 1252 and the church registers date from 1579.
Askham Hall, which was near to the site of the present Askham Grange, was the home of the York architect John Carr. John Carr (1723-1807) was the son of Robert Carr, a stonemason and quarry owner from Horbury. John trained as a mason and

was making designs in 1748, when he was employed by Edwin Lascelles of Gawthorpe Hall at Harewood. Carr was Lord Mayor of York in 1770 and 1785 and surveyor of bridges in both west and north ridings. He died at Askham Hall leaving £150,000 to his nephews and nieces: the hall passed to his nephew William Carr. When he was in old age John Carr would make long country tours showing his buildings to his great-nieces. Carr's local work included Hazlewood alterations for Sir Walter Vavasour, Gledhow Hall, Bramham Park, Leventhorpe Hall and Methley Hall.

The Hall became the property of the Swann family in the 19th.century. John Swann, a Commander in the Royal Navy, lived from 1793 until 1872 and when he died he was buried in the local churchyard. There are also tombs to Robert Swann, who died 1897 and Blanche who died in 1878.

Sir Andrew Fairbairn bought Askham Old Hall and estate in 1879 and with increasing problems of dry rot, decided to demolish and build a larger house nearby. Sir Andrew (1828-1901) completed the Hall, which displays the date 1886 over the front entrance. He also built the present St.Mary's Primary School, after donating the land for the building - the school opened in January 1899.

Sir Andrew Fairbairn was the son of Sir Peter Fairbairn, Mayor of Leeds when Queen Victoria opened Leeds Town Hall in 1858 - the event on September 7th. brought the Mayor a knighthood and he paid for the banquet himself. Andrew was born in Glasgow and married Clara, daughter of Sir J. Lambton-Loraine 8th.Baronet, in 1862. He was Chairman of Fairbairn-Lawson-Combe-Barbour Ltd and was Mayor of Leeds in 1866 and 1867. He resigned this post on September 25th.1868 when his term was completed by Thomas George. Andrew Fairbairn was the first Chairman of the Leeds School Board, Director of the Great Northern Railway Co., High Sheriff of Yorkshire, JP for the West Riding and Leeds MP for the East Division of the West Riding and a Captain in the Yorkshire Hussar Yeomanry. Andrew Fairbairn was knighted in 1868 is recognition of his reception of the Prince of Wales when he opened the Leeds Art Exhibition. The title appeared in the Gazette on September 1st.1868.

Peter Fairbairn was born in Kelso in 1799 and was apprenticed to a millwright, coming to Leeds in 1828. Samuel Lawson had established the Hope Foundry on Mabgate Leeds in 1812. When Peter came to the City, he opened in Lady Lane making flax spinning machinery and later took over the 1828 Wellington Foundry. This foundry turned to making woollen machinery and rope yarn.

In 1845 James Combe founded his Belfast company and joined James Barbour in 1851. In 1861 Peter Fairbairn died: followed five years later by Samuel Lawson's death.

In 1900 the Leeds and Belfast companies amalgamated to become Fairbairn-Lawson-Combe-Barbour. During the First World War the factory made shell fuse caps and

machine tools for boring tank guns. In 1921 the firm amalgamated with Urquart Lindsay and Robertson, Orchard of Dundee - the Dundee factory closed in 1958. The company reverted to munitions during the Second World War and was to start producing textile machinery for export again. In 1980 Fairbairn-Lawson of Leeds went into receivership and liquidation followed in 1985. The factory on Wellington Road was demolished in 1990 and redeveloped.
When Sir Andrew died on May 28th. 1901 the property went to his uncle William Wailes (1862-1933), who added the Fairbairn name to his own. William's son Neville was 21 years old in 1913 and his father had the west wing built with a swimming pool to mark the occasion. Neville was killed in a hunting accident in November 1939 aged 47 and his widow Margaretta leased the Grange to be a military orthopaedic hospital. Margaretta died aged 73 in 1970.
The hospital opened in 1940 with three wards run by the No.8 Company of the Royal Army Medical Corps. There were 30 personnel, 20 ATC and 10 Queen Alexandra's nurses, commanded by Major Tapley with Sister Bell being the Acting Matron. The hospital closed in June 1946.
In 1947 Askham Grange became the property of the Home Office and opened as a women's open prison on January 6th.1947. The clearing of the hospital was achieved using some German SS POW's. Mary Size was the first governor of the prison when there were only three inmates. It was the first such prison in the country with a Mother and Baby Unit attached.
The Askham Richard estate was sold in August 1969 and sold again soon afterwards to a firm in Cheshire: there being two tenanted farms and one which is rented.
In the mid 19th.century there were three inns at Askham Richard: the "Saddle" (John Palfreeman licensee), "New Inn" (Emanuel Marris as licensee) and "Rose and Crown", where John Leadley held the licence - it was Stephen Leadley in 1904. There is only one inn remaining today and the "Rose and Crown" was rebuilt by order of the Fairbairn family. There is a reminder in the inn today that it had been in the possession of one family for 300 years. It was an inn during Elizabethan times and a hospital during the Civil War.
One of the old inns was west of the village pond and close by the Methodist Chapel. The chapel is now closed and used for storage purposes, as part of Tudor Cottage. The village had a tannery at the south end and there is a village pump house on the green, built by Sir Andrew Fairbairn. Sir Andrew died in London and is buried in Kelsall Green cemetery.

Askham Bryan is associated with Brian Fitz-Alan, a descendent of Alan Rufus the builder of Richmond Castle. Bryan was a soldier and statesman and was Lord Lieutenant of Scotland and Lord of Bedale. He died in 1306 and is buried with his wife in St.Gregory's Church at Bedale.

In the Domesday Book Askham Bryan is known as plain Ascham and belonged to the great Percy family. It later belonged to the de Mowbrays and through marriage to the Stapletons.
In 1636 John Geldart, a York alderman had the Manor and built a moated manor house west of the church, which was burnt down: there are a few remains today of this site. In 1750 Samuel Clark, twice Lord Mayor of York, held the Manor and lived at the new Manor House. The Manor was abolished in 1811, in the same year that the village was affected by the Enclosure Act. In 1600 the village had 16 tailors, 15 shoemakers, 10 millers and blacksmiths, 9 butchers, 5 publicans and many farmers. About 250 years later there were two inns remaining, one blacksmith and one butcher. At the present time there is no shop, school, post office or vicarage.
The oldest building in Askham Bryan is the Norman Church of St.Nicholas. The rights of administration were granted to St.Mary's Abbey York, which held rectorial tithes within the parish.
The so called "chapelry" of St.Nicholas was served by this abbey until the Dissolution of the Monasteries in the 1530's. In 1433 there is a record of Dom Thomas ministering in the capella of Askham Bryan. In 1510 Seth Clayton was appointed chaplain by the Abbot of St.Mary's Abbey. Askham Bryan Church was served by the vicars of Askham Richard from 1565 until 1737.

Askham Bryan Church

The church has a Norman south doorway, with two orders of colonettes and zig zag pattern on the arch. The aisleless nave is linked to the chancel and there is a small bellcote built in 1611. There are three Norman windows in the east wall and a small "vesica" or fish window above. A lych gate was erected at the church in 1897 to mark Queen Victoria's Diamond Jubilee but was taken down in 1952 after being found to be unsafe.
Inside the church there is a 1634 pulpit and an Oak reredos dating from 1916. There are many memorials within the church to the local Preston family, who are also buried outside in the graveyard.
The first vicarage was built in 1794 and the later building was sold in 1982 and is a private house. The nearby Methodist Chapel is dated 1893 and became the Village Hall. The adjacent village shop served the whole community but it closed in 1987, the same year as the by-pass road nearby.
The first school dated from 1756 and there was a new school and schoolhouse completed in 1856 and became a private house following the sale in 1972.
The village almshouses near the church were built for the poor in 1862. Opposite the church is the village pond, made in the early 19th.century following the demolition of houses once on the site.
The Manor House stands north of the main street opposite the road from Askham Richard and the College. This was the home of the Preston family and during the War was a centre for knitting for the troops.
Early members of the Preston family included Thomas who was organist at York Minster, he died in 1691. His son was Darcy Preston who bought the Askham Bryan property about 1725. By his two wives Catherine and Mary he had 21 children: the later Preston line continued through his marriage to Mary. Their eldest son was John Preston, a prebend at York and his son was Admiral Darcy Preston (1762-1847).
Askham Bryan Hall is set back from the road and was once the home of the Payne-Gallway family, although it was the original home of the Prestons, who retained the property and rented it out. In 1900 it was the home of the Hon.Mrs.A.Jebb. The Payne-Gallways were tea planters and are remembered for their many acts of kindness within the village, including the donation of Christmas trees. In 1927 the hall was the home of Herbert Payne-Gallway and was also tenanted by Hon.Reginald Parker, the son of the 6th.Earl of Macclesfield. He was one of three aristocrats who founded the Tower brewery at Tadcaster of which he became a director until he retired in 1941. The hall was converted into two flats in the early 1960's and the stables were modernised to form Askham Court. Members of the Payne-Gallway family are buried in the churchyard.
In more recent times Dorothy Preston (1897-1961) - she was the daughter of Col.Darcy Preston (1860-1932) - married Major C.O'Callaghan of the Green Howards (1897-1978) and their daughter Patricia married Lt.Commander Peter Bell,

who died in January 1992 at Yeabridge Close Somerset and was buried in the family plot at Askham Bryan Church. In the churchyard is also the grave of Rear-Admiral Darcy Spence Preston, who was born in 1827 and died in 1890. There are still two farms within the parish owned by the Preston family. The Preston Charity was founded under the will of Rev. Rowland Mucklestone, in memory of his aunts Jane and Anne Preston.
One of the best preserved houses is the "Doctor's House" built in 1750 and a good example of Georgian architecture. In the Second World War the house was taken by the army but the family returned in 1945.
There was a small chapel, built in the grounds of the Little House in 1836, which stood derelict for many years. In 1967 it was converted into a modern house.
The "Nag's Head" is now the only public house and was once called the "Barstow Arms". It dates back to about 1800 and became the Nag's Head around 1900. Originally there were two houses and the pub - one house was a shop and the other the post office. The cottages were converted into a restaurant and there have been further alterations. The other inns at Askham Bryan were the "Windmill" and "Fox and Hounds"
On Westwood Lane stands "The Lodge" which achieved fame in 1991 as the location filming for the "Darling Buds of May" TV series.

Askham Bryan College of Agriculture and Horticulture was completed overlooking the main road in 1939 - the foundation stone was laid on November 21st.1936 by Sir Percy Jackson. He was the Chairman of the Yorkshire Council for Agricultural Education. During the last War the buildings were used for training for the Women's Land Army and as the Headquarters of the National Institute of Agricultural Engineering. It became an Agricultural College after the War and from 1954 concentrated on both the west and north ridings of Yorkshire.
Askham Bryan College consists of three farms: Westfield, East Barrow and Poplar Lodge. There is arable cropping, a herd of 180 Freisian/Holstein dairy cows, beef and pig units. There is a Forestry training centre at Redhouse Wood and research facilities for agriculture, horticulture and science. The College has five centres at Bedale, Harrogate, Easingwold, Pickering and Guisborough. There are 244 single study bedrooms, library, student's union and support services. The courses offered include BTEC Higher National with advancement to a degree validated by Leeds University.
The College Conference Centre was opened in February 1974 by the Duchess of Kent.

Askham Bryan windmill once stood on Mill Lane east of the present College, where Mill Farm was an active concern. A water tower now stands on the site, where John

Gilson was once the miller.

North of Askham Bryan was once the Rufforth airfield, formerly opened in November 1942. It was the home of No.4 Group Bomber Command with No.158 Squadron flying their Halifax M Mk IIs. with an initial raid on Genoa. On January 9th.1943 a Halifax lost power on take off and crashed on the main York Road near Copmanthorpe. 158 Squadron left Rufforth in February 1943 having lost nine crews. In March 32 Halifax planes were based at Rufforth: on August 9th.1944 one of the Halifax planes crashed at Askham Richard and on November 1st. another crashed at Askham Bryan after overshooting the runway. After the War the airfield was used by a gliding school and Austers of 664 Squadron operated until 1954. The airfield was sold to a farmer after a short period as a car racing circuit.

Copmanthorpe is south of the main road and astride the old Roman Road to York. The village is entered from the main road from Top Lane on the westbound carriageway: the "Fox and Hounds" is a recent building replacing the older "Queen's Arms" Inn or "Ginger Beer House".
In the Domesday Book Copmanthorpe was known as Copemantorp or the hamlet of Chapmen: they were itinerant traders who bought and sold goods in the many small hamlets and farms. By 1200 the name had changed to Coupmanetorp, closer to the Old Scandinavian "Kaupmannatorp".
In the 13th.century Copmanthorpe was given by William de Ros to the Knights Templars and the manor became Temple Copmanthorpe. The suggested site of the Templar's preceptory is in the village centre or in Drome Road: there are stones in village walls and buildings taken from the old preceptory.
From 1312 it became the property of the Knights Hospitallers until 1536. There were two manors and the second became the property of the Malbis (Malebisse) family and then through marriage to the Fairfax family, who were the owners for two centuries until 1526. In that year Thomas Vavasour became Lord of the Manor - he died in 1558 and was buried at St.Mary's Church Bishophill.
The Copmanthorpe Vavasour line started when Henry Vavasour of Weston married Matilda Bunney of Copmanthorpe. Their son Richard and his wife Margaret lived in the village, where Richard died in 1526. Their children included William who became a priest (died 1544), Richard who lived at Askham Richard and Thomas. He married Margaret Smyth and their eight children included Henry, whose son was Sir Thomas Vavasour of Copmanthorpe. It was Sir William Vavasour of Copmanthorpe, Thomas's son, who was created a baronet in 1643 and when he was killed at the battle of Copenhagen the title and Copmanthorpe line became extinct in 1659.
In 1651 John Barnard, a Hull merchant, acquired Copmanthorpe. In 1709 John Wood became Lord of the Manor for the Barnard family and he lived at the Manor

House Farm, which he demolished in 1710 and rebuilt the dwelling. The Tudor Manor House is now demolished. At the start of this century the Lord of the Manor were the trustees of the late Cpt.Albert C.Wood of Hollin Hall Ripon.

St.Giles' Church was founded in 1180 in late Norman England. The East stained glass window is by Charles Eamer Kempe (1837-1907) and the church was fully restored in 1889 by Hodgson Fowler. There was a new chancel, a vestry was added and a modern porch protected the old Norman doorway at a cost of £600. During the restoration an early Norman window was uncovered in the south aisle. A churchyard for burials was only allowed in 1750, prior to that folk were buried at York.

St.Giles Church was a chapel of ease to St.Mary's Church Bishophill Junior at York and became a Parish Church in 1866. There is a new church hall and the churchyard has the old bell, together with a grave to a resident who died aged 101. There is also the grave of Stephen Foster, gunner on the "Somerset", man of war - the oldest seaman in His Majesty's service: he died aged 94 in 1808.

The old school in Church Street opened in 1815 but was sold in 1821 to be a Methodist Chapel. A new school opened in 1869 and in recent times the Junior School opened in 1968 and the Infants in 1972.

The old Methodist Chapel became a Community Hall in 1958, when a new chapel was built.

Part of Copmanthorpe is a Conservation Area having seven listed buildings. These include the Church, the Post Office occupying a building dating from 1680, Paddocks House and Manor Farm House. The "Royal Oak" Inn was built in 1793 as a private house and was known as the "Oak Tree" inn about 1830. In 1921 it was taken over by the Tadcaster Tower Brewery and once had a brewhouse and blacksmith.

The new £35,000 public library is a great success, 1230 folk joined in the first two months.

Copmanthorpe railway station opened on May 29th.1839 and was one of the first lines into York. The station was rebuilt in 1904 but closed to passengers on January 5th.1959 and completely closed in May 1964.

In the First World War Copmanthorpe became a replacement landing ground for B Flight 33 Squadron of the RFC moving from the Knavesmire in May 1916 with their BE2C planes until September 1916. They were taken over on June 8th. 1916 by No.57 Cheltenham Squadron RFC - commemorated by a church plaque who moved to France with their FE2D planes in December 1916 and all of the group were killed in action. 76 Squadron A flight RFC operated from Copmanthorpe from September 1916 until March 1919, when the airfield was closed, facilities dismantled and land sold. The concrete foundations for the old hangars were once visible and the last hangar burnt down in 1921.

North of the main road to York is Askham Bog, the first nature reserve of the

Yorkshire Naturalists Trust - now the Wildlife Trust. Askham Bog was given to the Trust in 1946, covering 64 acres of the 120 acres: the remainder is by agreement with the owner. Access is through a gate in a hedge near the railway bridge, across the Pike Hills golf course and onto the causeway through the Bog. The reserve is a remnant of a larger marshy area between the two arms of a glacial moraine. The bog shows most stages in a succession from open fen to raised bog. The management maintains the water table and habitats by rotational clearing and cattle grazing. The Yorkshire Wildlife Trust now administers 59 reserves and has over 8000 members. It is the County Nature Conservation Trust for Yorkshire and North Humberside and was founded in 1946. The total acreage of the Trust's reserves is about 5000 acres and includes the station yard at Bolton Percy. It is a partner in the RSNC Wildlife Trusts Partnership of 48 Wildlife Trusts, 50 Urban Wildlife Groups and WATCH - the Junior Branch.

Pike Hills Golf Club by the main road was formed in 1920 playing on land at Hob Moor. They moved to their present site in 1948 and the course was extended to 18 holes in 1971. The Club was formed originally by the York Railway Institute and the Club is still a section of this Institute. There are 80 acres of land of which 70 acres is for the golf course. In the centre of the course is the Askham Bog Nature Reserve.

Acaster Malbis or High Acaster is a village on the River Ouse south east of Copmanthorpe. It was known as Acastre in 1086, meaning the Roman fort of Aca: Malbis was added in the 12th. century, when the Manor was held by the Malebisse family meaning "ill beast". The Malbisse family came into the Manor through the marriage of Richard de Malbysse with Maud, the daughter of Richard de Acaster. In 1166 Acaster was held by William Malbis and his son Richard was a courtier of King John. Holy Trinity Church is amongst trees by the river and is a 14th. rebuilding of an earlier Norman Church. The Victorian bell tower contains bells that once were said to have rung in York Minster. The church was repewed in 1831 and restored by C.Hodgson Fowler in 1886 at a cost of £1400. The church registers date back to 1656.

The churchyard has the graves of many local folk including the Cundall - Horatio and William Cundall were farmers at Mount Pleasant, Mawson, Farrer and Cowper families. The Cowpers were joiners, farmers and carriers, running a local service. The graves of the Raimes family include Frederick, Cyril, John and Herbert who were all born in the 19th. century. The Raimes were Lords of the Manor and lived at the Manor House and at "Southmoor". In the 1920's Dr.Alwyn Raimes was Lord of the Manor. There is also the box-tomb of Joseph Buckley who was an "eminent and ingenious mason of the City of York: died 1842".

In the church is the tomb of Sir John Malbys, who died in 1316 and is said to have founded the church. The Fairfax family held the Manor until the mid-18th. century.

During the Civil War the Scots were at Acaster, where they ravaged the area wrecking homesteads and eating the animals. Landlord Viscount Fairfax of Gilling excused his Acaster tenants from the payment of a year's rent in compensation for the losses during the disaster. It is said that Archbishop John Sharp of York preferred to come from Bishopthorpe to pray in the quiet of Acaster Malbis Church in 1691. The old brick pinfold was restored in 1987 and the nearby Memorial Institute opened in 1927. The Methodist Chapel was built in 1880 at a cost of £1138 donated by Lord Wenlock, who owned the salmon fisheries in the village. The dwellings of "The Old Mill" and "The Old Vicarage" are reminders of the past. The Manor House is converted into a Country Guest House and there is a new complex of buildings opened recently on the road past the Manor.
Acaster Malbis airfield was opened in January 1942 as a satellite for Church Fenton. The only RAF Fighter Command Squadron based at Acaster Malbis was No.601 from Duxford. The unsuitability of the location caused many accidents. The airfield reopened for Bomber Command in 1943 but had no operational units. In November 1944 the field went to Bomber Command Training Group but the site was used to store bombs. The field closed on February 28th.1946 and there are many buildings still intact. The concrete runways are still seen and the reopened road to Acaster Selby crosses the main runway. There are several small businesses which operate at Acaster airfield including a pig farm, haulage firm and farm.

Sim Balk Lane is the access to Bishopthorpe, known as Torp in 1086 and by 1275 was Biscupthorp. In 1226 Archbishop Walter de Grey bought the manor of Thorp St.Andrew from Kirkstall Abbey and built his manor house and chapel. They were given to the Dean and Chapter of York in 1241 and the chapel is still in use today. It has been altered over the years and has a wall carving and cross from the Oberammergau school. The Russian ikon of St.George was given to Archbishop Garbutt in 1943. The stained glass is late 19th.century by Charles Kempe, mainly showing the great northern saints.
Thomas Rotherham built the north wing near the end of the 15th.century and more was added in the 17th.century after the Civil War.
The palace assumed its present form in 1763/69 during the time of Archbishop Drummond, by architect Thomas Atkinson: he removed the Early English front of the Medieval building and built the front seen today. The gatehouse was built at the same period with stone from the dismantled Cawood Castle
Bishopthorpe Palace has been the home of the Archbishops in recent years: Archbishop Ramsay (1956 - 1961) decided to live in the Palace and afterwards the top floor was modernised with the palace becoming office and home set in 20 acre grounds. Archbishop Coggan (1961-1975) was followed by Stuart Blanch who retired in 1983 :he was born in February 1918 and died in June 1994. He accepted

a life peerage in 1985 becoming Lord Blanch of Bishopthorpe. Archbishop John Habgood will retire in August 1995 - he was appointed in 1983.
The Palace was the scene of the trial of Archbishop Richard Scrope, for his part in the rebellion against the King. King Henry IV, present at the trial, asked Lord Chief Justice William Gascoigne of Gawthorpe Hall to pronounce sentence. He refused to carry out this order and the King asked lawyer Sir William Fulthorpe to pass the death sentence. Archbishop Scrope was beheaded near Bishopthorpe Palace. He was taken to his place of execution sitting backwards on his horse and singing psalms. Thomas Mowbray was beheaded first, followed by Scrope on June 8th.1405.
Bishopthorpe's Church of St.Andrew was built in 1898/1902 by Charles Hodgson Fowler. He had demolished a previous church designed in 1768 by Thomas Atkinson: this being the second Bishopthorpe Church and subjected to occasional flooding on its riverside position. The altar position is marked by a tall cross inscribed: "On this spot there stood for centuries the parish church of St.Andrew Bishopthorpe. Rebuilt 1899." In 1892 a decision was taken to build a new church in 15th.century style. The west front of the old church was left standing together with the outline foundations and the new church retains a 15th.century font and a 13th.century piscina. There are a few graves on the old church site including William Thomson Archbishop of York, born in 1819 and was Archbishop from 1862 - he died at Bishopthorpe on Christmas Day 1890. There is a brass memorial to this Archbishop in the new St.Andrew's Church.
There is some interesting stained glass in the new church including the west window to Archbishops Thomson, Walter de Gray and William Dalrymple Maclaren - the 88th.Archbishop. Windows in the south aisle remember Jessie Oliver, Headmistress of St.Thomas School Stepney - there are four scenes from school life in 1350, 1693, 1846 and 1950. An adjacent window shows the trial of Richard Scrope at Bishopthorpe Palace in 1405. North aisle windows show Archbishop de Gray repealing the Game Law and renaming the village Bishopthorpe in 1226. Another window shows King Charles 1st at Bishopthorpe in 1633 with the ceremonies for healing those with King's Palsy. The ancient two bells and font in the church came from the demolished church of St.Crux Pavement in York. The church stood on the corner of Pavement and Shambles: the site is now the parish room built with stone from old church. It was first mentioned in 1087, probably rebuilt in the 15th. century and was pulled down in 1887.

The first building on the main York Road into the City east of the railway is the York Sixth Form College. This opened in September 1985 in the original Ashfield Secondary School buildings.
"Ashfield" was a large house now sited in the grounds of York College of Further Education and was the property of Sir Lycett Green. He was Master of the York and

Ainsty Hounds between 1886 and 1909.
West of the main road is the early 1990's development of supermarkets, where there is a Park and Ride service into the City.
East of the main road, adjacent to "Ashfield" stood Middlethorpe Lodge, the home of Sir John Grant-Lawson. He was once the Deputy Speaker of the House of Commons.
The other large house in the area was "Dringthorpe" home of Col.Sir Charles Read. It was used by the army in the last War and is now the site of the Wilberforce Home for the Blind.
Dringhouses was known as Drengus in 1234 meaning the "houses of the Drengs". A Dreng was a man holding land in ancient Northumbria by a tenure partly military and partly servile. The tenure of a Dreng was known as drenage: the word derives from the Old Norse "drengr" meaning a young man.
The Dringhouses toll house was on the site of No.100 "Tollgarth": the house served the end of the Tadcaster-Hob Moor turnpike trust. The payment of tolls ended in 1872 and the house was demolished in 1905, to be replaced with the present home built in 1910.
The Forte Posthouse York was opened in 1966 and has 139 en suite bedrooms. The site was the old Manor House and the property of Col. E.Wilkinson, who was Lord of the Manor. There was a paddock and farm, which were included in the grounds of adjacent "Goddards". The Manor House garden was once surrounded by a high thorn hedge. On January 13th.1941 Col.Wilkinson died and the estate was sold for £24,175 and was broken up.
On the west side of the main road are "The Fox" and "The Cross Keys" inns. The Fox was sold in 1873 to William Yates, who sold it to Tadcaster Tower Brewery in 1875. The Cross Keys was bought by the John Hunt Brewery in 1899 and is now part of J.W.Cameron brewery.
The nearby Dringhouses Library was once the local school, opened in 1852 - the school had been founded by Mrs.Trafford-Leigh in 1849. Dringhouses was enclosed in 1822 and the local pinfold has been restored with a plaque opposite the library.
The first chapel at Dringhouses was built in 1472 and replaced in 1725, built by Francis Barlow, Lord of the Manor. He dedicated the church to St.Helen north east of the present church of St.Edward. The foundation stone for the new church was laid in August 1849 and built from Clifford stone. The dedication was in memory of Frances Leigh's late husband Rev.Edward Leigh. The architects were Vickers and Hugill in the English Gothic Decorated style. Charles Vickers had a Pontefract practice and designed the Seacroft parsonage in 1846 and a church at East Knottingley in 1847/48.
"Goddards" was built by York architect Walter H.Brierley in 1926 for Noel Goddard and Katharine Terry. The gardens are by George Dillistone of Kent, who had

worked at Castle Drogo. After Noel Terry died in 1980 the Terry Trustees sold the house to the National Trust in 1984 and it is the Yorkshire Regional Office with 50 staff. Walter Brierley lived at Bishopthorpe and was buried at St.Andrew's Church - he died on August 22nd.1926, four years after the death of his wife Gertrude.
The tram terminus was near the Chase Hotel, run by horses until 1911 and the conversion to electricity - trams stopped running in 1935.
The 112 room York Swallow Hotel was once a private house known as The Hollies and owned by Major John Close of the Steel Works Forge in Leeman Road. His original house was on the site of the Royal Station Hotel and when the North Eastern Railway Co. built their hotel in 1866, they also built The Hollies for Col.Close in 1874.
In the 1920's the house was bought by two ladies who ran Harker's Hotel in St.Helen's Square: the site is now Betty's Restaurant - Betty's was founded in 1919 and marked the 75th. anniversary by a series of special events in June 1994. Col.Close's house now became "Harker's Hotel" and after the War was run by Renwick Hodgson. The hotel was sold in 1952 to Mr.Morris, who ran the White Swan in Piccadilly. His son Major Phillip Morris took over the "Chase Hotel", added more building and erected the large leather saddle as his trade mark. Swallow Hotels bought The Chase in 1987 with modernisation costing £8 million.
The Knavesmire was named after a Danish settler called Knorr and was known as Knaresmire: by 1625 it assumed the present form. The Knavesmire is a part of the common land called Micklegate Stray and extended over Hob Moor.
John Carr, the York architect, designed a new grandstand in 1757, following money raised by the Marquess of Rockingham. His design was preferred to those of James Paine and Thomas Robinson. In 1925 the lower storey was moved to its present position in the Paddock. The new grandstand was built in 1964-65.
Racing was held at Clifton Moor from 1633 but the occasional flooding prompted its transfer to the Knavesmire in 1731. In 1730 the area was a long undrained bog on which the poor of nearby villages held their grazing rights. Alderman John Telford laid out a racecourse from the streams and hollows. The house on the north end of the Knavesmire is the Herdsman's Cottage from 1840.
The area to the west is called Hob Moor after the effigy of a knight who gave the moor to the poor of Micklegate ward: the knight was probably one of the de Roos family. The stone was probably a 16th.century plague stone and erected in the 18th.century.
The Knavesmire once had a 9 hole golf course, which was moved as the York Golf Club to Strensall. The Knavesmire was used for aircraft in 1912, when two all steel Type E monoplanes built at the Blackburn Olympia Works in Roundhay Road were tested by the chief test pilot Reginald W.Kenworthy. The plane was too heavy to take off and the project was an initial failure. The area was also a short lived landing

ground for B flight of 33 Squadron RFC during April and May 1916 with their BE2C planes. It was part of the Home Defence Organisation protecting York from attack by Zeppelins. When there was a Zeppelin L21 attack on York on May 2nd/3rd 1916, it was decided to move the flight to Copmanthorpe as the flarepath would attract more possible raids on York. In the Second World War the Knavesmire was used by an AA battery.
On the western edge of the Knavesmire by the roadside is a simple stone inscribed: "TYBURN". It was named after the namesake at Marble Arch in London: the first hanging at Tyburn London was on May 5th.1760, when Earl Ferrers was executed for murdering his steward; he was the last nobleman to die a felon. A map of 1625 shows a ditch across the Knavesmire known as the Tyburn. The first execution took place here in 1379: it was Edward Hewison. The last was in 1801 with the hanging of Edward Hughes. The gallows saw the deaths of John Nevison in May 1684, Richard "Dick" Turpin in 1739 and Eugene Aram in 1759. The highwayman Dick Turpin was hung for the murder of an innkeeper from Epping: he was buried as John Palmer. The gallows were erected in 1802 outside York Castle. Between 1537 and 1680 many martyrs lost their lives at Tyburn, including 30 secular priests, 17 laymen, two Carthusian monks and two Jesuits. It is said that St.Margaret Clitherow often prayed at Tyburn perhaps in preparation for her own martyrdom in 1586.
Two Catholic martyrs hung at Tyburn were Father Peter Snow and Ralph Grimston, whose skulls were later to be displayed in Hazlewood Castle Chapel. They are seen today in a glass case in the north sanctuary, having been spiked on top of Micklegate Bar in 1598.
After the battle of Culloden in 1746 many captured Jacobites were brought to York for trial. Twenty two of these men were executed at Tyburn: the head of Cpt. James Hamilton was sent to Carlisle while those of William Conolly and James Mayne were spiked on Micklegate Bar and stayed there for seven years. On the stretch of moor in Invernesshire the Young Pretender Charles Stuart was defeated by the Duke of Cumberland.

The Mount School belongs to the Quaker Society of Friends. The first school was founded by William and Esther Tuke in their own home to provide a good liberal education for the daughters of Friends. The York Quarterly Meeting Girl's School was founded in 1831 at Castlegate - the house is still to be seen. The land on the old Driffield estate on The Mount was bought in 1857 for £1400: the 20 acre site is bounded by Dalton Terrace, Driffield Terrace, Love Lane and the railway. The governing body is responsible for the girl's boarding, weekly and day school 11-18 The Mount and for the brother school of Bootham. The co-educational 3 - 11 Junior Department is "Tregelles" and opened in 1991. The school motto is "Fidelis in parvo".

The Mount is the continuation of Tadcaster Road to Blossom Street or Dringhouses and is where many Roman stone coffins have been discovered over the centuries. It was once known as The Street of Tombs and later as South Prospect Street. In 1861 a Roman tombstone was found of a 13 year old girl called Corellia Optata; another coffin was discovered inscribed to the 10 month old daughter of Felicius Simplex of the 6th.Legion Victorious; in 1884 a limestone altar was found set up by Lucius Celerinus Vitalis in honour of Silvanus, a god of hunting and the wild
St.James' Chapel stood on the highest point on The Mount but the exact position is unknown. It was probably granted to the monks of Holy Trinity by King Stephen and served as a chapel of ease for the parish. Executed criminals were often buried in the churchyard and the enthronement processions of new archbishops started at this chapel.
On Blossom Street the Odeon Cinema dates from 1936 designed by Harry Weedon. The oldest convent in England is the Bar Convent and is on the east of the road near Micklegate Bar. It was founded in 1611 by the nuns of the Institute of the Blessed Virgin Mary started by Mary Ward (1585-1645). She was a pioneer of both women's education and of apostolic orders for women. A school was established on the site of the present Bar Convent before the days of state education. The Georgian building was designed by Thomas Atkinson in 1787 and the main glory is the chapel, completed in 1769. The Bar Convent was open to the public from 1987 but financial difficulties caused the closure of the public section in 1994. The five nuns of the order sold a 19th. century painting of The Crucifixion by the 17th. century artist Eustache Le Sueur. The Order was given this painting in the 1870's more than 200 years after the artist's death and it was once attributed to his tutor Simon Vouet until it was exhibited at Leeds Art Gallery. The painting realised £397,500 on June 10th. 1994 at the auction at London's Christies and will secure the future of the museum and the education courses run by the Bar Convent. The painting was sold to the National Gallery via a London dealer.
Blossom Street is derived from Ployhsuaingate in use at the end of the 13th.century. It became Ploxswaingate meaning Ploughman's Street and was noted as one street at York where a horse and plough could be turned.
The Hospital of St.Thomas of Canterbury was east of Micklegate Bar between the city walls and Nunnery Lane and was demolished in 1862 for road widening. It was founded in 1391 and run by the Corpus Christi Guild, catering for the poor and travellers. In 1547 it passed under the control of the city corporation. The old hospital was replaced in 1863 by a new building in Nunnery Lane.
St.Catherine's Hospital stood about 130 yards from the Bar Convent by the corner of Holgate Road. It was a leper house for both sexes and was open by 1333. In 1652 it was rebuilt as a home for poor widows and in 1835 was pulled down with new almshouses opening on Holgate Road.

The lower part of Micklegate Bar dates from the 12th.century: the barbican partly collapsed in 1810 and was taken away in 1826. The bar gates were removed in 1827 and the small statues on the top date from 1950, when they replaced some eroded figures. The arms displayed are those of King Edward III and the City; the lower arms representing the bar's restoration in 1737 and the then Lord Mayor Sir John Lister-Kaye. The side arches were cut in 1753 and completed by John Carr. At one time the top floors were used as a prison for noblemen and the practice of displaying traitor's heads on spikes was stopped in 1754. On December 30th. 1460 was fought the battle of Wakefield Green in the shadow of Sandal Castle. The Lancastrians under Lord Clifford killed Richard Duke of York - amongst 2000 killed that day. The Duke's head was severed and with a mock paper crown was taken to York and put on top of a spike on Micklegate Bar. The end of Act 1 of Shakespeare's King Henry VI Part 3 are the words:"Off with his head and set it on York gates; so York may overlook the town of York."
Micklegate Bar marks the end of the road from Leeds, Tadcaster to the City of York or Eboracum.

ACKNOWLEDGEMENTS

JOHN GILLEGHAN would like to thank the following for their help in writing this book:

LEEDS LOCAL HISTORY LIBRARY
Anne Heap, Jennifer Horne, Sandra Smith, Moya Barker and Colin Price

Alwoodley, Moor Allerton, Moortown, Pannal and Sandmoor Golf Clubs
Asda Group PLC
Askham Bryan College
Borthwick Institute of Historical Research (York University)
Browning House (Diocese of Ripon)
Chapel Allerton, Cross Gates, Halton, Harrogate, Selby, Tadcaster
Wetherby and York Libraries
I.J.Dewhirst Ltd.
Dunlopillo (Pannal)
Headmistress Gateways School
Ken Jones (Collingham)
Leeds Diocesan Archives
Leeds & Holbeck Building Society
Leeds Industrial Co-operative Society
Leeds Permanent Building Society
Leeds City Council Planning Department
Leeds City Museum
Leeds Skyrack Express
Robert Maltby Leeds University School of Classics
Canon Joseph Lyons St.Gemma's Hospice
Lloyds Bank PLC
Mansfield Brewery PLC
Midland Bank PLC
Mount Charlotte Investments PLC
National Westminster Bank PLC
Rudding Park
Mary Sampson (Hambleton)
Roger Shaw (Kitson & Partners)
Rev.Paul Summers (Vicar of Whitkirk)
Strikes Gardens Centres
Sutton Housing Trust
Tetley Pub Company
West Yorkshire Archive Service
Yorkshire Bank PLC
Yorkshire Electricity
Yorkshire Post Newspapers (Archives)
Yorkshire Water PLC

Also the great number of folk who have so willingly offered their time and memories in the compilation of this unique local history.

OTHER TITLES BY JOHN GILLEGHAN HAVE INCLUDED:

SCENES FROM EAST LEEDS
INTRODUCING THE YORKSHIRE DALES
THE MAGIC OF THE YORKSHIRE DALES
TIME TRAVELLER IN THE YORKSHIRE DALES
GUIDE TO SAXTON CHURCH
GUIDE TO LEDSHAM CHURCH
GUIDE TO ABERFORD CHURCH
HAZLEWOOD CASTLE NATURE TRAIL
A WALK IN THE PARK
A WALK IN THE COUNTRY